DIVERSIONS OF GALWAY

AMSTERDAM STUDIES IN THE THEORY AND HISTORY OF LINGUISTIC SCIENCE

General Editor
E. F. KONRAD KOERNER
(University of Ottawa)

Series III - STUDIES IN THE HISTORY OF THE LANGUAGE SCIENCES

Volume 68

Anders Ahlqvist (ed.)

Diversions of Galway

DIVERSIONS OF GALWAY

PAPERS ON THE HISTORY OF LINGUISTICS
FROM ICHoLS V, GALWAY, IRELAND, 1-6 SEPTEMBER 1990

Edited by

ANDERS AHLQVIST

in collaboration with

KONRAD KOERNER
R. H. ROBINS
IRÈNE ROSIER

JOHN BENJAMINS PUBLISHING COMPANY
AMSTERDAM/PHILADELPHIA

1992

Library of Congress Cataloging-in-Publication Data

International Conference on the History of the Language Sciences (5th : 1990 : Galway, Ireland)

Diversions of Galway : Papers on the History of Linguistics from ICHoLS V, Galway, Ireland, 1-6 September 1990 / edited by Anders Ahlqvist, in collaboration with Konrad Koerner, R.H. Robins, & Irène Rosier.

p. cm. -- (Amsterdam studies in the theory and history of linguistic science. Series III, Studies in the history of the language sciences, ISSN 0304-0720; v. 68)

Includes four contributions in French and two in German.

Includes bibliographical references and indexes.

1. Linguistics--History--Congresses. I. Ahlqvist, Anders. II. Title. III. Series.

P61.I57 1990

410'.9--dc20 92-24473

ISBN 90 272 4555 X (Eur.)/1-55619-363-7 (US) (alk. paper) CIP

John Benjamins Publishing Co. · P.O. Box 75577 · 1070 AN Amsterdam · The Netherlands

John Benjamins North America · 821 Bethlehem Pike · Philadelphia, PA 19118 · USA

Table of Contents

Foreword
Anders Ahlqvist ix

List of Participants xiii

Conference Committees xxi

Conference Programme xxiii

Opening Address
Brian Ó Cuív 1

The Priscian Text Used in Three Ninth-Century Irish Donatus Commentaries
Rijcklof Hofman 7

Speculative Lexicography: Difficulties in Following the Historical Path of a Linguistic Idea
Werner Hüllen 17

Carolingian Grammarians and Theoretical Innovation
Vivien Law 27

On the Origins of the Medieval Concept of Transitivity
Anneli Luhtala 39

Jean Charles Thiebault (de) Laveaux: The Revolt of a Jacobin Grammarian and Lexicographer against the Académie Française
Herbert E. Brekle 49

The First Grammar of Frisian (1681)
Rolf H. Bremmer Jr 59

Latinisme ou gallicisme ? Les méthodes translinguistiques latin – français au XVIIIe siècle
Bernard Colombat 73

The Hibernian Connection: Irish Grammaticography in Louvain
Jan de Clercq & Pierre Swiggers 85

Harmonic Dictionaries and Grammars in Semitic Linguistics
Yaakov Gruntfest 103

A Grammar without a Tradition? Fernando de la Carrera's *Arte de la lengua yunga* (1644)
Even Hovdhaugen 113

Étude historiographique des Manières de Langage
Barbara Kaltz 123

L'Ordre Naturel and Charles Batteux: à bas les philosophes
L.G. Kelly 135

Grammaire normative/grammaire descriptive dans la linguistique espagnole du XVIIe siècle
María Dolores Martínez Gavilán 145

How to "Improve" a Language: The Case of Eighteenth Century Descriptions of Greenlandic
Elke Nowak 157

Lichtenberg on Language and Reason: One Aspect of the Crisis in German Enlightenment
Johannes Roggenhofer 169

John Wallis' *Grammatica Linguae Anglicanae* (1653): The New Science and English Grammar
Joseph L. Subbiondo 183

Theory and Description in the Dutch Grammatical Tradition: The Case of the Passive
Marijke J. van der Wal 191

Animal Language: a Chapter from the Controversy between Rationalism and Sensualism
Helmut Weiß 203

The "Poznań School" of Structural Linguistics
Wiesław Awedyk & Camiel Hamans 213

Salomon Stricker's Motor Theory of Language
T. Craig Christy 227

Victor Henry et les lois phon(ét)iques
Piet Desmet 237

The Role of Acoustics and Apperception in Franz Boas' Theory of Phonetics
Michael Mackert 251

The Beginning and Development of Persian Syntactic Descriptions
Mehdi Meshkot Dini 261

Thirty-Five Years of English Auxiliaries: A Small History of Generative Grammar
Stephen J. Nagle 269

Dutch Linguists and the Origin of Language: Some Nineteenth-Century Views
Jan Noordegraaf 279

"Maschine" vs."Organismus". Einige Überlegungen zur Geistes- und Sprachwissenschaftsgeschichte im 18. und 19. Jahrhundert
Peter Schmitter 291

Zur Geschichtsschreibung der Sprechakttheorie: der Fall Reinach
Frank J.M. Vonk 309

Linguistics vs. Philology in an 1864 Student Paper by Jan Baudouin de Courtenay
Joanna Radwańska Williams 319

Abstracts 329

Index Linguarum 367

Index Nominum 369

Index Rerum 380

Foreword

ANDERS AHLQVIST
University College, Galway

THIS VOLUME contains a selection of papers presented at the Fifth International Conference on the History of Linguistics, which was held at the University College, Galway campus of the National University of Ireland, from Saturday 1 to Thursday 6 September 1990, under the auspices of the College's Department of Old and Middle Irish and Celtic Philology. Previous conferences in this series have been entitled *International Conferences on the History of the Language Sciences (=ICHoLS).*[1] Mainly for reasons of linguistic economy,[2] I chose to divert from this by calling it the *Fifth International Conference on the History of Linguistics (=ICHoLs V)* . However, I trust that intelligent librarians and other readers will understand that it nevertheless forms part of the series of meetings that began in Ottawa (cp. Koerner 1980:v–vi) in 1978. All our scholarly sessions took place in the Quadrangle Building of the College, the plenary ones[3] in the Aula Maxima and the poster ones in the New Boardroom.

[1] Or the equivalent in another congress language, cp. e.g. Koerner & Niederehe 1990:xiii.

[2] At the same time, I have to confess that my very uneven but in all cases quite non-native "Sprachgefühl" for English, French and German has very divergent feelings about the degrees of appropriateness pertaining to the terms *Language Sciences, Sciences du Langage* and *Sprachwissenschaft(en),* but I shall prefer to develop these thoughts further on another occasion. In the meantime, it should be clearly understood, firstly, that I alone was responsible for this in itself not unprecedented (cf. Schmitter 1992:132) slight change and, secondly, that it in no way implicates anyone among my coeditors, my fellow-members of the various conference committees or indeed my publishers.

[3] All these were recorded during the conference: the tapes are kept in the Sound Archive of the Teanglann (Language Centre) of University College, Galway.

In his "Opening Address", Brian Ó Cuív (p. 2 below) put forward the expectation "that when the Proceedings appear we will find grouping of papers under headings such as Classical Period, Medieval Period, Renaissance, Seventeenth Century, and so on". However, these groupings have been somewhat simplified in what follows. Thus, the Opening Address naturally forms a group apart, before papers on classical and mediaeval linguistics (pp. 7–48), which are followed by ones on early modern themes (pp. 49–212) and those (pp. 213–328) dealing with what I personally should like to describe as present-day linguistics, i.e. the last two centuries; within these last three groups papers are given according to alphabetical order of authors' names. Moreover, for the sake of presenting a reasonably full record of the proceedings of the conference, abstracts of other papers presented have (with one exception) been included (pp. 329–366) at the end of the volume, together with information about their places of publication in full, whenever available. Two abstracts of papers not presented at the conference are included, for their authors were prevented from coming to Galway by illness and subsequent death: these are by Thomas Frank and Leslie Seiffert, whose memories I wish to salute in this fashion.

On behalf of the organisers, I should like to place on record our very sincere gratitude to all our sponsors: the President of University College, Galway, Dr Colm Ó hEocha, for making the facilities of University College, Galway available to ICHoLs V, the organiser of ICHoLS IV, Professor Hans-J. Niederehe, for placing the surplus funds from the previous conference at our disposal, the Irish Tourist Board, for contributing towards a reception, Murphy's Brewery, for generously allowing us to sample their fine products at the informal get-together on the eve of the conference and, finally, Kenny's Bookshops[1] and Art Galleries, for a wonderfully hospitable reception. It is my sad duty to put on record the death, shortly before writing these words in October

[1] The nature of this bookshop cannot be understood by those who do not know the place. However, a small pointer may be provided by the fact that our colleague Juneidah Ibrahim there found a copy of Pringle 1896, a work apparently not available until then in the library of the Malay Language Planning Institute in Kuala Lumpur.

1991, of Mr Desmond Kenny Sr, whose family are, I am happy to say, continuing all his good work.

As organising secretary of the conference, I am very conscious of my deep gratitude to my fellow-members of all the various committees, in and outside Galway, (see below, p. xxi), without whose unstinting help before, during and after the conference it would simply not have been possible. Naturally, I am also very grateful to all the colleagues from many countries, who contributed to the conference itself, by presenting papers, chairing sessions, contributing to the discussion and participating in other ways, not least by enjoying themselves in Galway.

Regarding the book itself, I must, first of all, express my very real indebtedness to my three fellow editors, all of whom have contributed enormously to whatever measure of success it may achieve, in ways far more numerous than I can relate here in full. Thus, Irène Rosier has helped me solve many problems, drawing unstintingly on her extensive experience (cf. e.g. Rosier 1988) of writing and editing scholarly works. To Bobby Robins, the doyen of our discipline, I owe the very perspicacious and generous suggestion that this volume should bear the title[1] it has. All historians of linguistics have exceedingly sound reasons to be thankful to Konrad Koerner. For my own part, I am immensely in his debt, for all he has done to help me produce this book, not least in connection with many time-consuming and important matters of editorial policy, but also because of the shining and inimitable example provided by his own unbending intellectual integrity, astounding attention to detail and fearlessly forthright frankness. I am likewise most grateful to the John Benjamins Publishing Company and especially to Yola de Lusenet, for much sound advice, generously and sincerely given.

[1] The title serves three different purposes. Firstly, it echoes the feeling, which I know to be widespread among the participants, that the town of Galway was singularly hospitable to the conference, so that this may most certainly reflect one sense of English *diversion*. Secondly, I hope that the book will not prove entirely unworthy of Robins's own splendid example of what real linguistic scholarship is all about: cf. his *Diversions* (1970:VI) for the excellent reasons why he then chose to adapt Tooke's (1786) title to his own collection of essays. Furthermore, there is a third sense in which the title may be appropriate, namely in that it echoes the slight change (already mentioned above) in the name of the conference itself.

Most of the papers published in this book were submitted on computer diskettes. Those that were received in typescript only were scanned and read with OmniPage on an Apple Scanner belonging to the Library of University College, Galway: I am grateful to the library authorities for permission to use this equipment. The book itself was computer typeset with Microsoft Word for Macintosh.[1] My last debt of gratitude is to my son, Jacob Ahlqvist, who has helped me greatly, not only with arranging and inserting graphics in the texts, but also in numerous other ways connected with the use of computers.

REFERENCES

Koerner, Konrad, ed. 1980. *Progress in Linguistic Historiography: Papers from the International Conference on the History of the Language Sciences (Ottawa, 28–31 August 1978).* Amsterdam: John Benjamins.

Niederehe, Hans-Josef & Konrad Koerner, eds. 1990. *History and Historiography: of Linguistics. Proceedings of the Fourth International Conference on the History of the Language Sciences (ICHOLS IV), Trier, 24–28 August 1987.* Amsterdam & Philadelphia: John Benjamins.

Pringle, A. E. 1896. *English and Malay Vocabulary.* Singapore: Singapore & Straits Printing Office.

Robins, R[obert] H[enry]. 1970. *Diversions of Bloomsbury: Selected Writings on Linguistics.* Amsterdam: North-Holland.

Rosier, Irène, ed. 1988 *L'Héritage des grammairiens latins de l'antiquité aux lumières : Actes du colloque de Chantilly 2–4 septembre 1987.* Louvain: Peeters.

Schmitter, Peter. 1992. "Ernüchterung statt Bildstürmerei — einige Beobachtungen zu Koerners Historiographie der Linguistik". *Beiträge zur Geschichte der Sprachwissenschaft* 2.132–136.

Tooke, John Horne. 1786. Ἔπεα Πτεροεντα *or, The Diversions of Purley.* Part I. London: J. Johnson.

[1] Most of the text was set in Times Roman. Moreover, wherever necessary, use was made of special characters from the Graeca, IPAKiel, IPAPlus, IPARoman, Roman and Semitica fonts. It is a condition of the licensing agreement with the maker of these fonts that its name, address and contact numbers should be listed here: Linguist's Software, Inc. PO Box 580, Edmonds, WA 98020-0580, tel +1 (206) 775-1130, fax +1 (206) 771-5911.

List of Participants

Anders AHLQVIST, Roinn na Sean-Ghaeilge, Coláiste na hOllscoile, GAILLIMH.
Judith AHLQVIST.
Jacob AHLQVIST.

Mark AMSLER, Department of English and Linguistics, The University, NEWARK, Delaware 19716, USA.

Julie ANDRESEN, Department of English, 314 Allen Building, Duke University, DURHAM, North Carolina 27706, USA.

Wiesław AWEDYK, Institute of English, Adam Mickiewicz University, Niepodległości 4, 61-874 POZNAŃ, Poland.

Martin J. BALL, Department of Behavioural and Communication Studies, The Polytechnic, PONTYPRIDD, Mid Glamorgan CF37 1DL, Wales.

Barrie E. BARTLETT, Department of French, Simon Fraser University, BURNABY, British Columbia V5A 1S6, Canada.
Marlène BARTLETT.

Brigitte BARTSCHAT, D-7062 LEIPZIG, Weißdornstraße 86, Germany.

Lucia BINOTTI, Department of Spanish and Portuguese, U.C.S.B., SANTA BARBARA, California 93106, USA.

Andrew BREEZE, Avda de Sancho el Fuerte 77-12F, E-31008 PAMPLONA, Spain.

Herbert BREKLE, Lehrstuhl für allgemeine Sprachwissenschaft der Universität, D-8400 REGENSBURG, Universitätsstraße 31, Germany.

Rolf H. BREMMER, Vakgroep Engels, Rijksuniversiteit Leiden, Postbus 9515, NL-2300 RA LEIDEN, The Netherlands.

Geoffrey L. BURSILL-HALL, 406, 2190 Bellevue Avenue, WEST VANCOUVER, British Columbia V7V 1C4, Canada.
Hilary BURSILL-HALL.

Mª Luisa CALERO VAQUERA, Dept. de Filología española, Facultad de Filosofía y Letras, E-14071 CORDOBA, Spain.

Jean-Claude CHEVALIER, 83bis, bvd Richard-Lenoir, F-75011 PARIS, France.
Mme CHEVALIER.

T. Craig CHRISTY, Department of Foreign Languages, 203 Wesleyan Hall, University of North Alabama, FLORENCE, Alabama 35632-0001, USA.

Jan De CLERCQ, Departement Linguïstiek, Blijde Inkomststraat 21, B-3000 LEUVEN, Belgium.

Miriam CLYNE, Templemartin, CRAUGHWELL, Co. Galway.

Bernard COLOMBAT, U.F.R. de Lettres classiques et modernes, Université Stendhal, B.P. 25 X, F-38040 GRENOBLE CEDEX, France.
Mme COLOMBAT.

Jacques COULARDEAU, Equipe de recherche en psychoméchanique du langage, Université de Lille III, B.P. 149, F-59653 VILLENEUVE D'ASQ CEDEX, France.

David CRAM, Jesus College, OXFORD OX1 3DW, England.

Piet DESMET, Departement Linguïstiek, Blijde Inkomststraat 21, B-3000 LEUVEN, Belgium.

Edeltraud DOBNIG-JÜLCH, Lehrstuhl für allgemeine Sprachwissenschaft der Universität, D-8400 REGENSBURG, Universitätsstraße 31, Germany.

Beate DREIKE, Department of German, University College, CORK.

Prof. Daniel DROIXHE, rue d'Erquy 38, B-4480 OUPEYE, Belgium.

Markku FILPPULA, Englannin kielen laitos, PL 111, SF-60101 JOENSUU, Finland.

Lia FORMIGARI, Via Clitunno 15, I-00198 ROMA, Italy.

Stefano GENSINI, Istituto di Filosofia – Magistero, Piazza d'Armi, I-09100 CAGLIARI, Italy.

Joachim GESSINGER, D-3000 HANNOVER 1, Im Moore 25, Germany.

Yaakov GRUNTFEST, Ha-Rav Ankuna Street 28/52, HAIFA 35849, Israel.
Mrs. GRUNTFEST.

Camiel HAMANS, Baronielaan 185, NL-4818 PG BREDA, The Netherlands.

R. HEINE, Institut für Lingvistik der Universität, D-7000 STUTTGART, Keplerstraße 17, Postfach 106037, Germany.
Mrs. HEINE-RAAB.

Yasuko HIO, English Dept., Shikoku Christian College, Zentsuji-shi, Kagawa-keu, 765 Japan.

Rijcklof H.F. HOFMAN, Ameland 109, NL-3524 UTRECHT, The Netherlands.

Even HOVDHAUGEN, Lingvistisk Institutt, Postboks 1012 Blindern, N-0315 OSLO 3, Norway.

Werner HÜLLEN, Fachbereich 3 der Gesamthochschule, D-4300 ESSEN 1, Universitätsstraße 12, Germany.

Mrs. Juneidah IBRAHIM, Dewan Bahasa dan Pustaka, 50926 KUALA LUMPUR, Malaysia.

Asiah IDRIS, Dewan Bahasa dan Pustaka, 50926 KUALA LUMPUR, Malaysia.

Astrid JAHREIß, Forschungsstelle für deutsche Sprachgeschichte der Otto-Friedrich-Universität, D-8600 BAMBERG, Hornthalstraße 2, Germany.

Kurt R. JANKOWSKY, Department of German, Georgetown University, WASHINGTON D.C. 20057, USA.
Mrs. JANKOWSKY.

William JOBLING, Departement of Religious Studies, The University, SYDNEY, New South Wales 2006, Australia.
Mrs. JOBLING.

John E. JOSEPH, Department of French and Italian, The University, COLLEGE PARK, Maryland 20742, USA.

Barbara KALTZ, Luther College, The University, REGINA, Saskatchewan S4S 0A2, Canada.

Aino KÄRNÄ, Saksan kielen laitos, Porthania, SF-00100 HELSINKI, Finland.

L. G. KELLY, Department of Linguistics, The University, OTTAWA, Ontario K1N 6N5, Canada.

Douglas A. KIBBEE, Department of French, 2090 Foreign Languages Building, The University, 707 South Mathews Avenue, URBANA, Illinois 6l801, USA.
Mrs. KIBBEE.

C. H. KNEEPKENS, Dept. of Classical Languages, The Catholic University, Postbus 9l03, NL-6500 HD NIJMEGEN, The Netherlands.

Konrad. KOERNER, Department of Linguistics, The University, OTTAWA, Ontario K1N 6N5, Canada.

Pierre LARDET, 6 rue Franquet, F-75015 PARIS, France.

Vivien LAW, Sidney Sussex College, CAMBRIDGE CB3 3HU, England.
Nicholas SHACKLETON.

Joan LEOPOLD, P.O.Box 24250, LOS ANGELES; California 90024, USA.

Barbara LEWANDOWSKA-TOMASZCZYK, Department of English, The University, Kościuski 65, PL-90 514 ŁÓDŹ, Poland.

Marinella LÖRENCZI, Facultà di Magistero, Piazza d'Armi, I-09100 CAGLIARI, Italy.

Anneli LUHTALA, Laivanvarustajankatu 10 H 104, SF–00140 HELSINKI, Finland.

Yola de LUSENET, John Benjamins B.V., Postbus 52519, NL-1007 HA AMSTERDAM, The Netherlands.

Peadar MAC AN IOMAIRE, Stiúrthóir na Gaeilge Labhartha, Coláiste na hOllscoile, GAILLIMH.
Máirín MHIC AN IOMAIRE.

Gearóid MAC EOIN, Roinn na Sean-Ghaeilge, Coláiste na hOllscoile, GAILLIMH.
Gimma MAC EOIN.

Seán MAC ÍOMHAIR, An Teanglann, Coláiste na hOllscoile, GAILLIMH.
Máire MHIC ÍOMHAIR.

Michael MACKERT, Department of Linguistics, The University, NEWARK, Delaware 19716, USA.

William E. McMAHON, Department of Philosophy, The University, AKRON, Ohio 44325-1903, USA.
Mrs. McMAHON.

Seosamh MAC MUIRÍ, Roinn na Nua-Ghaeilge, Coláiste na hOllscoile, GAILLIMH.

Síle MHIC DHONNCHA, Roinn na Gaeilge, Coláiste na hOllscoile, GAILLIMH.

Jaap van MARLE, P.J. Meertens-Instituut, Postbus 19888, NL-1000 GW AMSTERDAM, The Netherlands.

Mª Dolores MARTÍNEZ GAVILÁN, Departamento de Filología Hispánica, Facultad de Filosofía y Letras, E-24701 LEÓN, Spain.

Brian MERRILEES, Department of French, Victoria, The University, 73 Queen's Park Crescent, TORONTO, Ontario M5S 1K7, Canada.

Mehdi MESHKOT DINI, Faculty of Letters and Human Science, Ferdowsi University, MASHAD 91384, Iran.

Jean-Claude MULLER, Fachbereich 7.1. (vergleichende Sprachwissenschaft und Iranistik) der Universität, D-6600 SAARBRÜCKEN, Germany.

Nicole MÜLLER, Corpus Christi College, OXFORD OX1 4JF, England.

Nuno NABAIS, Faculdade de Ciencias, Departamento de Educação, Edificio C 1 3 piso, Campo Grande, 1700 LISBOA, Portugal.

Stephen NAGLE, The University of South Carolina, P.O.Box 1954, CONWAY, SC 29526, USA.

Brigitte NERLICH, Department of Linguistics, The University, NOTTINGHAM, NG7 2RD, England.

Jan NOORDEGRAAF, Vrije Universiteit, Faculteit der Letteren, Postbus 7161, NL–1007 MC AMSTERDAM, The Netherlands.

Elke NOWAK, Institut für Lingvistik der Universität, D-7000 STUTTGART, Keplerstraße 17, Postfach 106037, Germany.

Máirtín Ó BRIAIN, Roinn na Nua-Ghaeilge, Coláiste na hOllscoile, GAILLIMH.

Conn Ó CLÉIRIGH, Dept. of Linguistics, University College, DUBLIN, 4.

Brian Ó CUÍV, School of Celtic Studies, 10 Burlington Road, DUBLIN, 4.

Donncha Ó hAODHA, Roinn na Sean-Ghaeilge, Coláiste na hOllscoile, GAILLIMH.
Máire Ó hAODHA.

Juan Ignacio SÁNCHEZ PEREZ, Calle Maestro Nicolás, 34 5°J., E-24005 LEÓN, Spain.

Raffaella PETRILLI, Via A. Aleardi 12/A, I-00185 ROMA, Italy.

Olga POMBO, Faculdade de Ciencias, Departamento de Educação, Edificio C 1 3 piso, Campo Grande, 1700 LISBOA, Portugal.

Erich POPPE, Dept. of Anglo-Saxon, Norse and Celtic, CAMBRIDGE, England.

Jana PŘÍVRATSKÁ, Na Brezince 18, 150 00 PRAHA 5, Czechoslovakia.

R. H. ROBINS, 65 Dome Hill, CATERHAM, Surrey CR3 6EF, England.

Johannes ROGGENHOFER, Lehrstuhl für allgemeine Sprachwissenschaft der Universität, D-8400 REGENSBURG, Universitätsstraße 31, Germany.

Haiim B. ROSÉN, Hebrew University, IL-91905 JERUSALEM, Israel.

Hannah ROSÉN, Hebrew University, IL-91905 JERUSALEM, Israel.

Irène ROSIER, 23 rue Manessier, F-94130 NOGENT-SUR MARNE, France.

Jacques-Philippe SAINT-GÉRAND, 42C2, rue de la Quintinie, F-75015 PARIS, France.

Hans SAUER, Institut für englische Philologie der Universität, D-8700 WÜRZBURG, Am Hubland, Germany.

Peter SCHMITTER, Institut für allgemeine Sprachwissenschaft der Universität, D-4400 MÜNSTER, Bispinghof 17, Germany.

Rüdiger SCHREYER, Institut für Anglistik der RWTH, D-5100 AACHEN, Kármánstraße 17-19, Germany.

Robin D. SMITH, Vakgroep Engels, Rijksuniversiteit Leiden, Postbus 9515, NL-2300 RA LEIDEN, The Netherlands.

Joseph L. SUBBIONDO, University of the Pacific, 3601 Pacific Avenue, STOCKTON, California 95211, USA.

Pierre SWIGGERS, Departement Linguïstiek, Blijde Inkomststraat 21, B-3000 LEUVEN, Belgium.

Daniel J. TAYLOR, Dept. of Classics, Lawrence University, Box 599, APPLETON, Wisconsin, USA.

Talbot J. TAYLOR, Department of English, College of William and Mary, WILLIAMSBURG, Virginia 23185, USA.

Ulrich TROJAHN, Am Bahnhof 1, 3211 ANGERN, Germany.

Mária TSIAPERA, Curriculum in Linguistics, The University of North Carolina, 318 Dey Hall 014A, CHAPEL HILL, NC 27514, USA.

Kees VERSTEEGH, Fakulteit der Letteren, Katolieke Universiteit, Erasmusplein 1, Postbus 9103, NL-6500 HD NIJMEGEN, The Netherlands.

Frank J. M. VONK, Fakulteit der Letteren der Rijksuniversiteit, Drift 13, NL 3512 BR UTRECHT, The Netherlands.

Marijke van der WAL, Vakgroep Nederlands, Rijksuniversiteit Leiden, Postbus 9515, NL-2300 RA LEIDEN, The Netherlands.

Zdzisław WĄSIK, Katedra Językoznawstwa Ogólnego, ul. Szewska 50/51, 50-139 WROCŁAW, Poland.

Helmut WEIß, Lehrstuhl für allgemeine Sprachwissenschaft der Universität, D-8400 REGENSBURG, Universitätsstraße 31, Germany.

Jan-Eric WIDELL, Djäknegatan 21, S-754 23 UPPSALA, Sweden.

Joanna Radwańska WILLIAMS, Department of Germanic and Slavic, S.U.N.Y., STONYBROOK, New York 11794, USA.

Isabel ZOLLNA, Institut für Romanische Sprachen und Litteraturen, D-6000 FRANKFURT am MAIN 11, Gräfstraße 76, Germany.

Conference Committees

INTERNATIONAL COMMITTEE:

Hans Aarsleff *(Princeton)*
Anders Ahlqvist[1] *(Galway)*
Julie Andresen *(Duke)*
Herbert Brekle *(Regensburg)*
Konrad Koerner[1] *(Ottawa)*
Hans-J. Niederehe *(Trier)*
W. Keith Percival *(Kansas)*
Ulrich Ricken *(Halle)*
R. H. Robins[1] *(London)*
Irène Rosier[1] *(Paris)*
Ramón Sarmiento *(Madrid)*
Brigitte Schlieben-Lange *(Frankfurt)*
Leslie Seiffert *(Oxford)*

GALWAY COMMITTEE:

Anders Ahlqvist[2]
Gearóid Mac Eoin[2]
Seán Mac Íomhair[2]
Nicole Müller
Seosamh Mac Muirí
Síle Mhic Dhonncha
Máirtín Ó Briain
Donncha Ó hAodha[2]

[1] Member of Programme and Editorial Committee.
[2] Member of Organizing Committee.

Conference Programme

Friday 31 August 1990

1700–2300: Registration and Informal Get-Together, in College Bar: stout and lager courtesy of Murphy's Brewery, Cork

Saturday 1 September 1990

	Plenary Session:	Poster Session:
0930–1000	Opening: Ó Cuív	
1000–1030	Amsler	
1030–1100	Bremmer	
	Chair: Ahlqvist	
1100–1130	Morning Coffee	
1130–1200	Droixhe	
1200–1230	Andresen	
1230–1300	Chevalier	
	Chair: Mac Eoin	
1300–1400	Lunch	
1400–1430	Brekle	
1430–1500	Dobnig-Jülch	
1500–1530	Roggenhofer	
1530–1600	Weiß	
	Chair: Ó hAodha	
1600–1630	Afternoon Tea	
1630–1700	Van der Wal	Brekle & al.
1700–1730	Hamans	
1730–1800	Awedyk	Jahreiß
	Chair: Nagle	Chair: Bartschat

Sunday 2 September 1990

1230–2230	Excursion, led by Miriam Clyne, to Clonfert and Clonmacnoise, followed by an evening meal in Hayden's Hotel, Ballinasloe	

Monday 3 September 1990

	Plenary Session:	Poster Session:
0900–0930	Petrilli	
0930–1000	Luhtala	
1000–1030	Kneepkens	
1030–1100	Law	
	Chair: Bursill-Hall	
1100–1130	Morning Coffee	
1130–1200	Meshkot Dini	Coulardeau
1200–1230	Saint-Gérand	Jankowsky
1230–1300	De Clercq	
	Chair: Robins	Chair: Ball
1300–1400	Lunch	
1400–1430	Desmet	Přívratská
1430–1500	McMahon	Colombat
1500–1530	Swiggers	Kaltz
1530–1600	Lardet	Jobling
	Chair: Rosier	Chair: Widell
1600–1630	Afternoon Tea	
1630–1700	Breeze	
1700–1730	Kibbee	
	Chair: Koerner	
1800–1930	Reception offered by Kenny's Bookshops	

Tuesday 4 September 1990

	Plenary Session:	Poster Session:
1000–1030	Binotti	
1030–1100	Gensini	
	Chair: Schmitter	
1100–1130	Morning Coffee	
1130–1200	Gruntfest	
1200–1230	Hovdhaugen	
1230–1300	Hüllen	
	Chair: Ó Cléirigh	
1300–1400	Lunch	
1400–1430	Martínez Gavilán	Hofman
1430–1500	Calero Vaquera	
1500–1530		Merrilees
1530–1600	Pombo	
	Chair: Zollna	Chair: Ó Cuív
1600–1630	Afternoon Tea	
1630–1700	Versteegh	D. J. Taylor
1700–1730	Muller	
1730–1800	Kelly	Rosén
1800–1830	Bartschat	
	Chair: Kärnä	Chair: Hüllen

Wednesday 5 September 1990

	Plenary Session:	Poster Session:
0930–1000	Nowak	
1000–1030	Sauer	
1030–1100	Smith	
	Chair: Brekle	
1100–1130	Morning Coffee	
1130–1200	Subbiondo	
1200–1230	Bartlett,	
1230–1300	Christy	
	Chair: Trojahn	
1300–1400	Lunch	
1400–1430	Vonk	Wąsik
1430–1500	Gessinger	
1500–1530	Leopold	Nabais
1530–1600	Mackert	
	Chair: Subbiondo	Chair: Hamans
1600–1630	Afternoon Tea	
1630–1700	Nerlich	
1700–1730	Noordegraaf	
1730–1800	Schmitter	
	Chair: Mac Muirí	
1930	Reception, offered by the Irish Tourist Board, followed by Conference Dinner (Chef de cuisine: Richard Wilkin)	

Thursday 6 September 1990

	Plenary Session:	Poster Session:
1030–1100	Schreyer	
	Chair: Awedyk	
1100–1130	Morning Coffee	
1130–1200	Nagle	
1200–1230	Williams	
1230–1300	Heine	
	Chair: Swiggers	
1300–1400	Lunch	
1400–1430	Joseph	Lewandowska-Tomaszczyk
1430–1500	Tsiapera	
1500–1530	van Marle	Filppula
1530–1600	Bouquet	
	Chair: Kelly	Chair: Poppe
1600–1630	Afternoon Tea	
1630–1700	T.J. Taylor	
1700–1800	General Meeting	
1800	Official Closure	
	Chair: Ahlqvist	

Opening Address

BRIAN Ó CUÍV
Dublin Institute for Advanced Studies

IN INVITING ME to address you in this opening session Dr Ahlqvist has done me a singular honour which I deeply appreciate. My appreciation is all the greater because I am well aware that there are others here today whose work in the field of linguistics might have gained them that honour. I lay no claim to being actively and primarily engaged in the area of theoretical linguistics. My academic training and background lie in the field of Celtic studies in which I had my formal initiation at university level fifty-five years ago. Over the years my career as teacher and lecturer, as research-worker and writer, has continued to be in that field, and more particularly in matters relating to the Irish language and its literature from Old Irish through later periods down to the current spoken dialects. I have had occasion to be lexicographer, palaeographer, historian, onomastic scholar, grammarian, phonologist, and student of metrics, but always with special reference to Irish. Accordingly, it is with a certain amount of awe that I contemplate the vast range of writings on linguistic matters that has been produced during my academic lifetime.

In considering what I should say in this opening address I have been recalling some other international gatherings such as this that I have attended. In 1948 I was present at the first post-war International Congress of Linguists in Paris where I saw in the flesh and heard discourses from eminent scholars including Louis Hjelmslev of the Linguistic Circle of Copenhagen and members of the Prague School such as Trnka who came from Czechoslovakia and Roman Jakobson who, along with André Martinet, represented the University of Columbia in New York. Among those representing the host country were Benveniste, Gougenheim, Sauvageot and Vendryes, and others present included Valentin Kiparsky from Finland, Devoto from Italy, Doroszewski from Poland, Debrunner from Switzerland, and Bonfante and Whatmough from the U.S. A.

In view of the great growth of interest and activity in linguistics and the study of different languages in the last forty years, it may be of interest to recall something of the programme in Paris. On that occasion the Congress was organised into eight plenary sessions in which topics estimated to be of wide interest were considered — four of them theoretical and four practical. On the theoretical side were discussions of general morphology with special reference to categories, the interrelations between phonemic and grammatical aspects of language, the interrelations between morphology, syntax and semantics, and the influence of the morphology of one language on that of another. On the practical side the topics were linguistic terminology, linguistic investigation with special reference to dialectal study and linguistic geography, linguistic statistics, and the question of an auxiliary international language.

Rather than spend time discussing later International Congresses of Linguists I pass on to the first in the present series of Conferences on the History of the Language Sciences which was held in Ottawa in 1978. I think that it is a sign of the success of that Conference, as much as of the world-wide interest in linguistic matters, that the series has continued regularly on a triennial basis so that we are meeting here in the Fifth Conference. I might point out that Galway has already been the venue for a conference in a separate linguistic series, for the Fifth International Conference on Historical Linguistics was held here in 1981. Our chairman today was the central figure in organising that Conference, just as he is again this year. We cannot but commend him for his unflagging energy.

An examination of the abstracts of communications to be presented in the coming days shows that the pattern of diversity shown in the first and subsequent conferences in this series has been maintained. I expect that when the Proceedings appear we will find grouping of papers under headings such as Classical Period, Medieval Period, Renaissance, Seventeenth Century, and so on. I have no doubt that even the most diligent among us will find the range and choice of papers more than adequate and that our knowledge and understanding of our subject will be enhanced during the week, not only by listening to papers and the subsequent discussions, but also by meeting old friends and, may I hope, making new ones.

At the outset of this address I said that the Irish language and its literature are my special field of study. In coming to Galway you have come to the one University College in Ireland which is situated within a relatively short distance of districts in which Irish has survived as a spoken language from pre-Christian times. To the majority of Irish people it is a matter of regret that circumstances in the past have resulted in a general replacement of Irish by Englishas the normal spoken language in our country. The death of any language must be a matter for regret, but in the case of Irish, which has the oldest extant vernacular literature in western Europe, it would be especially regrettable. However, we have not yet reached that stage and I do not expect *rigor mortis* to be pronounced in my lifetime. And now, in order to introduce a somewhat lighter note into this talk, I would like to tell you briefly about a visit paid to Ireland early in the present century by the greatest English philologist of his day, Henry Sweet.

One of the results of our country's unfortunate history was that at the beginning of this century there were comparatively few opportunities for Irish people to get training in their own country in a number of areas of academic activity, including palaeography, philology, and phonetics. An effort to provide a remedy was made when a German, Professor Kuno Meyer, and an Englishman, Professor John Strachan, founded a "School of Irish Learning" in Dublin with the intention of giving courses of training and instruction from time to time in selected subjects. It was in this connection that Sweet came to Ireland, for in September 1903 he gave here a three-week course in practical phonetics, the main purpose of which was to stimulate research on spoken Irish dialects.

It is not with the course that I am concerned here, but with a by-product of Sweet's visit to Dublin. He came to Ireland at a time when there was considerable political activity in a national effort to gain self-government from England, and co-incidentally there was a growing realisation of the significance of the Irish language as a mark of national identity, with the result that even speaking Irish in public might be regarded by the authorities as a sign of disaffection towards the British government. Sweet was obviously a very observant person, and in the few weeks he spent in Dublin he learned quite an amount about the spirit of unrest and political change in this country. On his return to Oxford he recorded some of his impressions in a little pamphlet which he had printed and which he circulated to friends and acquaintances The title-page gives a hint of the less than serious nature of its contents. It reads: "Home Rule in Ireland. Before & After. by Open-minded", and it bears the imprint "University Press, Clontarf 3145." I might add that Clontarf was the scene of a battle in the year 1014 which put an end to the threat of domination of Ireland by Scandinavian invaders.

Sweet's pamphlet consists of a fanciful outline of the history of Ireland down to the 32nd century A.D., commencing with the imposition of self-government on a reluctant Irish people, and including successive periods of oppressive foreign rule by a South African Boer General and by a Yankee Emperor who made the Yankee language compulsory in all the schools and universities of Ireland, and finally an era of relative peace with the establishment in the year 3011 of the United States of Europe of which Ireland was an autonomous member. The destruction by order of the Yankee Emperor of the whole of the literature of Western Europe had left much of the history of Ireland a blank, but a precious piece of evidence from the past had been discovered during recent excavations in the ancient capital. This consisted of fragments of a diary estimated to date from as far back as the twentieth century whose author was revealed as being an English academic who was engaged in giving a course in Dublin on what he described as "the phonetics of Modern Irish".

It is with certain passages in the diary which puzzled the 32nd-century writer that I am particularly concerned here, but as a prelude to speaking about them I must mention the term "native speaker" which had been coined during the 19th century to designate an Irishman whose first and normal language was Irish. Students of the language valued "native speakers" as the repository of the living speech. At this point I must quote from Sweet's pamphlet:

> The frequent references in our diary to "native speakers," and the evident pride and satisfaction with which the diarist announces that he has one of them in his class — as if a "native speaker" were something rare and precious — points clearly to the extraordinary and hitherto unsuspected fact that by "Modern Irish" is meant a language radically distinct from Englishand Yankee... Am I too sanguine in expressing a hope that the excavations now being carried on may unearth further specimens of this deeply, tantalizingly interesting language?

One other passage must be quoted. In it the 32nd-century author described the current linguistic situation in Ireland. He said:

> At the present time there is only one language which is understood all over Ireland — that is, Yankee; although the praiseworthy efforts of the English League to restore the old national language show every sign of being eventually crowned with success, especially in the West, where the old language still lingers as a popular dialect. I was astonished and pleased to find, during my visit to the Island of Aran last summer, that the dialect spoken there is pure English of a very archaic type: strong verbs and irregular plurals preserved, polysyllabic as well as monosyllabic roots, preservation of the sounds of *th* in *this thing*, of *v* in the disyllabic *never*. The Islanders ridicule the speech of the mainland with its *dis tĭ, neb, gwine* for *going* (Aranese *goin)*, and its other Yankeeisms.

In Sweet's time, as he well knew, Irish was the everyday language of over 90% of the population of the Aran Islands which you have probably already seen some twenty-five miles from here out in the ocean. About a quarter of the population were Irish-speaking monoglots — very precious "native speakers". Irish is still commonly spoken in the Islands today, so any of you who care to make the journey out there can combine your participation in this Conference with the experience of hearing in daily use this "tantalizingly interesting language". In the meantime may I express the hope that you will fully enjoy your time in Galway.

The Priscian Text Used in Three Ninth-Century Irish Donatus Commentaries*

RIJCKLOF HOFMAN
University of Utrecht

THREE IRISH scholars teaching on the Continent around the middle of the 9th century A.D. play the leading parts in this contribution. After a brief sketch of the general background (cf. e.g. Riché 1989:47–118) and the activities of these three teachers, I will concentrate on the quotations in their works from the sixth-century Latin grammarian Priscian.

In the period from the 6th until the 8th century, the cultural level of the inhabitants of the European Continent had gradually declined. During the last decades of the eighth century, Charlemagne decided to improve the educational system in his Empire, but he could not find many capable teachers in his own realm.

In the British Isles, however, teachers had been experimenting for two centuries giving lessons in Latin to pupils with a different mother tongue. Moreover, in the British Isles the same manual was generally used for second language acquisition purposes as on the Continent, namely the *Ars Grammatica* written by the 4th-century Latin grammarian Donatus.[1] Therefore Charlemagne and his successors invited Insular grammarians to help them with their educational programme. But Donatus's manual was remarkably unfit for the use that it was put to: it had originally been written by a Roman for Roman children who used Latin as their first language. This text was commented on as early as

* The research for this article was supported financially by the Netherlands Organization for Scientific Research (NWO). The English version of this paper was revised by Robert Tausk.

[1] On this section cf. Holtz (1981:264–326), with ample bibliography and Law (1982). On the Carolingian period cf. also Holtz (1988) and Law (this volume).

the seventh century in the British Isles. Some of the tracts written between the seventh and the ninth century were more elementary than others, but here only one type is discussed, written for more advanced students. I will pay attention to the authors of three commentaries on Donatus's grammar, who all arrived on the Continent between 835 and 850 A.D. We know the names of two of them: Murethach (henceforth: Mur.) and Sedulius Scottus (Sed.). The third commentary, *Ars Laureshamensis* (Laur.), has been transmitted anonymously.[1] The three texts are closely related, and all three are adaptations of a now lost, so-called "common source", which was written in Ireland and perhaps never left the island.[2]

The three commentaries, and probably their common source too, are constructed in the same fashion: the author first quotes a phrase from Donatus, which he paraphrases. He then explains the literal meaning, and finally he discusses the implication of Donatus's words, or confronts him with quotations from other grammarians. Almost every phrase that Donatus has written is commented on in this way.[3]

I will now concentrate on the quotations from the 6th. century Latin grammarian Priscian in the texts of our three authors. Sometimes a quoted passage is interrupted because one of the sentences in it is paraphrased, or it differs from its source-text in that a few words are added which are missing in the original. These additions, however, cannot always be attributed to our three authors (or their common source). The doubt about their originality is connected with the history of the transmission of Priscian's *Institutiones Grammaticae:* many Priscian-MSS contain a great number of glosses. Such glosses were not added all at once; instead, they reflect the activities of several generations of glossators. Whenever the text of Priscian was copied, new glosses were added; at the same time the glosses already present in the "Vorlage" were transcribed together with the main text. On the other hand, no two

[1] Edited by Holtz (1977a) and Löfstedt (1977a,b).

[2] Cf. Holtz (1972:59–72); cf. also Löfstedt (1977a:xiii) for a modification of one of Holtz's conclusions.

[3] Cf. Holtz (1977b:72–73) for a more elaborate description of the technique and its possible source.

MSS contain exactly the same collection of glosses, as scribes omitted glosses which they did not think useful.[1] It will now be examined whether the added words in the quotations from Priscian in our three texts are in fact glosses which were integrated into the quotations.

The Priscian-text used by the common source belonged to the so-called 'Irish recension' of Priscian, that is to say to the version of the text as reflected by the six Priscian MSS with Irish connections.[2] This fact is clear from a comparison between the quoted Priscian-fragments in our three commentaries and the variant readings in the critical apparatus in Hertz's (1855–59) edition of Priscian. This conclusion is corroborated by the fact that at least ten significant additions to the quoted fragments can be compared to glosses in an Irish Priscian-MS presently kept in St. Gall (Stiftsbibl., MS 904 = henceforth MS G).

To illustrate my point I will discuss two examples which combine three advantages: they touch upon linguistic concepts, they exemplify that things are not as simple as one might wish, and they show how Irish scholars handled words with Greek affinities.[3]

EXAMPLE 1

> Donatus, *Ars Maior II,3* (Holtz 1981:616.1): *Alia patronomica, ut Atrides, Pelides.*
>
> (Laur., *In Don. Mai. II* [Löfstedt 1977a:16.28–31] = *Prisc.* [Hertz 1855]:62, 15–17).
>
> Sedulius Scottus, *In Don. Mai. II* (Löfstedt 1977b:85.98–4): *Patronomica dicuntur quasi patrilega vel patrum legalia.* Νόμος *enim grece lex dicitur. Patrilega autem ideo dicuntur, quia ex patribus fiunt et ex patris scripturis aliquid retinent. Patronomicum est, quod a propriis tantummodo derivatur patrum nominibus secundum formam*

[1] On the different layers of the glosses in the Irish St. Gall Priscian cf. Strachan (1903). Draak (1967) provides us with a good impression of the techniques used by the glossators. The character of a ninth century Continental gloss-commentary on Priscian is sketched in Gibson (1981).

[2] The relevant MSS (except the 'Ambrosian fragment') are described in Hofman (1988:809–812).

[3] On glosses over Greek lemma-words in Priscian's text in MS G, cf. Ahlqvist (1988).

grecam; resolvuntur etiam per genitivum primitivi et significant filium vel nepotem.
Murethach , *In Don. Mai. II* (Holtz 1977a:64.32–33).
patronomica dicuntur quasi patrum legalia, eo quod legem et vim nominationis primi patris retineant, ut .. etc.
Priscian, *Inst. Gr.* (Hertz 1855:62,15–17): *Patronymicum*) est quod a propriis tantummodo derivatur patrum nominibus secundum formam graecam, quod significat**) cum genitivo primitivi filius vel nepos.*
MS G, p. 30b: *) 30b24 z (left margin):*b- patronomicum dicitur ut in alio* and **) 30b26 bb (right margin) *.i. ciall genitivi nominis cétnaidi conacomol fris indí as filius vel nepos issi fil isind aitherrechtaigthiu* "i.e. the meaning of the genitive of the primitive noun with the addition to it of *filius* (son) or *nepos* (grandson), that is what is found in the patronymic."
MS K, f. 15r. (right margin): *b- patronomicum dicitur eo quod a nomine patris trahit nominationem.* νεμει *enim grece nomen dicitur ut omonima sinonima síc patronomica. b- patronomica paterna legalia pater et nomos .i. genitor et lex. trahunt legem sive* [leg. *et vim?* cf. Mur.] *nominationis et significationis vel á patribus vel ab avís reliqua.*

Example 1 is taken from the comments on Donatus's enumeration of the various kinds of common nouns. Donatus lists the so-called 'patronymic' among them, but he does not explain what a patronymic is. Laur. quotes Priscian's definition literally, stating that a patronymic is a noun derived from a proper name, which usually means "the son — or the grandson — of ...". Sed also quotes the first part of Priscian's definition literally, but replaces the second part by a paraphrase which is a Latin translation of an Old Irish gloss in MS G. Before giving the definition, however, he provides us with a curious etymology of the word "patronymic", which resembles the comment in Mur.

It is obvious that both authors draw from the same source, which departs in its etymologizing from the erroneous spelling *patronomicum* instead of *patronymicum* and considers the word as a compound from *pater* "father" and the Greek word νόμος "law", translated into Latin as *lex* "law". That a derivation to that effect was popular in Ireland has been known for a long time: Ascoli (1879:l) has suggested that the Old Irish calque on *patronomicum*, which is used in our example and which is found several times in MS G, *aitherrechtaigthe*, necessarily departed from a compound *pater* + νόμος, a suggestion repeated by Stokes and Strachan (1903:84 fn. g).[1]

But, although we can designate the Priscian-glossators as the source of Mur. and Sed, we cannot simply hold them responsible for the "invention" of the etymology. In order to find the inventor we have to turn to another ninth-century Irish copy of Priscian, presently kept in Karlsruhe (Badische Landesbibl., MS Aug. cxxxii = MS K). In that MS we find two glosses which explain *patronomicum* and which are both preceded by the source-indication *b-*. The first of these two is the complete version of an abbreviated gloss in MS G, which, however, does not help us any further. But the second gloss in MS K clearly goes back to the same source as our two authors, viz. "b-".

EXAMPLE 2

> Donatus, *Ars Maior I,2* (Holtz 1981:604.11): *Sunt autem <sc. semivocales> numero septem, f l m n r s x.*
> Sedulius Scottus, *In Don. Mai. I* (Löfstedt 1977b:12,35–37): *x: Nam ab i littera incipit per anastrophen greci nominis xi, quia necesse fuit, cum sit semivocalis, a vocali incipere et in se terminari*
> Murethach, *In Don. Mai. I* (Holtz 1977a:16.79–84): *Ut quid autem x non ab e incipit sicut ceterae semivocales? Quia per conversionem factum est, ut a fine converteretur in caput. Ab Augusto quippe inventa et a grecis chi x* [sic MS D] *mutata, i quod habebat in fine apud grecos voluit idem doctor ut haberet apud* Latinos *in capite et loco duarum consonantium fungeretur.*
> Laur. *In Don. Mai. I* (Löfstedt 1977a: 156,66–69): *Quaeritur, quare sola x non ab e, sed ab i incipit. Ad quod dicendum, quia ab Augusto inventa est et ex greco xi mutata, id est vocata, est ix; voluit enim idem doctor, ut hoc, quod apud grecos habeat in fine, hoc apud* Latinos *haberet in capite.*

[1] One may add that the 'inventor' of the etymology may have been someone without a proper knowledge of Greek: in one of many lists in yet another fourth-century grammarian who was known in Ireland, Charisius, we read *lex* νόμος *legis* (Barwick 1925:49.25).

Priscian, *Inst. Gr.* (Hertz 1855:8.11–14):... *absque x, quae* <*sola* [add. MSS GLK]> *ab i incipit per anastrophen**) *graeci nominis* ξῖ, *quia necesse fuit, cum sit semivocalis, a vocali incipere et in se terminari* [sic MSS GK cf. Sed *terminare* Prisc.] *(...), quae novissime***) *a* Latin*is assumpta post omnes ponitur literas.*
MS St. Gall 904, p. 4b: *) 4b12 m *per anostrophen: .i. tre impúth* ".i. by inversion"; **) 4b15 q *novissime: in tempore Augusti inventa est x.*
Cf. Isidore (Lindsay 1911: *Etymologiae*, I,4,14): *X littera usque ad Augusti tempus nondum apud* Latinos *erat*, ..
Cf. Donatus Ortigraphus (Chittenden 1982:17.220–224 = Priscian 8.11–14; 17.229–232 = Is., *Et.*, I,4,14).

Example 2 has been taken from the comment in our authors on Donatus's section on the letters of the alphabet. Donatus not surprisingly, mentions the letter *x* among them, and in connection with that letter our three authors address the question why it irregularly begins with an *i*, and not with an *e*.

Fortunately, they found an answer among Priscian's remarks on the letter *x*. Priscian observes two things: (1) that *x* begins with an *i* because the letter was borrowed from the Greek Ξ, with a reversal of the place of the accompanying vowel; (2) that *x* was assigned a place at the end of the alphabet because it was adopted into Latin at a recent date. Sed. copies Priscian's first observation only; Mur. and Laur. paraphrase both observations, and add some extra information. Their comments resemble each other very much, and we may safely assume that the common source is responsible for the original paraphrase. Moreover, this source depends on a glossed Priscian-text: Priscian used the difficult word *anastrophe* "reversing of letters", which Laur. omits altogether, but which Mur. (and his source?) replace by the synonym *conversio*, probably because of pedagogic considerations. The common source was perhaps inspired by a gloss explaining *anastrophe* which he read in his Priscian MS. A gloss to that effect, *tre impúth* "by inversion", is still transmitted in MS G (gloss*).[1]

[1] Cf. also the gloss on *per anastrophen* in the Irish Priscian MS Leiden BPL 67, f. 10v: *.i. reversionem* (added in a ninth-century Carolingian hand under Irish influence).

Mur. and Laur. replace the rather vague *novissime* "recently" in Priscian's second observation by something more concrete, which can be rendered as follows: "*x* was invented by Augustus and changed by him from the Greek ξι. For this same doctor wanted the *i* — at the end in the Greek letter name — to be at the beginning in the Latin one". The common source found the addition in his Priscian MS. This is clear from a gloss, on *novissime*, in MS G (gloss**). Especially significant is the use of the word *inventa*. However, the common source did not understand the implication of the gloss, for he called the great first Roman Emperor "a doctor". The information which is summarized in the gloss can be found in extenso in one other place, namely in the first Book of the *Etymologies* of the 6th century Spanish bishop Isidore of Seville. The fact that the Irish scholar who originally wrote the gloss used Isidore is confirmed by an independent witness, viz. an anonymous grammar written by an Irishman, probably in the early 9th century, which is known as *Donatus Ortigraphus* (Chittenden 1982). In this book, in the section on the letters of the alphabet, our passage from Priscian is quoted by name. Immediately following it, the passage from Isidore is quoted in full, also by name.

It is time for some conclusions now. A comparison between glosses on a classical Latin grammar and phrases in a Medieval Latin text may seem a modest enterprise at first sight, but it does reveal a number of interesting things. In the first place, glosses in the St. Gall Priscian sometimes agree with additions in our three texts, but there are many St. Gall glosses which have not been incorporated in them. Moreover at least one gloss which is present in the Karlsruhe Priscian only, is integrated in an explanation that goes back to the common source. Apparently, the author of the common source used a Priscian MS which is not extant any more, but which resembled the MSS of the Irish recension of Priscian. This conclusion is corroborated by a consideration to which I have not yet called attention: it is noteworthy that almost all the additions which can be traced back to glosses occur in quotations from Books I and II in Priscian. We can tentatively conclude that the author of the common source used a copy of Priscian's work in which only the first two books had been glossed. As far as the originality of our three authors is concerned, it is becoming clear now that very often phrases or theories which seem to be individual contributions are in fact just glosses which have been integrated in a clever way in a given fragment quoted from a classical grammarian. And yet this conclusion is not entirely a negative one: it means that we can consider the work of Sedulius and his comrades the final result of the labour of the Irish Priscian-glossators, who have, during a period lasting for several generations, woven a web around the Priscian-text that grew denser with every generation. The fact that some glosses occur in a single MS only, whereas others are shared by a number of MSS, indicates that the practice of gloss-writing goes back a long time. In any case the modest aspirations of the glossators have ensured one thing: the continuity of linguistic thought.

REFERENCES

Ahlqvist, Anders. 1988. "Notes on the Greek Materials in the St. Gall Priscian (Cod. 904)". *The Sacred Nectar of the* Greek*s* ed. by Michael W. Herren, 195–214. London: King's College *(King's College London Medieval Studies*, 2.)

Ascoli, G.I. 1879. "Il codice irlandese dell' Ambrosiana. II: Appendici e illustrazioni". *Archivio Glottologico Italiano* VI. Roma: Loescher.

Barwick, Karl, ed. 1925. *Charisii Artis Grammaticae Libri V*. Leipzig: Teubner.

Chittenden, John, ed. 1982. *Donatus Ortigraphus, Ars Grammatica*. Turnhout: Brepols *(C[orpus] C[hristianorum] C[ontinuatio] M[ediaevalis]* 40D).

Draak, Maartje. 1967. "The Higher Teaching of Latin Grammar in Ireland during the 9th Cent.". *Mededelingen der Kon. Ned. Academie van Wetenschappen*, afd. Letterkunde, Nieuwe Reeks, Deel 30, nr. 4, 107–144.

Gibson, Margaret. 1981. "Rag- Reads Priscian". *Charles the Bald*, edd. Margaret Gibson & Janet Nelson, 311–316 Oxford: BAR Int. Ser., 101.

Hertz, Martin, ed. 1855–59. *Priscianus. Institutiones Grammaticae. Grammatici Latini II, III*. Leipzig: Teubner (Repr., Hildesheim: Olms, 1961).

Hofman, Rijcklof. 1988. "Glosses in a 9th Cent. Priscian MS Probably Attributable to Heiric of Auxerre (d. ca. 876) and their Connections". *Studi Medievali*, 3a Serie, 29:2.805–839.

Holtz, Louis. 1972. "Sur trois Commentaires irlandais de l'Art Majeur de Donat au IXe siècle". *RHT* 2.45–72.

—. ed. 1977a. Murethach *[= Mur.]*. *In Donati Artem Maiorem* Turnhout: Brepols *(CCCM* 40).

—. 1977b. "Grammairiens irlandais au temps de Jean Scot : quelques aspects de leur pédagogie". *Jean Scot Erigène et l'histoire de la philosophie*, 69–78. Paris: CNRS.

—. 1981. *Donat et la tradition de l'enseignement grammatical*. Paris: CNRS.

—. 1988. "Les Innovations théoriques de la grammaire carolingienne : peu de chose. Pourquoi?". *L'Héritage des grammairiens Latins de l'Antiquité aux lumières,* ed. Irène Rosier, 133–145. Louvain: Peeters.

Law, Vivien. 1982. *The Insular Latin Grammarians*. Woodbridge: Boydell Press.

Lindsay, Wallace M., ed. 1911. *Isidori Hispalensis Episcopi Etymologiarum sive Originum Libri XX*. Oxford: University Press.

Löfstedt, Bengt, ed. 1977a. *Ars Laureshamensis [=* Laur.*]. Expositio in Donatum Maiorem*. Turnhout: Brepols *(CCCM* 40A).

—. ed. 1977b. Sedulius Scottus *[=* Sed.*]. In Donati Artem Maiorem*. Turnhout: Brepols *(CCCM* 40B).

Riché, Pierre. 1979. *Ecoles et enseignement dans le Haut Moyen Age*. Paris: Aubier Montaigne (2nd ed., Paris: Picard, 1989.)

Stokes, Whitley, and Strachan, John, eds. 1903. *Thesaurus Palaeohibernicus*. Vol. II. Cambridge: University Press (Repr., Dublin: Institute for Advanced Studies, 1975.)

Strachan, John. 1903. "On the Language of the St. Gall Glosses". *ZCPh* 4.470–492.

Speculative Lexicography: Difficulties in Following the Historical Path of a Linguistic Idea

WERNER HÜLLEN
Universität-Gesamthochschule-Essen

ANGLO-SAXON WRITTEN culture starts (as in fact does European written culture) with glosses, as is well-known. They served as translation aids for the understanding of Latin texts, but almost certainly also as teaching aids. Interlinear and marginal glosses were soon arranged in lists, first in textual, later in alphabetical order. Such lists mark the beginning of the bilingual alphabetical dictionary and thus started an important lexicographical tradition (Stein 1985).

Though, in some cases, it is difficult to assess why a special Latin word needed a written translation whereas others apparently did not, it is obvious that some glosses are not just meant to be translation or teaching aids. This is the case when semantically similar lexemes or lexemes from various semantic fields but in a topical order are collected. We find "nests" of such related glosses, for example, in the *Leiden Glossary* with words designating gems or animals (Hüllen 1989a). An interest in facts, in encyclopedic knowledge (in the widest sense) can be assumed to be at work behind such glosses, particularly when enlarged into whole glossaries. A good example is *Archbishop Alfric's Vocabulary* with its 2157 lemmata in 15 chapters.[1] Obviously,

[1] This is the title that T. Wright gave to the glossary in 1857 mistakenly attributing it to Archbishop Aelfric although E. Dietrich had already proved in 1855 that the Author was Aelfric, abbot of Eynsham, who flourished about 1006 (Stein 1985:33/34). Its subtitles are:
De Instrumentis Agricolarum
Nomina Omnium Hominum Communiter
Nomina Ferarum

the aim of the compiler(s) was to assemble as many lexemes/words as were meaningful and useful but not necessarily difficult to understand for people of the 10th and 11th century. Certainly, not all of these words needed written translation from Latin into Anglo-Saxon, but obviously all of them were useful to know. This is confirmed by the fact that, even within the chapters, we find a meaningful sequence of lexemes, e.g. (Roman) state offices in a hierarchical order or sicknesses according to the danger which they can have for humans. Another example is Alfric's *Glossary* whose (about) 1300 lemmata somehow cover the whole world.[1] Whereas the first vocabulary seems to follow a more practical purpose, the latter is philosophically oriented.

De Nominibus Insectorum
Nomina Vasorum
De Generibus Potionum
Nomina Avium
Nomina Herbarum
Nomina Arborum
Nomina Armorum
Nomina XII Ventorum
Nomina Tricti Sunt
Vestium Nomina
Nomina Colorum
Nomina Navium

[1] The following is a brief overview of the contents, with original subtitles:
Nomina: 19 lemmata about God, heaven, earth, mankind.

Nomina Membrorum: 101 lemmata about parts of the body; 33 lemmata about persons and church offices; 36 lemmata about family relationships; 132 lemmata about persons in society, artisans (including musical instruments and their players, parts of ships etc.); 42 lemmata again about persons, and similar words; 45 lemmata as before, but with words about intellectual work; 67 lemmata about characteristics of persons; 66 lemmata about natural phenomena, the weather and seasons.

Nomina Avium: 46 lemmata.

Nomina Piscium: 19 lemmata.

Nomina Ferarum: 74 lemmata obviously ordered according to the size of animals.

Nomina Herbarum: 68 lemmata mainly for flowers and herbs.

Nomina Arborum: 83 lemmata.

Nomina Dormorum: 232 lemmata about houses, in particular monasteries, churches (including utensils for mass, clerical vestments etc.); 33 lemmata about arms, tools, towns, castles, metals; 66 lemmata which defy grouping, but which contain a number of theological terms.

The glossary ends with the sentence (in Anglo-Saxon):

Such glossaries mark the beginning of a lexicographical tradition which is less notorious than the tradition of alphabetical dictionaries but which has been nevertheless present in an unbroken chain from the early period of glosses down to today. The members of this chain are topical glossaries or dictionaries, thesauri, taxonomies, ideological dictionaries, terminological classifications or other types of non-alphabetical word-lists.

This second lexicographical tradition can be called "speculative" in parallelism to the well-known medieval speculative grammar. The gist of speculative lexicography is the idea of reconstructing the world in words and to do so in such an arrangement that the world's order, as understood and assumed to be the case at a certain time, is reflected in it. Such topical word-lists then become a mirror *(speculum)* of reality just as language with its grammar, in particular with its word-classes, was supposed to be a mirror of the world, in particular its ontological categories.

Generally speaking, we can say that alphabetical lexicography and even more speculative lexicography gave rise to and reinforced two important linguistic ideas (Waswo 1987):

i. Words are understood to be the names for things (Ullmann 1962/1972). They are in language what the object is in the world. They are labels attached to such objects in order to identify them. This explains the predominance of nouns in early lexicography. It is also characteristic that the scene in Genesis where Adam gives names to animals and plants in paradise has for such a long time served as the explanation for the essence of language.

We can only speculate on the reasons why early understanding of language was as utterly word-centred as it appears. Certainly man's involvement in nature as reflected in early philosophy and natural history was of overriding importance. It is a view of language that reflects man's dependence on natural and artificial objects.

Looking at words as the names of things also means that they (words) can take their (things) place, that language can be used as a

"We cannot however write all names nor even imagine them." (Zupitza 1880/1966)

surrogate for reality. This leads to an epistemological dualism of an objective world and a mental language which face each other (Harris 1980).

ii. As the world was supposed to be orderly, vocabulary was necessarily supposed to be at least susceptible to the same order. What has been called the "Great Chain of Being" (Lovejoy 1936/1964) is the idea that the world as a creation of God must be homogeneous, without leaps or gaps, with every item in its proper place. The idea of the "Great Chain of Being" has its corollary in the "Great Chain of Words", i.e. in the assumption that there is a proper order for the lexemes of a language which mirrors the order of reality. Of course, there are no theoretical deliberations on such paradigmatical preconditions of lexicographical work, but we may assume them because otherwise topical glossaries and the activity of culling them from texts do not make sense.

There is, so far, no history of such topical glosses, apart from an introductory essay by Dornseiff (1943) in his thesaurus of German vocabulary.[1] But it would certainly be worth-while writing one.

Speculative lexicography is a permanent idea in the history of general European linguistics which, however, appears time and again in different apparel depending on a wider context. I shall try and enumerate some of its types.

First, there are topical glossaries/dictionaries which are what they are and nothing else. At least they do not give any hint of a wider use. They list large corpora of words in a philosophical/encyclopedic order, moving from the early Latin-Anglo-Saxon nominals to other bi- and multilingual arrangements. An outstanding example of the latter is Junius' *Nomenclator, omnium rerum propria nomina* (1577) which, besides the Latin lemma, lists German, ("Belgian"), French ("Gallic"), Italian, Spanish, and English equivalents.

Second, there are those dictionaries with a didactic purpose. An outstanding example of this type is John Withals' *A Shorte Dictionarie*

[1] McArthur (1986a) deals with topical glossaries and dictionaries but as a description of cultural history rather than a work in lexicography (see also McArthur 1986b).

for yonge begynners (1553) with English-Latin word pairs. Its interesting "Prologue" has the following sentence:

> ... I have drawen as diligently as I coulde, the propre names of thynges cunteyned vnder one kynde, and disposed them in such ordre, that a very childe beyng able to reade, may with little labour perfitely imprinte them in memory: whiche shall not be onlie profitable for them nowe in theyr tendre age, but hereafter when they shalbe of more iudgement and yeres, it shalbe vnto them a singular treasure: for the lacke whereof they shalbe compelled as also in familiar communication to vse in the stede of the proper and naturall woorde, a paraphrase or circumlocution. (A II^{V})

This is an early example of a teaching and learning theory which maintains that learning vocabulary is facilitated by a speculative arrangement of lexemes. This prefigures the Comenian idea that you learn a language better the closer the relation is between the word and the thing. Interest in matter as aroused by a meaningful (non-alphabetical) arrangement is, thus, supposed to support interest in language learning.

In fact there are many examples where topical word-lists were expanded into teaching dialogues, as e.g. *Dialogues in French and English* by William Caxton (about 1420) or James Bellot's English and French *Familiar Dialogues* (1586) (Hüllen 1989b). From this point of view, Comenius loses somewhat his position as the instigator of modern language teaching because he is now found to be a member of a long tradition. His merit is still to have given philosophical and pedagogical foundations to an established habit.

In fact, topical dictionaries with didactic purposes seem to be the most frequently used type of speculative lexicography, because there are countless examples all through the centuries of such word-lists accompanying grammars, teaching dialogues, etc.

Thirdly, there is John Wilkins's monumental work of "Tables" meant to be the semantic underpinning of his universal language but in fact also a comprehensive thesaurus of English lexemes according to philosophical principles. It picks up another tradition, that of scholastic summae and Ramistic systems of terms — just as Dalgarno does in the same context — but develops them into an extensive thesaurus of English words (Hüllen 1986, 1989c:195–245).

Fourthly, there are thesauri in the narrower sense as have become notorious in Roget's epoch-making work which has found followers in almost all the important languages of the world. But it also had its predecessors, as, for example, *De La Fabrica Del Mondo* by M. Francesco Alunno (1570) with about 6000 entries, each of which consists of a sometimes quite long row of synomyms. Besides their overall speculative arrangements such thesauri exploit synonymy in language and gear their word-lists to such practical purposes as e.g. stylistic exercises.

Fifthly, there are so-called ideological dictionaries which, in a sometimes loose connection with Humboldt, try to arrange their entries in such a way that the national culture and world view, supposedly incorporated in a language, become visible (Proceedings 1956). Admittedly, such ideological dictionaries, e.g. in Rudolf Hallig and Walther von Wartburg's plan (1952), were more linguistic ideas than lexicographical practice, but as a powerful idea they gave the tradition of speculative lexicography a special facet (Hüllen 1990). They mirror a new epistemological relation between language users and their world.

Lastly, recent linguistic work in the field of artificial intelligence and network semantics should be mentioned with its attempt to arrange lexemes in the way in which they are assumed to be stored in the human brain (e.g. Hoffmann 1986).

This list of types of speculative lexicography is loosely arranged in historical sequence, but they can almost all be found side by side at our present time. This proves the universal validity of an essential lexicographical idea. The difficulties in writing a history of such topical glossaries consist in differentiating between a perennial idea and its time-related context and describing a lexicographical paradigm in such attires as have been given to it by the wider purposes to which it has been put. There is, at the moment, no methodological framework for an undertaking like this. One reason for this is in fact that lexicographical practice in the various contexts mentioned only rarely belongs to linguistics proper. It either belongs to other disciplines like pedagogy, psychology, or sciences, or it is part of the layman's way of handling language-related problems. Although susceptible to so many ideas, the linguistic basis of lexicographical work discussed here remains the same through the many centuries. Even today, in such contexts, language is looked upon as consisting of words which are the names for things, an idea that is still convincing for engineers, scientists or even foreign language teachers, however (after Wittgenstein) of course not for linguists proper.

The intersections between the perennial lexicographical idea and its time-related contexts are to be found in the various arrangements that were given to vocabulary. They were taken from traditional cosmo–logical ideas, from ancient philosophy and the Bible, from natural history, from various folk taxonomies, from more recent scientific classifications, from cultural anthropology, psychological ideas on learning and simulations of language processing, from the hard facts of machines, tools, etc. and from still other sources. Note, for example, the difference between the overall plan of Alunno (1570) and Roget (1852):

Alunno: Dio	
	Cielo
	Mondo
	Elementi
	Anima
	Corpo
	Huomo
	Qvalita
	Qvantita
	Inferno
Roget:	Abstract relations
	Space
	Matter
	Intellect
	Volition
	Emotion, religion and morality.

The sequence of (sub)titles gives the world view away which dominated the two books. The plan of the book repeats the plan of the world.

For a long time, such schemata were arranged in lists with various means of indicating logical hierarchies between (groups of) entries. In John Wilkins's well-known tables we find the beginnings of a branching arrangement. Again, different arrangements become necessary when language is supposed to mirror psychic reality in a network of lexemes (Table 1).

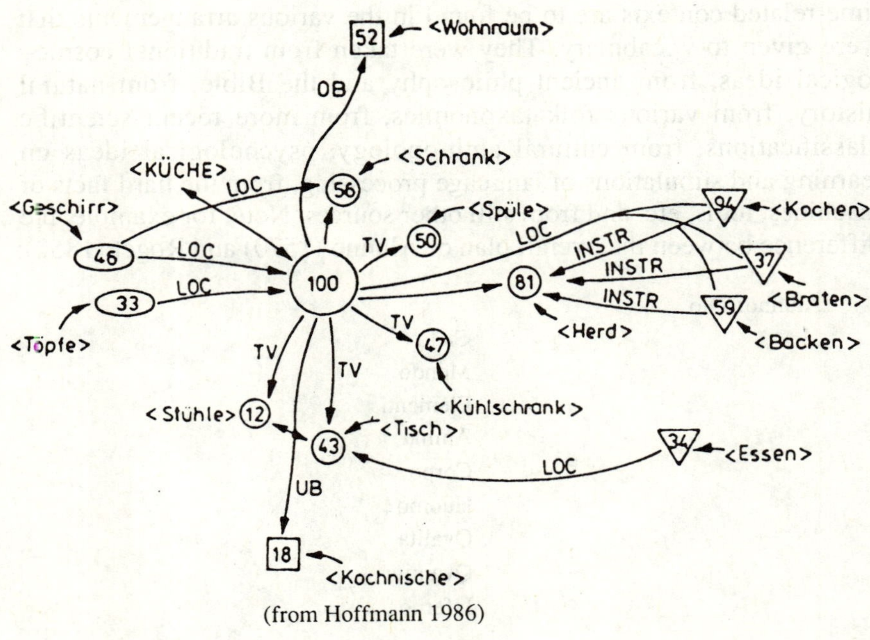

(from Hoffmann 1986)

It is certainly difficult to disentangle all this on a historiographically satisfying level of description. But it seems worth-while trying because "speculative lexicography" is an important part of our linguistic history, both the layman's and the expert's.

REFERENCES

Alvnno, M. Francesco. 1570. *Della / Fabrica / Del Mondo /* Di M. Francesco Alvnno / Da Ferrara / Libri X. / Ne'quali Si Contengono Le Voci Di / Dante, del Petrarca, del Boccaccio, del Bembo, & d'altri buoni / autori, mediante lequali scriuendo si possono esprimere con facilità / & eloquenza tutti i concetti dell'huomo di qualunque cosa creata. / Di Nvovo Ristampati, Corretti, Et Ampliati / di piu di 1500 uocaboli, cosi Latini come volgari, tratti da diuersi / buoni & approuati scrittori. / Con Vna Dictiaratione Di Molte Voci Che / mancauano nell'altre impressioni aggiunta a beneficio de gli / studiosi della lingua volgare. / Et Con Le Particelle Della Medesima / nostra lingua porte nel fine dell'opera. / In Veneta / Apresso Iacopo Sansovino il Giouane. / MDLXX.

Arntz, Reiner & Heribert Picht. 1989. *Einführung in die Terminologiearbeit.* Hildesheim: Olms.

Bellot, James. 1586. *Familiar Dialogues, for the Instruction of the(m), that be desirous to learne to speake* English, *and perfectlye to pronou(n)ce the same.* Set forth by James Bellot Gentleman of Caen. Imprinted at London by Thomas Vautrollier, dwelling in the black friars.

Caxton, William. approx. 1483. *Dialogues in French and English.* Ed. by Henry Bradley, London 1900 *(EETS,* Extra Series LXXIX).

Dornseiff, Franz. 1943. "Wortschatzdarstellung und Bezeichnungslehre". Introduction to: *Der deutsche Wortschatz nach Sachgruppen,* 29–66. Berlin: Walter de Gruyter. (Repr. 1970.)

Hallig, Rudolf & Walther von Wartburg. 1952. *Begriffssystem als Grundlage für die Lexikographie./Système raisonné des concepts pour servir de base à la lexicographie.* (2nd revised and enlarged ed.), Berlin: Akademie-Verlag, 1963.

Harris, Roy. 1980. *The Language Makers.* London: Duckworth.

Hüllen Werner. 1986. "The Paradigm of John Wilkins' Thesaurus". *The History of Lexicography,* ed. by R. R. K. Hartmann, 115–125. Amsterdam: Benjamins.

—. 1989a. "In the Beginning was the Gloss. Remarks on the Historical Emergence of Lexicographical Paradigms". *Lexicographers and their Works,* ed. by G. James vol. 14, 100–116. University of Exeter.

—. 1989b. "Von Glossaren und frühen Lehrbüchern für den fremdsprachlichen Unterricht". E. Kleinschmidt,, ed. *Fremdsprachenunterricht zwischen Sprachenpolitik und Praxis,* 112–122. Tübingen: Narr.

—. 1989c. "Their Manner of Discourse". *Nachdenken über Sprache im Umkreis der Royal Society.* Tübingen: Narr.

—. 1990. "Rudolph Hallig and Walther von Wartburg's *Begriffsystem* and its non-/acceptance in German linguistics". P. Schmitter, ed. *Essays towards a History of Semantics,* 129–168. Münster: Nodus.

Hoffmann, Joachim. 1986. *Die Welt der Begriffe.* Weinheim: Beltz.

Junius, Hadrianus. 1577. *Nomenclator, Omnivm Rervm Propria Nomina Variis Lingvis Explicata Indicans:* Multo quam antea emendatio ae locupletior: Antverpiae: Ex officina Christophori Plantini, Architypographi Regij.

Lovejoy, Arthur O. 1936. *The Great Chain of Being*. Cambridge, Mass.: Harvard University Press (repr. 1964).

McArthur, Tom. 1986a. *Worlds of Reference: Lexicography, Learning and Language from the Clay Tablet to the Computer*. Cambridge: University Press.

— . 1986b. "Thematic Lexicography". *The History of Lexicography*, ed. by R. R. K. Hartmann, 157–166. Amsterdam: Benjamins.

Proceedings of the Seventh International Congress of Linguists London, 1–6 September 1952. (1956). Part I and II. London: Published under the auspices of C.I.P.L. with the assistance of U.N.E.S.C.O.

Roget, Peter Mark. 1852. *Roget's Thesaurus of English Words and Phrases*. (New edition prepared by Susan M. Lloyd. London: Longman, 1982.)

Stein, Gabriele. 1985. *The* English *Dictionary before Cawdrey*. Tübingen: Niemeyer.

Ullmann, Stephen. 1962. Semantics. *An Introduction to the Science of Meaning*. Oxford: Blackwell. (Repr. 1972.)

Waswo, Richard. 1987. *Language and Meaning in the Renaissance*. Princeton: University Press.

Withals, John. 1553. *A Shorte Dictionarie for yonge begynners*. Gathered of good authours, specially of Columel, Grapald, and Plini. London: Thomas Berthelet

Wright, Thomas & Richard Paul Wülcker, eds. 1968. *Anglo-Saxon and Old English Vocabularies*. 2nd ed., Darmstadt: Wissenschaftliche Buchgesellschaft.

Carolingian Grammarians and Theoretical Innovation*

VIVIEN LAW
Cambridge University

HOW DOES ONE recognise theoretical innovation? It is rarely completely new; more often it grows out of existing work, identifiable as a shift of emphasis, a new set of questions, techniques transferred from another discipline. Much recent historiography devoted to Chomsky's place in linguistics has focussed on the continuities with the thought and approach of his predecessors rather than the much vaunted discontinuities. If there is room for dispute over a development which took place within our lifetimes, then how much more difficult the assessment of an earlier period is likely to be.

The problem is particularly acute for the earlier Middle Ages, the period from roughly 600 to about 1100. It is not just that most of the texts have not yet been printed; the basic groundwork of establishing which the important texts are is only now being carried out, and a sketch (let alone a comprehensive study) of the development of grammatical doctrine between Priscian and Petrus Helias has yet to be written. More specialised studies, generally written by medievalists for medievalists, are beginning to fill in the gaps, even though we still lack such useful tools as a census of grammatical manuscripts comparable to Bursill-Hall (1981) for the later Middle Ages. Most historians of linguistics seem to take the view that the period can safely be left to medievalists. Louis Holtz, the editor of several important Carolingian grammars, has recently attempted to bridge the divide by confronting the question of theoretical innovation in Carolingian linguistics (1988),

* I wish to thank Irène Rosier for some bibliographical suggestions, and the staff of the Archivo de la Corona de Aragón, Barcelona, and the Bayerische Staatsbibliothek, Munich, for their help.

spanning the years from 751 to some time in the tenth century. He concluded that, despite their innovativeness in other areas, the Carolingian were remarkably unenterprising in their grammars of Latin, failing to raise any new questions or to arrive at fresh insights. Considering what the Carolingians achieved in other areas — script reform, textual studies, revival of Classical Latinity and texts, development of rhetoric, dialectic and the theory of music, introduction of theological and philosophical speculation — this is really very odd. Did they really have nothing new to say about language? The problem merits another look.

In the seventh and eighth centuries the most important task facing teachers had been the transmission of a knowledge of Latin, without which the Church could not have operated (or not at any rate in the form it chose to). Theoretical innovation was the least of their worries; all their effort and originality went into working out the most efficient way to describe Latin morphology. Of course, they needed a certain number of the basic grammatical concepts elaborated in Antiquity, and to this end they studied Donatus's *Ars minor* and the more advanced *Ars maior* in detail. Theoretical issues were of secondary importance. Pre-Carolingian teachers had enough to do in arriving at an adequate description of the forms of Latin, and it is there that their originality lies (Law 1986).

Toward the end of the eighth century, under Charlemagne, there are signs of greater linguistic confidence. Elementary language teaching had to continue, of course, for each generation had to master Latin anew, but there were now enough teachers and enough appropriate textbooks to release the energies of some individuals for more advanced studies. Ancient grammars previously forgotten were brought back into circulation, and grammarians took to glossing and commenting on grammars by authors other than Donatus — Eutyches, Phocas, Priscian. Priscian's great *Institutiones grammaticae,* a university-level grammar if ever there was one (in over a thousand pages) attracted attention once more. It differed from other grammars not only by its sheer bulk and detail, but in the fact that it drew upon the language of dialectic, something that was to strike a particular chord with the Carolingians. Over the next two centuries one of the chief activities of grammarians consisted in getting to grips with Priscian through commentary and gloss, abbreviated versions, florilegia and paraphrases, a process inaugurated for the Carolingians by the Anglo-Saxon scholar Alcuin of York. Alcuin and his circle seem also to have been instrumental in arousing interest in two of the Liberal Arts which in the seventh and eighth centuries had been recognised in name only, the other two *artes sermocinales,* rhetoric and dialectic (Bischoff 1981:157; Marenbon 1981). The extent to which rhetoric influenced the study of grammar from this point on has not yet been investigated. Dialectic is known to have been of central importance in the study of grammar at least from the mid-eleventh century, and sporadically from an earlier date (Gibson 1975; Markowski 1981:38; Marenbon 1983). What is still unclear is what part the Carolingians played in developing the resources offered by dialectic for the comprehension of grammar.

Whereas in the seventh and eighth centuries dialectic was apparently studied only in the potted digests included in encyclopedias such as Martianus Capella's *Marriage of Philology and Mercury* (IV), Cassiodorus's *Institutiones* (II iii), and Isidore of Seville's *Etymologiae* (II xxii to end), around 800 we start to meet with signs of renewed interest (Lewry 1981; Gibson 1982; Marenbon 1983). Boethius's translations of two important works, Porphyry's *Isagoge* and Aristotle's *De interpretatione,* came into circulation together with Boethius's commentary on them; and the paraphrase of Aristotle's *Categories* from the circle of Themistius, known as *Categoriae decem,* also became available, lent additional authority by its ascription to St Augustine. All three works were concerned, primarily or incidently, with language. The well-known discussion of the relationship between language, thought and reality at the opening of the *De interpretatione* seems not to have influenced the study of grammar as immediately as the other works.[1] The *Categories* begin with a glance at the terms *aequivoca, univoca* and *denominativa,* before working systematically through the ten categories — *substantia, quantitas, qualitas, ad aliquid, facere, pati, situs, locus, tempus, habere.* In the *Isagoge* Porphyry ex-

[1] The definitions of the noun and verb are paraphrased by Alcuin in his grammar (859B and 874A) and Usuard (p.87: noun only).

plores five fundamental terms used by Aristotle throughout the *Categories: genus, species, differentia, proprium, accidens*. The overlap with grammatical terminology was plain. But how was the grammarian to go about integrating this new teaching into his own discipline? It is not easy to see at once how the findings of a new discipline can best be applied to one's own; intellectual history is littered with false starts. Ninth-century grammarians seem to have found their inspiration in Priscian. Priscian — or as often as not his Greek sources — is more methodologically explicit than most other Late Latin grammarians, a fact which is apparent from the opening lines of the *Institutiones grammaticae*. He begins with two definitions of *vox,* upon which he immediately comments:

> Philosophi definiunt, uocem esse aerem tenuissimum ictum uel suum sensibile aurium, id est quod proprie auribus accidit. Et est prior definitio a substantia sumpta, altera uero a notione, quam Graeci ἔννοιαν dicunt, hoc est ab accidentibus *(GL* II 5,1–4).

This and similar passages could not but make his Carolingian readers curious. Why are definitions so important? What are the rules governing their formulation? The theory of definitions became their way in to dialectic.

Dialectic, traditionally described as the art of telling truth from falsehood, taught the techniques of argumentation, among them the formulation of definitions. As one commentator put it, "those philosophers who are called dialecticians are the only ones who know how to make definitions; none of the others know" *(Septem* ΠΟΡΙΟΧΑΙ f.258v). Midway through the fourth century Marius Victorinus had catalogued some fifteen types of definition in his *De definitionibus,* and his list was repeated by Cassiodorus and Isidore. Ancient and medieval grammarians depended heavily upon definitions. With a couple of exceptions, ancient grammarians tend to work in a largely unselfconscious manner. Although they may define *definitio,*[1] or ana-

[1] E.g. Charisius (ed. Barwick p. 192,21f.), Diomedes *(GL I* 420.25–421.2), Scaurus (f. 53v), Marius Victorinus *(GL VI* 4.9–11), Audax *(GL VII* 3f.).

lyse the elements of a particular definition one by one, they have no consistent metalanguage and make little use of the terminology of dialectic. Their method is exemplified by this passage from Servius's commentary on Donatus:

> *Nomen est pars orationis cum casu corpus aut rem proprie communiterue significans.*[1] In omnibus partibus orationis definitiones ita esse debent, ut et segregent ab aliis partibus et ipsius partis quam definiunt aliquam proprietatem dicant. Igitur quod dixit nomen partem esse orationis, segregauit a sibilis plausibus et quidquid confusae uoci datur. Quod autem dixit *cum casu,* segregauit a uerbis aduerbiis praepositionibus coniunctionibus. Quod autem dixit corpus aut rem significare, hoc ipsius proprium est *(GL* IV 406.22–29).
>
> "The noun is a part of speech with case signifying an object or a concept, and is either proper or common." Definitions ought to be like this for all parts of speech, both distinguishing them from other parts and specifying the unique property of the part being defined. Thus, in saying that the noun is a part of speech, he distinguished it from whistles, clapping and whatever is produced with an inarticulate sound. In saying "with case" he distinguished it from verbs, adverbs, prepositions and conjunctions. In saying that it signifies an object or a concept, this is proper to it.

The nearest Servius comes to a technical term is the word *proprietas;* such markedly dialectical terms as *genus, species* and *differentia* are absent. His seventh- and eighth-century successors are similarly chary of the language of dialectic. Paradoxically, although Alcuin's introduction to dialectic includes a brief discussion of definitions, he follows Marius Victorinus in regarding them as pertinent only to dialecticians and rhetoricians — not to grammarians. They find only passing mention in his own grammar. Thus, although Alcuin's role in reintroducing dialectic in the Carolingian period is undoubted, he

[1] Here and in subsequent passages the lemma, or text being commented upon, will be italicised in the Latin text and placed within inverted commas in the translation.

seems to have played little part in helping to assimilate it into grammar. The first positive signs are to be found in a series of treatises by or associated with the *Scotti peregrini,* the Irish scholars active in the Frankish kingdom toward the middle of the ninth century: Murethach, Clemens Scottus, Sedulius Scottus, the anonymous authors of the *Ars Laureshamensis,* the *Ars Brugensis, Donatus Ortigraphus* and several others. These writers (or more usually their lost sources) adopt several of Victorinus fifteen types of definition. Some take over just two *(definitio substantiae* and *definitio soni),* others three (adding *definitio numeri),* but several work with a more elaborate schema that involves six types. Sedulius Scottus exemplifies them thus:

> Definitionis autem genera secundum grammaticos sunt sex: prima substantialis, ut "nomen est pars orationis cum casu"; secunda soni, ut 'nomen dictum est quasi notamen'; tertia specialis, ut "corpus aut rem proprie communiterue significans"; quarta accidentalis, ut "nomini accidunt sex"; quinta numeralis, ut "partes orationis sunt octo"; sexta etymologiae, ut 'homo dictus est ab humo et humus ab humore' *(CCCM* 40B, 64.16–23).

> The types of definition according to the grammarians are six in number. The first is definition according to the substance [essence] e.g. "a noun is a part of speech with case". The second is definition according to the sound, e.g. "the noun is, as it were, a note". The third is according to its specific properties, e.g. "signifying an object or concept and either proper or common". The fourth is in terms of its accidents, e.g. "the noun has six accidents". The fifth is quantitative, e.g. "there are eight parts of speech". The sixth is etymological, e.g. "*homo* is so called from *humus,* and *humus* from *humor*".

With a few exceptions this analysis becomes fairly routine, but it testifies to a growing awareness of the metastructure of grammatical discourse, visible even in grammars intended for use at a relatively low level of instruction. The following excerpt demonstrates the meticulous thoroughness with which some teachers sought to introduce their pupils to these basic notions:

> *Quid est oratio?...* Quid requirit *quid?* Substantiam. *Nomini quot accidunt? vi. Quae? Qualitas et reliqua.* Quid est *nomini quot accidunt?* i. quot accidentia accidunt nomini. Quid requirit *quot?* Certum numerum. Quid est *vi?* Diffinitio numeri *(Magnus quae uox,* f. 166r).

But what of the doctrine itself? Was the Carolingian understanding of language, or at any rate of grammar and its categories, altered or enhanced by the teachings of dialectic? Later in the ninth century and during the tenth — most of the texts have as yet to be securely dated — grammarians begin to experiment with the doctrine contained in texts such as the *Isagoge*[1] and the *Categories*. A short text in a manuscript from St Gall, a centre with a lively and long-lasting interest in dialectic (Piper 1882;[2] De Rijk 1963), reveals the new approach. It opens with a statement of the relationship between grammar and dialectic:

> Octo partes orationis in grammatica quales in se ipsis dictiones sint liquido ostendunt; decem uero Aristotilis cathegoriae, quae ad logicam pertinent, quid ipsae partes orationis extra se significent, deinde quales per se sint ipse. Hunc ordinem in pueris natura ostendit, qui prius intellegunt ea uox que est *homo* unde predicaetur quam in ipsa uoce fieri discant hanc flexionem: *homo hominis homini hominem ab homine*. Et a prima origine linguarum omnes se ad intellectum solum sermonum ferebant. Postea aliqui ceperunt de ipsa quoque uoce sermonum tractare *(Distributio* p. LXXVI).

> The eight parts of speech in grammar show clearly what words are in themselves. Aristotle's ten categories, which pertain to logic, show first what those parts of speech signify beyond themselves, and then what they are in themselves. Nature shows us this same sequence in children: they learn to understand what the word 'man' is predicated of before

[1] Sedulius Scottus introduces his readers to the *quinque species isagogae* in his commentary on the *Ars minor* (8,2–9).

[2] To the two manuscripts used by Piper for his edition a third can be added: Luxembourg, Bibliothèque Nationale MS latin 10444 (provenance Echternach), ff.85r–87r. It contains the text from p. LXXIX line 21 *Pluriuoca uero...* to p. LXXXIX line 3 ... *Patronomicum est/*. I am grateful to Jean-Claude Muller for bringing this fragment to my attention.

> they learn its inflection... Ever since languages originated everyone has exerted himself to understand utterances; only later did a few people begin to investigate the form of the utterances.

Dialectic thus occupies an epistemologically prior position, even if grammar is, in the words of Isidore of Seville, 'the origin and basis of all the Liberal Arts'. In the body of the treatise the author takes a standard grammatical classification scheme, Priscian's list of the subtypes of common noun — corporeal, incorporeal, homonyms, synonyms, collective, local, temporal, etc. — and tries to map these classes onto the ten Aristotelian categories, assigning each to one or more of the categories. The numerous difficulties encountered are analyzed at some length, always elucidated by means of concepts drawn from dialectic.

In another text, a Priscian commentary from an eleventh-century manuscript from the Catalan monastery of Ripoll (barely twenty miles away from Vich, where Gerbert of Aurillac studied logic in the third quarter of the tenth century), dialectic has penetrated still further into the fabric of grammar, though not without the author's retaining awareness of the process. In the passage quoted below the commentator begins by quoting Priscian, who is commenting upon his own definition of *oratio:*

> *<Oratio est ordinatio dictionum congrua sententiam perfectam demonstrans.> Est autem haec diffinitio generalis quae in species siue partes diuiditur* et cetera. Queritur cur ambigue posuit *in species siue partes:* utrum ideo, quia secundum philosophos abusiue species pro partibus et partes pro speciebus ponitur, cum quantum ad proprietatem significationis pertinet species in genere, pars in toto ponitur? Sed quaerendum utrum orationem naturaliter in partes partiri oportet, sicut totum diuiditur in partes, an etiam in species sicut genus. Sed et hoc dicere possumus, quod oratio et in partes potest partiri et in species *(Septem* ΠΟΡΙΟΧΑΙ f. 266r).

> "Speech is a well-formed sequence of words expressing a complete thought. This is a generic definition which is divided into species or parts" et cetera. Why did he use the ambiguous expression "in species or

> parts"? Was it because philosophers hold that it is wrong to write "species" for "parts" and "parts" for "species", when properly speaking a species belongs within a genus and a part within a whole? We should ask whether it is in accordance with the nature of speech to divide it into parts, just as a whole is divided into parts, or into species too, as a genus is. This we can also say: speech can be divided into both parts and species.

The commentator moves swiftly from the wording of Priscian's text to the issue raised by the ambiguity he has observed: is speech a whole or a genus? He concludes (with assistance from the teachings of Boethius's *De divisione)* that the answer depends on your standpoint. A grammarian sees speech as a whole with parts — the eight parts of speech — whereas a rhetorician (like Priscian in his *Praeexercitamina)* will see it as a genus with ten species. Throughout the discussion the tone is that of an independent thinker who wants to keep his distance, even from so eminent an authority as Priscian: shades here of William of Conches's famous complaint about the obscurity of Priscian's definitions.

These and similar texts from the Carolingian period make it plain that the systematic application of the techniques and categories of dialectic to grammar began, not some time during the eleventh century, but in the middle of the ninth. Grammarians found their incentive to grapple with the works on dialectic now re-entering circulation in their study of Priscian's *Institutiones grammaticae,* and in their increasingly critical scrutiny of the definitions used by Priscian and other grammarians.

This story has implications which extend far beyond the Middle Ages. The Carolingians became aware as they tackled the new discipline of dialectic that they had inherited two sets of categories, one linguistic, the other — as they saw them — mental/real-world. Naturally they wanted to discover how these two sets of categories related to one another, especially given that the linguistic ones were through their philosophical origin closely related to the mental/real-world ones. The Carolingians were the first to grapple with this problem not just at the philosophical-psychological level that we find in commentaries on the *De interpretatione,* but in the challenging domain of relating linguistic structures and categories directly to mental categories. This to us is a very modern problem, the stuff of generative grammar and cognitive semantics. It was the Carolingians who sensed, however dimly, the relevance of dialectic to our understanding of language, and who perceived and developed some of its implications. Whilst trying out a new set of tools for the study of language they introduced a new set of questions into the mainstream, and on and off those questions have remained central to linguistics ever since. This alone justifies the inclusion of the Carolingian era among theoretically innovative periods in the history of linguistics.

REFERENCES

1. Primary Sources

Alcuin. 1851. *Dialogus Franconis et Saxonis de octo partibus orationis. Patrologia Latina* 101.849–902.

Charisius. 1964. *Artis grammaticae libri V.* Ed. by Karl Barwick, with addenda and corrigenda by F. Kühnert. Leipzig: B.G. Teubner.

Distributio omnium specierum nominum inter cathegorias Aristotilis. 1882. Ed. by Paul Piper. *Die Schriften Notkers und seiner Schule I: Schriften philosophischen Inhalts,* LXXVI–LXXXIX. Freiburg i. Br. and Tübingen: J.C.B. Mohr. Completed by P. Piper. 1890. "Zu Notkers Rhetorik". *Zeitschrift für deutsche Philologie* 22.277–86.

GL = *Grammatici Latini.* 1855–80. Ed. by Heinrich Keil. 7 vols. Leipzig: Teubner.

Magnus quae uox. Munich: Bayerische Staatsbibliothek. Clm 14737, ff.157v–183v.

Sedulius Scottus. 1977a. *In Donati artem maiorem.* Ed. by Bengt Löfstedt. *Grammatici hibernici carolini aevi,* Pars III.1 *(=C[orpus] C[hristianorum] C[ontinuatio] M[ediaevalis],* 40B). Turnhout: Brepols.

Sedulius Scottus. 1977b. *In Donati artem minorem. In Priscianum. In Eutychem.* Ed. by Bengt Löfstedt. *Grammatici hibernici carolini aevi,* Pars III.2 *(=CCCM,* 40C). Turnhout: Brepols.

Septem ΠΟΡΙΟΧΑΙ (sic!). Barcelona, Archivo de la Corona de Aragón. Ripoll 59, ff.257v–288v.

Usuard. 1964. Ed. by Josep M. Casas Homs. "Una gramàtica inèdita d'Usuard". Miscel·lània Anselm M. Albareda, 2 *(=Analecta Montserratensia, 10),* 77–129.

2. Secondary Sources.

Bischoff, Bernhard. 1981. "Die Hofbibliothek Karls des Grossen". In his *Mittelalterliche Studien* III, 149–69. Stuttgart: Anton Hiersemann.

Bursill-Hall, Geoffrey L. 1981. *A Census of Medieval Latin Grammatical Manuscripts*. Stuttgart–Bad Cannstatt: Fromann-Holzboog.

De Rijk, L.M. 1963. "On the Curriculum of the Arts of the Trivium at St Gall from c.850–c.1000". *Vivarium* 1.35–86.

Gibson , Margaret. 1975. "The Continuity of Learning circa 850–circa 1050". *Viator* 6–13.

—. 1982. "Latin commentaries on logic before 1200". *Bulletin de Philosophie Médiévale* 24.54–64.

Holtz, Louis. 1988. "Les innovations théoriques de la grammaire carolingienne: peu de chose. Pourquoi?". *L'Héritage des grammairiens latins de l'Antiquité aux Lumières,* ed. by Irène Rosier, 133–45. Paris & Leuven: Peeters.

Law, Vivien. 1986. "Originality in the medieval normative tradition". *Studies in the History of Western Linguistics in Honour of R.H. Robins,* ed. by Theodora Bynon and F.R. Palmer, 43–55. Cambridge: University Press.

Lewry, Osmund, OP. 1981. "Boethian logic in the medieval West". *Boethius: His Life, Thought and Influence,* ed. by Margaret Gibson , 90–134. Oxford: Basil Blackwell.

Marenbon, John. 1981. *From the Circle of Alcuin to the School of Auxerre: Logic, Theology and Philosophy in the Early Middle Ages*. Cambridge: University Press.

—. 1983. *Early Medieval Philosophy 480–1150: An Introduction*. London: Routledge & Kegan Paul.

Markowski, Mieczysław. 1981. "Sprache und Logik im Mittelalter". *Sprache und Erkenntnis im Mittelalter* I, 36–50. Berlin–New York: W. De Gruyter.

On the Origins of the Medieval Concept of Transitivity

ANNELI LUHTALA
University of Helsinki

1. INTRODUCTION

THE CONCEPT OF transitivity in the description of the verb first appeared, as far as we know, in the grammar of Apollonius Dyscolus in the 2nd century A.D. It was introduced into the Latin tradition in the 6th century by Priscian whose account of transitivity will be the main concern of this paper. We will approach his work primarily from a medieval perspective. During the Middle Ages the concept of transitivity developed into a general tool of syntactic description and it is worth asking just how much the analysis of the medieval grammarians is supported by Priscian, whose work was their main authority.

Priscian applies transitivity terminology in a number of contexts. I shall argue that some of them are well-established whereas others are less so. The established ones are the two contexts familiar from the work of Apollonius, namely the transitivity of the verb and of the pronoun. Priscian also introduces a discussion of the transitivity of prepositions. In these contexts transitivity terminology is employed consistently. The less established uses of terms lend themselves to interpretations such that nominals are construed (in)transitively between themselves and that a transitive clause consists of two relationships, intransitive and transitive. In high medieval syntactic theory the transitive clause *Socrates percutit Platonem* is understood as consisting of the intransitive relationship *(Socrates percutit)* and of the transitive relationship *(percutit Platonem)*. As to nominal constructions,[1] those showing agreement *(Socrates albus)* were analysed as intransitive and those not showing agreement as transitive *(filius Socratis).*

I shall argue that the status of these medieval uses of these terms is accidental. They contradict Priscian's general position and would seem to derive from his ambiguous employment of terms.

2. APOLLONIUS DYSCOLUS

I shall first briefly introduce the Apollonian transitivity contexts. The concept of transitive action is crucial for Apollonius's discussion of verbal voice, διάθεσις, whereby he characterizes as truly active those verbs showing transitive action, that is, action proceeding from one person to another. It is from such verbs that the passive διάθεσις is derived (GG II.2:395.12ff).[2]

The state of affairs involving transitive action with two participants can be identified as one of the two simple clause types familiar from Diogenes Laertius's exposition of Stoic predicate types (VII, 64, cf. GG II.2:274.1ff; 395.12ff). The Stoics distinguished between verbs that form a complete statement with the nominative alone and those that additionally require an oblique complement. The latter kind of verbs are now known as transitive verbs and are indeed often described in terms of action proceeding from the nominative case to one of the oblique cases (e.g., GG II.2:413.3). Another frequent mode of expression places the emphasis on the verb which is said to require certain cases (e.g., GG II.2:410.11). However, it is assumed in Apollonius's theory that the nominative is understood in the finite verb when not overtly expressed (GG II.2:447.9ff), so that a more accurate view seems to be that the oblique depends on the nominative rather

[1] The details of how these constructions came to be introduced into medieval grammar are not a concern of this paper. For the various ways in which they were defined, see, e.g., Kneepkens (1990); Covington (1984:44–61); Rosier (1983:166–198).

[2] References to Apollonius's work are based on *Grammatici Graeci* (ed. Uhlig & Schneider), those to Priscian on *Grammatici Latini* (ed. Hertz). The volume, the page number and the line are given.

than the verb. The transitivity of the verb would therefore seem to amount to the transitivity of a simple clause.

Apollonius refers to the transitive state of affairs with such terms as διάβασις/μετάβασις τοῦ προσώπου (GG II.2:280.6) as well as a number of adjectives (e.g. διαβιβασμός, διαβιβαστικός and διαβατικός).[1] However, his vocabulary is not well established and he frequently resorts to paraphrases of the type "the verb which requires an oblique" (GG II.2:410.9ff).

The verbs which form a complete statement with the nominative alone are less clearly defined in terms of διάθεσις. They are mentioned as less prototypical active verbs since their action does not proceed towards another person — this is why they do not form the passive (GG II.2:395.12ff). The weak position of these verbs in respect of the transitive verbs is reflected in the poverty of expressions referring to them. While there is a host of expressions for transitivity, I have come across only two occurrences of the term intransitive, ἀδιαβίβαστον (GG II.2:411.7ff; 409.11). In his discussion of verbal voice he refers to these verbs by the term αὐτοτελής, absolute (GG II.2: 402.7).[2]

In view of the later medieval developments of these terms, the question arises whether these terms were applied to refer to the internal structure of a clause. This would not seem to be the case. The two terms, transitive and intransitive, refer to two types of action depending on whether one or two persons are involved in the action. They serve to constitute two types of complete statements and it would in fact seem a contradiction in terms to use these terms to refer to any part of a clause, that is, to an incomplete statement. But there is, rather surprisingly, an instance in which the incomplete nominative verb relation is referred to in terms of διάθεσις (GG II.2:147.14ff). According to this passage, a transitive clause manifests two διαθέσεις one realized by the

[1] It is interesting that the Greek equivalents given by Priscian for the Latin terms *transitivum* and *intransitivum* (GL II:552.25) are μεταβατικός and ἀμετάβατος which appear only in Apollonius's discussion of pronominal transitivity. This fact lends support to my claim that Priscian's treatment of verbal transitivity leans heavily on Apollonius's discussion of pronominal transitivity.

[2] For the double origin of this term in ancient grammar, namely as the equivalent for the Greek terms ἀπόλυτος and αὐτοτελής, see Kneepkens 1988.

nominative–verb relation and the other by the verb–oblique relation. However, the two διαθέσεις remain unlabelled.

I now want to draw attention to a less well-known context for the employment of this concept, namely Apollonius's discussion of pronouns. He refers to compound reflexive pronouns such as ἐμαυτόν and simple pronouns such as ἐμέ as intransitive and transitive respectively on account of their behaviour in a transitive state of affairs (GG II.1:44.1ff). Apollonius' argument is as follows. The μετάβασις proceeding from the nominative towards the oblique cases takes place either as involving a change of person, whereby a simple or transitive pronoun appears in the postverbal position, or as involving one person only, whereby a compound or intransitive pronoun is used. In the latter case we are dealing with a reflexive construction, αὐτοπάθεια.

Finally, a crucial context for our inquiry is Apollonius's discussion of grammaticality in which he focuses his attention on the phenomenon of concord (ἀκολουθία, τὸ κατάλληλον) (GG II.2:280–281). His argument is that a major source of ungrammaticality is that the various parts of speech exhibit various inflectional patterns, some for case and number, others for number and person while others for gender. In the process of sentence construction, the inflecting parts of speech tend to show agreement so that, for instance, a plural verb is associated with a plural nominal as in γράφομεν ἡμεῖς. According to him, there is agreement because the constructibles refer to the same referent. By contrast, in the transitive state of affairs agreement is not required. The oblique complement present in such a clause need not agree in number with the nominative so that it is possible to say either τύπτουσι τὸν ἄνθρωπον or τύπτουσι τοὺς ἀνθρώπους.

In Apollonius's framework, concord serves to distinguish the constructibles pertaining to the same referent whereas lack of concord between the constructibles implies the presence of various referents.[1] Apollonius applies these criteria also to constructions consisting of nominals. In this kind of relationship the constructibles referring to the

[1] This argumentation would seem to illustrate his rational position which sees linguistic phenomena in correspondance with real world phenomena (cf. Blank 1982:21–39).

same referent agree in case, gender and number. In constructions such as οὗτοι οἱ ἄνδρες and ἡμῶν αὐτῶν ἀκούουσιν we understand that the words showing agreement refer to the same referent, whereas the lack of agreement in τούτους γυνὴ ὕβρισε and ἡμῶν αὐτὸς ἀκούει implies that there are two different referents involved.

2. Priscian

We now proceed to discuss Priscian's role in introducing this concept into the Latin tradition. We have stated that his contribution to these terms consisted in reproducing the two Apollonian contexts and in adding a new one, the transitivity of prepositions.[1] Furthermore, in comparison with Apollonius's account of transitivity, Priscian marks a considerable advance in making use of a consistent vocabulary throughout his discussion. He makes regular use of the expressions *transitio, verbum (in)transitivum* as well as the adverbs *(in)transitive* whereas the noun *intransitio* is absent from his work. However, when examining how the Apollonian contexts came to be presented by Priscian, his role in transmitting this concept turns out to be distinctly ambivalent.

In Priscian's work the description of the two Stoic clause types in terms of transitivity is fully established. The verbs which require the presence of an oblique case to complete their meaning are regularly labeled transitive. The verbs forming a complete statement with the nominative alone are labeled intransitive or absolute. In an Apollonian manner, the description of the (in)transitive clause is framed either in terms of the presence of one or two participants involved in a state of affairs ("per unam personam" vs. "ab alia ad aliam personam", "transitio personae ad personam" GL III:210.11; 211.22;17.22) or in terms of the opposition of morphological cases ("a nominativis actus proficiscentes ad obliquos" GL III:15.10). Just like Apollonius, Priscian often expresses himself so that the oblique depends on the verb but his theoretical position, in accordance with Apollonius, requires that the

[1] Priscian's discussion of prepositions falls out of the scope of this study.

oblique depends on the nominative understood in the verb (GL III:17.21ff).

We have discussed similarities in the presentations of the two grammarians. Let us now consider some of the differences. I would like to claim that Priscian assigns the criterion of coreferentiality a more prominent role so that it now figures in all transitivity contexts whereas in Apollonius's work it was relevant to some contexts only. The new emphasis manifests itself in the definition of the intransitive clause and in Priscian's introduction of the reflexive clause type alongside the intransitive and transitive types.

It is illuminating to compare the following two presentations of the intransitive clause. The first of them is based on morphological and syntactic criteria resembling the Apollonian way of defining a complete statement: "Absoluta, sive activae sive passivae sint vocis, cum nominativo perfectam habent constructionem, ut *Plato vivit*" (GL III:270.11ff). In the second one, the construction is labelled intransitive and the pragmatic criterion *per unam personam* has entered into its definition: "Nominativus et vocativus absoluti sunt, id est per unam personam intransitive possunt proferri, ut *ego Priscianus ambulo*" (GL III:210.11ff).

In assigning a more prominent role to coreferentiality Priscian would seem to be influenced by Apollonius's discussion of pronouns. As a result, the reflexive clause now establishes itself as one of the construction types. The following quotation which could be regarded as a most typical presentation of Priscianic construction types, is a direct translation from Apollonius' discussion of pronouns:

> evenit enim, ut a nominativis actus proficiscentes ad obliquos sive in transitione personarum intellegantur sive in una eademque persona. in transitione, ut *Aristophanes Aristarchum docuit* ... in una quoque eadem persona hoc idem fit, ut *Phemius se docuit*, docendi enim transitio non ad alteram fit personam, sed ad ipsum Phemium reciprocatur... (GL III:15.9ff).[1]

[1] The position of the reflexive clause remains ambiguous. It is, of course, transitive from the formal point of view: the oblique case is present. However, it is in-

As to the construction type named *retransitio,* listed by the medieval grammarians as a fourth type, my impression is that Priscian does not present it as a fourth construction type along with the intransitive, transitive and reflexive.[1] His references to retransitivity are called forth by his observations of the use of the Latin reflexive pronoun *se*. He distinguishes between two uses of this pronoun, namely reflexive and "retransitive" (GL II:584.2ff; III:165.27; 168.26; 171.14; 176.4). A retransitive state of affairs occurs when the reflexive pronoun appears in a subordinate clause referring not to the subject of the subordinate clause but to the acting person in the main clause (e.g. "Orare iussit era, si se ames, ut ad se venias", GL II:584.9).

The ambivalence of Priscian's role in introducing a technical vocabulary into the various contexts is manifest in the way he deals with Apollonius's discussion of grammaticality. The relationship between the nominative and the verb discussed in terms of agreement by Apollonius, is labeled intransitive by Priscian:

> quae sunt igitur declinabiles ... orationis constructione, id est dispositione, ad aptam coniunctionem ferri debent, ut puta singulare ad singularem et plurale ad pluralem, cum ad unam eandemque refertur personam intransitive, ut *ego Priscianus scribo intellegens* et *nos oratores scribimus intellegentes.* (GL III:182.26ff).

Although his examples in this connection refer to complete statements, his discussion will permit the medieval grammarians to identify any relationship of agreement as intransitive. Furthermore, in the following statement — unique in its kind — Priscian provides support for analysing as intransitive even a nominative–verb relation which does

transitive from the pragmatic point of view: one and the same person is acting and undergoing action. The medieval authors who understood it as a subtype of the intransitive construction (Kneepkens 1990), adopted the semantic interpretation of transitivity. They could base themselves on such Priscianic passages in which he constrasts the transitive pronouns (ἀλλοπαθής) with the reflexive ones (αὐτοπαθής) equating the latter with intransitivity (GL III:15.24ff).

[1] The retransitive type is absent from Baratin's exposition of Priscianic construction types (1989:471–475) whereas it has traditionally appeared in modern presentations of Priscianic syntax (Covington 1984:8; Percival 1987:68–69).

not form a complete statement: "ordo quoque naturalis eis datus est: quippe nominativus, quem primum natura protulit, ipse primum sibi locum defendit, unde verbis quoque intransitive iste quasi egregius adhaeret" (GL II:186.13ff).

The medieval grammarians could, then, claim Priscianic origin for analysing as intransitive any relationship of agreement between the nominative and the verb. But what about the agreement between nominals which came to be labeled *intransitio personarum?* There would not seem to be any explicit statement in favour of such a view but, once again, a couple of ambiguous passages readily suggest themselves as sources of these medieval interpretations.

In his discussion of grammaticality Priscian — just like Apollonius — applies the same defining criteria to the construction of nominals as he applied to the nominative-verb relation. That is, agreement between nominals occurs when they refer to the same referent. However, when illustrating agreement in gender and case, he does not use the term *intransitive*. "Cum igitur ad unam eandemque personam et casus et genera et numeri referuntur, supra dicta consequentia est observanda" (GL III:183,15ff). I would hence conclude that the verb is always present in Priscian's conception of (in)transitivity.[1]

Of all the interpretations of transitivity that we have characterized as medieval the least amount of support can be found in Priscian for the analysis known as *transitio personarum* in medieval syntactic theory. The unique example which we will proceed to quote is indeed a curious one as it highlights the effects of Priscian's occasional vague wordings. Although it appears in an unexpected environment, it can be shown to have attracted the attention of the medieval grammarians and to have been used for the very purpose of justifying the new analysis.[2]

[1] This would seem true concerning yet another ambiguous passage (GL III:32.22ff).

[2] It is interesting that Petrus Helias singles out the first example to the exclusion of all the others: "Ecce illa tota divisio que dicit *aquile devolaverunt altera ab oriente, altera ab occidente* per obliquos casus prolata est, et pro verbo positum est hoc participium *volantium*, et transitiva est constructio quia transitive construuntur he dictiones *celeritas* et *aquilarum*. Non tamen ibi est transitio actus, sed personarum tantummodo, et casuum fit ibi transitio quia alterius casus est *celeritas*,

The context of this occurrence is Priscian's discussion of partitive expressions, or more precisely, a digression in this discussion. Priscian, rather unexpectedly, sets out to discuss how the example sentence *aquilae devolaverunt, haec ab oriente, illa ab occidente* can be transformed so that both the noun *aquilae* and the verb *devolaverunt* appear in oblique cases. As the verb cannot be inflected in case, it must be turned into the participle in order to be inflected in case:

> itaque si et quod dividitur et illa in quae dividitur, volumus per obliquos casus proferre, necesse est participio uti, quod loco verbi accipitur obliquis adiungendum, et transitionem facere, ut *aquilarum volantium, ... similis est celeritas* vel per dativum *aquilis volantibus ... relinquitur occidens* et accusativo *aquilas volantes ... misit occidens* (GL III:126.2ff).

In labeling all the resulting constructions (italicized above) transitive Priscian would seem to equate rather carelessly the two expressions *obliquis adiungendum* and *transitionem facere* and by doing so he would seem to understand a nominal construction, *aquilarum volantium celeritas* as transitive.

We concluded above that some Apollonian contexts give slight support for the analysis according to which a transitive clause is said to manifest two διαθέσεις. One of these contexts is reproduced by Priscian who takes the further step of labeling the nominative–verb relation intransitive and the verb-oblique relation transitive thus arriving at what might be termed a medieval analysis. "Quemadmodum nomina sic etiam pronomina per singulos casus similiter cum verbis construuntur. et nominativis quidem intransitive, obliquis vero transitive verba coniunguntur" (GL III:147.12ff).[1]

et alterius *aquilarum* de cuiusmodi constructione superius dictum" (CIMAGL 27:46).

[1] There is another instance of the same type for which I have not been able to find an Apollonian antecedent (GL III:213.7ff).

REFERENCES

Apollonius Dyscolus. *Apollonii Dyscoli quae supersunt*. 3 vols. Ed. by Richard Schneider & Gustav Uhlig (= *Grammatici Graeci* II.1 & 2.) Leipzig: Teubner 1878–1910. (Repr., Hildesheim: Olms, 1965.)

Baratin, Marc. 1989. *La naissance de la syntaxe à Rome*. Paris: Les Éditions de Minuit.

Blank, David L. 1982. *Ancient Philosophy and Grammar: The Syntax of* Apollonius *Dyscolus*. (= American Philological Association; *American Classical Studies,* 10.), Chico, California: Scholars' Press.

Covington, Michael A. 1984. *Syntactic Theory in the High Middle Ages. Modistic Models of Sentence Structure. (=Cambridge Studies in Linguistics,* 39) Cambridge: University Press.

Diogenes Laertius. *Lives of Eminent Philosophers.*. Ed. & transl. by R.H. Hicks. (Loeb Classical Library.) London: Heinemann, 1925.

Kneepkens, C.H. 1988. "Absolutio: A Note on a History of a Grammatical oncept". *L'Héritage des Grammairiens Latins de l'Antiquité aux Lumières. Actes du colloque de Chantilly 2–4 septembre 1987,* ed. by Irène Rosier, 155–169. Paris: Bibliothèque de l'information grammaticale.

—. 1990. "Transitivity, Intransitivity and Related Concepts in 12th Century Grammar. An explorative study". *De Ortu Grammaticae: Studies in Medieval Grammar and Linguistic Theory in Memory of Jan Pinborg,* ed. by Geoffrey L. Bursill-Hall et al., 161–189. Amsterdam & Philadelphia: John Benjamins.

Percival, Keith. 1987. "On Priscian's Syntactic Theory: the Medieval Perspective". *Papers in the History of Linguistics (= Proceedings of the Third International Conference on the History of the Language Sciences, Princeton, 19–23 August 1984,* ed. by Hans Aarsleff et al., 65–74. Amsterdam & Philadelphia, John Benjamins.

Petrus Helias. *The Summa of Petrus Helias on Priscianus Minor*. Ed. by James E. Tolson with an introduction by Margaret Gibson (= *Cahiers de l'institut du moyen-âge grec et latin = CIMAGL,* 27). Copenhagen: Université de Copenhague, 1978.

Priscian. *Prisciani Grammatici Caesariensis Institutionum Grammaticarum Libri XVIII*. Ed. by Martin Hertz. (= *Grammatici Latini* II–III.) Leipzig, Teubner, 1859.

Rosier, Irène 1983. *La Grammaire spéculative des modistes*. Lille: Presses Universitaires.

Jean Charles Thiebault (de) Laveaux: The Revolt of a Jacobin Grammarian and Lexicographer against the Académie Française

HERBERT E. BREKLE
Universität Regensburg

1. HIS LIFE AND WORK

LAVEAUX WAS BORN in Troyes (Champagne) on November 17th, 1749. In his early youth he entered the Order of the Dominicans and pursued his studies in Clermont (Auvergne). Probably before 1775 he left the Dominicans for good; he got his first position as a teacher of French at the University of Basle (1775–77). Between 1782 and 1785 he taught French at Berlin and it is from 1782 onwards that Laveaux entered the career of a grammarian, critic, and above all a lexicographer, mostly on a free-lance basis. His first work — *Leçons de langue françoise données à quelques académiciens et autres auteurs françois de Berlin* — appeared in 1782 anonymously at Francfurt (no publisher indicated). Laveaux' aim was to criticise the — in his opinion — decadent and corrupt French as it was written and spoken at Frederic's Berlin Academy and in related literary circles. It was with his *Leçons* that Laveaux entered his lifelong feud with the ancien régime — not only in linguistic subject matters. In the same vein Laveaux criticizes in great detail the *style réfugié* in the writings of French clergymen and members of the Berlin Academy in his journal *Maître de langue* (published between 1783 and 1785). The gist of his criticisms concentrates on conservative tendencies which Laveaux is eager to detect in French publications in German-speaking countries. In order to remedy the lexical and stylistic deficiencies in such writings he even proposed to establish a separate section at the Berlin Academy for the cultivation of the French language. The tasks of such an institution would have consisted in working out a linguistically adequate bilingual dictionary (French–German and German–French) and in publishing a literary journal. This plan was, however, never carried out although Laveaux must have felt himself to be qualified for it: in 1784/85 he published the second revised and enlarged edition of a *Dictionnaire françois-allemand et allemand–françois* (1st edition 1779/80) published by a "Société de gens de lettres" on the basis of the dictionary of the Académie française and of Schmidlin's *Catholicon* (1771). In 1789/1790 appeared the 3rd edition, again revised and enlarged by Laveaux.[1]

His engagement as a literary critic was documented in the collection *Critique de quelques auteurs françois qui écrivent en Allemagne* (1787);[2] this work contains also a number of critiques on the lively discussions centering around Rivarol's and Schwab's prize-essays on the universality of the French language.[3]

In 1785, by the intervention of Frederic II, Laveaux obtained the position of professor of French at the Hohe Karlsschule in Stuttgart. In order to promulgate his own linguistic and didactic ideas in his French courses Laveaux wrote — on the Duke's order — a comprehensive, partially bilingual elementary text-book. Let me quote the French title-page in full:

> Leçons méthodiques de langue françoise pour les allemands; contenant tout ce qui est nécessaire pour apprendre et enseigner cette langue. A l'usage de l'Université-Caroline de Stouttgard. Ouvrage entrepris par ordre de Son Altesse Sérénissime Monseigneur Le Duc régnant de Wirtemberg. Par M. De La Veaux Professeur de Belles-Lettres à la dite Université. Stouttgard: de l'Imprimerie de l'Université-Caroline 1787/1788.

[1] For further editions of this *Dictionnaire* and for bibliographical details see the article Laveaux in our *Bio-bibliographisches Handbuch* (Brekle et al.).

[2] First published in Laveaux' *Cours théorique et pratique de langue et littérature* (1784/1785); which itself is the book-form publication of his journal *Maître de langue*.

[3] See further Piedmont 1984:17 ff.

Together with some of his colleagues and students he successfully tried to disseminate from 1790 onwards revolutionary ideas in public circles.[1] Kuhn In view of the Duke Karl Eugen's strict surveillance of his "Hohe Schule" it was only natural that Laveaux' situation became untenable. He submitted his resignation and was removed from his office on October 10th, 1791.

Laveaux left Stuttgart for Strasbourg where he joined — together with some of his students — the Jacobins' club. During the years 1791–1793 he served the revolutionary cause on both sides of the Rhine as the editor of the *Courrier de Paris* and of the *Courrier de Strasbourg*. In 1793 he went to Paris where he edited the Jacobin newspaper, the *Journal de la Montagne;* besides he held a position in the Ministry of War.

In 1793 he had to defend himself against the charge of not being a true Jacobin. He published his *Réponse de J.Ch. Laveaux à un écrit anonyme intitulé Portrait de Laveaux,* in which he explains in great detail the reasons why he came back to France only in 1791.[2] Somehow Laveaux managed to survive the period of "la Terreur". Judging from his later publications he must have worked in Paris as a grammarian and lexicographer until his death in 1827.[3]

2. LAVEAUX' IMPORTANCE AS A LEXICOGRAPHER AND CRITIC OF THE ACADÉMIE FRANÇAISE

As we have already seen, his first attempts as a lexicographer date back to his years in Berlin when he saw through the press several editions of a bilingual French-German and German-French dictionary. The relative success of this work can be measured against the fact that between 1784/85 — when the first editon revised by Laveaux was published — and 1812 we have been able to locate at least eight editions in such places as Berlin, Braunschweig and Strasbourg.

[1] For details see Kuhn et al. (1989:147, 151–163).

[2] For details and quotations see Gough (1974) and Kuhn et al. (1989:153–163).

[3] It is unfortunate that for so far we have been unable to consult Hugh Gough's unpublished 1974 Oxford dissertation: *Jean-Charles Laveaux (1749–1827): A political biography*.

It was in 1802 when Laveaux published in Paris his two-volume *Nouvelle édition, augmentée de plus de vingt mille articles* of the *Dictionnaire de l'Académie française*. This edition must be seen as a preparatory work for his *Nouveau dictionnaire de la langue française* (Paris 1820, 2 volumes, approx. 2.200 columns). Reduced versions of this dictionary were published in 1823 and 1825, both in Paris.

The second edition, revised, corrected and enlarged, was seen through the press one year after his death by Laveaux' daughter Rose-Dorothée Thibault-Laveaux, Mme Jean Baptiste Marty, in 1828.

The structure and types of information that can be found in the dictionary are clearly indicated on the title-page:

> 1°. Le Recueil de tous les Mots de la Langue usuelle, dont un grand nombre ne se trouve point dans les autres Dictionnaires, avec leurs définitions, et des exemples propres à en indiquer l'usage et la construction; — 2°. Les Étymologies nécessaires pour l'intelligence de ces mots, tirées des langues anciennes ou étrangères; — 3°. Un grand nombre d'Acceptions non indiquées ni définies jusqu'à présent, justifiées par des passages d'auteurs classiques, et auxquelles ces passages servent en même temps de fondement et d'exemples; — 4°. L'explication détaillée des Synonymes; — 5°. Des Remarques sur la Prononciation et l'Orthographie, lorsqu'elles s'écartent des règles générales; — 6°. La Solution des principales Difficultés grammaticales; — 7°. Les Noms des Outils et Instrumens [!] des Arts et Métiers, avec l'indication de leurs usages divers; — 8°. Les Termes des Arts et des Sciences, avec les définitions ou les descriptions des objets qui sont soumis aux procédés des uns et aux spéculations des autres; — 9°. La Critique de plusieurs Mots recueillis ou insérés mal à propos dans quelques Dictionnaires modernes, etc., etc. (Laveaux 1820: title-page).

In the preface to his *Nouveau Dictionnaire* Laveaux in the first place argues in favour of descriptivism; a reliable and representative dictionary should be founded on sound empirical work:

> le lexicographe ne doit ni proposer, ni inventer des mots et des acceptations nouvelles [...] il faut qu'il recueille dans toutes les classes, dans tous les arts, dans toutes les industries, tout ce qui est approuvé par

la raison, par le goût, par l'utilité, tout ce qui rentre dans les règles générales du langage (Laveaux 1820: I).

From this clearly follows the necessity of a new dictionary-structure (as indicated on the title-page); above all a dictionary should meet the demands of the general public. This again implies that Laveaux must needs reject Vaugelas' and to a still greater extent the Academy's application of the criterion of "la cour et la ville". He also disagrees with d'Alembert who wants to exclude the terminologies of the arts and sciences from a dictionary. Contrary to d'Alembert, Laveaux sticks to the principle that a national language should be "une et indivisible" (my wording); there should not be "deux langages différens [...] entre moi et les hommes qui me procurent les besoins et les commodités" (Laveaux 1820: V). In this passage — and in many others[1] — of his *Discours préliminaire* the connection between Laveaux' political convictions as a democrat and his lexicographical axioms is obvious.

In his opinion a dictionary should also reflect partial vocabularies of a sociolectal and technical nature; as to the latter he is, however, eager to distinguish encyclopaedic from dictionary information: it is the task of a dictionary to give such semantic explications of a technical term so that the layman may understand them; in contrast, an encyclopaedia should provide its user with optimally detailed theoretical and procedural informations about a given technical term. As to the textual or literary sources for the lemmata and examples of his dictionary entries Laveaux relies heavily on Enlightenment authors like Voltaire, Diderot, Rousseau and Condillac, without, however, neglecting authors

[1] For instance, when justifying the etymological parts of his dictionary entries Laveaux is eager to point out their usefulness for the general public; again he pleads in favour of one unified language and its conscious and transparent usage. In the case when "les racines étant puisées dans les langues que le peuple ne comprend pas, les dérivés et les composés ne lui paraissent pas plus compréhensibles; et s'il y attache quelque idée, c'est toujours d'une manière vague, imparfaite, et sans connaître la signification précise des élémens. Alors les mots formés de racines étrangères restent toujours en quelque sorte, séparés du langage commun; ils s'y mêlent plus difficilement; de sorte qu'il existe dans la nation deux langages dont les différences et la séparation sont d'autant plus sensibles, que le nombre des mots dérivés des langues mortes ou étrangères est plus considérables. C'est ici qu'il est souvent nécessaire d'indiquer les étymologies". (Laveaux 1820:VII)

of the seventeenth century such as Molière, Arnauld, Nicole and the great moralists.

He explicitly mentions Voltaire's lexicographical dictum that "un dictionnaire sans citations est une squelette" (Laveaux 1820:V) and consequently blames the Academy's dictionary for not having followed this principle.

Based on his intimate knowledge of the historical development of the Academy's dictionary work[1] which he criticizes as being theoretically inconsistent and empirically hopelessly inadequate, Laveaux considers his own *Nouveau dictionnaire* as being superior to any other existing French dictionary.

Laveaux' second major lexical work is his *Dictionnaire raisonné des difficultés grammaticales et littéraires de la langue française.* Its bibliographical history is quite remarkable: 1st edition Paris 1818 (810 pages), 2nd edition "revue, corrigée, et considérablement augmentée" Paris 1822 (2 volumes, 1353 pages!), then, revised by his grandson Charles Marty-Laveaux, four more revised editions between 1846 and 1910 (from 1847 onwards the publisher was Hachette). Based on these bibliographical facts alone we may venture the hypothesis that the lexicographer and grammarian Laveaux must have influenced and guided generations of French writers, teachers, and pupils during the nineteenth and well into the twentieth century.

In his preface to the first edition Laveaux discusses at some length problems of the correctness of usage in connection with the phenomenon of linguistic change (mostly changes of lexical and stylistic usage) and argues against the Academy's strong — and in Laveaux' opinion misguided — normative tendencies. He criticizes the linguistic work of the Académie française wholesale: their dictionary always lagged behind the developments of the "bon usage", the people working on it certainly were not the brightest minds, and, above all, the Academy never managed to produce a really good French grammar. Laveaux is quite explicit about this:

[1] We cannot here go into the "chronique scandaleuse" in and around the Académie française (Richelieu and his "côterie" against Corneille and Racine) which Laveaux relates in considerable detail.

> [...] l'Académie française [...] a totalement manqué son but. Elle a composé un dictionnaire sans avoir fait une grammaire, c'est-à-dire établi des conséquences sans avoir reconnu de principes, élevé un édifice sans avoir posé de fondemens. (Laveaux 1818:V).

In contrast to his own lexicographical work with its fine-grained semantic, syntactic and stylistic differences, Laveaux harshly criticizes his colleagues from the Académie:

> On y prenait, par le moyen des définitions, une idée assez juste de la signification plus ou moins générale d'un grand nombre de mots usuels, mais les exemples ajoutés à ces définitions n'indiquaient ni les différentes places que ces mots peuvent occuper dans le discours, ni les nuances ou les reflets qu'ils peuvent recevoir, ou de ses places, ou de leur union avec certains mots, ou de leur opposition à d'autres, ou enfin des différens tours dans lesquels ils peuvent figurer. (Laveaux 1818: V).

He furthermore complains that writers and grammarians were divided:

> Vaugelas, Bouhours, Ménage, les écrivains de Port-Royal, furent divisés; Furetière s'éleva contre l'Académie française; de nos jours, Desfontaines, Fréron et Geoffroi; contre les meilleurs écrivains de notre siècle; La Harpe contre Voltaire, son maître; et Domergue contre plusieurs de ses contemporains (Laveaux 1818: IV).

By the way, the main sources for Laveaux' examples, decisions on grammatical correctness, and stylistic adequacy are Voltaire, Marmontel, Jaucourt, La Harpe, and above all, Condillac.

Laveaux criticizes not only the various lexicographical deficiencies of the Academy's dictionary-work, he also deplores in a rather polemical tone the fatal consequences of the Academy's authoritarian influences on the development of French as a living language. His chain of accusations runs as follows.

> [...] ne pouvant justifier ou défendre un grand nombre de leurs bizarres décisions, ils voulurent en faire des dogmes, [...] . Alors on vit s'élever une sorte de superstition grammaticale et littéraire qui fit regarder le Dictionnaire de l'Académie comme le recueil unique et sacré de toutes

> les beautés et de toutes les délicatesses de la langue, et l'Académie comme un conseil grammatical perpétuel, contre les décrets duquel il était défendu de s'elever sous peine d'anathème. [...] les hommes faibles et timides, et c'est toujours le plus grand nombre, se courbèrent devant l'idole; [...] On n'osa plus hasarder d'autres expressions que celles qui se trouvaient dans le Dictionnaire de l'Académie; tout ce qui ne s'y trouvait pas fut déclaré barbare et mal sonnant, et la langue resta comme stationnaire devant cette barrière magique. (Laveaux 1818:V f.)

A piece of fine rhetoric, fully imbued with the spirit of the Enlightenment; all the anti-authoritarian and anti-clerical key-words are there. At the time when Laveaux wrote this — 1818 — he was, moreover, quite optimistic as to the future positive developments of the French people, its language and its usage; he is confident that

> [...] la raison a fait des progrès, et que les lumières se sont étendues sur toutes les classes. Il est bien encore quelques hommes qui en ont conservé le langage, mais c'est, ou par intérêt, ou par politique, ou par vieille habitude. La croyance n'y est plus, et le ridicule attend quiconque tenterait de la faire renaître. (Laveaux 1818:VI)

This is not the place nor the time to inquire into the truth of Laveaux' evaluations and prophecies. With his grammatico-stylistic encyclopaedia he certainly had his share in liberating the French and their language from the grammatical and lexical supremacy of the ancient Académie.[1]

REFERENCES

Brekle, Herbert Ernst; Dobnig-Jülch, Edeltraud; Höller, Hans Jürgen; Weiß, Helmut, (forthcoming). *Bio-bibliographisches Handbuch der Grammatiker, Sprachtheoretiker und Lexikographen des 18. Jahrhunderts im deutschsprachigen Raum mit Werkbeschreibungen ihrer sprachwissenschaftlichen Arbeiten.*

[1] Due to restrictions of space we cannot analyze Laveaux' *Dictionnaire synonymique de la langue française* (1826). See the article on Laveaux (2.12) in our *Bio-bibliographisches Handbuch* (Brekle et al.).

Gough, H. 1974. *Jean Charles Laveaux (1749–1827). A Political Biography.* Unpublished D. Phil. diss. Oxford.

Kuhn, A., ed. 1989. *Revolutionsbegeisterung an der Hohen Carlsschule.* Stuttgart-Bad Cannstatt: Holzboog.

Laveaux, Jean Charles Thiebault (de), ed. 1791–1793. *Courrier de Paris.*

—, ed. 1791–1793. *Courrier de Strasbourg.*

—. 1787. *Critique de quelques Auteurs qui écrivent en Allemagne.* Berlin: Arnold Wever.

—, ed. 1802. *Dictionnaire de l'Académie française ... Nouvelle édition, augmentée de plus de vingt milles articles.* Paris: Moutardier.

—, ed. 1784–85 (2nd ed.). *Dictionnaire françois–allemand & allemand–françois à l'usage des deux nations. ...* Berlin: A. Wever.

—. 1818. *Dictionnaire raisonné des difficultés grammaticales et littéraires de la langue françoise...* Paris: Lefèvre.

—. 1826: *Dictionnaire synonymique de la langue française, ...* Paris: Alexis Eymery ... et à la Librairie Française.

—, ed. 1793. *Journal de la Montagne.* Paris.

—. 1782. *Leçons de langue françoise données à quelques academiciens et autres auteurs françois de Berlin.* Par un Maître de langue. *Ouvrage utile à toutes les personnes qui désirent de se perfectionner dans la langue françoise.* Frankfurt.

—. (1783–85) *Le Maître de langue ou remarques instructives sur quelques ouvrages françois écrits en Allemagne.* Berlin: A. Wever.

—. 1820. *Nouveau dictionnaire de la langue* française *ou l'on trouve 1°. Le Recueil de tous les Mots de la Langue usuelle, dont un grand nombre ne se trouve pas dans les autres Dictionnaires ...* Paris: Deterville. (First ed., 1818.)

—. 1793. *Réponse de J. Ch. Laveaux à un écrit anonyme intitulé: "Portrait de Laveaux,..."* Paris.

Piedmont, René M. 1984. *Beiträge zum französischen Sprachbewußtsein im 18. Jahrhundert. Der Wettbewerb der Berliner Akademie zur Universalität der französischen Sprache von 1782/84.* Tübingen: Gunter Narr (=Lingua et Traditio 7).

Schmidlin, Johann Joseph. 1771. *Catholicon ou Dictionnaire universel de la langue françoise, oder französisch-deutsches Universalwörterbuch der französischen Sprache.* 9 vols. Hamburg: Isaac Etienne.

The First Grammar of Frisian (1681)*

ROLF H. BREMMER JR
Rijksuniversiteit Leiden

IN THE COURSE OF the later Middle Ages, the loose federacy of the seven semi-independent Frisian farmers' republics were annexed one by one by neighbouring powers. The present-day province of Fries-land in The Netherlands was annexed by the Duke of Saxony in 1500, and as a result Low German became the language of administration. In 1525 the Habsburg Emperor Charles V bought Friesland from the Saxons and introduced Dutch. After 1550 no official documents in Frisian are any longer found. The language soon disappeared from the public domain. Dutch became the dominant language, especially after Friesland had joined Holland politically and religiously in its rising against the Spanish. In the seventeenth century only some four books entirely written in Frisian were published. The most important one of these was the *Friesche Rymlerye* (1667), the poetic works of Gysbert Japix (1603–1666), a school principal. In 1681 Simon Abbes Gabbema, the State Historiographer of Friesland, published a revised and augmented edition of the *Rymlerye* in two volumes (Breuker 1989, I).[1] Vol. 2 begins, according to the title-page, with a *Friesche Grammatica;* item 2 is an Old Frisian law text presented synoptically from two manuscripts; item 3 contains a collection of letters from Japix to Gabbema; items 4 and 5 are two prose texts, translated from French into Frisian by Japix. This paper deals with the first item only.

* An extended and fully annotated version of this paper will appear in Frisian in *Philologia Frisica Anno 1990* (Ljouwert: Fryske Akademy, 1991). I gladly express my gratitude to my brother Marius, a latter-day Maecenas.

[1] Breuker (1989, I) contains a facsimile reprint of these two volumes, originally published by Kerst Tjallings and Gerrit Heegslag in Leeuwarden. I refer throughout to Breuker's pagination of the reprint.

HET TWAEDE DIEL,
Fen dy
FRIESCHE
WIRKKEN
Behelſjende ijn zig

I. Frieſche Grammatica,
II. Dae Liordera bota,
III. Frieſche Brieuwen.
IV. Hiſtorje fen DORILIS in CLEONICE,
V. PHILIPS fen MORNAY, Heer fen Pleſſis. fen Libben in Stearren.

Trog
Mr. GYSBERT JAPIX,
Schooltjenner in forlezzer binne Boalſert.

In nu, ney zijn deæd, wt zijn eyne Schriften ijn't ljeuwgt [illegible]*brægt;*
Trog
SYMEN AEBBES GAEBBEMA Hiſt: Fr.
Nooyt for dezen ijn druwk weſt.

TO LEUWARD,
By KERST TJALLINGS in GERRIT HEEGSLAG, Bockforkæpers. 1681.

(By courtesy of Leiden University Library)

On closer inspection, it appears that *Grammatica* is too good a word for two small chapters or tracts, both written in Latin. Tract 1 (henceforth

T1) is called: *"Quaedam ad Grammaticam Spectantia Lingam (!) Phrysicam, & Prima Elementa, ante Centum Quinquaginta & Quod Excurrit Annos Conscripta"* "Some Things on the Grammar, Concerning the Frisian Language, and the First Elements, Described 150 Years Ago and Further Back" (Breuker, I, 1989:285–95). Tract 2 (= T2) is entitled: *"Fargmentum (!) de Literis Frisicis"* "A Fragment on the Frisian Letters" (Breuker I, 1989:296–303).

A number of questions must be asked concerning these tracts, either because they have not been asked before or, because they have not yet been properly answered, such as: what is the size and scope of the Grammar? What is the intended audience? Is the Frisian really 150 years old as the title of T1 claims? Who is the author? It is the purpose of this paper to provide some possible answers.

SIZE AND SCOPE

The size of the tracts is too modest to be of much help in learning even the basic principles of Frisian. The traditional components of grammars at the time comprised: (1) orthography, (2) etymology (i.e. morphology), (3) prosody and (4) syntax. We can therefore conclude at once that the *Friesche Grammatica* is far from complete, as it does not contain sections on prosody and syntax. Furthermore, the section on etymology should have contained at least some eight or nine subsections, dealing with the various word classes, such as nouns, adjectives, adverbs, verbs, pronouns, conjunctions, prepositions, etc. In reality, the first tract only contains information on nouns, adjectives and numerals. The *Fragmentum,* divided into eight short chapters, belongs to the field of orthography, and is fairly complete. In the Priscian tradition it discusses the *figura* "shape" and *potestas* "value" of the letters omitting their *nomen* "name", however. Here it is a mixture of a description of origin (ch. 1) and pronunciation (chs. 2–8) of all the Frisian vowels and some of the consonants.

The scope of the Grammar may have been to present a fully-fledged description of Frisian: what we have is not much more than an abortive attempt.

INTENDED AUDIENCE

In view of this first conclusion, the Grammar can hardly have been intended for the use in schools. This observation tallies with external evidence, for, as far as we know, Frisian was never taught at school in early modern times.

Both tracts are written in Latin, so that we may assume a certain level of education on behalf of both the author and the reader. On more than one occasion Latin *sive* or *vel* is abandoned in favour of Frisian *of* "or". Such slips seem to betray an author who has either an imperfect command of Latin or one who has kept too little distance from the object he wants to describe.

Affinity with the subject is also shown by the author's occasional use of the 1st pl. as opposed to his preponderant, more descriptive use of the 3rd pl. In his description of the genitive, after having mentioned which words use an *-s* to form the genitive, he carries on (p. 293): "Cætera nomina genitivum non habent, nec enim dicimus, *di leerdez treppen. de Mounles vioec*. Sed pro genitivo utimur in omnibus particula *Fen* ..." "The remaining words have no genitive, for *we* do not say: the ladder's rongs, the mill's wing. But instead of the genitive *we* use in all instances the particle 'of' ...". Such a use of the 1st pl. perhaps indicates that the tract was not written by one Frisian for another, but by a Frisian who seeks to explain the essentials of the language to someone who is still ignorant of it. In T2 the use of "we" is much more frequent than in T1, betraying an even greater engagement with the subject on behalf of the author.

A final indication that the tone of the tract is informal, or at least not too formal, is found in the section on the declination of the cardinals. The author explains that the masculine and feminine forms of *arst* "first" add an *-e,* while the neuter form does without one. He then repeats this information for the words for "second" up to including "fifth", and then lists the epicine forms and the neuter ones from "sixth" through "seventeenth". At this point one would think that the rule is clear. But for the sake of security, the author (editor?) has printed oblong beside the remaining cardinals the following instruction (p. 295): "Si ultima[m] demas literam, hoc est E, habes genus neutrum" "If you take away the final letter, that is E, you will get the neuter gender". Such a piece of advice seems appropriate for someone who wants to learn the language actively, and it is the only time in the tract that the reader is directly addressed.

Both T1 and T2 exhibit an interest in matters Frisian that is also reflected in the rapid increase of Frisian historiography towards 1600. I suspect they were aimed at the same readership, i.e. the educated upper- and middle classes. This was a growing group, not least owing to the foundation of a university in Franeker in 1585.

THE DATE OF THE LANGUAGE

According to the caption of T1, we would be dealing here with Frisian as it was used about 150 years ago or even further back. If we take 1681, the year of its publication, for a starting point, we would arrive at 1531, or further back, for the year of origin of the first tract.[1] As I mentioned in my introduction, the early sixteenth century was a period of rapid decline of Frisian as a written medium, not only in public documents but also in private writings such as letters, ego documents and wills. What is presented in T1, however, does not tally with the kind of Frisian from ca. 1525. It must be early seventeenth century for a number of reasons.

1. Of pluralization, it is said that nouns which end in a consonant make their plural by adding the "particle" *-en*. This indeed is true for early sixteenth-century Frisian. But then the section carries on with the exceptions and it is stated that a number of nouns, 18 to be precise, get an *-s* plural. The majority of this list, 16, are nouns ending in *-ir/-er*, most of them agent nouns. There is something conspicuous about these exceptions. The *-s* is not an original plural marker for Frisian, but was borrowed from either or Low German, or, more probably, these two neighbouring dialects together enhanced the import of plural *-s* (cf. Bremmer 1989:78, fn. 3). The first instances of such an *-s* that I have been able to find date from 1502. Practically all of these concern nouns

[1] Latin *conscripta* also allows another interpretation, viz. that it is a grammar of Frisian as it was written 150 years ago. As I will show the latter interpretation is equally unlikely.

ending in *-er,* but they are few and far between. From a fairly short text (Vries/Oosterhout 1982), I collected *bakkeren* "bakers", *dragheren* "carriers", *glesfensteren* "window panes", *helpren* "helpers", *presteren* "priests", *schomakeren* "shoemakers", *Switseren* "men from Switzerland". Plural *-s* is shown in the loanword *stuvers* "kind of coins" and in the native words *wakers* "watchmen" and *borghers* "burghers, citizens". This state of fluctuation between *-s* and *-en* plurals, however, did not escape the author. In a subsection, 8 nouns ending in *-er* are listed that are said to have both *-s* and *-en*. Remarkably, none of these are agent nouns. As the Grammar assumes *-s* to be an ordinary plural morpheme, it must have been written well after 1500.

2. As for gender, the author makes a daring statement: nouns have no gender, but are all epicene. He demonstrates this statement by four examples:

> *in Moy tzirl* "a handsome chap" (m.)
> *in moy Feynt* "a handsome bachelor" (m.)
> *in moy Faam* "a beautiful girl" (f.)
> *in moy Spicir* "a beautiful granary" (m.)

The examples make clear why he arrives at an observation which is factually incorrect, for Frisian at the time still had three genders, masculine, feminine and neuter. But the fact that neither the indefinite article nor the adjective show inflectional endings where they should have appeared, at least according to Latin grammar, will have led to this drastic conclusion. The selection of examples is not exactly representative: 3 out of 4 are masculine, only one is feminine. No neuter examples are given. Had the author given this matter some thought, he might have realized the absurdity of his statement. The endingless adjectives are at first sight remarkable, especially because one would have expected them to end in *-e.* I have not yet found early sixteenth century examples of such adjectives in this position that shed their endings and thus retain their monosyllabic form. But analysis of the *Burmania Proverbs* from 1614 (Brouwer 1940) reveals that this process of desinential erosion by that time was well on its way. Some 85% of the monosyllabic adjectives preceded by an indefinite article and followed by a noun, irrespective of gender, have a zero ending.

3. Frisian, according to the grammarian (p. 287), has no cases apart from the genitive, which is formed by adding *-s*. From the ensuing examples it appears once more that we are dealing with a stage of language that has progressed much in the shedding of inflections. Instead of **dis caêls stirt, *dis baêms virtil* "the root of the tree", he writes *dat caêls stirt, dy baêms virtil:* the determiner is not inflected as might have been expected according to the rule of concord between determiner and noun.

4. The non-neuter def. art. in the *Grammatica* is *dy* and *de*. The former presents the older, the latter the younger form. Although Japix used both forms, the *Burmania Proverbs* from 1614 have practically only *de*. A collection of chronicles (Meijering 1986), representative for Frisian from ca. 1525, does not yet have *de* at all. On the basis of these four linguistic arguments I conclude that the language in T1 cannot date from the early sixteenth century, but cannot be much later than the beginning of the seventeenth century, either.

AUTHORSHIP

The fact that Simon Gabbema included these two tracts in the collected work of Gysbert Japix suggests that Japix would be the author. True, Japix was a schoolmaster and he certainly will have taught grammar to his pupils, and as a poet he was very sensitive to language, but was he a grammarian? The collected works, as we have seen, also include some 25 letters written by Japix to Gabbema. The very first of these (Breuker, I: 324–5), and the only one written in — the remaining 24 are in Frisian — includes a passage in which reference is made to the Grammar. Apparently Gabbema had sent Japix T1, for all the remarks concern matter of the first tract. Japix proved very enthusiastic and expressed the joy he would experience if Gabbema and he could spent some time together discussing its contents more thoroughly. At the same time he is critical of what the Grammar has to say and, for example, objects to the grammarian's usage of <v> for /w/. Whether Japix also discusses T2 in his letter, as Breuker (1989, II:60) suggests, is doubtful. The only possible reference to it concerns Japix' remark about the pronunciation of *th*. Gabbema had apparently pointed out to Japix that *th* could best be read as *d*. He was not the first to do so. Sibrandus Siccama (1617:88, Tit. III) had formulated this suggestion similarly (and was in all probability Gabbema's authority in this matter):

> ... the ancient Franks, Frisians and Saxons always used a *t* for *d*, as the Frisians and English still do today. For, where the pronounce *door, dien, dat, dese, deerne, dulden, dingen,* our ancestors with aspiration said *troch (!), thi, thira, thiorne, thilden, thingien* ...[1]

However, Japix does not agree with Gabbema on the pronunciation of *d*, and adduces Frisian examples to prove that *th* is now pronounced as *t* in Frisian. Apparently, he had misunderstood Gabbema, who, like Siccama, referred to the pronunciation. Letter 1 is the only undated one, but on good grounds Breuker (1989, II: 249–50) has argued that the letter must date from 1660. As it was Gabbema who had sent the Grammar to Japix, we must now ask whether Gabbema was its author as has frequently been suggested and is commonly believed, but has never been demonstrated.

Simon Abbes Gabbema (1628–1688) grew up in Leeuwarden, the capital of Friesland, and from 1647 to 1651 he studied classical philology at the universities of Groningen, Deventer, Utrecht and Leiden, but never obtained a degree. Back in Leeuwarden in 1652, he acquired a reputation of great learning. He published editions of Petronius' *Satyricon* (1654) and the works of Catullus (1659) as well as a number of mainly poetic works, such as a versification of The Song of Songs (ca. 1659). In 1659 he was appointed Historiographer of Friesland. This function implied his having access to many public records and documents that had been collected by his predecessors. These he actually had at his disposal and he kept them in his private abode.

[1] "...nam veteres *Franci, Frisij, Saxones* semper *t* pro *d* usurpabant, quod etiam nunc *Frisij & Angli* observant. Nam ubi Belgae [...] pronunciant, majores nostri [...] cum aspiratione efferebant".

It has been suggested that Gabbema concocted the Grammar, perhaps to create a pretext in order to get into touch with the renowned Gysbert Japix. Even Franciscus Junius, the well-known philologist, had come to Japix for almost two years (1647–48; cf. Breuker 1990) to be instructed in Frisian, of which fact Gabbema had later been informed by Junius himself (Breuker 1989, I: 274). As we have seen, Letter 1 must in all probability be dated to 1660, and therefore the argument of the Grammar as a means of attracting Japix' attention becomes invalid, because their correspondence began in 1654. What I suspect is that Gabbema found both T1 and T2 among the papers of his predecessors, sent T1, or a copy thereof, to Japix purely out of interest for the language. He probably wanted to have Japix's opinion of it. According to Breuker (1989, II:60), it is almost impossible for Gabbema to be the author of either tract, because the Frisian in it is too good to be of Gabbema's hand. Breuker's intuition, however, can be supported by philological arguments.

1. The spelling of Frisian in T2 differs markedly from T1. For example, initial /w/ is in T2 always written <w>, as opposed to T1 where it consistently appears as <v>. This spelling is so conspicuous around 1660 that even Japix in Letter 1 took offence to it. In all the Frisian that flowed from Gabbema's pen between 1649 and 1688 I have not come accross it. Actually, this latter spelling is a feature of sixteenth-century Frisian, albeit not a common one. The last instance I have found occurs in a private letter from 1578.

2. In T1, the adjective for "Frisian" is found twice, and is spelled *Phrysic-,* both times with a <ph> and <y>. In T2 the adjective always is spelled with an <f> and an <i>, a further indication that the two tracts are in all probability not by the same author, or, at least, not written at the same time.

3. T2 strikes one as more learned in contents than T1. The author quotes a number of books, enabling us to get an impression of his knowledge. In ch. 1 he discusses the *figura,* the shape, of the Frisian letters, and states that it is without doubt that the ancestors of the Frisians, like all Asian nations, used the Greek alphabet. The idea of an Asian origin for the Frisians goes back to medieval legend, but was extremely popular in Friesland around 1600. At that time, though,

serious historians such as Ubbo Emmius, sufficiently proved on the basis of classical texts that this idea was fictitious. By 1625 Frisian historians had accepted the truth that there was no Oriental ancestry for their people (cf. Waterbolk 1952:189). As is clear, the author still believes it, and thus provides us with a dating *post quem non*.

4. Many nations, the author carries on, borrowed their alphabet from the Greeks, such as the Goths, of whom the Frisians are either settlers *(coloni)* or relatives *(suggeneres)*. The Gothic alphabet resembles the Greekone so much that it must have been borrowed. The Anglo-Saxons, according to the author, had an alphabet which was quite different from that of the Goths. The Frisians, — still according to the author — because they use almost the same language as the Anglo-Saxons ("cum ea lingua pene usi sint"), must therefore have had an alphabet resembling either that of the Goths or that of the Anglo-Saxons. It is interesting to note that we find mention made of the affinity between English and Frisian, a notion which grew in popularity in the course of the sixteenth century (Bremmer 1990).

More interesting, perhaps, is the author's awareness of Gothic. He knows that it is written in Greek letters, and quotes as his authority from *Scriptores Frisiorum* (Cologne 1593) by Suffridus Petrus (1527–1597), a Frisian who worked as a professor of history at the university of Cologne. Petrus wrote a number of books on the history of the Frisians, and is among the first to report the existance of the Codex Argenteus. Also derived from Petrus is the author's information that the influential Frisian diplomat Joachim Hopper (1523–1576) would have possessed a copy of the Lord's prayer in Gothic letters. In ch. 2 we find a further important source quoted, viz. Bonaventura Vulcanius' *De Literis & Lingua Getarvm, siue Gothorum* (Leiden 1597). Vulcanius' book, with all its samples of texts in the ancient Germanic dialects known at the time, was the first attempt to study Gothic seriously. The third source explicitely mentioned is Justus Lipsius' *De Recte Pronunciatione Linguae Latinae* (Leiden 1588; with many reprints, though). A fourth, unacknowledged source which provided the author with his Old High German forms in ch. 8, is Paulus Merula's *Willerami Abbatis in Canticum Canticorum Paraphrasin Gemina* (Leiden 1598). All four books, therefore, date from the close of the sixteenth century

This fact provides further evidence that T2 was written around the turn of the seventeenth century, particularly as no later works appear to have been used. It also still expires the thrill of the newly discovered Gothic, and as such is a document overlooked by Van de Velde (1966).

6. It has escaped attention, for instance, that the author never refers to the edition of the Gothic gospels by Junius from 1664. Had Gabbema been the author, this would be odd, for we do know that he possessed a copy of it. In fact, Gabbema owned quite a number of books relating to Germanic philology, such as Junius' edition of the Old English "Caedmonian" poems (Amsterdam, 1655); Junius' *Observationes in Willerami* (Amsterdam 1655), a philological commentary on the Old High German paraphrase of the Song of Songs; Mauritz Opitz' edition of the Middle High German *Annolied* (Danzig 1639); Flacius Illyricus' edition of Otfrid's Old High German Gospel harmony (Zurich 1571) and Conrad Gesner's *Mithridates* (Basle 1555), to mention some (cf. Feitsma 1965:229–230). Nothing from the contents of these books emerges in T2. Yet Gabbema knew them well. In his long preface to his edition of Japix' works — in fact, a eulogy on the Frisian language — he circumstancially refers to them (Breuker 1989, I:264, 272–3). Surely, were he the author of T2, Gabbema would have found the opportunity between 1660, when we first hear of its existence, and 1681, when it was printed, to have brought the information contained in T2 up to date somehow, if only to show off his erudition. That he has not done so, shows his respect for the text as he must have found it. He has treated it like any other document in his possession.

7. A final argument against Gabbema's alleged authorship can be found in Junius' scholarly legacy. Or rather, as Thomas Tanner reports about it in 1697 in a long list of the Juniana kept in the Bodleian Library, including "De literis Frisicis ex Gabbemae chartis" (Breuker 1989, II:60–1). *Ex chartis* ["from the documents"] to me suggests that Gabbema must have sent it to Junius along with a number of Old Frisian manuscripts that he had asked for, probably around 1661 (Breuker 1990:62), shortly after Japix' Letter 1 to Gabbema.

As I have said above, Gabbema must have found the tracts among the documents of his predecessors. That we must look for an author who possessed many Old Frisian texts, becomes clear from a remark in passing in T2, ch. 2, where the author says that he has studied the ancient Frisian laws both in print (this is a reference to the incunable with legal texts from ca. 1480) and in manuscripts. Only a State Historiographer, or someone closely connected to him — the afore-quoted Siccama springs to mind — would have had sufficient material of this kind at his disposal.

Further arguments could be adduced to disclaim Gabbema's authorship, but this will do for the present. I have tried to show that the two tracts in all probability belong to the beginning of the seventeenth century. As such they belong to a peak in the production of books dealing with Friesland, its history and its culture (cf. Waterbolk 1952). Yet, we are still stuck with the information in the title that the Frisian described in these tracts is 150 years old, or even older. If Gabbema's hand must be detected somewhere, it is in the title. One possible interpretation is that he realized that the tracts were old, but had no clue as to their actual age and therefore made an uninformed guess. Alternatively, but less likely, one of the features of Frisian that struck philologists at the time was its age. It is usually referred to as "the ancient Frisian language". Perhaps this is what Gabbema wanted to express in the title.

The context, though, in which the two tracts appear should not be overlooked. They appear in a book which combines all the features of the Frisian language. There is poetry of a high level, both secular and religious, frivolous and serious. There is devotional prose as well as a pastoral novelette, there is correspondence. Included also are samples of law texts in Old Frisian. What the book seems to signal is this: "Look, reader, you may have thought that Frisian was a language of the past, and today perhaps good enough for use among farmers. But here is solid proof to the contrary. All genres can be practised in Frisian — it can even be the object of linguistic analysis. Frisian is as good as Dutch. Dutch may have its grammars, but we have one that is so much older". That is how I would like to interpret the claim for age for the Grammar. Its inclusion in Gabbema's edition of Japix' works is motivated by a self-consciousness of the rights and the possibilities of the Frisian language. Unfortunately, the pious wish at the end of T2: *Reliquia desiderantur* — perhaps best translated as "We want more!"

— remained unfulfilled. Unfortunately, too, for the Frisians and their language, the signal the book gave was never really received by its reader. Serious grammatical interest in Frisian would only start in the nineteenth century.

REFERENCES

Bremmer Jr, Rolf H. 1989. "Is de Nederlandse meervouds *-s* van Engelse komaf?", *ABäG* 28.77–92.

—. 1990. "Late Medieval and Early Modern Opinions on the Affinity between English and Frisian: The Growth of a Commonplace", *FLH* 9.167–191.

Breuker, Philippus H. 1989. *It wurk fan Gysbert Japix. I: Tekst yn facsimile. II Oerlevering en ûntstean.* Ljouwert: Fryske Akademy.

— . "On the Course of Franciscus Junius' Germanic Studies, with Special Reference to Frisian". *Aspects of Old Frisian Philology* , ed. by Rolf H. Bremmer Jr, Geart van der Meer and Oebele Vries [= *ABäG* 31–32], 42–68. Amsterdam: Rodopi/Grins: SFFYRUG.

Brouwer, Jelle H. 1940. "De Burmania-sprekwurden". *De twadde jiergearkomste fen de Fryske Akademy,* ed. by Pieter Sipma et al., 82–182. Assen: Van Gorcum.

Feitsma, Antonia et al., eds. 1965. *Johannes Hilarides en syn Naamspooringen van het Platte Friesk,* I–II. *Estrikken* 37–38. Grins.

Meijering, Henk D., ed. 1986. *Oudfriese kronieken uit het handschrift Leeuwarden RA Schw. 3992. Co-Frisica 1A-B.* Amsterdam/Kiel.

Siccama, Sibrandus 1617. *Lex Frisionum sive Antiquae Frisiorum Leges.* Franeker: Johannes Lamrinck.

Van de Velde, Roger 1966. *De studie van het Gotisch in de Nederlanden.* Gent: Koninklijke Vlaamse Academie voor Taal- en Letterkunde.

Vries, Oebele and Meint G. Oosterhout, eds. 1982. *De Leeuwarder Stedstiole 1502–1504. Estrikken* 60. Grins.

Waterbolk, Etzo H. 1952. *Twee eeuwen Friese geschiedschrijving.* Groningen: Wolters.

Latinisme ou gallicisme ?
Les méthodes translinguistiques latin – français au XVIIIe siècle

BERNARD COLOMBAT
Université Stendhal, Grenoble

1. LE FAIT QUE la description des langues classiques ait été pendant longtemps pratiquement seule en usage a eu des conséquences importantes sur la description linguistique en général. Cela a en particulier retardé l'élaboration d'un moule adéquat pour la description des vernaculaires. De là l'intérêt des historiens pour analyser les progrès dans la description de ces dernières, progrès conçus pratiquement toujours comme un affranchissement du modèle classique. Mais on s'est assez peu intéressé jusqu'ici à l'évolution même de la description des langues qui ont servi de base, du moins avant l'essor de la grammaire historique et de la grammaire comparée.

Or la description des langues classiques a connu une crise à partir du moment où se sont élaborées d'autres descriptions qui ne pouvaient plus se satisfaire du modèle ancien. Un moment très important de cette crise se produit au XVIIIe siècle à cause des centres d'intérêt qui se développent alors et de l'inadéquation des méthodes jusqu'ici utilisées. Le XVIIIe siècle français se passionne à la fois pour la pédagogie en général, pour l'enseignement du latin, pour la comparaison des langues et la recherche d'universaux linguistiques. En même temps, l'enseignement du latin connaît une crise, car les trois traditions d'apprentissage du latin qui s'affrontent alors ne donnent pas satisfaction. La grammaire de Despautère (1460–1520), encore utilisée au travers de ses nombreux adaptateurs et traducteurs, a subi des modifications, mais celles-ci n'ont fait qu'obscurcir un texte obsolète. La *Nouvelle Méthode latine* de Port-Royal reste un ouvrage diffus et contradictoire du fait que Lancelot (1616–1695) n'a fait qu'ajouter des remarques inspirées

(1523–1601) à un ouvrage originellement tiré de Despautère. Une troisième tradition, plus récente — elle remonte aux alentours de 1650 — relève purement de la pédagogie. Il s'agit de méthodes qui se proposent de trouver la traduction latine correspondante pour des mots français difficiles parce qu'ils n'ont pas de correspondants exacts en latin. Ces "méthodes", qui n'ont souvent rien de "méthodique", connaissent un succès relativement important dans les collèges où la crise de l'enseignement du latin se développe. Mais leur totale vacuité théorique en fait la cible des "philosophes" qui condamnent ces "inventions" des "grammatistes" que sont par ex. le "*que* retranché" ou "la particule *on*". Parallèlement se développe ce qu'on peut appeler "le mythe du latin sans grammaire". On rêve d'un enseignement du latin par imprégnation, en citant constamment l'exemple de Montaigne (1533–1592), les théories de Locke ou l'enseignement donné par Lefebvre de Saumur (1615–1672) à son fils et fondé presque exclusivement sur la pratique de la version. De plus, le développement de la grammaire générale conduit à la recherche d'universaux linguistiques. La comparaison du latin, plus elliptique et à l'ordre des mots plus libre, et du français, qui n'a plus les marques casuelles pour marquer les fonctions, est au centre des discussions. L'analyse de ces différences est à l'origine de l'idée qu'on doit pouvoir établir des "passerelles" d'une langue à l'autre, grâce aux traductions interlinéaires. Nous voudrions ici aborder à la fois la question pédagogique de l'apprentissage du latin et la question théorique de la langue de référence. Pour cela nous examinerons d'abord ces méthodes représentatives des préoccupations pédagogiques de l'époque, puis nous les mettrons en rapport avec les notions d'idiotisme, gallicisme, latinisme.

2. LES INTERLINEÁIRES

2.1. *Principe*

Rapprocher, à la fois matériellement (typographiquement) et conceptuellement (en opérant des modifications syntaxiques) les deux langues : latin et français ; par conséquent opérer une série de transformations soit sur le texte latin, soit sur le texte français, soit sur les deux.

2.2. *Schématisation des données*

Dans le rapprochement des deux langues nécessité par l'interlinéaire, il y a essentiellement deux procédures mises en oeuvre : addition ou soustraction, et modification de l'ordre des mots. Inévitablement, il nous faut, pour faciliter la comparaison, opérer une schématisation des données. Pour le latin, on peut distinguer les états suivants, comme nous invitent à le faire les auteurs eux-mêmes : L.O. latin original; L.R. latin "reconstruit", *i.e.* dont l'ordre des mots a été modifié (remède aux "inversions") ; L.R.S. latin "reconstruit et suppléé", *i.e.* dont les mots prétendus manquants ont été rétablis (remède aux "ellipses"). Pour le français, nous avons dû déterminer nous-même un peu arbitrairement les états suivants : F.E. Français élégant ; F.L. Français littéral ; F.A. Français agrammatical. Ces différents états de langue peuvent être classés en fonction d'un degré d'acceptabilité exactement inverse au degré de rapprochement : plus ils sont proches, moins ils sont acceptables ; plus ils sont acceptables, moins ils sont proches (cf. SCHEMA 1).

SCHEMA 1 : LES ADAPTATIONS DES DEUX LANGUES

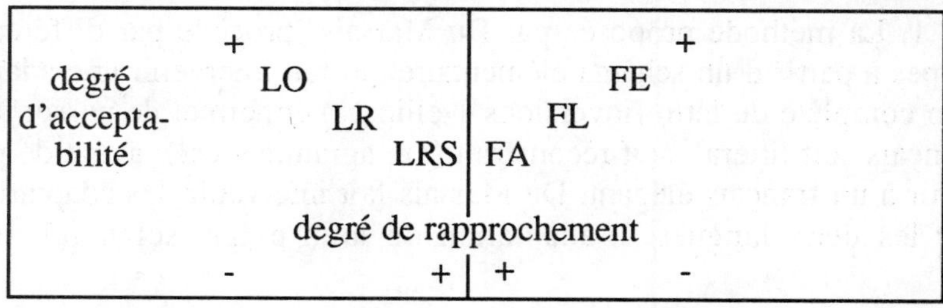

Autre point important : la mise en page et la présentation des données. Quels que soient les textes examinés (simples recueils de textes en interlinéaires, ouvrages plus théoriques ou "plans d'éducation"), les auteurs attachent toujours beaucoup d'importance à la mise en page des données, que nous avons schématisée sur deux exemples[1] (cf. SCHEMA 2).

SCHEMA 2 : LA MISE EN PAGE

DE LAUNAY (1756-1761)

diction-naire	(FE) / FL / LR	+	notes syntax-iques
	LO		
	FE		

RIVARD (1760)

LRS / FA/FL
identification morphologique des mots
en note: FE

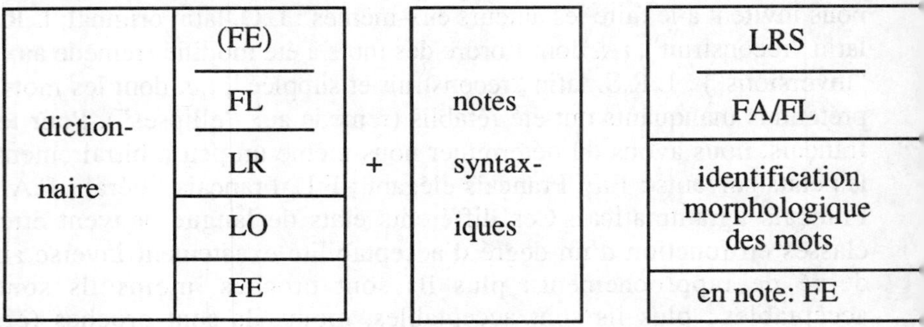

Nous avons sélectionné huit auteurs que nous étudierons par référence au premier et plus important, Du Marsais.

2.3. ANALYSE DES DONNEES.

2.3.1. La méthode proposée par Du Marsais[2] procède par différentes étapes à partir d'un schéma élémentaire qui fait intervenir une adaptation complète du latin (inversions + ellipses) et permet de passer à un français soit littéral, soit reconstruit (*i.e.* agrammatical), avant de parvenir à un français élégant. Du Marsais fait intervenir des adaptations sur les deux langues. L'adaptation du latin exige, selon lui, trois

[1] Nous ne pouvons, pour des raisons de place, donner la totalité des schémas, pas plus que l'itinéraire recommandé par l'auteur pour passer d'un état de langue à un autre. Pour un exposé plus complet, on se reportera à notre thèse d'Etat *Les figures de construction dans la syntaxe latine, 1500-1780*, Univ. de Paris VII (1991). Pour la mise en page chez Du Marsais (1676–1756), cf. Douay-Soublin 1988:38–42.

[2] 1722 : Horace, *Carmen Saeculare*, in *Exposition d'une nouvelle Méthode* [=1797:vol.1:42–65]; 1729 : Phèdre, *Fables, Prologue*, in *Préface d'une méthode* [=1987:15–19]; 1731 : Jouvency, *Appendix: Epitome de diis et heroibus poeticis* [1797:vol.2]).

opérations: établir des “supplétions”; modifier l’ordre des mots; résoudre les latinismes (1797 vol.1.7–25).

a) L’ellipse reste une explication interne au latin. Ainsi Du Marsais justifie le rétablissement de *in* dans *in illo tempore* par la référence aux auteurs et par l’anecdote selon laquelle “Auguste lui-même avait coutume d’exprimer les prépositions qu’il est plus élégant de sous-entendre“ (1797 vol.1.156).

b) Le rétablissement de l’ordre des mots n’est pas opéré en fonction d’un ordre canonique de la phrase latine, ni calqué sur le français, mais rétabli en fonction de “l’ordre universel, qui est de tout pays” (1797 vol.1.159).

c) S’il est possible de définir un ordre des mots naturel et universel, il est beaucoup plus difficile de ramener les idiotismes à une forme qui serait une expression neutre et intermédiaire entre toutes les langues: là où le français dit *crier au feu,* le latin dit *clamare aquas* (1797 vol.1.22).

Du fait que ce n’est pas le français la langue de référence (c’est du moins ce dont Du Marsais se défend énergiquement), des interventions sont aussi nécessaires de ce côté, et certains exemples montrent que Du Marsais ne “tire” pas le latin vers le français, mais qu’il a pour but d’adapter les deux langues aux exigences d’une théorie générale du langage (à l’avenir = TGL). *Quod* “parce que” est glosé *<propter illud negotium secundum> quod* et traduit : “à cause de cette chose, selon laquelle”. Ce système complexe d’ellipses n’a pas pour objet de rapprocher le latin du français (il suffirait pour cela d’admettre que *quod* peut se traduire par “parce que“ à côté de “que”), mais de renvoyer à une TGL qui n’admet pas la recatégorisation des morphèmes et selon laquelle *quod/que* est toujours relatif et suppose un antécédent. Cependant assez souvent se pose le problème des limites des reconstructions. Un subjonctif en phrase libre est complété soit par un verbe et une conjonction *(precamur ut),* soit, plus légèrement, par *utinam* (1797 vol.1.49,51). Cette réduction à des universaux de langage n’implique pas le fixisme théorique que revendiquera Beauzée (1717–1789). Certes il faut rechercher les fondements d’une TGL, mais la différence entre les langues ne se manifeste pas ultimement dans leur expression, mais déjà au niveau du “tour d’imagination” (1797 vol.1.116).

2.3.2. [1] DUMAS (1674–1744) propose (1732–3) une interlinéaire volontairement fruste qui fait correspondre syntagmes français et syntagmes latins, sans se préoccuper de les faire coïncider exactement, car il veut éviter l'inconvénient des "métodes où l'on est obligé de doner de deus sortes de latin, et souvent trois sortes de *françois*" (1732–3 vol.4.ii). Mais le défaut essentiel reste celui que présentent les ouvrages antérieurs à ceux de Du Marsais: les mots ne se répondent pas de langue à langue. [2] C'est dans la critique de la méthode de Du Marsais que réside le principal intérêt de l'ouvrage (1756–61) de DE LAUNAY (env.1700–1767). Ce qu'il reproche à son prédécesseur, c'est de ne pas respecter le texte latin original et d'y mettre de l'embarras par l'introduction de mots sous-entendus. Ainsi, aux 39 mots dont le *Prologue* de Phèdre est composé, Du Marsais en ajoute 30 autres, ce qui introduit des confusions avec le texte original et compromet la latinité de l'ensemble (1756–61:1, *Avert.*10). Il ne faut donc pas suppléer les mots latins sous-entendus. Cependant on peut mettre le latin original dans l'arrangement qui convient à l'élève (LR préféré à LO). Le français obtenu est très peu acceptable (FA plutôt que FL) et sera doublé par des expressions moins littérales. De Launay ne place pas la discussion sur un plan théorique: s'il admet le principe de l'inversion et celui de l'ellipse, la pédagogie ne tolère pas de rétablir dans le texte latin les mots ellipsés. [3] VANIÈRE (?–1768) s'insurge ([1]1759) contre l'alternance des lignes de français et de latin et propose de disposer chacun des deux textes sur des colonnes séparées: une 3e colonne contient un mélange de latin et de français avec renvoi par un système alphanumérique à une grammaire. Le latin est reconstruit, mais non suppléé. [4] RIVARD (1697–1778), qui n'a pour intention que de faciliter la connaissance de textes religieux, complète son interlinéaire (1760) par un double renvoi à des notes grammaticales de bas de page et à une syntaxe en 60 règles. La forme latine originale (LO) n'intéresse pas par elle-même l'auteur qui recherche uniquement l'efficacité dans le passage de langue à langue. De ce fait, le latin est reconstruit (selon l'ordre français, Rivard ne se souciant pas de la recherche d'un ordre universel) et suppléé. C'est donc en fonction du résultat (la traduction française) que les opérations sur le latin ont lieu. [5] De la méthode (1768) de DE RADONVILLIERS (1709–1789), on ne retiendra que le souci de progressivité. Progressivité dans le passage de langue à langue, qui impose de prendre en compte les quatre différences essentielles entre le latin et le français (1768:69–73) : les mots ; le "méchanisme" ou "emploi des inflexions et des particules pour lier les idées" ; le "style", *i.e.* l'expression de la pensée par des idées différentes ; l'arrangement des mots. Progressivité dans la pédagogie qui impose un passage par quatre niveaux d'étude. Ce que recherche De Radonvilliers, c'est une simple méthode de traduction, par rapprochement empirique des deux langues, et non la référence à une TGL explicite, comme Du Marsais. Entre les deux auteurs, il y a la différence qui sépare un "méchanicien" d'un "métaphysicien". [6] MATHIAS (1777) se déclare en faveur d'un latin reconstruit et suppléé, mais préfère, comme Rivard, une traduction mêlant étroitement latin et français. Comme De Radonvilliers, il élabore une méthode très progressive avec un appareil pédagogique complexe (notes, analyse morphologique, études des synonymes). [7] La méthode (1780) d'ADAM (1716–1792) présente la particularité d'être entièrement dépendante de sa grammaire française, dont l'étude doit nécessairement précéder, et de faire intervenir quatre textes répartis sur quatre pages de deux cahiers, ce qui permet des interactions incessantes entre les différents états. De plus, cette méthode, qui est à la fois une méthode de thème et de version, présente l'intérêt de montrer la vanité d'un rapprochement des deux langues : LR est du latin avec la construction française: ce n'est donc plus du latin ; FA est du français avec la construction latine : ce n'est donc plus du français (rarement un auteur a poussé aussi loin notre langue dans l'agrammaticalité). Il y a donc "croisement" des reconstructions, et non leur superposition. On est loin de l'entreprise de Du Marsais à la recherche d'une TGL.

3. LA QUESTION DE LA LANGUE DE REFERENCE

3.1. *Le traitement des deux langues*

Mise à part la méthode très élémentaire de Dumas qui refuse toute modification sur les deux langues, tous les auteurs admettent qu'on peut réorganiser le texte latin selon l'ordre français ou un prétendu ordre universel. C'est même une condition *sine qua non* de l'efficacité de l'interlinéaire. Quant au parti de "suppléer" le latin, seulement trois auteurs le prennent, les autres le refusant, soit tacitement, soit explicitement, comme De Launay, qui admet qu'il y a des ellipses en latin, mais veut qu'elles soient exprimées en français ("les mots sous-entendus doivent être en *françois*" 1756–61:1, *Avert.*11). Sous cette formulation maladroite, il touche à une question cruciale: faut-il situer l'ellipse dans une conception intralinguistique ou dans une conception translinguistique de la figure? Le français subit aussi son lot de transformations, la plupart des auteurs (Du Marsais, De Launay et surtout Adam) n'hésitant pas à recourir à un français carrément agrammatical[1].

3.2. *L'utilisation d'un vocabulaire spécifique*. Qu'on ait affaire aux auteurs de méthodes interlinéaires, à leurs détracteurs, ou aux auteurs de méthodes ordinaires, dans tous les cas, on observe l'utilisation d'un vocabulaire spécifique. Ce vocabulaire, c'est "faire la construction" (e.g. Du Marsais 1987[1729]:25), "un latin sans inversion" ou "ôter les inversions" (e.g. Rivard 1760:v). De là les expressions: "latin rangé selon la construction simple" (Du Marsais 1987[1729]:24), "latin décomposé" ou "latin déconstruit". Expressions couramment admises par la majorité des praticiens, même si quelques-uns, comme Pierre Chompré, se plaignent de ces textes "disloqués" ou de ces auteurs "renversés". L'utilisation constante de ce vocabulaire amenait à poser la question de la langue de référence, et plus généralement de l'écart d'une langue particulière par rapport aux universaux linguistiques, la grammaire latine devenant de plus en plus une "description par différence" soit par rapport à une grammaire générale, soit par rapport à une grammaire française dont l'élaboration progresse très rapidement au XVIIIe siècle. Cette différence est désignée par les termes *latinisme* ou *gallicisme,* selon le point de vue auquel on se place. Aussi vaut-il la peine de s'intéresser à l'emploi de ces termes.

[1] Les interlinéaires ont suscité à la fois de vives critiques de la part de ceux qui refusent la modification des textes latins (Pierre Chompré [1698–1760] et Noël-Antoine Pluche [1688–1761]) et des réserves sur leur efficacité pédagogique, par exemple de la part de Morelly (fl. milieu XVIIIe s.), Changeux (1740–1800), Diderot (1713–1784), Guyton de Morveau (1737–1816) et Beauzée.

3.3. Idiotisme, latinisme, gallicisme.

3.3.1. Les progrès de la grammaire générale et de la grammaire française amenaient à poser la question de *l'idiotisme,* mot qui, comme les termes qui le particularisent, comporte plusieurs sens, entre autres ceux-ci : 1) locution propre à un groupe linguistique particulier, 2) locution d'une langue indûment importée dans une autre langue. Dès leur origine, les termes *latinisme* et *gallicisme* sont eux aussi porteurs d'une ambiguïté originelle : à la fois 1) construction ou emploi propre à la langue latine, ou à la langue française, et 2) construction calquée, dans une autre langue, sur le modèle d'une construction latine ou française. Or l'utilisation de ces trois termes est révélatrice d'une hiérarchie des langues dans la réflexion linguistique, comme on le montrera par l'exemple de ces trois auteurs : Du Marsais, Lhomond (1727–1794) et Beauzée.

3.3.2. Du Marsais hésite entre les deux sens répertoriés. S'il utilise le sens 2 dans l'article *anglicisme* de *l'Encyclopédie,* l'utilisation des termes *gallicisme* et latin*isme* dans ses ouvrages pédagogiques a évolué. Dans la 1ère éd. de *l'Exposition* (1722=1797:vol.1.2–41), le latin est sans cesse ramené au français, et le terme latin*isme* est constamment utilisé, à l'exclusion de *gallicisme.* Cette approche modifiait considérablement la perspective traditionnelle qui avait jusqu'alors tendance à juger les structures françaises comme un écart par rapport au latin. Du Marsais au contraire évaluait le latin par rapport au français, qui tendait à se constituer, spécialement en ce qui concerne l'ordre des mots, en langue idéale. Or certaines critiques *(e.g. Journal des Savants,* janv. 1724) l'ont conduit à recentrer son analyse autour du couple latinisme–gallicisme, latin et français étant dans la même position (au moins théoriquement) par rapport aux universaux de langage (1729=1987:44–45). Une fois établi sur ces bases saines, l'idiotisme ne devrait plus poser de problème. Il y a une faculté de langage à laquelle correspondent des universaux de langage dont chaque langue s'écarte par ses idiotismes. Cette perspective idéale n'est pas dans la pratique si facile à tenir, car elle soulève la question de la spécificité de l'idiosyncrasie. Si les langues se réduisent à des collections d'idiotismes, que deviennent les universaux syntaxiques?

3.3.3. Dans la vulgate pédagogique persiste l'idée que l'idiotisme est quelque chose qui dans une langue ne correspond à rien de précis dans une autre. Ainsi les "particules" — le terme est révélateur — françaises *que* et *on* sont autant de "gallicismes" parce qu'elles n'ont pas de correspondant exact en latin. De plus la tradition pédagogique, qui avait à disposition une tradition descriptive beaucoup plus forte pour le latin que pour le français, privilégiait nettement le rapprochement vers le latin. Ainsi Lhomond (1780), nullement influencé par la grammaire générale qu'il rejette, ne parle que de *gallicismes*. Il pose dans l'absolu la langue latine par rapport à laquelle sont décrits les tours français — justement qualifiés de "gallicismes" — nécessaires à connaître pour passer d'une langue à l'autre; c'est précisément l'objet de la "méthode latine" que de proposer une étude de ces tours.

3.3.4. C'est Beauzée qui fournit la réponse la plus approfondie sur l'idiotisme[1]. Il refuse le sens 2 et affirme que "le *Gallicisme* en français est à sa place". Une fois fondée la validité de l'idiotisme, il pose la question de sa reconnaissance et de sa délimitation et établit pour cela dans l'article *idiotisme* une distinction entre *idiotisme régulier* quand "les règles immuables de la parole y sont suivies" et *idiotisme irrégulier* quand "les règles immuables de la parole y sont violées". La distinction permet de fonder un modèle linguistique général indépendant de la fréquence des usages constatés dans les langues. Prenant comme exemple l'adjectif après la copule, il considère que l'absence d'accord en allemand (emploi adverbial) est un idiotisme régulier, car "l'esprit considère l'attribut d'une manière vague et sans application au sujet", alors que l'accord de l'adjectif en cette position, dans la plupart des autres langues, constitue certes une "phrase commune", mais n'en est pas moins un *idiotisme irrégulier* qui suppose le rétablissement d'un substantif dans l'attributif (ex. *ego sum <homo> miser ;* cf. SCHEMA 3).

[1] Cf. les articles de *l'Encyclopédie* qu'il a consacrés à la question, à savoir *gallicisme, hébraïsme, hellénisme,* et surtout *idiotisme.*

SCHEMA 3 : L'IDIOTISME SELON BEAUZEE

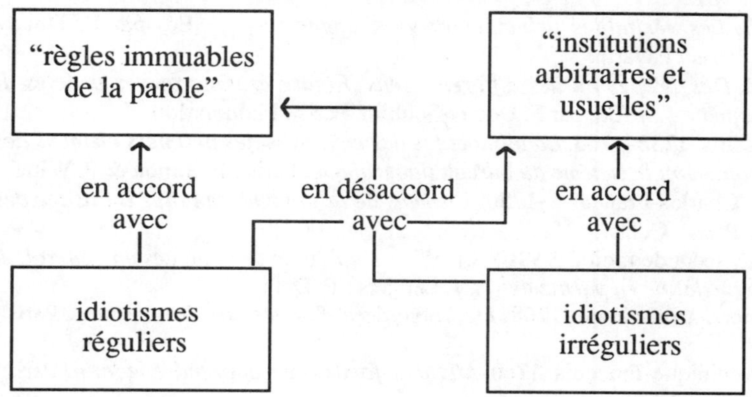

4. Ainsi conçue, la question de l'idiotisme est affinée, mais loin d'être réglée, la définition des "règles immuables de la parole" posant quelques problèmes. Surtout la pédagogie, qui avait des réponses urgentes à donner, ne pouvait se satisfaire de cette tentative de défini–tion des universaux linguistiques. Si bien que deux tentations inverses, à la fois d'expliquer les phénomènes français dans le vieux cadre de la grammaire latine, et de réorganiser la phrase latine selon l'ordre des mots français, cohabiteront, parfois dans le même ouvrage, contribuant à créer une interlangue hybride dont il est bien difficile de démêler les composantes. Après 1780, on parlera encore longtemps dans la grammaire latine scolaire à la fois du "*que* retranché" et des ellipses ou des inversions latines.

REFERENCES

Adam, Nicolas. 1780. *La vraie manière d'apprendre une langue quelconque [...], Grammaire* latine. Paris : Benoît Morin [et autres ouvrages publiés chez le même éd. de 1780 à 1787].

De Launay [= Pipoulain Delaunay], Pierre. 1756–61. *Nouvelle Méthode [...] latine.* Paris : veuve Robinot et Babuty. 4 vols.

Diderot et al. 1751-1772. *Encyclopédie,* Neuchâtel : Briasson.

Douay-Soublin, Françoise, éd. : cf. Du Marsais 1987 et 1988.

Du Marsais, César Chesneau. 1797. *Oeuvres*. éd. par Duchosal & Millon. Paris : Pougin. 7 vols.

— . 1987. *Les véritables principes de la grammaire [...]*. Ed. par F. Douay-Soublin. Paris : Fayard.

— . 1988. *Des Tropes ou des différents sens, Figure et vingt autres articles de l'Encyclopédie [...]*. Ed. par F. Douay-Soublin. Paris : Flammarion.

Dumas , Louis. 1732–1733. *La biblioteque des enfans, ou les premiers elemens des lettres, contenant le sisteme du bureau tipografique*. Paris : P. Simon & P. Witte.

Lhomond, Charles-François. [2]1780. *Elémens de la grammaire latine à l'usage des collèges*. Paris : Colas.

Mathias [fl. seconde moitié XVIIIe s.]. 1777. *De l'étude des langues en général, et de la langue latine en particulier [...]*. Langres : P. Defay.

Radonvilliers, Lyzarde de. 1768. *De la manière d'apprendre les langues*. Paris : Saillant.

Rivard, Dominique-François. 1760. *Méthode facile pour apprendre le latin*. Paris : Butard.

Vanière, Ignace. [4]1799 [[1]1759]. *Cours de latinité*. Paris : A. Boudet.

The Hibernian Connection: Irish Grammaticography in Louvain*

JAN DE CLERCQ & PIERRE SWIGGERS
K.U. Leuven – Belgian National Science Foundation

THIS PAPER is intended as a contribution to the history of Irish grammar in the seventeenth and eighteenth centuries. At that time Irish grammar underwent a radical change in function and orientation: whereas medieval grammars of Irish were conceived as tools for literary instruction, the exile of Roman catholics to the Continent in the second half of the XVIth century caused a need for another type of grammar: *descriptive* grammars which could serve as reliable guides for the clergy separated from the homeland, providing them with a "structural memento" of their native tongue.

This new phase in the history of Irish grammar is linked with a number of prominent places on the Continent, where the Irish intelligentsia in exile found refuge. Important settlements of Irish Roman catholics are to be situated in the southern Low Countries (Douai, Antwerp, Lille, Louvain), in France (Paris, Bordeaux, Poitiers, Toulouse, Nantes), in Spain (Salamanca, Madrid), and in Italy. In Louvain the presence of *Hiberni,* who were housed in three colleges (the "Collegium pastorale Hibernorum", the college of the Dominican fathers, and the Franciscan "Coláiste San Antoine"), was a culturally and intellectually very marked one, and it was especially in the latter college that an important scientific activity developed. We shall first

* For kind advice and help with our work on these Louvain grammars of Irish, we are indebted to Father Brendan (O.F.M.) and Brother Isidore (O.F.M.) of St. Anthony's College in Louvain, to Father P. Ó Súilleabháin (O.F.M.) and Father Benignus Millett (O.F.M.) of Dún Mhuire, Killiney, to Prof. Brian Ó Cuív (Dublin), and to Dr Erich Poppe (Marburg and now Cambridge).

sketch the general scientific contribution of St. Anthony's College, before focusing on the grammatical activity connected with the College.[1]

As most Irish colleges on the Continent, the Franciscan college of Louvain had a twofold function: it was an educational center for young Minor Friars, and given the concentration of teachers and scholars, it was also intended to stimulate scientific work. In Louvain the Irish Franciscans had a major asset in promoting intellectual activity: in 1514, some eight years after the obtainment of the royal privilege to build a convent in Louvain, the Franciscan friars could rely on their own printing press, using the Gaelic fount *(cló Gaelach)*.[2] The Louvain Franciscans published an impressive series of catechetical works, including the *Suim Riaghlachas Phroinsiais*, Florence Conry's [Flaithrí Ó Maoil Chonaire] *Sgáthán an Chrábhaidh* (1616), and Hugh Mac Caghwell's [Aodh Mac Aingil] *Scáthán Shacramuinte na hAithridhe* (1618). The latter scholar laid the foundations of a long-standing tradition of philosophical and theological research, inspired by the scholasticism of Duns Scotus. Next to theology and philosophy, we have to mention the important hagiographical contribution of the Irish Franciscans from Saint Anthony's College. This activity must be seen in the light of a monumental project conceived by Hugh Ward [Aodh Mac an Bhaird], viz. that of a hagiographical series relating to Scotland and Ireland. This project of *Acta Sanctorum veteris et maioris Scotiae seu Hiberniae* involved the edition of all the available sources, and to achieve this several collaborators were sent out to various European monastic libraries, in order to copy manuscripts. The main publication resulting from this activity is the compilation by the "Four Masters" in

1 On the history and the cultural achievements of the College, see De Buck (1869), Jennings (1925), O'Briain (1928), Mooney (1969), Conlan (1977), and De Clercq & Swiggers (1990). On the place of the college in Irish Renaissance scholarship, see Silke (1973).

2 In a letter, published by Gilbert (1874:604), and probably dating from around 1613–14, we read: "Wee have of late erected heere a new Irish printe, whence wee hope will ensue manifould fruites, redounding to the great good and glorie of our church and catholike contreyman". Presumably, the printing fount had previously been used by Jacob Messen in Antwerp, who in 1611 published the first Irish catechism by Bonaventure O'Hussey; a second edition was published in 1614 in Louvain.

which Michael O'Clery [Micheál Ó Clérigh] had a prominent rôle. The work, *Annála Ríoghachta Éireann,* or "Annals of Donegal" (also the "Annals of the Four Masters") is indeed a detailed history of the Irish kingdom, ranging from the first occupation of the isle up to 1636.

The didactic and scientific function of the Franciscan college in Louvain also involved a grammatical component.[1] The Louvain friars have left us a number of manuscripts and printed works from approximately 1610 to 1728, when Hugh Mac Curtin [Aodh Buidhe Mac Cruitín] published his *Elements of the Irish Language*, in which an attempt at a synthesis of grammatical doctrine is made. It may be worthwhile to note that the first printed grammar of Welsh has also some ties with Louvain: Gruffydd Robert, the author of a *Gramadeg Cymraeg* published between 1567 and 1584 in Rome, was an exiled Catholic who had studied in Louvain and in Milan.

1. The first Irish grammatical product stemming from Louvain is Bonaventure Hussey's [Giolla Bríghde Ó hEósa] manuscript *Rudimenta Grammaticae Hibernicae*. The work is intended as an elementary grammar for the Irishmen in exile, and has strong links with the Bardic tradition.[2] Hussey's grammar never reached print, but it circulated in a number of manuscript copies, just like a few other grammatical and prosodical tracts written in Louvain. Father Felim O'Briain (1933) compiled a list of manuscripts containing grammars and prosodies composed by the Louvain friars, and now preserved at the British Museum, the Royal Irish Academy or Trinity College.[3] Of these the tract conserved in manuscript D. 4.35 (TCD) contains an Irish

[1] For a survey of Irish grammaticography by the Louvain Franciscans, see Tourneur (1905:60, 72), and Lambert (1987:23–24). For grammatical tracts based on the Louvain *Rudimenta*, see Egan (1968:xxi–xxv) and the *Catalogue of Irish Manuscripts in the Royal Irish Academy* (General index, p. 802).

[2] On the *Rudimenta* and its author, see Wall (1942), Ó Cuív (1956:99–104), Egan (1944; ed. 1968:ix–xxv), Ó Concheanainn (1968). On Bardic grammaticography, see Thurneysen (1892), Ó Cuív (1965; 1973; 1980; 1987), Adams (1970), Ahlqvist (1979–80; 1983). Several grammatical tracts have been edited by Bergin (1915–1955) and McKenna (1944).

[3] O'Briain (1933:107) gives the following list: B.M., Egerton 162, 168, 192; Add. 18, 951, etc.; R.I.A. 3B 30; 23A 24; 23I 13; Stowe, A.IV.2, etc.; T.C.D. D4. 35; H4. 15; H4. 24; H4. 29; H6. 7. Cf. the list compiled by Egan (1968: xv–xix).

prosody; the manuscript was taken to Rome by Father Patrick Tyrell, who put it at the disposal of Francis O'Molloy [Proinsias Ó Maolmhuaidh]. To O'Briain's list we should add two copies of Hussey's *Rudimenta* conserved in the Marsh Library in Dublin (manuscripts Z. 3.5.3. and Z. 3.4.19, of which only the latter contains the prosody; cf. Scott–White 1913:61; 63), and another one conserved in Trinity College (H. 5.20), to which Edward Lhuyd had already drawn the attention (Lhuyd 1707:IX, 299; Abbott–Gwynn 1921:259–261). The latter copy as well as the manuscript of Marsh Library containing the prosody show striking resemblances to the contents of the first printed grammar of Irish, the *Grammatica Latino-hibernica* of Father Francis O'Molloy.

Bonaventure Hussey's *Rudimenta* constitute a fairly comprehensive survey of Irish grammar, covering phonetics, morphology, syntax, and prosody. Only the latter part, specifically intended for advanced students, is written in Irish. The other parts, written in Latin, are aimed at a public in want of systematic information on the structure of Irish. In contradistinction to the Bardic tradition Hussey's grammar is a work not conceived for poets, and this explains the deviations from the model of Bardic grammar. The principal deviation lies in the adoption of a Latin-based model of parts of speech, as opposed to the tripartite division in the Bardic grammars.

> Partes orationis Hybernis sunt septem, videlicet, *airteagal* .i. articulus; *ainm* .i. nomen; *insgne* .i. pronomen; *briathar nó pearsa* .i. verbum; *reimhbriathar* .i. adverbium; *coimhc[h]eangal* .i. coniunctio; *iarmbéarla* .i. praepositio. Veteres autem tres tantum rece[n]sent orationis partes quas vocant *trí hiarnaile na gaoidhilge* nimirum, *focal*, *pearsa* et *iarmbéarla*. Per *focal* intellegunt nomen, pronomen et adverbium; per *pearsa*, solum verbum; per *iarmbéarla*, praepositionem, coniunctionem et articulum (ed. Egan 1968:15).

Although he retains the term *iarmbéarla*, Hussey restricts its extension to the prepositions in the modern sense (such as *dó, aige, leis,* etc. cf. ed. Egan 1968:66–68). The most explicit rejection of the native tradition concerns the order of presentation of the finite verb forms. In the Bardic tradition the following order was invariably adopted (see

Bergin 1938:211): 1. Future indicative/present subjunctive; 2. Secondary future/past subjunctive; 3. Present indicative with negative of the preterite; 4. Imperfect indicative; 5. Preterite (or perfect). Hussey proceeds in accordance with the Latin order of presentation, going from Present Indicative, Preterite Indicative, Future Indicative, to the Imperative and the other moods, and then discussing the infinitive and the gerund. His decision is motivated by a purely pragmatic factor, viz. his readership:

> Hiberni Graecos imitantes coniugationes verborum incipiunt a futuro, tum quia a futuro plura videntur derivari quam a reliquis temporibus, tum etiam quia prius natura res est futura quam presens aut preterita. Nos tamen quia hic scribimus in gratiam eorum qui sunt in lingua Latina versati, Latinorum ordinem sequemur (ed. Egan 1968:50).

The description of the tenses, including the negative forms, is very detailed and contains many examples. But there are a number of shortcomings in the systematization, such as the inclusion of the emphatic mood (corresponding to the English construction *It is I/you (...) who ...*) under the future Indicative,[1] and the treatment of series which run across the divisions of tenses and moods. This is the case for instance of what Hussey labels the "Future Conjunctive" (form with *súil),* which is a superimposed mood on the forms of the Imperative or Consuetudinal moods. An even more cumbersome problem, that of the use of analytic forms, consisting of the third person form and the personal pronouns, is dealt with by Hussey in an ad hoc way: he simply notes the alternation (characteristic of the Ulster dialect) existing between these analytic forms and the fully conjugated "normal" forms.

> In omni enim modo et tempore, quamlibet personam circumloqui possum per tertiam singularem istius temporis, et pronomen importans praedictam personam, ut *<gonuidh mé>, gon[u]id[h] thú, gon[u]id[h] sé, <gonuidh sí>, gon[u]id[h] sinn, siad,* &c. <pro *gonuim, gonae, gonuidh, gonmaoid* etc.>; *do ghon mé, do g[h]on sinn, sibh, siad* etr. pro

[1] As Hussey notes, these forms (*as mise g[h]onas, as sinne g[h]onas ...*) could have been treated as a "seventh mood", the *modus relativus.*

> *do g[h]onas, do g[h]onamar,* etc.; <*gonfaidh mé, thú,* etr. pro *gonfad, gonfamáoid*> et sic de reliquis. Iste modus est familiaris Ultoniensibus et notandus pro iis qui habent penuriam verborum (ed. Egan 1968:56–57).

The strength of Hussey's description lies in its "realistic" conception, its tendency to fully exemplify the descriptive account, and in the thorough attempt at systematization. Hussey's realism is evident from his sober definitions of word classes, his exclusion of the ablative as a separate case,[1] his sporadic references to dialect variants[2] or to popular usage (e.g., of *gu* + negative future instead of the Conjunctive) and the stress laid on correct spelling.

The richness of Hussey's account is another merit of the *Rudimenta*. Hussey deals with two principal mutations — lenition (or "aspiration" as he calls it), and eclipsis —, and mentions the respective written notations. Also, his account of the *species* and *figura* of the nouns, as well as his description of the verb is well documented.[3] He fails however to give an adequate account of the forms of the copula, and has unfortunately chosen not to dwell on irregular verbs.

The attempt at systematization is the third and probably the most important merit of Hussey; it is the more remarkable since the author had to take into account the native tradition and the Latin model more suited to his readership. In his syntax, Hussey sticks to the medieval Latin distinction between *concordantia* and *regimen*. Both phenomena are discussed in an analytical way, one part of speech being dealt with after the other. Greater systematicity combined with exhaustiveness is found in the chapter on prepositions, in which Hussey gives an account of the contractions between prepositions and articles. Another instance of systematic description is the linking of verbal forms in terms of

[1] See ed. Egan (1968:27): "Casus nominum sunt quinque: *ainm uathaidh no iolruidh* .i. nominativus singularis vel pluralis; *tuilréim* .i. dativus; *taoibhréim* .i. genetivus; *réim* .i. accusativus; *gairm agallm[h]a* .i. vocativus. Non dignoscimus ablativum a dativo, nec Graeci".

[2] See, e.g., ed. Egan (1968:18) on the derivational particle *-in*.

[3] One can add to this the account of the emphatic pronoun (ed. Egan 1968:46–47).

deleting one ending and adding another.[1] Hussey's main contribution lies in providing a five-declensional system of nouns, which was taken over by Mac Curtin and O'Donovan, and through these by most of the later works. Hussey's five-declensional system is as follows:

> 1. Nouns ending in a vowel (broad or slender), with no inflectional variation in the singular: type *bogha;* 2. (Mostly feminine) Nouns ending in a vowel and inflected in the singular: type *dearna;* 3. Masculine nouns ending in a velarized consonant: type *foghmhar;* 4. Feminine nouns ending in a velarized consonant: type *inghean;* 5. Nouns ending in a palatalized consonant: type *foghlaidh.*

As Ó Cuív (1956) has shown, the treatment is inadequate, and inferior both to the previous Bardic tradition, and William Haliday's seven-declensional system *(Uraicecht na Gaedhilge,* 1808). But he also noted that Hussey's inadequacy should be seen in the light of the fact that he "was breaking new ground in this attempt to synthesize where his forerunners had analysed" (1956:104).

2. O'Molloy's *Grammatica Latino-hibernica* was published in 1677 by the printing press of the Congregation "de Propaganda Fide". The author was a Franciscan priest, professor of theology in the College of S. Isidore, and an agent for the Irish Catholics at the papal court in Rome.[2]Ó In 1676 he had published a catechism in Irish (*Lucerna Fidelium, seu Fasciculus decerptus ab Authoribus magis versatis qui tractarunt de Doctrina Christiana*, Rome), and his grammar was intended as a tool for Catholic missionaries who wanted to study the religious documents written in Irish (1677:3^{v}–4^{r}). O'Molloy relied

[1] See, e.g., ed. Egan (1968:53–54): "Secunda singularis potest formari mutando *ad* in *ae* et *ead* in *e*, ut *gonfad, gonfae, buailfead, buailfe*; et tertia ijsdem mutatis in *aid[h]* et *id[h]*, ut *gonfad, gonfaidh, buailfead, buailfidh*; et prima pluralis inserendo *maoi* inter ultimam consonantem *d* et vocalem vel dypthongum <praecedentem>, ut a *gonfad, gonfamaoid*, a *buailfead, buailf[e]amaoid.* Secunda pluralis formatur a secunda singulari mutando *ae* in *aithe* et *e* in *ithi*, ut *gonfae, gonfaithi, buailfe, buailfithi*, vel in *t[h]aoi* quando *ad* purum habetur in prima singulari, ut ab *ioméorae, ioméort[h]aoi*; et tertia pluralis a tertia singulari convertendo *dh* in *d* purum, ut *gonfaidh, gonfaid, buailfidh, buailfid*".

[2] On Francis O'Molloy, see Ó Casaide (1933), Egan (1946–47; 1955–56; 1967).

heavily on copies of Hussey's manuscript work, both for the grammatical section and the prosody. The treatment of prosody reflects his dependence on manuscript Z. 3.4.19, Marsh Library, and on manuscript D. 4.35., Trinity College; as to the grammatical sections, especially those dealing with the *figura* of words and with the "particles", O'Molloy has made extensive use of D. 4.35 and of H. 5.20 (also Trinity College). All these sources thus point to a Louvain connection, and one can safely state that O'Molloy made good use of Hussey's *Rudimenta,* in one or the other of its copies. There is another link with Louvain, which is pervasive throughout the first chapters of the *Grammatica Latino-hibernica.* These chapters deal with the topic of phonetics (tackled from the point of view of the graphical representation). The treatment is a traditional one, in terms of *nomen, figura, potestas* of the *litterae.* This is also the scheme adopted in the *Rudimenta.* But O'Molloy's treatment of vowels, diphthongs and consonants is particularly indebted to a dialogue on the pronunciation of Latin by the Humanistic scholar Justus Lipsius. Lipsius's *De recta pronunciatione Latinae linguae dialogus* (1586) has in fact been plagiarized by O'Molloy, as Father Egan (1955–56) has shown. O'Molloy did, however, more than simply applying Lipsius's account of Latin pronunciation to Irish. This should be stressed, since modern scholars have tended to be extremely critical of O'Molloy's achievements: Bergin (1938:206) dismisses the work as being "not a good grammar", and Egan (1967) considers it to be unoriginal and "very defective". But originality is rare in seventeenth-century grammars, especially in those written for a general public, assumed to be familiar with the Latin descriptive model. It is also true that O'Molloy's grammar does not show the same sense of detail as the *Rudimenta,* and that the exemplification is often far from accurate. But one should appreciate the *Grammatica* as an elegantly written booklet ("opusculum" in the author's words), the main purpose of which is to give an idea of the pronunciation and grammatical build-up of Irish. The fact that O'Molloy relied on Lipsius's dialogue for the phonetic section shows that his grammar is written for an intelligentsia familiarized less with Irish (and its dialects) than with problems of orthography and orthoepy and with the lineaments of grammatical manuals proceeding from sound to parts of speech. O'Molloy's attitude with respect to the native Irish tradition is ambiguous: on the one hand, he faithfully incorporates the Irish grammatical terminology, and he also mentions for instance the poets' division of consonants into eight classes (1677:56–58), but on the other hand he discards the tripartite division of the Bardic grammarians into *focal, pearsa* and *iarmbéarla,* and posits seven parts of speech.[1]

O'Molloy's description of Irish phonetics is extensive, but not well organized. He explains the principle of broad and slender "harmony" (*caol le caol, leathan le leathan*),[2] and has some interesting observations on the pairing of voiced and voiceless (*t*/*d*, *k*/*g*, 1677:20–21). But his phonetic description suffers from the concentration on the written language, which in addition is looked at from the point of view of the functional value(s) of the letters of the Latin alphabet. Of course, this leads to a distorted treatment of the consonant mutations. Of these, lenition is dealt with in the paragraph on the letter *H*. O'Molloy treats lenition in a very analytic way, discussing the values of the graphical representations *<dh>, <fh>, <mh>, <ch>,* etc. A major shortcoming is that O'Molloy does not account for the conditioning of the lenition process. The other mutations, viz. eclipsis and aspiration, are not dealt with under the specific letters of the alphabet, although this could easily have been done for aspiration. In fact, O'Molloy never touches upon the problem of initial aspiration (of the type *a hathair* "her father"), except for his brief discussion of the distinction between *a* "his" (which involves lenition) and *a* "her" (involving aspiration). But he only gives

[1] "Lingua Hibernica septem admittit partes orationis, scilicet articulum, nomen, praepositionem, personam seù verbum, adverbium, coniunctionem, & pronomen (...). Vetustiores tres tantùm orationis ponebãt partes vtpotè principaliores, nempe dictionem seù nomen, pronomen, & personam, seù verbum; per pronomen autem intelligebant promiscuè omnia, quae nec nomina sunt, nec verba, sed de his infrà" (1677:82–83).

[2] "Hoc est dicere, si posterioris syllabae prima vocalis fuerit subtilis; similiter prioris seù antecedentis syllabae vltima vocalis debebit esse subtilis; pariformiter si larga, larga; alias vitium erit tùm in enunciatione, tum in orthographia: non tamen requiritur quod vtraque vocalis semper sit eiusdem speciei, vel numeri, tametsi multoties contingat quòd sint, sed sufficit quòd ambae sint largae, vel ambae subtiles" (1677:50–51).

examples for the feminine possessive *a* "her" followed by initial *l*, *r*, or *n*, and notes that the initial consonants are produced *fortiter*. The mutations which O'Molloy deals with — apart from the already mentioned lenition — are *eclipsis, mersio* and *suppressio*. The latter term (Irish *cadad)* refers to de-aspiration, caused by an adjacent consonant. As to *eclipsis* and *mersio*, they are complementary aspects, as O'Molloy notes, since the former term refers exclusively to initial mutations, and the second to medial mutations.

The morphological portion of O'Molloy's grammar is not very satisfactory, except for the paragraphs on derivation, which discuss morphologically complex formations from the point of view of their meaning. O'Molloy does not give more than one nominal declension[1] and only one verbal conjugation, leaving out the problem of the various verb tenses. The main drawback of his morphology, however, is the lack of paradigmatic organization; the reader is lost in the prose text of the *Grammatica,* which discursively aligns a number of phenomena that could easily have been presented in a synoptic scheme. A case in point is O'Molloy's treatment of the article: instead of accounting for the differences between the various *an*-forms (Masc. Nom. sg., Masc. Gen. sg., Masc. Dat. sg., Fem. Nom. sg., Fem. Dat. sg.) in terms of initial mutations,[2] O'Molloy prefers an elaborate discussion which, by focusing on the problem of gender-identification, misses the crucial issue:

> Articulus enim *an*, modò praeponatur substantivo nominativi casus, & nomen illud incipiat à consonanti aspirabili, tunc aspiratur consonans, seù mortificatur per litteram *h,* dummodò nomen fit foeminini generis,

[1] O'Molloy attributes 6 nominal cases to Irish: "Casus tot habent Hiberni, quot Latini, nominatiuum, genitiuum, datiuum, accusatiuum, vocatiuum, ablatiuum, numero sex, vulgò *an cas ainmuightheach*, *gineamhonach*, *tabhtharthach*, *gioramach*, *garmach*, & *diobhalach*" (1677:118–119).

[2] This would have given a scheme such as the following:

	Masc.	Fem.
Nom. sg.	*an (t-)*	*an*^{L}
Gen. sg.	*an*^{L}	*(na*^{H}*)*
Dat. sg.	*an*^{N}	*an*^{N}

> dummodò verò fuerit masculini generis, nequaquam. Dignoscitur igitur quòd *fhear,* Latinè *vir,* sit masculini generis; *bean* verò foeminini generis, quia non dicitur *an fhear,* sed *an fear,* nec dicitur *an bean,* sed *an bhean,* & sic de aliis (1677:112–113).

On this point O'Molloy's grammar is strikingly inferior to the *Rudimenta.*

3. O'Molloy's grammar appeared at a moment when the scholarly activity of the Louvain Franciscans decreased. But in 1728 an Irish grammar was printed in Louvain by Martin Van Overbeke, who served as a printer to the Irish Franciscans. The work constitutes the first autonomous Irish grammar written in English, and it was composed by a scholar interested in the history of his native Ireland. The author, Hugh Mac Curtin, belonged to the family that had kept the office of chronicler of the O'Brien family since the fourteenth century.[1] His work is directly based on O'Molloy's *Grammatica* for the phonetic part, and on the *Rudimenta,* partly for the phonetic section and especially for matters of morphology and syntax. Mac Curtin's grammar is not aimed at a public of missionaries in need of a grammar of their native tongue; it is written for an audience of scholars interested in the ancient history — called "Antiquities" by Mac Curtin — of Ireland, and in reading the ancient records (such as the *Annals,* to which reference is made in the preface). Mac Curtin also aims at restoring the Irish language in its rights by showing how it can be laid down in rules, and by showing its rich and original structure.[2] Mac Curtin deplores the fact that native Irishmen, especially in the higher classes of society, have abandoned their language, and he presents his grammar as the most satisfactory account of a language which has to be preserved. In Mac Curtin's view, this preservation should not involve a simplification of the old orthography, of which he stresses the linguistic usefulness (the orthography reflects the "underlying" historical forms), the historical relevance (direct access to the oldest texts), and the "sociolinguistic"

1 On Mac Curtin's grammar, see further Bergin (1938:220–223), and Ó Cuív (1956:104–106). For biographical information, see Ó Cuív (1986:395, 396–397).

2 Cf. Mac Curtin (1728:31): "The Irish being a most elegant, independent, copious, and ancient language, which doth not easily admit of mixtures".

importance (the standard orthography allows one to preserve the "true Dialect"). Reacting against E. Lhuyd's proposals for an orthographical reform, Mac Curtin writes:

> I answer, the Dialect, and Idioms of the Language necessarily require to keep close to its Ancient Orthography. And if those Gentlemen would consider the great inconveniences that would unavoidably follow the omission of initials and other letters in Irish words, they should not prescribe such Methods or Alterations: first, by omitting the initial consonant of a word (altho in their opinion it could be well pronounced without it) the Radix is lost, and consequently the reader cannot arrive to the sense or Primitive therof. Secondly if this Alteration, thus proposed and recommended, had been taken and practiced, al our Ancient Histories and Poëtry would soon grow useless and altogether unknown to Posterity. Thirdly this omission would clearly destroy the true Dialect insomuch, that in process of time it would prove strange to the very Natives themselves. (1728, Preface, [*10–*11]).

As a grammarian, Mac Curtin is far from original. His grammar is a typical Louvain product, in that it derives from Hussey's *Rudimenta*[1] and, to a lesser extent, from O'Molloy's *Grammatica*. In line with Hussey, Mac Curtin quotes the Irish grammatical terminology, and offers an adequate exemplification. Mac Curtin has also inherited Hussey's sense for paradigmatic presentation, and adds to his systematization by dividing diphthongs and triphthongs according to their initial element into "Apthongs", "Epthongs", "Ipthongs", "Upthongs" and "Opthongs" (cf. Lhuyd 1707:299). We must also mention his account (in terms of distribution) of final vowels in Irish words (he gives a list of 22 attested vocalic endings). The phonetic section offers an adequate description of the sounds, and of the principal mutations. It is followed by a morphological section, which gives a prominent place to the discussion of the "accidents" of the word classes, and by a syntactic section, both directly based on the *Rudimenta*. Mac Curtin adopts,

[1] In addition, the grammar is followed by a reprint of Hussey's catechism of 1611.

among others, Hussey's five-declensional system, his division of moods and tenses (noting also that there are "incident, or supervenient Moods to other Moods, and so Moods of Moods", 1728:58),[1] his bipartition of syntax into "concord" and "government". But contrary to Hussey, he posits an ablative case (e.g., after the preposition *gan* "without").

Mac Curtin has written his grammar for an audience acquainted with English and, to a lesser extent perhaps, with Irish, and he proceeds patiently in explaining the difficulties of the Irish language. Perhaps the best illustration of this can be found in the passage dealing with the gender of nouns. Mac Curtin considers this problem from the point of view of the learner who has to recognize the gender of a noun (excluding nouns referring to human beings) on the basis of contextual information. He posits five "rules" allowing to recover the gender of the noun (1728:38–40):

(1) the initial mutation caused by the article in the nominative (e.g., *an bhean* = an^L before a feminine noun; *an fear* = $an^{(t)}$ before a masculine noun);

(2) for nouns beginning with *s*: anteposition of *t* (with feminine nouns after the article *an);*

(3) the coupling with the genitive forms: *an - an* (masculine); *an - na* (feminine);

(4) the presence or absence of aspiration in the genitive (an^L: masculine; na^H: feminine);

(5) aspiration by *na* in the Genitive singular of the feminine.

These are analytic rules (in fact rules 3 and 5 should be viewed as one procedure for identifying the gender), all dealing with forms attested and observed in context. To these Mac Curtin has added another

[1] Such as the Relative Mood (with *ar/ear* + copula), or the Conjunctive Mood (see, Mac Curtin 1728:67).

"discovery procedure", which goes beyond the direct context and which involves the interparadigmatic correlation with the pronouns *é* (Masc.) or *í* (Fem.):

> It is the most common distinction of the Genders of Nouns, to observe the difference between *é & í, he & she*. For when *é* agrees with the Noun, it is Masculine; and when *í* agrees with the Noun, it is Feminine: as *is é mó chean,* it is *my head*, Masculine; *is í ma chos,* it is *my foot,* Feminine.This Rule is infallible alwayes, whether the thing signifyed be male or female (1728:40).

As to the detail of description, Mac Curtin does not go beyond his principal model, the *Rudimenta*. He also refrains from giving an account of the irregular verbs.

4. We have examined three grammars of Irish, written in a time-span of two centuries and showing intertextual relationships. The three grammars have a basic converging feature: they are all connected with the Irish College in Louvain, and more particularly with the grammatical activity clustered around Bonaventure Hussey. The latter's manuscript grammar, written around 1610, is the starting point of a new "tradition" within Irish grammar, characterized by a progressive abandonment of the Bardic tradition and a gradual "Europeanization" of Irish grammaticography. O'Molloy's grammar and Mac Curtin's work are directly dependent on Hussey's manuscript work. The model underlying these grammars is a composite one: it is a combination of the Bardic tradition (maintained, e.g., in the description of the mutations, the account of the noun and verb systems) and the Latin tradition (underlying the parts of speech model, the description in terms of *accidentia,* and the division of syntax into concord and government). To this one must add, in the case of O'Molloy's work, the direct influence of Lipsius's treatise on the correct pronunciation of Latin.

These three grammars thus constitute a homogeneous series, connected with Louvain. But within this series, we can recognize some variation, which can be accounted for in terms of three parameters: *audience, scope, intention.* The *Rudimenta* and O'Molloy's grammar are aimed at a public of missionaries, who want to have a description of the language in which they have to preach when going back to their native country; Mac Curtin's grammar, on the other hand, is intended for a learned public which should appreciate the qualities of the Irish language. As to the scope, we can distinguish between panoramic accounts and descriptions involving systematization. O'Molloy's grammar is a cursory treatment of problems of the Irish language, and this explains the absence of paradigms; on the other hand, the *Rudimenta* and the *Elements* want to provide their readership with a systematic description of Irish phonetics, morphology and syntax, and this is achieved through a well-articulated division of the contents of the grammar, through the inclusion of synoptic paradigms, and the definition of the descriptive units. The third parameter, the intention underlying the activity of grammar-writing, is also a factor of variation. Hussey's and O'Molloy's works were written for the instruction of young missionaries who "have to know more about" their native language. Mac Curtin's grammar reflects a different intention: it is propagandistic in a different way, since its aim is to vindicate the rights of the Irish language at a moment when the language was in decay.

These differences in audience, scope and intention are reflected in the specific contents of the three grammars, and they also explain the use of the metalanguage for description: Latin in the case of Hussey's and O'Molloy's work, aimed at a public familiar with Latin, and having already a basic knowledge of Irish, English in the case of Mac Curtin's grammar, written for a learned audience interested in the history of the Irish people, and in need of being reminded of the antiquity of their language, and of the cultural autonomy of Irish in the face of English.

REFERENCES

Aarsleff, Hans et al., eds. 1987. *Papers in the History of Linguistics. Proceedings of the Third International Conference on the History of the Language Sciences (ICHoLS III), Princeton, 19–23 August 1984*. Amsterdam/Philadelphia: Benjamins.

Abbott, Thomas Kingsmill & Gwynn, E.J. 1921. *Catalogue of the Irish Manuscripts in the Library of Trinity College, Dublin*. Dublin: Hodges & Figgis.

Adams, G. B[rendan]. 1970. "Grammatical Analysis and Terminology in the Irish Bardic Schools". *FL* 4.157–166.

Ahlqvist, Anders. 1979–1980. "The Three Parts of Speech of Bardic Grammar". *Studia Celtica* 14/15.12–17.

— 1983. *Histoire de la linguistique : la tradition irlandaise. (= Travaux d'Histoire des Théories Linguistiques 2)* Paris: Université Paris 7.

Bergin, Osborn, ed. 1915–1955. "Irish Grammatical Tracts I–IV". Published as Supplements to *Ériu* 8 (1916); 9 (1921–1925); 10 (1928); 14 (1946); 17 (1955).

— 1938. "The Native Irish Grammarian". *Proceedings of the British Academy* 24.205–235.

Catalogue of Irish Manuscripts in the Royal Irish Academy. 1926–1958. Dublin: Royal Irish Academy.

Conlan, Patrick. 1977. *Saint Anthony's College of the Irish Franciscans at Louvain*. Dublin: Assisi Press.

De Buck, Victor. 1869. "L'archéologie irlandaise au couvent de Saint Antoine de Padoue à Louvain". *Etudes religieuses, historiques et littéraires* 14.408–437; 586–603.

De Clercq, Jan & Swiggers, Pierre. 1990. "Het Sint-Antoniuscollege van Leuven". *Museumstrip Leuven* 17.69–75.

Dillon, Myles et al. 1969. *Catalogue of Irish Manuscripts in the Franciscan Library, Killiney*. Dublin: Institute for Advanced Studies.

Egan, Bartholomew. 1944. "Rudimenta Grammaticae Hibernicae". O'Brien, ed. 238–242.

—. 1946/1947. "An t-Athair Froinsias Ó Maolmhuaidh". *Franciscan College Annual* 1946/1947.13–17.

—. 1955–1956. "Notule sur les sources de la Grammatica Latino-Hibernica du Père O'Molloy". *EC* 7.428–436.

—. 1967. "O'Molloy, Francis". *New Catholic Encyclopedia*, vol. VI.1014.

—. ed. 1968. *Graiméir Ghaeilge na mBráthar Mionúr*. Dublin: Institute for Advanced Studies.

Gilbert, J.T. 1874. "The Manuscripts of the Former College of Irish Franciscans, Louvain". *Appendix to the Fourth Report of the Royal Commission on Historical Manuscripts* 1874. 599–613. London: Stationery Office.

Jennings, Brendan. 1925. *The Irish Franciscan College of Saint Anthony at Louvain*. Dublin: Browne & Nolan.

Koerner, Konrad, ed. 1980. *Progress in Linguistic Historiography. Papers from the International Conference on the History of the Language Sciences (Ottawa, 28–31 August 1978)*. Amsterdam: Benjamins.

Lambert, Pierre-Yves. 1987. "Les premières grammaires celtiques". *HEL* 9.13–45.

Lhuyd, Edward. 1707. *Archaeologia Britannica, giving some account Additional to what has been hitherto Publish'd, of the Languages, Histories and Customs of the Original Inhabitants of Great Britain. Vol. I. Glossography*. Oxford: Printed at the Theater for the Author.

Mac Curtin, Hughes. 1728. *The Elements of the Irish Language, Grammatically Explained in English*. Louvain: Van Overbeke (reprint 1972, *English Linguistics 1500–1800*, no. 351, Menston: The Scolar Press).

Mac Aogáin, Parthalán = Egan, Bartholomew.

McKenna, Lambert ed. 1944. *Bardic Syntactical Tracts*. Dublin: Institute for Advanced Studies.

Moody, T.W. & Vaughan, W.E., eds. 1986. *A New History of Ireland. IV. Eighteenth-century Ireland, 1691–1800*. Oxford: Clarendon Press.

Mooney, Canice. 1969. "St. Anthony's College, Louvain". *Donegal's Annual* 8.18–48.

O'Briain, Felim. 1928. "Irish Franciscan Historians of St. Anthony's College, Louvain. Father Hugh Ward". *The Irish Historical Record* 32.113–129.

—. 1933. "The Louvain Grammarians. A Link with Tadhg Dall". *The Irish Book Lover* 21.107–109.

O'Brien, Sylvester ed. 1944. *Measgra i gCuimhne Mhichíl Uí Chléirigh. Miscellany of Historical and Linguistic Studies in Honour of Brother Micheal Ó Cléirigh, O.F.M. Chief of the Four Masters, 1643–1943*. Dublin: Assisi Press.

Ó Casaide, Séamus. 1933. "Father Francis Molloy and Lucerna Fidelium". *The Irish Book Lover* 18.5–17.

Ó Concheanainn, Tomás. 1968. Review of Egan (1968). *Éigse* 12.339–344.

Ó Cuív Brian. 1956. "Grammatical Analysis and the Declension of the Noun in Irish". *Celtica* 3.86–125.

—. 1965. "Linguistic Terminology in the Mediaeval Irish Bardic Tracts". *TPS* 1965.141–164.

—. 1973. "The Linguistic Training of the Medieval Irish Poet". *Celtica* 10.114–140.

—. 1980. "A Mediaeval Exercise in Language Planning". Koerner, ed. 23–34.

—. 1986. "Irish Language and literature, 1691–1845". Moody & Vaughan, eds. 374–423.

—. 1987. "The Observations of Medieval Irish Scholars on Sandhi Phenomena in Irish". Aarsleff et al. (eds.) 107–115.

O'Molloy, Franciscus. 1677. *Grammatica Latino-Hibernica, Nunc compendiata*. Romae: Ex Typographia S. Cong. de Propag. Fide.

Scott, John Russell – White, Newport J.D. 1913. *Catalogue of the Manuscripts Remaining in Marsh's Library*. Dublin: Thom.

Silke, John J. 1973. "Irish Scholarship and the Renaissance, 1580–1673". *Studies in the Renaissance* 20.169–206.

Thurneysen, Rudolf. 1892. "Le terme *iarmbérla* dans la grammaire irlandaise". *RC* 13.267–274.

Tourneur, Victor. 1905. *Esquisse d'une histoire des études celtiques*. Liège: Vaillant-Carmanne.

Wall, Thomas. 1942. "Bonaventure O'Hussey". *The Irish Ecclesiastical Record* 59.36–48.

Harmonic Dictionaries and Grammars in Semitic Linguistics

YAAKOV GRUNTFEST
University of Haifa

HARMONIC DICTIONARIES and grammars — a kind of linguistic works in vogue in sixteenth and seventeenth century European Semitology — were an important stage in the development of the comparative approach to language.

These works were not the first attempt in this field. Comparative description of Semitic languages — Hebrew, Aramaic and Arabic — had already been practiced by Jewish philologists in the 10th to 12th centuries. Their achievements were significant: they succeeded in establishing all sound shifts and described a number of grammatical correspondences in the three languages. However, after the extinction of the Jewish-Arabic culture in Spain and North Africa, these comparative studies came to a standstill. The works of the mediaeval Jewish philologists were forgotten and, when the centre of Semitological studies shifted to the West, European scholars had to start again from the beginning.

A renewed approach to comparativism was made as early as the sixteenth century — i.e. in the dawn of a serious acquaintance with Oriental languages in Europe — in the form of parallel, though separate, grammatical description of various Oriental and European languages. A pioneer in this field was Guillaume Postel (1506–1585). In 1538 he published an introduction to twelve languages, a half of them Semitic. In the next year an analogous book by Teseo Ambrogio (1469–1540) appeared. Semitic languages were also represented in various multilingual works in vogue at that time, such as collections of the text of the *Pater Noster* (the most famous of them being that by

Hieronymus Megiser (1555–1616), the multilingual dictionaries by Megiser and Ambrogio Calepino (1435–1511) etc.

The objectives of these multilingual works were to demonstrate to the reader the variety of languages in the world, both those newly discovered and those long-familiar, and to provide elementary manuals for their initial study. In addition, the parallel presentation of the linguistic material, accompanied by the authors' remarks, was ment to provoke reflection on the interrelation between languages and their mutual similarity.

At the same time there appeared comprehensive surveys of the languages of the world. Of these the most significant were the works of Theodor Bibliander (Buchmann, 1504–1564; *De ratione communi omnium linguarum et literarum commentarius,* 1548) and Conrad Gesner (1516–1565; *Mithridates,* 1555), in which an attempt to characterize the connections between the languages of the world was made.

In Semitic philology the parallel description of languages became more specific and took the form of a straightforward comparison of linguistic phenomena.

The first steps were somewhat tentative. Angelo Canini (1521–1557) entitled his book, which appeared in 1554, *Institutiones linguae Syriacae, Assyriacae atque Talmudicae una cum Aetiopicae atque Arabicae collatione*. But, in fact, the comparison with Ethiopic and Arabic was made only in few — albeit essential — instances. At the same time, Hebrew, Greek and, to a lesser extent, Latin, which were not mentioned in the title, were widely used for elucidation of Aramaic grammatical phenomena.

Pierre-Victor Palma (1525–1610), in his description of four "principal Oriental languages" (Arabic, Armenian, Syriac and Ethiopic), used a mixed device. The presentation of the four Oriental languages is parallel, but separate; on the other hand, all of them, especially Armenian, which the author regards as cognate to the three others, are compared with Hebrew, their common source.

Comparative works appearing at the beginning of the seventeenth century were more highly developed and comprehensive. The special character of such works is expressed in the term *harmonic* (i.e. built on similarities, reflecting similarities), which often appears in the titles of these early comparative works and can be accepted as a generic term for all works of this kind.

The term *harmonic* was used for the first time by Etienne Guichard (d. at the beginning of the seventeenth century) in his *L'harmonie étymologique* of Hebrew, Chaldaean, Syriac, Greek, Latin and a number of new European languages (1606). The purpose of his work was purely theoretical, namely to present etymological evidence for the generally accepted thesis that all languages of the world originated from Hebrew. Specifically Semitological *harmonic* works usually had different objectives: pedagogical — to facilitate the study of a second or third Semitic language; philological — to provide additional means for better understanding the Holy Scriptures; linguistic — to demonstrate the similarity between Semitic (or Oriental, as they were then called) languages.

The first large-scale comparative work, *Lexicon pentaglotton* by Valentin Schindler (d. 1604) was published posthumously in 1612. This *Lexicon* embraced Hebrew, Chaldaean, Syriac, Talmudic-Rabbinical and Arabic and was a great scholarly achievement for its time. From a technical point of view the *Lexicon* had a deficiency: the Syriac and Arabic words were given in Hebrew transcription. In spite of — or possibly due to — this, Schindler's wordbook enjoyed great popularity and was reprinted three times (the last in 1695).

In 1628 there appeared a grammar of Hebrew, Chaldaean and Syriac, "compared between themselves", by Louis de Dieu (1590–1642). From a structural point of view this work may be regarded as a unified grammar of three languages, or rather as three grammars interwoven into one fabric. The comparison of Aramaic and Hebrew is almost exhaustive, only specific Syriac phenomena being excluded.

But the true Golden Age of *harmonic* works began with the appearance of the famous *Biblia Sacra Polyglotta*, published by Brian Walton (1600–1661) in 1653–1657. This monumental opus, huge even by present-day standards, comprised the texts of the Old and New Testaments in their original languages and in eight versions. The vast textual material contained in Walton's Bible stimulated linguistic research. Moreover, this material could only be used effectively for philological and theological purposes with the help of an appropriate linguistic apparatus. In a relatively short time, on the basis of *Biblia Polyglotta,* two large linguistic works were compiled: a seven-language *harmonic* lexicon by Edmund Castell (1606–1685), to which a vast grammatical supplement was appended, and *Hodogeticum Orientale harmonicum* by Johann Friedrich Nicolai (1639–1683). To this period also belong two important *harmonic* works by Johann Heinrich Hottinger (1620–1667): a *Grammar* (1659) and a *Lexicon* (1661). In addition to this, Walton provided his *Biblia Polyglotta* with an extensive *Prolegomena*. The Linguistic questions discussed in Walton's Prolegomena, their sequence and, to a certain degree, the proposed solutions correspond to the initial chapters of Bibliander's *Commentarius,* which appeared more than a hundred years previously and was, in all probability, used by Walton as a base to build on. These *Prolegomena* may be regarded as an updated contemporary summary of general linguistic concepts accepted in certain leading Semitological circles.

Walton's ideas on the development of languages can be briefly summarized as follows: language is the main attribute peculiar to the human being; language could have appeared due to natural development, but the Holy Scriptures testify that it was given to the First Man by God; it is impossible to establish which was the first language — it was not Hebrew, but Hebrew is very close to this primary language (though important traces of primacy are also evident in Chinese); peoples' desire to glorify themselves and thus avoid dispersion was the cause of the building of the Tower of Babel; the consequences were the precise opposite: the multiplication of languages and the dispersal of peoples and languages throughout the world; it is difficult to establish the number of the initial languages, yet, according to widespread scholarly opinion it was seventy or seventy two; various factors influenced the later development of languages: the course of time which alters everything, the intermingling of peoples, natural environmental conditions; the principal languages of the world are: Hebrew, Greek, Latin, Teutonic (i.e., German), Sclavonic, Tartaric and Chinese.

In the above scheme two sources of contemporary linguistic views are clearly discernible: the information provided by the Holy Scriptures and their commentators, and direct observation of languages and their development. This two-fold approach is also evident in a more specific problem — the definition of the Semitic linguistic family (i.e. languages which originated directly from Hebrew). Following his principal authority, Bibliander, Walton includes in this linguistic group Chaldaean (Syriac), Canaanite, Punic (both known by name only), Arabic, Armenian, Ethiopic and, to some degree, Persian.

The inclusion of Armenian in the Oriental (i.e. Semitic) group of languages had a long tradition, based primarily on the similarity of the ethnonyms, Armenian and Aram, and a number of false etymologies (e.g., Palma 1596:81–90). But Armenian version was not represented in *Biblia Polyglotta* and Walton did not dwell on this question. The problem of Persian — the language of one of the eight versions — is dealt with at length (Walton 1653–1657 vol. VI:105). Persian seemed, like Janus, to have two faces. The Semitic lineage (i.e. the descent from the patriarch *Shem)* of the ancient Persians (presumably biblical *Elam)* was unanimously regarded as being attested by the Bible. A number of lexical resemblances between Persian and Aramaic were found by European philologists (actually they were due to borrowing and occasional phonetical similarity). On the other hand, in the middle of the seventeenth century the connections between Persian and Western languages, particularly German and English, were quite obvious. Walton found a balanced solution to the problem. The Persians, he states, are the progeny of *Elam* and *Cuth,* who, in their turn, are descended from *Shem,* like the Hebrews and Arameans. Due to many fluctuations, both ethnic and linguistic, a lot of words penetrated into Persian from Arabic, Turkish, Greek, Latin, and Tartaric. Walton avoids giving a direct answer to the question: why the Persian language is so similar to German and English, saying that the problem is too difficult. Nevertheless, he is ready to accept the opinion of Marais Zuerius Boxhorn (1602–1653) according to which these words were borrowed into both Persian and German from the languages of the Scythians or Tartars due to their frequent incursions into neighbouring territories.

As for the way the linguistic material is presented in the fundamental *harmonic* works, the least original, or most traditional, approach was that of Castell. His *Lexicon heptaglotton,* built, like all classic Semitic dictionaries, on the root-principle, contains rich lexicographical material, as well as textual references (for Hebrew). In the grammatical supplement about two thirds are devoted to the verb and the rest to the noun and pronoun. The verb, an area of grammar most suitable to systematization, is presented in the form of Comparative tables accompanied by commentaries. In accordance with the general composition of Walton's *Biblia Polyglotta,* the Persian language is dealt with on a par with the six Semitic languages, but in both the grammatical and lexicological sections it is presented separately.

For Castell's contemporaries his *Lexicon* must have been an invaluable handbook for the study of biblical and other religious texts, due to the vast volume of linguistic material contained therein and to the clear and essentially traditional mode of its presentation.

The *harmonic* works of Hottinger appeared before Castell's *Lexicon.* They were not orientated to Walton's *Biblia* and did not comprise Persian. Of special interest is Hottinger's *Lexicon heptaglotton,* which includes Hebrew, four dialects of Aramaic, Arabic and Ethiopic.

The structural concept of Hottinger's *harmonic* dictionary was, and remains to the present day, unique in Semitological literature. It is built in a pattern of five columns. The first column presents abstract biconsonantal nuclei ('', 'B, 'G etc.): *radix inusitata et aliis linguis vicinis restituenda.* The second column comprises *Rhizologia,* i.e. Hebrew roots and words, derived from the abstract nuclei of the first column by addition of the third root-consonant. In the remaining three columns we find various categories of *harmonic* words from Semitic languages other than Hebrew. Hottinger's *Lexicon* was an attempt at a deductive presentation of the inventory of Semitic roots. A deductive approach to the dictionary, but of a different kind, was earlier applied by the prominent mediaeval philologist al-Khalîl ibn Aḥmad (c. 718–791) in his wordbook of Arabic *Kitāb al-'Ayn.* Al-Khalîl's wordbook, even its basic concept, could not be known to Hottinger.

Castell, Hottinger and Schindler were renowned philologists, occupying high academic positions. As distinct from them, the fourth author of a fundamental *harmonic* work, Johann Friedrich Nicolai, is less known in Orientalistics. Born in 1639, he studied in Leipzig and, for a certain period of time, occupied the post of *Dozent* of Oriental languages in Jena. Later he abandoned his academic career, moved to Lüneburg to serve as a *Prediger* and ended his days as a *Superintendent* at the age of fortythree. Nicolai's comparative work, *Hodogeticum Orientale harmonicum,* was written in his Jena period on the initiative of his university tutor Johann Ernst Gerhard (1621–1668), himself an author of a *harmonic* grammar.

Hodogeticum is the most universal and systematic of the great *harmonic* works. It comprises lexical, grammatical and textual sections. All three sections are structured on the same pattern: in six parallel vertical columns are adduced *harmonizing* data from Hebrew, Chaldaean, Syriac, Arabic, Ethiopic and — as with Castell — Persian languages. The lexical section includes two additional columns containing various deviations and Latin translation. These tables of *harmonisms* occupy about half a page. In the lower half the non-*harmonized* words and forms are adduced. In certain cases Nicolai compares pure inflections and not word forms, as his predecessors used to do. As a method of systematization of linguistic material and of highlighting the *harmonic* phenomena, Nicolai's work was unmistakably a step forward.

Regarding the systematization of concrete grammatical forms, the authors of *harmonic* works were faced with a dilemma: what to accept as the basis for *harmonization* — the form or the meaning. In many cases, especially in verbal conjugation, the problem was neutralized by the fact that the structure of the forms and that of the meaning were essetially identical. In such cases the *harmonization* turned into a formal comparison. In other cases the authors of the *harmonic* works usually based their comparisons on meaning. In relatively complex cases, when it was necessary to *harmonize* morphological schemes which were only partially homologous in the compared languages, the authors sometimes failed to find, or to invent, a sound principle for *harmonization*. For example, dealing with verbal stems, Hottinger (1659:50–91) begins by adducing the stems in four languages (Hebrew, Chaldaean, Syriac, Arabic) separately, according to the standard grammars *(haec serie coniugationes vulgo ponuntur),* then, for the benefit of the students, he establishes correspondences between Hebrew and Arabic verbal stems in a simplified, and not always accurate, way;

and finally, he presents comparative tables of the stems in all the four languages, taking the traditional Hebrew system as a base and intermingling the passive forms of inner and outer formation. Nicolai, the systemizer, presented the verbal stems (1670:II, 14–15) in one comparative table, also based on the Hebrew traditional system; but, since the Arabic and Ethiopic traditional systems differ from that of Hebrew, he adduced full lists of the Arabic and Ethiopic stems — including the forms which appeared in the *harmonic* table — in the section of the "absence of *harmony*".

Notwithstanding certain deficiencies, the work of the early comparativists deserves positive appraisal. Like their mediaeval predecessors, they found no difficulty in establishing all the Semitic sound shifts and the correlation between the main grammatical elements. For Semitic languages this task was facilitated by the triliteracy of Semitic root structure and the predominantly agglutinative technique of joining morphological units.

A modern Semitologist, bred in the tradition of comparative-historic linguistics, may be disappointed by the contrast between the huge amount of linguistic material assembled in the monumental *harmonic* works of the seventeenth century and the relatively low level of its theoretical evaluation therein. This discrepancy between the amount of factual and theoretical material is explained partly by the predominantly philological inclinations of the Semitologists of this epoch, partly by the relatively small number of Semitic languages known at the time, but above all by the general nature of thinking of pre-Boppian linguistics. The authors of *harmonic* works did not pursue any explanatory-historic objectives. As distinct from comparative-historic linguistics, their method may be called comparative-demonstrational.

Harmonic works continued to appear at the end of the seventeenth and on into the eighteenth centuries, but their heyday was already over. Undoubtedly, these works paved the way for the comparative-historic approach to language in Semitology, but *harmonic* linguistics per se could hardly develop into historical linguistics. A "theoretical mutation" — to use the expression of Sylvain Auroux (1990:223) — was needed. This "mutation" occured in Semitology only in the middle of the 19th century under the influence of Indo-European linguistics.

The theoretical limitations do not diminish the historical importance of the *harmonic* works. The great *harmonic* lexicons and grammars were the outstanding achievement of Semitic philology of the seventeenth century and had no equivalent in contemporary European linguistics, either in the amount of material dealt with or in the scope of the application of the comparative approach.

The works of Schindler, Castell, Hottinger and Nicolai were passed down to us as great monuments of an epoch. They demonstrate the highest level that pre-Boppian comparativism was capable of attaining and, at the same time, the limitations of its potential. Each of these authors could have concluded his work with the words: *feci quod potui, faciant meliora posteri.*

REFERENCES

Auroux, Sylvain. 1990. "Representation and the Place of Linguistic Change before Comparative Grammar". *Leibniz, Humboldt, and the Origins of Comparativism (Studies in the History of the Language Sciences,* 49) ed. by Tullio de Mauro and Lia Formigari. Amsterdam & Philadelphia: John Benjamins.

Castell, Edmund. 1669. *Lexicon heptaglotton, Hebraicum, Chaldaicum, Syriacum, Samaritanum, Aethiopicum, Arabicum, conjunctim et Persicum, separatim.* London: Thomas Roycroft.

Hottinger, Johann Heinrich. 1659. *Grammatica quattuor linguarum, Hebraicae, Chaldaicae, Syriacae et Arabicae, harmonica.* Heidelberg: Adrian Wyngaerden.

—1661. *Etymologicon Orientale sive Lexicon harmonicum heptaglotton.* Frankfurt: sumptibus J.W. Ammonii & W. Serlini.

Nicolai, Johann Friedrich. 1670. *Hodogeticum Orientale harmonicum.* Jena: Johann Jacob Bauhofer.

Palma (Cayet), Pierre-Victor. 1596. *Paradigmata de quattuor linguis Orientalibus praecipuis, Arabica, Armenica, Syra, Aethiopica.* Paris: S. Prevosteau.

Schindler, Valentin. 1612. *Lexicon pentaglotton, Hebraicum, Chaldaicum, Syriacum, Thalmudico-Rabbinicum et Arabicum.* Hanau: typis J.J. Henei.

Walton, Brian, ed. 1655–1657. *Biblia Sacra Polyglotta.* London: Thomas Roycroft.

A Grammar without a Tradition? Fernando de la Carrera's *Arte de la lengua yunga* (1644)

EVEN HOVDHAUGEN
University of Oslo

MOCHICA OR YUNGA is the name of a language which was spoken on the Pacific coast of Peru from the Sechura desert in the north to approximately Trujillo in the south. The Mochica-speaking territory was conquered by the Quechua-speaking Incas about 80 years before the Spanish conquistadors arrived. Originally spoken over a large territory and by a number of speakers, Mochica started to yield to Spanish in the eighteenth century. At the beginning of our century, it was only spoken in the isolated village of Eten in northern Peru. Today there are no fluent speakers left and the few semi-speakers will most certainly be dead before the turn of the century.

Our information of Mochica consists of two types of sources: first, texts and grammars from the sixteenth and seventeenth century. The oldest preserved source is a number of religious texts published in Oré (1607). The second source is Carrera (1644), which contains a quite extensive grammar, all the basic religious texts, psalms, confessional formulas, as well as some brief dialogues and a number of sentences in Mochica. We also have information about a Spanish–Mochica–Quechua catechism from 1596 and two other grammars, but apparently these grammars were unknown to Carrera (if they ever existed!) because he wrote that nobody could deprive him of the glory of being the first to write a grammar of Mochica (Altieri 1939:4).

The other kind of sources on the language are word lists and phrases from the end of the nineteenth and the first quarter of the twentieth century. The most extensive source is Middendorf (1892). All these materials show a dying language only used in limited spheres of communication and where all components were heavily influenced by Spanish.

Accordingly, our main sources for the knowledge of this ancient South American language is Carrera 1644. Carrera's grammar was published in Lima in 1644 with the title *ARTE DE LA LENGVA YVNGA DE LOS VALLES del Obispado de Truxillo del* Peru, *con vn Confessonario, y todas las Oraciones Christianas, traducidas en la lengua, y otras cosas.* The book was printed in two versions. One was dedicated to the king and probably consisted of copies destined for Europe. The other was dedicated to the cantor of the cathedral in Trujillo. There are a few discrepancies between the two editions besides the dedications suggesting that some minor (and rather unmotivated) changes were made in the text between the printing of the two editions. Since both editions are full of misprints (especially in the spelling of the Mochica words), it is probable that Carrera never had the opportunity to read proofs of the text; moreover, the strange and unmotivated differences between the two editions (which never correct the numerous misprints found in both editions) suggest that Carrera himself had no hand in the final production of either.

We do not know how many copies were printed of the book, but today only four copies are known to exist (one in British Museum in London, one in Biblioteca Nacional in Madrid, and two in private ownership in South America). Carrera's grammar was partly or completely reprinted three times in Peru between 1879 and 1921. It also formed the basis of Middendorf (1892), in which Carrera's paradigms were checked and attempts were made to translate his texts with the help of old Mochica-speaking informants in Eten. In 1939 a critical scholarly edition of Carrera's grammar appeared (Altieri 1939).

We know very little about the author. D. Fernando de la Carrera Daza was born in Trujillo in 1604. His parents were Juan de la Carrera and Jerónima Daza Carvajal, both descendants from the first Spanish families in the city. He was a fluent speaker of Mochica which he learned as a native speaker in Lambayeque (close to Chiclayo and Eten) where he grew up (Altieri 1939:6). Carrera was a priest, from 1633 in the small town of Reque (close to the village of Eten and the modern town of Chiclayo). The last time his name is mentioned is in a document dating from 1665.

In his grammar Carrera does not refer to other languages than Latin and Spanish. Those seem to have been the only languages he knew besides Mochica. We cannot exclude the possibility that he had some knowledge of Quechua and might have read some Quechua grammars, but there is no positive indication to that effect. Carrera mentions that he has had the opportunity to discuss his linguistic work with several Jesuits, but apparently none of them knew Mochica. According to Carrera (Altieri 1939:6), there were only four Spanish clerics at his time who knew Mochica.

The book is structured as follows:

Statements of approval, censorship and dedication followed by an introduction (pp. xiv–xxxiv), which gives his reason for writing the grammar, a survey of the places where Mochica is spoken, and rules for the pronunciation of the language.

The first part (pp. 1–27) gives the rules of declension for nouns, adjectives and pronouns and the corresponding paradigms.

The second part (pp. 28–29) treats gender of nouns and since there are no grammatical genders in Mochica this part is very short.

The third part (pp. 30–105) treats the conjugations of the verbs mainly through paradigms and then presents a more general survey of the rules for the formations of verbal forms. This part ends with a survey of the word classes and aspects of the syntax, mainly the position of pronouns and the copula and the relationship between passive and active sentences.

The fourth part (pp.107–142) purports to treat everything in the syntax of Mochica that can be accommodated to Latin and ends up with extensive lists of prepositions, adverbs etc, and an unordered sample of grammatical problems not treated earlier. Then follows an extensive list of nouns (in nominative and genitive) and verbs (1st and 2nd sg. pres., 1st sg. past and past participle) as well as illustrative phrases, irregular or variant forms etc. After the confessional formulas (Mochica and Spanish), Carrera adds a list of nouns for human body parts, directions, numerals, and parts of day and night.

Carrera's purpose for writing the grammar is made clear in the introduction where he tells how shocked he was at discovering that people in Reque and the surrounding areas had after one century of Christianity completely misunderstood the basic principles of the Christian religion, believing, for example, that the saints were all gods and having no idea of the Holy Trinity. The purpose of the *Arte* is purely practical and several times in the book he points out that the reason why certain grammatical topics or words are included is that they are necessary for understanding the holy texts, carrying out confession etc. Furthermore, he stressed that he has presented what could be described and included from this very difficult language according to the rules of Latin grammar, but that he had found it necessary to add some letters to the alphabet and give some other letters a new pronunciation. He stressed that he had used this revised orthography in order to teach the Mochicas to read and write their own language successfully. His role as an alphabet innovator was also the aspect of his work stressed in the introductory statements to his grammar by the few other experts of Mochica.

Carrera's whole grammar and programme was in many respects a failure. His promised dictionary of Mochica never appeared and there is no evidence that his alphabet was used by anyone or that any further publications in Mochica appeared. The reason behind this was partly a change in language policy in Peru. From a religious linguistic tolerance and an eagerness to use all languages to save as many souls as possible in the beginning, the Church slowly moved to the adoption of a more practical and centralised linguistic attitude of the bureaucracy, tolerating only two languages in the country: Spanish and Quechua. But Carrera was not completely without blame in this failure either. No matter how good and interesting his grammar is for us and was for his very few contemporaries who knew Mochica, it was largely useless for all the others. Carrera had really "gone native". He understood the Mochicas and his translations of the Christian religious texts are very free and masterly adapted to Mochica customs and ways of thinking. But he frequently forgot to translate his examples (words as well as sentences) and the texts. What was intended as an introductory textbook became an advanced grammar for those who already knew Mochica.

One of Carrera's most impressive achievements is his Mochica alphabet in which he partly invented new letters, partly gave Latin letters new phonetic values and partly used combinations of letters to express phonemic distinctions. The phonemic system of Mochica was as follows:

VOWELS:		i						u	
			e		ə		o		
					a				
CONSONANTS:	p		t				ts	tš	k
							ţş	ţš	
	m		n						ŋ
			ɲ						
	f		s				š		
			ş				ş̌		
				r		l			
						ļ			
				ð					

There is, furthermore, a possibility that there was a retroflex affricate /tş/.

This phonemic system is represented as follows in Carrera's alphabet:

a = /a/	*c* /*qu* = /k/	*ç*/*z* =/ş/	*æ* = /ə/
ch = /ts]/	*cɥ* = /ţš/	*d*= /d, ð/	(*tr* = /tş/)
e = /e/	*f* = /f/	*i* = /i/	
l = /l/	*ll* = /ļ/	*m* = /m/	
n = /n/	*ñ* = /ɲ/	*o* = /o/	
p = /p/	*r*/*rr* = /r/	*s*/*ss*/*z* = /s/	
t = /t/	*tzh* = /ts/	*tzhi* = /ţş/	
u/*v* = /u/	*x* = /š/	*xll* = /ş̌/	

As we see, except for the opposition /s/ – /ʂ/ (which is rather marginal in Mochica), this is an almost perfect representation of the distinctive phonological oppositions. And Carrera was well aware of the importance of the distinctive function of sounds:

> Esta letra siguiente es una h al revés, de diferente sonido que las nuestras, muy necesaria y forzosa para diferenciar esta pronunciación *chido* ... [been] etc. de la *h* al revés, como *cɥapa* [roof] ... (Altieri 1939:11)

Carrera's phonetic explanations, although far from being sufficient, show a better awareness of the function of the basic articulatory organs than what most of his contemporary grammarians had:

> Para pronunciar *tzhæich* [your] se ha de comenzar con la lengua en el paladar junto a los dientes, y acabar con los labios abiertos. (Altieri 1939:11)

In the morphology and syntax, there are numerous instances in which Carrera simply copies the Latin or Spanish classifications applying them automatically to Mochica. An example is the case paradigms where we find the six cases of Latin although "accusative, vocative and ablative are identical with nominative in all declensions" (Altieri 1939:13). And when distinguishing between the postpositions governing accusative and those governing ablative (Altieri 1939:60–61), Carrera based the classification on which cases the (semantically) corresponding prepositions govern in Latin!

Carrera only knew some very elementary linguistic terminology and had probably not read any more advanced grammar. He had very vague ideas about syntax. From our point of view, this leads to some rather serious shortcomings in his description. He assumes the dative to be a separate case although the Mochica dative consists of a postposition *pæn* added to the genitive. But the locative is formed in the same way with a postposition *nic*. Carrera, however, was unfamiliar with the term locative and did not see the structural parallelism. Similarily, Carrera was not able to see ergative as a separate case, but observing that in some words ergative was formally identical with genitive, he analysed ergative as a second genitive. He also had to operate with two nominatives in Mochica because all nouns in Mochica have two stems: a possessed stem and a non-possessed stem. In some words, the possessed is basic and, in other words, the non-possessed is basic: *fanu* "dog" — *fanuss* "someone's dog" but *efquic* "father" — *ef* "someone's father". But Carrera's description of these phenomena is more than satisfactory for us to grasp the function of the forms involved:

> El primiero nominativo es general, en todo genero de cosas, como *col* [horse] ... etc. en los cuales no hay propiedad ni señorio, porque dice generalmente el caballo, ... etc.
>
> Y asi, si el caballo es mio, o la manta, u otra caso en que yo o aquel, o el otro, o Pedro, o Juan etc., tengamos dominio o propriedad, no se dice *mæiñ col ang mo* [this is my horse] ... porque son barbarismos y de ninguna manera se habla asi.
>
> El secundo nominativo sale del primero, y en los acabados en vocal o en el diptongo *æ*, se forma con sólo añadir dos *ss* [...]
>
> Esto supuesto, digo que todas las oraciones que tuvieren propriedad de la cosa que se quiere decir, se han de hacer con los seguendos nominativos y no con los primeros ... (Altieri 1939:14–15)
>
> Item se advierte que los genitivos que acaban en *eio*, se vuelven en *en* para las oraciones de pasiva, porque la persona que parece por activas, se pone por pasiva en el secundo genitivo ... (Altieri 1939:16)
>
> La persona que hace por activa se pone por pasiva en genitivo, y el acusativo que era por activa se pone en nominativo, y se concuerda con el verbo, teniendo advertencia dė empezar siempre por el genitivo, que es el que en la lengua Latina había de estar en ablativo con preposición. (Altieri 1939:52)

Carrera's morphological rules are pedagogical and descriptively quite adequate. Let us take one example:

> El pretérito perfecto se forma del presente con la partícula *da* y *ed*. La primera persona es *meteiñ* [I carry], entra en medio del verbo y de la persona esta partícula *da,* u dirá *metedaiñ* [I carried]. La secunda es *metaz* [you carry] ... y entrando entre la *t* y la *a,* en el primero modo, esta partícula *ed,* dirá *metedaz* [you carried]. (Altieri 1939:45).

In many instances, it seems that Carrera developed his descriptive ability in the process of writing, and several times he returns to a grammatical problem mentioned earlier and presents another and more extensive explanation.

His ability to describe complex phenomena in Mochica which have no parallel in Latin is also quite impressive like, for example, his description of the impossibility of having pronouns and suffixed verbal forms combined (Altieri 1939:51–53), or his analysis of the particle *ô* which marks non-dependent phrases (65–68). Although he lacked the technical terms for phenomena like causative, ergative, benefactive, etc. and he sometimes offered somewhat complicated rules, Carrera's description of the phenomena as well as his information about their meaning is so comprehensive and exact that there are few problems for a linguist of the twentieth century to understand and reformulate it in his/her own terms.

Carrera was himself a bit hesitant in formulating rules (cf. also Altieri 1939:24).

> Los más verbos de esta lengua tienen derivativos, que son aún más usados que los principales; y porque no tienen formación cierta y determinada, no la pongo aquí por cuanto si se formasan fuera del uso de los indios, era enseñar que no se entendiese y así para dar luz de ellos, pongo los ejemplos siguientes, ... (Altieri 1939:39).

Carrera's grammar is simple and naïve in its technical vocabulary and builds on a rudimentary knowledge of Latin grammar. But precisely this uneducated linguistic background combined with the author's native knowledge of the language he described may be the main reason behind his success. His thoughts were not imprisoned and subjugated by the burden of the tradition of centuries of intensive grammar writing and language philosophy.

The study of this grammar faces historiographers of linguistics with some interesting problems. One approach is to analyse this grammar on the background of what the author knew about grammar, which sources he had and how he used them. We may assume that Carrera had studied both Spanish and Latin grammars, but we do not know which ones. We do not know if he had known other grammars, but it is not likely. The numerous grammars of Quechua and Aymara we have from the sixteenth and seventeenth centuries are in structure very similar and very orthodox in their faithfulness to the classical model of Latin grammar. Several of these were also to some extent influenced by Nebrija (1492). Carrera's grammar is more disorganized, and apparently its main structure follows the author's idiosyncratic set up. As a result, this grammar is only marginally, if at all, part of a linguistic tradition.

What does this tell us who are doing the history of linguistics? At least one thing can be said: man's ability to think independently about linguistic matter and analyse linguistic problems may be more important than generally assumed. Or to put it another way: there might have been a few more Carrera's in the history of linguistics and the wheel may have been invented more times than generally assumed. Accordingly, our hunt for precursors, background sources, influence from previous thinkers, and the like may be out of the place here. Perhaps what we need is a typological characterization of grammars to put grammars like Carrera's correctly on the map.

Let me give the last word to Carrera. His way of expression is not quite clear and a bit clumsy, but his problems as a descriptive linguist have a familar ring to many of us.

> Yo estuve determinado, de poner en esta lengua más verbo que el substantivo, pero déjelo de poner, por no añadir confusión a la que la misma lengua tiene, que cierto es bárbara o irreducible a términos, en la cual el que más sabe ignora mucho. Pero si yo fuera el que la leyese, por este arte, o por otro, si lo hubiera, yo diría el modo como gobernarse, con el verbo substantivo, platicándole y dándolo a entender; y esto no es posible poder escribir, si no es llenando de confusión, lo que quisiera hacer fácil, y así no hay que reparar en esto, sino seguir los preceptos

que se ponen, que algún día, el que la llegare a saber, conocerá que no voy yo descaminando. (Altieri 1939:53)

REFERENCES

Altieri, Radamés A. 1939. *Fernando de la Carrera Arte de la lengua Yunga (1644)*. Reediciòn, con introduction y notas por Radamés A. Altieri. (= Universidad nacional de Tucuman, Publicacion no. 256) Tucuman, Argentina: Instituto de Antropologia.

Carrera, Fernando de la. 1644. *ARTE DE LA LENGVA YVNGA DE LOS VALLES del Obispado de Truxillo del Peru, con un Confessonario, y todas las Oraciones Christianas, traducidas en la lengua, y otras cosas*. Avtor el beneficiado don Fernando de la Carrera, natural de la dicha ciudad de Truxillo, Cura y Vicario de S.Martin de Reque, en el Corregimiento de Chiclayo. Lima. Joseph de Contreras.

Middendorf. Ernst W. (1830–1909) 1892. *Das Muchik oder die Chimu-Sprache*. (=*Die einheimischen Sprachen Perus,* 6.) Leipzig. F. A. Brockhaus.

Nebrija, Antonio de. 1492. *Gramática sobre la lengua castellana*. Salamanca: eponymous press.

Oré, Luis Hieronimo de [Ore, Ludovicus Hieronimus 1554–1629]. 1607. *Ritvale, sev manvale pervanvm, et forma brevis administrandi apud Indos sacrosanta Baptismi, Pœnitentiæ, Euchaeistiæ, Matrimonij, & Extremæ vnctionis Sacramenta*. Iuxta ordinem Santæ Romanæ Ecclesiæ per R.P.F. Lvdovicvm Hieronymym Orerium, Ordinis Minorum Concionatorem, & Sacræ Theologiæ Lectorem accuratum. Neapoli. Apud Io. Iacobum Carlinum, & Constantinum Vitalem.

Étude historiographique des Manières de Langage*

BARBARA KALTZ
Luther College, University of Regina

1. HISTOIRE DES IDEES LINGUISTIQUES, HISTOIRE DE LA LANGUE ET HISTOIRE DE L'ENSEIGNEMENT DES LANGUES ETRANGERES

QUELLE LEÇON pouvons-nous tirer des *Manières de langage (MDL)* pour l'histoire des idées linguistiques? Rédigés pour l'enseignement des vernaculaires en tant que langues étrangères, d'abord pour l'enseignement du français en Flandre puis en Angleterre dès le XIVe siècle, ensuite pour d'autres langues parlées en Europe, ces ouvrages témoignent de l'impact croissant des vernaculaires à partir de cette époque, tout comme les premiers vocabulaires, les traités orthographiques, les grammaires et les recueils de lettres modèles[1].

Les avis sur l'intérêt des *MDL* sont toutefois partagés. Certains les ignorent tout simplement, affirmant que l'enseignement des vernaculaires en tant que langues étrangères au Moyen Age est une quantité négligeable et que le besoin d'un enseignement des langues modernes ne s'est fait sentir qu'à la Renaissance (Titone 1980:23). Selon Rickard (1976:16), la valeur de ces ouvrages, "pleins de grossières fautes de français" et laissant "le chercheur sur sa faim", serait "minime". D'autres études philologiques (e.g. Stengel 1879) et

* Ce texte est une version remaniée et abrégée de ma communication au congrès de Galway. Je tiens à remercier le Service culturel de l'Ambassade de France à Bonn (R.F.A.) de m'avoir attribué une bourse de courte durée en 1988, ainsi que Luther College et le Conseil de recherches en sciences humaines du Canada qui m'ont accordé des subventions en 1989 et 1990. Mes remerciements vont également à H.-J. Niederehe de l'Université de Trèves (R.F.A.) pour son aide et ses conseils, ainsi qu'à D. A. Kibbee (University of Illinois) et B. Merrilees (University of Toronto) pour leurs remarques pertinentes lors du congrès de Galway.

[1] Pour plus de détails, je renvoie le lecteur à Kibbee (1991).

pédagogiques (e.g., Lambley 1920, Riemens 1919, Rothwell 1968), ont depuis longtemps établi l'importance des *MDL* pour le domaine de l'histoire du français et de l'histoire de l'enseignement du français langue étrangère.

En mettant à profit bon nombre de ces recherches d'orientation pédagogique ou philologique, j'entreprendrai par la suite de relire une série de *MDL* dans une perspective historiographique. Comme l'a montré Niederehe (1990), la séparation entre l'historiographie linguistique et l'étude de l'histoire de la langue est de toute manière artificielle et risque d'atrophier la recherche. Auroux (1989:31) pose le problème de façon plus directe encore en notant "qu'une histoire des sciences du langage digne de ce nom devra, tôt ou tard, intégrer le travail sur la langue". Les *MDL* sont, me semble-t-il, des témoins d'un tel travail sur la langue, ne serait-ce que sous forme d'ébauche, et méritent d'être étudiées de plus près à ce titre. A propos du domaine de l'enseignement des langues secondes, Bursill-Halla d'ailleurs souligné dès 1977 que l'historiographie linguistique ne peut se permettre, pour quelque époque que ce soit, de passer sous silence la production d'ouvrages pédagogiques.

2. Manières de langage, colloques, dialogues

Avant de présenter la série des textes regroupés ici sous la désignation de *MDL*, quelques remarques d'ordre terminologique s'imposent. A quoi cette désignation renvoie-t-elle, en quoi se distingue-t-elle des autres termes désignant ces textes, tels que *dialogues, colloques, manuels de conversation* ? Une lecture des occurrences de l'expression *MDL* — ainsi que de la tournure équivalente *maniere de/du parler* — dans *La manière de langage* (1396) montre que *maniere* n'a nullement le sens de manuel que lui attribuent Södergård (1953:203) et Rickard (1976:15). Par *MDL*, l'auteur anonyme du texte de 1396 désigne au contraire les tournures dont il préconise l'emploi dans telle ou telle situation de discours, par exemple en parlant à un enfant ou en demandant son chemin. Par ailleurs, des choix sont assez souvent proposés qui permettent de varier l'expression d'une intention ou d'une demande, caractéristique qu'on note également dans des textes plus tardifs (e.g., Holyband 1576/1609). La tournure *MDL* se retrouve avec le même sens dans des ouvrages ultérieurs de ce type (e.g. *Un petit livre; Lytell Treatise),* traduisant ainsi l'approche *directe* et la finalité pratique de cette tradition pédagogique, qui vise en premier lieu une compétence orale dans la langue cible. La désignation *MDL* caractérise de façon particulièrement heureuse ce type d'ouvrage pédagogique[1] si bien qu'elle sera retenue par la suite pour parler de tout texte rentrant dans cette catégorie.

3. MDL, VOCABULAIRES, RECUEILS DE LETTRES MODÈLES ET GRAMMAIRES

Par ailleurs, il importe de bien distinguer ce type de texte des autres ouvrages destinés à l'enseignement des langues étrangères, et notamment des vocabulaires et des grammaires. Bien entendu, il n'est pas question de nier les liens multiples entre la tradition des *MDL,* celle des vocabulaires et celle des premiers ouvrages grammaticaux pour les vernaculaires. Ainsi, les vocabulaires, tels *l'Introito e porta* (1477) ou le *Dictionnaire des huict langaiges* (1552), contiennent souvent un certain nombre de tournures. Il reste que ce sont essentiellement des listes de mots classés par groupes thématiques, suivant la tradition des *nominalia.* Inversement, certains ouvrages qui se rattachent en premier lieu à la tradition des MDL (e.g., le *Lytell Treatise* et les *Coloquios familiares)* renferment des listes de mots rangés par groupes. De toute façon, les titres sont souvent trompeurs. Ainsi, le *Vocabularium* de 1514 se compose en fait d'un *nominale* Latin-français-allemand et d'une *MDL* français-allemand. Il arrive aussi que vocabulaire et dialogues soient regroupés dans un même recueil et que le titre l'indique (e.g., Berlaimont 1558). Notons au passage qu'à partir du XVIe siècle, on trouve également *dialogues* et dictionnaire alphabétique réunis dans un seul ouvrage (e.g., *Colloquia,* 1576). Si les vocabulaires, les dialogues/colloques et, accessoirement, les recueils de lettres, parfois regroupés avec les *MDL* (e.g., *Colloquia,* 1576), poursuivent bien entendu le même objectif, celui d'enseigner une langue étrangère,

[1] Cf. Merrilees (1985:105, 114).

il faut néanmoins retenir les différences fondamentales dans l'approche pédagogique et l'organisation du matériau linguistique.

4. LE CORPUS: CRITÈRES DE SELECTION

L'objectif de ce travail est d'ébaucher une vue d'ensemble pour une série de *MDL*[1]. Il ne s'agit pas, bien entendu, de minimiser l'intérêt des recherches qui se limitent à l'examen de la situation pour une seule langue (e.g. Lambley 1920 et Kibbee 1989a/b pour le français en Angleterre) ou pour une paire de langues (e.g. Gessler 1931 pour le français et le flamand ; Pirozynski 1981 pour le polonais et l'allemand). Une approche plus globale devrait toutefois nous permettre de mieux saisir les constantes et les variantes du type de texte en question. Ainsi, la périodisation retenue pour ce travail (milieu XIVe siècle – fin XVIe siècle) fait ressortir que la tradition des *MDL,* établie au Moyen Age, sera maintenue pendant la Renaissance et au-delà. Cette tradition ne s'arrête d'ailleurs pas à la fin du XVIe siècle. Bien au contraire, la production de *MDL* connaîtra un essor considérable par la suite, et notamment au XVIIe siècle. D'autre part, cette périodisation permet de souligner les liens existant entre la tradition des *MDL* et la production grammaticale et lexicographique des temps modernes. Enfin, si le français est représenté dans tous les textes examinés, il m'a semblé indispensable d'inclure également des ouvrages renfermant d'autres vernaculaires européens, ainsi qu'un exemple de *MDL* comprenant une partie latine, qui illustre les liens entre l'enseignement du latin langue seconde et celui des vernaculaires. Quant aux ouvrages plurilingues, ils nous permettent de mieux comprendre à quel point les débuts de la lexicographie et de l'enseignement des vernaculaires étaient une *affaire européenne*.

5. LES CARACTERISTIQUES SECONDAIRES DES MDL

Ayant posé que les ouvrages retenus pour cette étude ont des caractéristiques communes qui justifient leur regroupement d'un point de

[1] Les textes retenus pour le corpus sont marqués d'un astérisque dans la bibliographie.

vue typologique, je propose par la suite d'en dégager quelques caractéristiques *secondaires*. J'entends par là les variations résultant du nombre de langues représentées, du public visé (enfants et/ou adolescents, commerçants, voyageurs, femmes), de la structure textuelle (organisation du matériau linguistique, structure exclusivement dialogique ou non) et de la nature de la langue présentée (langue quotidienne, langue spécialisée)[1].

5.1 LE PUBLIC VISE PAR LES MDL

Selon Fisher (1985:45), les auteurs de grammaires des langues vulgaires du XVIe au XVIIIe siècle se seraient toujours adressés à l'adulte, "jamais peut-être" à l'enfant. La situation se présente de façon tout à fait différente pour les *MDL*. En effet, la *MDL* la plus ancienne, le *Livre des mestiers*, est présentée par son auteur comme un ouvrage "mout proufitable a tous enfans aprendre" (éd. Gessler 1931:51). Par la suite, une série de *MDL* s'adressera également de manière explicite aux enfants *(Petit livre, Profitelijck boexcken, Dialogues francois, Douze dialogues)*. Si les auteurs de ces ouvrages indiquent d'une manière ou d'une autre à quel public ils s'adressent, ces renseignements nous manquent dans d'autres cas, et nous sommes réduits à émettre des hypothèses à partir du contenu des ouvrages. C'est ainsi qu'on peut penser que l'auteur du *Lytell Treatise* a destiné son texte à la fois aux enfants et à un public adulte. L'ouvrage comprend en effet, à côté des parties "standard" d'une *MDL* (salutations, pour vendre et acheter, pour demander son chemin) un "booke of curtesye", d'ailleurs fort amusant, pour les jeunes enfants. De la même manière, le French *Littelton* (1576/1609) contient un dialogue "Des Escholiers & Eschole", alors que les autres parties sont clairement rédigées à l'intention des voyageurs et des commerçants. Il est difficile d'établir à quelle tranche d'âge appartenaient ces apprenants. C'est le cas aussi pour les *escoliers* auxquels s'adresse l'auteur de la *Maniere de langage* de 1396 (1934:44). Les *Dialogues* français de 1415 visaient également un

[1] Dans la présente version abrégée de ma communication, seules pourront être traitées la question du public visé et celle de la nature de la langue présentée.

public d'élèves ou d'étudiants. La polyvalence des ouvrages destinés à l'enseignement des langues vernaculaires que souligne Pirozynski (1981:12–13) pour la Renaissance est sans doute également caractéristique des textes antérieurs à cette époque: les ouvrages écrits en premier lieu pour la jeunesse devaient souvent s'adresser aussi à un public adulte.

La plupart des chercheurs s'accordent pour dire que ce public adulte était surtout constitué de personnes désirant voyager à l'étranger et faire du commerce. Dans le cas des destinataires des premières *MDL* rédigées en Angleterre, le motif du voyage n'était peut-être pas toujours le commerce. Streuber (1962:76) estime en tout cas que parmi les Anglais désireux de voyager en France et d'apprendre la langue à cet effet, il y aurait eu aussi des étudiants (notamment en droit). Lusignan (1986:110–111) va plus loin en posant une "destination en quelque sorte juridique et administrative" des premières *MDL*.

Les *MDL* ont-elles eu un public féminin? Curieusement, cette question ne semble pas avoir été soulevée par les chercheurs qui se sont intéressés aux *MDL*. Peter Erondell *(The French Garden: for* English *Ladyes and Gentlewomen to walke in,* 1605/1621), s'étonne dans son avis au lecteur de ce que personne avant lui n'ait pensé à rédiger des dialogues pour les Anglaises qui voudraient apprendre le français. Si son ouvrage est peut-être le premier à proposer un contenu spécifiquement féminin (e.g. vêtements pour femmes et enfants ; soin des bébés), il semble peu probable que les *MDL* antérieures à ce texte n'aient pas été utilisées dans l'éducation féminine, d'autant que leur emploi ne se limitait pas à l'étude en milieu scolaire. Un vocabulaire de 1516, *l'Introductio quaedam utilissima,* s'adresse de façon explicite aux femmes. Selon son auteur, l'ouvrage serait un "tres util vocabuliste a aprendre pour ceulx qui desirasse [sic] sans aler alescole comme artisans et femmes". Enseignants et apprenants des vernaculaires, en milieu scolaire ou non, avaient sans doute recours à toute la gamme d'ouvrages didactiques (vocabulaires, *MDL,* recueils de lettres modèles, grammaires). Dans ces circonstances, les filles et les femmes ont sans doute fait partie du public des *MDL* bien avant le début du XVIIe siècle.

5.2 LA NATURE DE LA LANGUE PRESENTEE DANS LES MDL

Haastrup, qui s'intéresse plus particulièrement aux guides de conversation danois–français du XVIIIe siècle, note (1989:33) que

> les dialogues dans les manuels d'enseignement des langues semblent être une source méconnue dans un domaine méconnu de la linguistique et de la lexicographie historiques, c'est-à-dire l'histoire de la conversation et de la langue parlée.

Il pense que les guides de conversation en général ont "mauvaise réputation" (1989:34), ce qui s'expliquerait en partie par le "manque d'intérêt pour les conversations familières, plus généralement la langue usuelle" de la part des chercheurs (1989:35). Ses remarques me semblent s'appliquer aussi aux textes qui nous intéressent ici. Dans certaines études, les *MDL* sont en effet abordées avec une sorte de parti pris normatif. Ainsi, on déplore le "français fort corrompu" (Rickard 1976:16), on relève la présence d'anglicismes, d'archaïsmes et de régionalismes dans les *MDL* rédigées en Angleterre (Lambley 1920:36, 39, 55), éléments pourtant caractéristiques des langues en contact, et on semble regretter la présence d'injures (Rothwell 1968:45), oubliant que la langue parlée n'a jamais respecté les normes et les conventions, quelles qu'elles soient.

La langue quotidienne est présente à des degrés divers dans tous les textes examinés ici, conséquence logique de l'orientation pratique des *MDL*, qu'elles partagent avec les premières grammaires du français et les dictionnaires plurilingues de l'époque. Témoins de cette langue quotidienne telle qu'elle était utilisée dans des situations de discours variées, les *MDL* mériteraient à mon sens d'être étudiées de plus près non seulement pour les indications sur le vocabulaire, la prononciation et la morphologie qu'elles fournissent à l'historien de la langue (cf. Marchello-Nizia 1979:39) mais aussi pour l'intérêt qu'elles présentent au niveau de l'analyse des structures discursives[1].

[1] Cf. Buridant (1986:19): "Il apparaît aussi qu'avec ces Colloques, Manières et Dialogues, proposant des modèles de discours, la lexicographie médiévale touche, bien sûr, à la rhétorique, avec laquelle la frontière est mouvante".

A côté de la langue quotidienne, on trouve également des éléments de langue spécialisée dans différentes *MDL*. En général, les dialogues traitant de la vente et de l'achat de marchandises ne renferment pas beaucoup de termes spécialisés et peuvent donc être considérés comme faisant partie du domaine de la langue usuelle. Mais certains textes dépassent largement ce domaine ; c'est le cas notamment de la *MDL* la plus ancienne que nous connaissions. Le *Livre des mestiers,* comprenant des termes spécifiques à des métiers très divers, porte donc bien son titre. Dans les *Dialogues françois* (1567), les conversations ont trait surtout à la vie quotidienne des enfants — ainsi, les trois premiers dialogues sont intitulés "Le lict, et les habitz", "La priere" et "La table ou le repas des escoliers" —, mais on trouve également, à la fin de l'ouvrage, un dialogue, assez long, sur "l'écriture et l'imprimerie"[1]. Enfin, les *Coloquios familiares* de G. Meurier contiennent, à côté des dialogues habituels destinés au voyageur (qui apprend ainsi à demander "ou sont les latrines ou priuez" et s'entend répondre: "Allez sur le fumier", 1568:17), de nombreux chapitres présentant des "deuiz bien propres" à diverses catégories professionnelles. Meurier y donne des échantillons de la langue particulière à des métiers aussi spécialisés que ceux des "Beurriers, Chandeliers, Graissiers, Fromagiers, Portiers, Iamboniers" (tel le titre du chapitre 22).

6. Conclusion

A partir d'un certain nombre de travaux d'orientation philologique et pédagogique portant sur les *MDL,* j'ai tenté d'attirer l'attention sur quelques aspects caractéristiques de ce type de texte, susceptibles d'intéresser l'historien des idées linguistiques, et de souligner pour le domaine des *MDL* que "la lexicographie de la Renaissance est loin d'être en rupture totale avec la tradition médiévale" (Buridant 1986:33). La nature de ces liens reste floue parce trop d'éléments nous échappent encore (Buridant, ibid.). La présente étude ne saurait constituer qu'un premier pas vers une relecture plus approfondie des *MDL,* qui devrait

[1] Voet (1981:305) estime qu'il s'agit du premier document présentant la terminologie de l'imprimerie en flamand et en français.

notamment élucider la question épineuse de la filiation des textes, préciser le profil de leurs destinataires du point de vue de l'histoire sociale[1], analyser de manière systématique la structure textuelle des *MDL* et plus particulièrement les éléments spécifiquement discursifs.

REFERENCES

I. TEXTES

*Anon. 1576. *Colloquia et Dictionariolum sex linguarum: Teutonicae, Latinae, Germanicae, Gallicae, Hispanicae & Italicae (...).* Anvers : Henricus Henricus. (flamand–latin–allemand–français–espagnol–italien).

*Anon. 1903. "Dialogues français composés en 1415". *Romania*. 32.49–53. (éd. P. Meyer). (français).

Anon. 1552. *Le Dictionaire des huict langaiges: grec, latin, flameng, francois, espagnol, italien, anglois, et aleman (...).* Paris : chez la veufue Guillaume le Bret.

Anon. 1516. *Introductio quaedam utilissima, sive vocabularius quattuor linguarum, Latine, Italice, Gallice et Alamanice (...).* Augsbourg : Erhart Oeglin.

Anon. 1477. *Introito e porta de quele che voleno imparare e cõprender todescho & latino cioe italiano (...).* Venise : Adam von Rottweil.

*Anon. 1931. *Le livre des mestiers de Bruges et ses dérivés. Quatre anciens manuels de conversation.* 6 vol. Bruges. (éd. Jean Gessler). (français–flamand).

*Anon. 1497 (?). *A Lytell Treatise for to Lerne Englisshe and Frensshe.* Westmynster. (rééd. Amsterdam : Da Capo Press, 1973). (anglais–français).

*Anon. 1934. *La manière de langage qui enseigne à bien parler et écrire le français : modèles de conversations composés en Angleterre à la fin du XIVe siècle.* Paris: E. Droz. (éd. Jean Gessler). (français).

*Anon. 1567. *La première et la seconde partie des dialogues françois, pour les jeunes enfans. (...).* Anvers : Christophle Plantin. (français–flamand).

*Anon. 1879. "Un petit livre pour enseigner les enfantz de leur entreparler comun francois". *ZNFSL* 1.10–15. (éd. Edmund Stengel). (français).

*Anon. 1953. "Une manière de parler". *NM*. 54.209–219. (éd. Östen Södergård). (français–anglais).

*Anon. 1514. *Vocabularium Latinis, Gallicis et Theutonicis verbis scriptum.* Lyon : Jehan Thomas. (français–allemand).

[1] Bien entendu, il faudrait aussi s'intéresser aux enseignants. Cf. Kibbee (1991) pour les premières *MDL*.

*Anon. 1558. *Vocabvlario, colloqvios o dialogos en qvatro lengvas, Flamengo, Frances, Español, y Italiano (...)*. Anvers : Ian Verwithagen. (flamand–français–espagnol–italien).

*Berlaimont, Noel van. 1552. *Een profitelijck boecxken om Francoys ende Duystsche oft Vlaems te leeren spreken (...)*. Anvers : Andries Luberts. (flamand–français).

Erondell, Peter. 1621 [[1]1605]. *The French Garden: for* English *Ladyes and Gentlewomen to Walke in: Or, A Sommer Dayes Labour (...)*. Londres : John Grisimond.

*Holyband, Clavdivs. 1609 [[1]1576]. *The French Littleton. A Most Easie, Perfect, and Absolvte Way to Learne the French Tongue*. Londres : Richard Field. (rééd. Cambridge : University Press, 1953). (anglais–français).

*Meurier, Gabriel. 1568. *Coloquios familiares muy convenientes y mas provechosos (...)*. Anvers : Jean Waesberge. (espagnol–français).

*Vivre, Gerard de. 1581. *Dovze dialogves, traitants de diverses matieres, tres-propres avx novveavx apprentifs de la langue françoise*. Anvers : Ian Waesberghe. (flamand–français).

II. ETUDES

Auroux, Sylvain. 1989. Compte-rendu de *Vaugelas and the Development of the French Language* de Wendy Ayres-Bennett (Londres : The Modern Humanities Research Association, 1987). *Bulletin d'information de la SHESL* 21.31.

Buridant, Claude, éd. 1986. *Lexique 4 : La lexicographie au Moyen Age*. Lille : Presses Universitaires.

Bursill-Hall 1977. "Teaching Grammars of the Middle Ages". *HL* 4:1.1–29.

Fisher, Sophie. 1985. "A qui et comment s'adressaient les grammairiens des 'langues vulgaires' ? A propos de grammaires des langues romanes (XVIe/XVIIIe siècles)". *Le Citoyen de demain et les langues,* 36–45. Paris : APLVEP. (Coord. Daniel Thomières.)

Haastrup, Niels. 1989. "Sur les guides de conversation". *Documents pour l'histoire du* français *langue étrangère ou seconde* 4.33–38.

Kibbee, Douglas A. 1989a. "L'enseignement du français en Angleterre au XVIe siècle". *La Langue française au XVIe siècle : usage, enseignement et approches descriptives,* éd. par Pierre Swiggers & Willy Van Hoecke, 54–77. Louvain: Leuven University Press.

—. 1989b. "Les manuels anglais du XVIe siècle et l'imprimerie". *Documents pour l'histoire du français langue étrangère ou seconde*. 4.18–20.

—. 1991. *For to Speke Frenche Trewely: The French Language in England, 1000–1600*. Amsterdam & Philadelphie : John Benjamins.

Lambley, Kathleen. 1920. *The Teaching and Cultivation of the French Language in England during Tudor and Stuart Times*. Manchester : University Press.

Lusignan, Serge. 1986. *Parler vulgairement. Les intellectuels et la langue française aux XIIIe et XIVe siècles*. Montréal : Les Presses de l'Université de Montréal.

Marchello-Nizia, Christiane. 1979. *Histoire de la langue française aux XIVe et XVe siècles*. Paris : Bordas.

Merrilees, Brian. 1985. "Le dialogue dans la méthodologie du français langue seconde au moyen âge". *Le Dialogue*. 101–115. Ottawa: Didier. (Série 3L, 7,éd. par Pierre R. Lévin & Paul Perron.)

Niederehe, Hans-Josef. 1990. "Zum Verhältnis von Wissenschaftsgeschichte und Sprachgeschichte". *Understanding the Historiography of Linguistics,* éd. par Werner Hüllen, 75–86. Münster : Nodus Publikationen.

Pirozynski, Jan. 1981. "Ein unbekanntes polnisch-deutsches Gesprächsbüchlein aus der 1. Hälfte des 16. Jahrhunderts in der Sammlung der Herzog August Bibliothek Wolfenbüttel". *Wolfenbütteler Beiträge* 4, éd. par Paul Raabe, 9–58. Francfort : Vittorio Klostermann.

Rickard, Peter. 1976. *Chrestomathie de la langue française au quinzième siècle*. Cambridge : University Press.

Riemens, K.-J. 1919. *Esquisse historique de l'enseignement du français en Hollande du XVIe au XIXe siècle*. Leyde : A. W. Sijthoff.

Rothwell, W. 1968. "The Teaching of French in Medieval England". *MLR*. 63.37–46.

Södergård, Östen. "Une manière de parler". *NM* 54.201–225.

Stengel, Edmund. 1879. "Die ältesten Anleitungsschriften zur Erlernung der französischen Sprache". *ZNFSL* 1.1–40.

Streuber, Albert. 1962. "Die ältesten Anleitungsschriften zur Erlernung des Französischen in England und den Niederlanden bis zum 16. Jahrhundert". *ZFSL* 72.37–86.

Titone, Renzo. 1980. *Glottodidattica. Un profilo storico*. Bergame : Minerva Italica.

Voet, Leon. 1980–1983. *The Plantin Press (1555–1589). A Bibliography of the Works printed and published by Christopher Plantin at Antwerp and Leiden*. 6 vols. Amsterdam : Van Hoeve. (Vol. II: 1981.)

L'Ordre Naturel and Charles Batteux: à bas les philosophes

L.G. KELLY
University of Ottawa

AMONG THE BEST loved and least remembered figures of eighteenth-century France is l'abbé Charles Batteux (1713–1780), professor of Rhetoric at Rheims, Professor of Greek and Latin at the Collège militaire royal. This list of his relevant works gives only the reprints listed in the British Library, Library of Congress, and the Bibliothèque nationale (Paris):

Cours de belles lettres, 1746/47, 1753
Principes de littérature, (an amplified version of the above) 1753, 1763, 1764, 1775, 1788, 1824, 1802, 1809, 1824
Translated into German, 1761,1762,1763, 1769
Translated into English, 1761
Translated into Spanish, 1797
Translated into French, 5 edition 1816
Principles of Translation. Edinburgh, 1760 (Part 3 §4 of his *Principes).*
De la construction oratoire, 1763
Traduction d'Horace, 1750, 1768, 1803, 1813, 1823
Les quatre poétiques d'Aristote, d'Horace, de Vidal & de Boileau, 1771, 1782, 1825
His remarks on Aristotle were translated and annexed to a Spanish verion of the Poetics (1778)
Nouvel examen du préjugé sur l'inversion, 1767
Traité de l'arrangement des mots, traduit du grec de Denys d'Halicarnasse, 1788
Translated into French, 1827

We know a fair amount about his life — the letter to his nephews prefaced to the posthumous edition of his Dionysius of Halicarnassus gives a rather engaging picture of a man who owed all to patronage and was quite happy to work within the system. His obituary and entries in the *Biographie universelle* and Chalmers's *Biographical Dictionary* give the image of a kindly scholar who was loved and respected for his academic and educational skill, his academic rigour and his devotion to his poor relations. The only sour notes in all this are adverse comments on the rather stiff style of his translations of the classics:

> The style is strongly tinged with a metaphysical air, a stiff and dry precision reigns through the whole, but a little tempered by choice examples by which the author has embellished his lessons (Chalmers 1812: s.v. Batteux).

And the autobiographical letter to his nephews hints that he had suffered from the skullduggery to which orthodox academics subject any scholar who dares swim against the current. Certainly, for a man who was asked to revise the language curriculum of the Royal Colleges, and whose works were published well into the nineteenth century, Batteux is intensely unknown, even in standard histories of linguistics.

It may well have been his own fault. It would seem that most of his career was devoted to a sustained attack on the rationalist view *la grammaire générale* had of word order (cf. Scaglione 1983:200). His *Réflections sur la langue française* prefaced to the posthumous Dionysius is quite blunt about his attitude to the contemporary rationalist climate in language study:

> L'étude de la Philosophie et des Philosophes anciens, de leurs recherches et de leur ignorance sur les objets les plus interessans de la vie, avoient augmenté en moi cette persuasion à tel point, que j'ai eu besoin de revenir à la philosophie du peuple, pour me défendre de celle des Philosophes, qui jetoit de noir sur mes pensées (Batteux 1788:208).

Cette persuasion was that

> ... notre langue étant fixée par ses formes dans l'arrangement des mots, et la Latine jouissant de la plus parfaite liberté,... ce n'étoit pas chez nous qu'il falloit chercher les loix que la nature préscrit sur l'arrange-

> ment des mots, & qu'on ne pouvoit les rencontrer, s'il y en avoit, que dans les langues libres... (Batteux 1788:208)

In spite of the seeming skepticism of *s'il y en avoit* in the above quotation Batteux is enough of an eighteenth-century academic to assume that sentence orders are naturally determined. For art follows nature, and language in all its manifestations is an art, hence the inadequacy of the completely rational *ordre métaphysique*. He applies his Aristotelian tag through the sensualist principle familiar from Condillac and Locke, *la pensée et l'expression sont l'image l'une de l'autre:*

> Le lieu et la liaison des idées ne tiennent point aux langues, elles ne tiennent qu'à l'esprit, au bon sens, au raisonnement. Or l'esprit et le raisonnement ont le même procédé en françois qu'en latin (Batteux 1753 V.239).

In the fifth volume of *Principes de littérature* Batteux attacked this question from two angles: a closely argued discussion of rhetoric as a theory of language, and a careful demonstration of translation as a language act. He sees three possible principles which theoretically may guide sentence order: grammar, metaphysics and *l'intérêt ou le point de vue de celui qui parle*. The grammatical order, that is subject followed by verb followed by object, he dismisses as artificial, unnatural and therefore harmful:

> L'ordre grammatical est une entrave donnée à l'esprit et aux idées, plutôt qu'une règle de construction. Attachée au génie de l'analogie particulière d'une langue, nulle part il n'est absolument le même. Il y a des langues où il est précisément le contraire de ce qu'il est dans d'autres langues : ce qui ne pourroit arriver s'il étoit naturel. (Batteux 1753 V.10–11)

Note the denial that there is such a thing as a grammatical universal. Batteux does not even bother to counter the philosophers' theory that a natural sentence being bound by the *ordre de l'entendement,* it began with the doer (the grammatical subject), continued with the action (finite verb), and finished with the result (the object). By implication he refutes Charles Maupas's famous principle that French was the only language that consistently followed this natural order, and ridicules the claim (cf. Cordemoy in *Discours physique de la parole)* that sound grammatical concepts followed nature. The metaphysical order too is outside the normal run of language use: "Il en est de même de l'ordre métaphysique. Il peut être bon quelquefois pour les savans, quand ils discutent ou qu'ils analysent leurs idées" (Batteux 1753 V. 11). And thus the third, le *point de vue de celui qui parle,* he claims as the only natural sentence order: "...l'arrangement naturel des mots est réglé par l'importance des objets." For only in this way can one attain the *naiveté* essential in language use.

Batteux speaks of the sentence as a process of constructing meaning. It begins with a *début* and goes to a *but*. The *début* is his *objet important,* which is not necessarily the grammatical subject, as the general grammarians taught, but can be any predominant idea represented by any part of speech. Thus while his sentences have beginnings they do not have ends, but expressive goals. Batteux's mentor for this flagrantly functional attitude is Dionysius of Halicarnassus, which explains why Batteux does not acknowledge Condillac, the more modern authority. He presents his translation of Dionysius as a supplement to the posthumous edition of *Principes de littérature*. Dionysius derives sentence orders from three expressive principles: intellectual priorities, affective priorities, and audial priorities. Batteux reduces them all to the one principle: "L'ordre naturel est que l'objet important soit à la tête" (Batteux 1788 V.§ 9). At least in appearance this idea could have been taken from Condillac. Certainly Batteux agrees with him that language is not a direct image of reality, but an image of the speaker's reaction to reality. It is for this reason that the audial aspect of language ranks with the intellectual and affective, and can override either. Though he admits that his ideas are much more congenial to the Classical Languages with their relatively free word-orders, he demonstrates quite convincingly that French is quite flexible enough to abandon the "grammatical word-order", and does so by inversion of normal sentence orders, a rather sensitive subject for both him and his adversaries.

The section on translation at the end of Part 3 of the *Principes de littérature* is based on a type of contrastive discourse analysis betweeen Latin and French. His English and German translators pay lip service to

French as the language of comparison used by the author, but make a spectacularly successful job of acclimatising Batteux to their own languages. Batteux's exploits to the fullest his principle that rhetorical priorities are more natural and universal than grammatical. His first axiom is that the translator must not meddle with

> ...l'ordre des choses, soit faits, soit raisonnemens ; puisque cet ordre est le même dans toutes les langues, & qu'il tient à la nature de l'homme plutôt au génie particulier des Nations (Batteux 1753 V.269).

His second rule is: "Qu'on doit conserver aussi l'ordre des idées, au du moins celui des membres..." (Batteux 1753 V.269). And the third is that one must preserve the periods of the source text in the target:

> ...parce qu'une période n'est qu'une pensée composée de plusieurs autres pensées, qui se lient entre eux par des rapports intrinsèques ; et que cette liaison est la vie de ces pensées, & l'objet principal de celui qui parle (Batteux 1753 V.269).

His first rule is obviously intended to deal with conceptual universals as expressed in sentences; rules 2 and 3 are concerned with particular manifestations of these universals in individual languages.

It is worth looking at what is meant by *pensée* here. Furetière 1690 s.v. *pensée,* gives two meanings of interest to us:

> Tout ce qui vient dans l'esprit, dans l'imagination, dans la mémoire. ...se dit aussi de quelque belle parole, de quelque dit notable d'un homme d'autorité.

Batteux uses both of these meanings. *Pensée* is clearly semantic, and not grammatical. *Idée* is a conceptual primitive usually expressed by a word no matter its part of speech, *membre* is a phrase or clause, *Choses, faits* and *raisonnemens* seem to be relatively general terms meaning ideas in isolation, or ideas connected one to another, no matter their part of speech. It is not surprising then that rule 4 enjoins preserving all the conjunctions unless they can be compensated for functionally.

In his version of Cicero's *Pro Archia* ii.3 offered as an illustration of his ideas on translation, Batteux 1753 V.271–272 also demonstrates his theories on language:

> Sed ne cui vestrum mirum esse videatur, me in quaestione legitima, & in judicio publico, cum res agatur apud Praetorem populi Romani lectissimum virum, & apud serenissimos Judices, tanto conventu hominum, ac frequentia, hoc uti genere dicendi, quod non modo a consuetudine judiciorum, verum etiam, a forensi sermone abhorreat: quaeso a vobis, ut in hac causa mihi detis hanc veniam, accommodatam huic reo, vobis, quemadmodum spero, non molestam; ut me, pro summo poeta, atque eruditissimo homine dicentem, hoc concursu hominum litteratissimorum, hac vestra humanitate, hoc denique Praetore exercente judicium, patiamini de studiis humanitatis ac litterarum paulo loqui liberius; & in eiusmodi persona, quae propter otium ac studium minime in judiciis periculisque tractata est, uti prope novo quodam est inusitato genere dicendi.

His translation of this sentence, made *sans la couper*, is:

> Mais comme l'affaire que je plaide est une question de droit, une cause publique, qui est porté au tribunal du Préteur du peuple Romain, & devant les Juges les plus austères ; & que cependant j'ai dessein de la traiter d'une manière qui paroitra peu conforme à l'usage du barreau : j'ai, Messieurs, à vous demander une grace, que vous ne pouvez me refuser, eu egard à la condition de celui que je défends, & dont j'espere que vous ne vous repentirez pas vous-mêmes : c'est qu'ayant à parler pour un poëte célèbre, pour un savant, en présence de tant de gens de Lettres, devant des Juges si polis, & un Préteur si éclairé, vous me permettiez de m'etendre avec quelque liberté sur le mérite des Lettres : & que, comme je représente un homme qui est etranger dans les affaires, & qui ne connoit que l'etude & les livres, vous trouviez bon que je m'exprime moi-même d'une manière nouvelle, & qui pourra paroître etrangere dans le barreau.

The Cicero gobbet is a good illustration of his methods; and his claims for it recall Cicero *De optimo genere oratorum* v. 14: "Si on la coupoit, les membres cesseroient d'avoir les mêmes formes & les mêmes regards, & le traducteur seroit infidele" (Batteux 1753 V.272). This principle of translation is not concerned with just rhetoric: it derives from the major pillar of Batteux's theory of language, the communicative importance of linkage between ideas or *pensées:* "cette liaison est la vie de ces pensées, & l'objet principal de celui qui parle" (Batteux 1753 V.27). Though his version of Cicero does seem to keep the Latin periodic structure, follow the order of its members, and preserve its legal rotundity in all its length, it shows extreme differences in clausal relationships: (Cicero's *cum res agatur...*, a clause of reason, becomes a relative clause, for example). As well there is considerable expansion of phrases into full clauses, as at the end of the passage. There Cicero's *prope novo quodam est inusitato genere dicendi* becomes *d'une manière nouvelle, & qui pourra paroître etrangere dans le barreau.* Batteux's claim that he has not cut the period is convincing only if one takes his punctuation at face value: I am sure a modern would put a full stop before *c'est:* Batteux's colon is a rhetorical punctuation mark not a grammatical, indicating a continuity of thought through the passage.

This linkage is clearly not tied to grammatical shape or function: even if one accepts that Batteux keeps Cicero's discourse priorities, his grammatical are changed as a result. Hence it is not until translation rule 11 that Batteux comes to grammar; and it is here that he shows how he avoids Latin*ismes* in French and *Gallicismes* in Latin. In a passage that looks forward to Sechehaye's *Structure logique de la phrase,* Batteux shows that just as an idea may be expressed by any part of speech, the mere fact that one language may use a certain part of speech does not bind the translator at all if he is to produce a text in conformity with the norms of his own language. In Volume IV of his *Cours* Batteux had already discussed this principle as it applies to word order in an individual language. Within the *pensée,* which corresponds to Vinay and Darbelnet's *unité de traduction,* any grammatical shape is possible. If necessary, the translator is to substitute one grammatical construction for another within the *pensée, pourvu qu'il conserve à la pensée le même corps & la même vie*. This he terms *métamorphose,* the *transposition* of moderns like Vinay & Darbelnet and Peter Newmark.

The anonymous English version of 1760 is for once quite unenterprising, calling the technique "alteration". Batteux obviously regards this section as central to his aim of teaching a rhetorically based theory of translation which will produce a natural target text. It is prefaced by a reference to Cicero *De optimo genere oratorum* v. 14, and heavily exemplified, for example:

> Itineri paratus & praelio : prêt à la marche & au combat. Cette traduction n'est point assez françoise; changeons les substantifs en verbes, prêt à marcher & à combattre. (Batteux 1753 V.279)

Strangely enough, he does not illustrate from his own Cicero passage, which yields a rich harvest of *métamorphoses: quaestione legitima* is *une question de droit,* the preposition *apud* becomes *au tribunal du,* and the adjectival phrase with its parenthetical clause, *vobis, quemadmodum spero, non molestissimam,* is completely realigned by making the parenthesis a main verb and the adjective a clause subordinate to it, *& dont j'espere que vous ne vous repentirez pas vous-mêmes.*

Where other rhetoricians and grammarians of the period had regarded grammar as the major structural principle of language, Batteux clearly gives that function to discourse, and subordinates grammar to it, claiming that grammar is the particular at the service of the universal, and the artificial at the service of the natural. The immediate result is the down-grading of grammar from an organising principle of language to the handmaid of expression. Therefore Batteux finds it easy to incorporate into his theories of language the Latin rhetorician's concept of *consuetudo,* or proper use of language according to the conventions. Thus Latinisms and Gallicisms are not merely linguistic entities in the narrow sense, they are social and behavioural as well.

In some ways Batteux is not unlike modern functionalists: in his eyes an utterance is an act of expression or communication, and all the rhetorical "extras" like elegance and energy are at the centre of the enterprise, not at the periphery. As a sentence is primarily a vehicle of meaning, universals are to be found in the way meanings are structured, not in the way they are expressed. From these considerations Batteux drew the obvious conclusion: that the predominant role France accorded grammar as the natural principle of language organisation was misguided. In rhetorical quarters, a rather popular doctrine, it would seem from the longevity of Batteux's work. By the consequent undercutting of the much pressed claim that French was superior to Latin by reason of its natural grammar, Batteux also flew in the face of the eighteenth-century flexing of the linguistic muscles of French, and, as we have seen, he was well aware of what he was doing. But in the long run, the grammatical establishment seems to have had its revenge and Batteux remains an interesting footnote in the history of both linguistics and translation.

REFERENCES

Auroux, Sylvain. 1986. "Actes de pensée et actes linguistiques dans la grammaire générale" . *Histoire de l'énonciation, HEL* 7 105–120.

Batteux, Charles. 1753. *Principes de littérature*. 5 vols. Paris: Sesaint & Saillart. (Reprint, Geneva: Slatkine, 1967.)

—. 1788. *Traité de l'arrangement des mots, traduit du grec de Denys d'Halicarnasse*. Paris: Nyon.

—. 1843. *Biographie universelle*. Nouvelle édition Paris: Desplaces.

Chalmers, Alexander. 1812. *The General Biographical Dictionary*. New edition London: Nichols et al., IV.159–160.

Cordemoy, 1668. *Discours physique de la parole*. Paris: Lambert.

Delesalle, Simone. 1984. "D'Henri Weil à Michel Bréal, ou de l'ordre des mots contre les mots d'ordre." *Matériaux pour une histoire des théories linguistiques*. ed. Auroux, Sylvain et al., 461–470. Lille: Presses universitaires.

Furetière, Antoine. 1690. *Dictionnaire universel*. 3 vols. (Ed. by Alain Rey. Paris: SNL Robert, 1978.)

Kelly, L[ouis] G[erard] 1979. *The True Interpreter*. Oxford: Blackwells.

Maupas, Charles de. 1607. *Grammaire françoise, contenant reigles... à la naïve connoissance et par usage de nostre langue*. Bloys: Philippes Caffereau.

Padley, G[eorge] A[rthur]. 1988. *Grammatical Theory in Western Europe, 1500–1700: Trends in Vernacular Grammar II*. Cambridge: University Press.

Ricken, Ulrich. 1984. "Linguistique et philosophie dans la grammaire de Condillac." Auroux, Sylvain. et al., eds. *Matériaux pour une histoire des théories linguistiques*, 337–446. Lille: Presses universitaires.

Scaglione, Aldo. 1983. "The Trivium Arts and Contemporary Linguistics: the Contiguity/Similarity Distinction and the Question of Word Order". *HL* 10.196–207.

Sechehaye, Charles Albert. 1926. *La Structure logique de la phrase*. Paris: Champion.

Grammaire normative/grammaire descriptive dans la linguistique espagnole du XVIIe siècle

MARÍA DOLORES MARTÍNEZ-GAVILÁN
Universidad de León

L'IDEE DE LA RENAISSANCE que la perfection de la langue se mesure à sa capacité d'être réduite à *l'art,* c'est-à-dire, à une mise en règles grammaticale, a abouti à l'apparition des traditions vernaculaires européennes. Outre l'attribution aux langues vulgaires d'un prestige semblable à celui des langues classiques, il existe une préoccupation commune à toutes ces langues: le choix du modèle idiomatique sur lequel il faut élaborer l'artifice grammatical.

Le problème de déterminer un niveau d'usage — littéraire, cultivé ou vulgaire — qui fournisse la base de l'établissement du système grammatical de la langue acquiert des caractéristiques propres dans chaque pays du fait de circonstances linguistiques, historiques et culturelles spécifiques.

Ainsi, par exemple, en Italie, très fragmentée politiquement et linguistiquement, la question préalable était le choix d'une variété dialectale comme standard littéraire et administratif, tandis qu'en France et en Espagne, étant donnée leur centralisation politique et le grand essor et la reconnaissance qu'avaient acquis respectivement le dialecte de la zone de Paris et le castillan, il n'était pas question de choisir une modalité diatopique mais d'élucider l'usage que l'on devrait instaurer comme norme grammaticale.

En Italie, le triomphe définitif de ce courant, dirigé par Bembo — qui préconisait le toscan archaïsant — fut possible grâce au prestige des grands lettrés du *Trecento* (Dante, Pétrarque et Boccace). Face à ce courant s'élevèrent les voix de ceux qui étaient pour le toscan actuel ou pour un pan-italien fondé sur l'usage des principales coupures du pays (v. Padley 1988:19–22). En France, face à l'absence d'autorités littéraires d'une telle taille, l'alternative était donc entre l'usage de la Cour et celui du Parlement et de la Chancellerie (v. Kukenheim 1974:94 et 210–211).

Dans les deux pays le débat tourne toujours autour des groupes ayant le prestige social et politique le plus important. En Espagne, cependant, selon la remarque de J. M. Yvancos (1986:80), le problème se manifeste sous la forme d'un affrontement entre la norme cultivée et la norme vulgaire. D'après cet auteur, les savants de l'époque ont adopté deux positions: *normativiste,* en faveur de l'usage des gens cultivés comme support de l'autorité, et *antinormativiste,* qui défend l'usage commun comme la seule source d'autorité en matière grammaticale[1]. Ces positions sont représentées respectivement par deux de nos plus importants humanistes : Nebrija et Juan de Valdés.

Pour Nebrija, l'artifice de la grammaire est le moyen d'assurer la subsistence du castillan et de le préserver de la corruption. La stabilité de la langue, qui "hasta nuestra edad anduvo suelta & fuera de regla, y a esta causa a recebido en pocos siglos muchas mudanças" (Nebrija éd. 1980:100), est possible au moyen de règles grammaticales élaborées selon l'usage et l'autorité des savants, principe de normativité inspiré de la doctrine de Quintilien[2] — qu'il avait déjà établi dans ses *Introductiones* Latin*ae* (1481)[3] —, et sur lequel il insiste dans la *Gramática de la lengua castellana* (Nebrija ed. 1980:105).

Par contre, Juan de Valdés, dans son *Diálogo de la lengua*, écrit vers 1535, participe de l'idée de l'usage commun comme source d'autorité idiomatique et, suivant les postulats du courant d'Erasme — dont il fut disciple —, il conçoit les adages et proverbes comme une concentration du savoir naturel et comme la plus précise expression du langage

1 Pozuelo (1986:87–90) remarque l'existence d'un troisième courant : le *rationaliste*, soutenu par Francisco Sánchez de las Brozas, nommé el Brocense [= Sanctius], pour qui la raison est au-dessus de l'usage et de l'autorité.

2 Quintilien, dans son *Institutio Oratoria* avait exposé les principes régulateurs du rôle de la grammaire ("Sermo constat ratione, vetustate, auctoritate, consuetudine"), où il soutenait l'usage en tant que sorti de l'approbation des érudits : "Ego consuetudinen sermonis vocabo consensum eruditorum, sicut vivendi, consensum bonorum" (I, IV).

3 Où il définit la grammaire comme "Scientia recte loquendi recteque scribendi ex doctissimorum virorum usu atque auctoritate collecta" (III, 1).

populaire. A ce propos, il affirme que "... para considerar la propiedad de la lengua castellana, lo mejor que los refranes tienen es ser nacidos en el vulgo" (Valdés 1535:48).

Les opinions pour ou contre l'un des deux courants ont été exposées non seulement dans des ouvrages sur le langage en général, mais principalement au sujet de la réforme orthographique (v. Pozuelo 1986:79), mais elles n'ont pas été fixées dans la grammaire proprement dite parce que toute la production espagnole du XVIe siècle est composée de manuels, publiés dans plusieurs pays européens, pour apprendre la langue aux étrangers, dont les objectifs didactiques conduisaient à écarter toute analyse théorique. Excepté un seul cas — l'ouvrage de Villalón, publié à Anvers[1] —, on n'envisage pas le choix d'un principe d'autorité comme support de la correction idiomatique.

Face au grand nombre de grammaires espagnoles qui voient le jour en Italie, en France, en Grande-Bretagne et aux Pays-Bas, il est surprenant de constater le peu d'attention accordée chez nous à l'étude de la langue elle-même au-delà des niveaux purement scolaires. C'est qu'en Espagne, d'après le témoignage, parmi d'autres, de Valdés lui-même, opposé à toute codification du vulgaire[2], on n'apercevait pas encore la nécessité d'une grammaire de la langue maternelle du fait que celle-ci, étant acquise de façon tout à fait naturelle — c'est-à-dire, par l'usage —, ne passait pas par l'apprentissage de règles grammaticales ; ce qui explique le peu de succès de l'ouvrage de Nebrija, qui n'a été reédité que plus de deux cents ans après.

C'est à partir du XVIIe que l'on publiera en Espagne d'autres grammaires qui lieront les deux tendances déjà mentionnées —

1 Qui adopte aussi le point de vue de Quintilien, tel qu'on l'observe dans le titre même : *Arte, o Gramática para saber hablar y escrevir enla lengua castellana: colegida dela autoridad de los Sabios, conforme ala costumbre y uso común dela lengua no corrompida* (Villalón ed. 1971:11).

2 "... ya sabéis que las lenguas vulgares de ninguna manera se pueden reduzir a reglas de tal suerte que por ellas se puedan aprender; y siendo la castellana mezclada de tantas otras, podéis pensar si puede ninguno ser bastante a reduzirla a reglas" (Valdés ed. 1969:72–73). Cf. Aldrete : "Bien cierto es, que para saber la lengua no es menester arte, ni escuela donde aprenderla en la tierra donde se usa ... En Castilla oi para hablar Romance no es menester acudir a maestros, que lo enseñen, que con el hablar mismo se sabe" (Aldrete ed. 1972:47).

normative/antinormative — et qui appliqueront à la systématisation et à la mise en règles du castillan les idées sur le principe d'autorité que l'activité grammaticale doit suivre. Cela sera possible grâce à Gonzalo Correas et Juan Villar. Avec Gonzalo Correas l'usage commun est, pour la première fois dans la tradition espagnole, l'objet de description grammaticale. Villar, en accord avec Nebrija, prétend préserver la pureté de la langue et éviter la corruption tout en imposant des normes de correction fondées sur l'usage cultivé. Les deux auteurs adoptent une attitude différente quant au but de la grammaire et au niveau d'usage sur lequel elle se fonde : grammaire du point de vue descriptif et grammaire du point de vue normatif. Je parlerai de ces deux points de vue, dans cet ordre.

L'*Arte de la lengua española* de Correas est un ouvrage d'une importance fondamentale pour notre historiographie linguistique. Bien que le poids de la tradition gréco-Latine soit remarquable, parfois excessive, dans l'analyse grammaticale qu'il pratique, il incorpore aussi d'autres innovations dont certaines surprennent par leur actualité. A mon avis, cet ouvrage est important pour l'histoire de la grammaire pour plusieurs raisons. D'un côté, il s'agit du premier auteur qui admet ouvertement, dans notre tradition vernaculaire, l'existence d'universaux linguistiques à côté de phénomènes particuliers, propres et spécifiques à toute langue, et il considère donc que la grammaire doit conjuguer ces deux aspects. D'un autre côté, sa mise au point descriptive et sa conception de la langue comme un diasystème constitué de modalités dialectales, sociales et stylistiques fait que Correas élabore une analyse extrêmement minutieuse de la langue espagnole, où toute diversité de langage est possible, ce qui constraste avec la rigueur de la grammaire normative, qui rejette tout ce qui n'est pas subordonné à un modèle de correction déterminé : le langage cultivé généralement.

L'orientation universaliste de Correas, présentée nettement dans le texte qui suit : "La Gramatica en lo general es comun á todas las lenguas, i una mesma en todas" (Correas 1625:9–10), a été attribuée par plusieurs auteurs à l'influence de El Brocense. A. Yllera soutient que l'*Arte* de Correas est "la mejor herencia en España de la *Minerva*", en tant qu'il s'agit de l'ouvrage "que pretende con mayor coherencia elaborar una gramática romance razonada y apoyada en los principios generales que se suponen comunes a todas las lenguas, puesto que se basan en la razón humana" (Yllera 1983:664 et 656)[1]. Etant donné que Correas croit à l'universalité des catégories linguistiques, il envisage la possibilité de faire l'étude de plusieurs langues successivement et selon la même méthode, car, selon leur essence, elles partagent toutes les mêmes règles grammaticales. C'est cela justement qui détermine la publication du *Trilingue de tres artes de las lenguas Castellana, Latina, i Griega, todas en Rromanze* (Salamanca, 1627), ouvrage qui correspond à l'idée selon laquelle l'étude préalable des préceptes au moyen de la grammaire de la langue maternelle aidera à l'apprentissage postérieur des langues classiques, étant donnée l'existence d'un ensemble de catactéristiques communes à toutes ces langues.

Le *Trilingue* n'est pas une grammaire générale, et moins encore l'*Arte de la lengua*. Mais une fois que son auteur accepte le postulat de l'existence d'universaux linguistiques, cela a ses répercussions sur l'élaboration d'arts particuliers. C'est le même cas que pour la *Minerva* de El Brocense, selon l'analyse de A. Yllera (1983:653–654) ; il s'agit d'une grammaire latine et, par conséquent, d'un art particulier, mais étant fondée sur la raison universelle, elle révèle des principes valables pour toute langue.

La conception de la grammaire que soutient Correas permet de conjuguer la description des caractéristiques particulières aux langues avec la considération des catégories grammaticales tenues pour universelles :

> (Las lenguas) convienen en lo xeneral, i maior parte de la Gramatica aunque sean sus vocablos i frases diferentes, i por esto pareze ser natural á los onbres su conzierto i convenienzia, i desconvienen en propiedades i cosas particulares. Arte de Gramatica se dize la que contiene i enseña los prezetos xenerales que convienen á todas las lenguas, i los particulares que pertenezen á sola aquella de que se trata (Correas 1625:129).

[1] Cfr. Padley (1988:187 et 1985:276–282). D'après la thèse d'Yllera, Correas et Villar, sous l'influence de El Brocense, appliquent à l'étude de la langue espagnole les principes rationalistes qu'il avait mis en pratique dans sa grammaire latine.

Bien que tout au long de l'ouvrage il fasse allusion à ces catégories générales, telles que les parties du discours (Correas 1625:133–134), dans la pratique, son analyse est centrée sur ce qui est propre et spécifique au castillan, à tel point que sa description de la langue espagnole est la plus ample et la plus minutieuse de l'époque. Et c'est justement dans sa profonde capacité d'observation des phénomènes linguistiques que la maîtrise de Correas se révèle au plus haut point.

Les passages où il montre sa conception de la grammaire comme une discipline purement descriptive et subordonnée à l'usage commun sont peu communs à son époque et, de ce fait, surprenants :

> Bien podemos conzeder que todos saben el uso de la Gramatica en las lenguas que se crian i son naturales sin atender á prezetos ni saber que los ai, que por eso las hablan i entienden solo por el uso rrexido con la sinple i natural arte, el qual en ellas es mas poderoso que los prezetos i rreglas que del mesmo salieron. Mas con los prezetos puestos en arte, ó con la natural arte advertida i puesta en metodo, ó conzierto se entienden mexor i conservan las lenguas, como suzede oi á la Hebrea, i Caldea, i antigua Araviga, i á la Griega, i á la Latina que dexaron de ser vulgares, i son dotrinales i se estudian por arte i prezetos como otra zienzia (Correas 1625:130).

Dans ce passage, Correas fait une distinction entre *art naturel* et *art grammatical*. L'*art naturel* consiste en la connaissance que le sujet parlant possède sur sa langue, c'est-à-dire, celui qui lui permet de parler et de comprendre la langue sans avoir besoin des explications du grammairien. L'*art naturel* n'est rien d'autre que l'usage, le "hablar natural ó usual de las xentes en sus lenguas", comme il le dira ailleurs, c'est à dire, l'ensemble d'habitudes linguistiques de la communauté parlante.

L'art grammatical, compétence du grammairien, à savoir, des érudits de la langue, n'est qu'une formalisation de l'art naturel par des règles et des préceptes. A partir de l'observation et d'une élaboration théorique postérieure, le grammairien explique, systématise, met en *método* ou *conzierto* les usages idiomatiques. De cette façon, la langue espagnole — de même que les langues classiques — se transforme en objet scientifique dans la mesure où elle est étudiée "por arte i prezetos como otra zienzia".

Correas adhère au courant qui défend l'usage comme principe suprême de la langue, à l'exemple de Valdés et Aldrete. Mais, tandis que pour ces auteurs la codification grammaticale de la langue maternelle n'est pas nécessaire puisque cette dernière est acquise par l'usage, la position de Correas est justifiée par l'idée de la Renaissance selon laquelle les langues ne subsistent ni n'atteignent la dignité des langues classiques qu'au moyen de l'art grammatical.

La priorité de l'art naturel sur l'art grammatical est nettement établie à partir du moment où Correas affirme que "el uso ... es mas poderoso que los prezetos i rreglas que del mesmo salieron". Sa position est donc fort éloignée des exposés de la grammaire normative, qui impose un modèle de correction auquel le sujet parlant doit se tenir. Mais, dans la conception de Correas, la grammaire n'est pas au-dessus de l'usage, bien au contraire : c'est de l'usage même — de l'art naturel — que proviennent les préceptes dont la grammaire est constituée. Dans ce contexte, les *rreglas o prezetos* qu'il mentionne constamment ne doivent pas être considérés comme des normes de correction auxquelles l'usage doit être subordonné, mais plutôt comme des principes explicatifs qui formulent et systématisent les phénomènes linguistiques, idée analogue à celle de El Brocense dans cette affirmation : "regla es aquella cosa que se explica brevemente; de suerte que el derecho no se tome de la regla, sino que se haga la regla a partir del derecho que ya existe" (El Brocense ed. 1976:46). Pour Correas la grammaire est donc une discipline purement descriptive. Mais, quel usage doit-il décrire ou subordonner à la codification grammaticale? Comme on peut le déduire du texte ci-dessous, l'auteur défend ouvertement l'usage commun :

> La Gramatica es arte, ó zienzia de hablar conzertada i propiamente en la orden de las palavras, considerada i sacada de la conformidad i conzierto del hablar natural ó usual de las xentes en sus lenguas (Correas 1625:129).

Ce sont les habitudes linguistiques de la communauté, propres à tous les sujets parlants, qui fournissent le fondement de l'établissement du système grammatical de la langue.

Ses critiques incessantes contre l'affectation du langage de la Cour et contre l'élaboration érudite du langage des gens cultivés (v., par exemple, Correas 1625:90, 144, 363 et 385) s'exerce surtout quand ceux-ci s'écartent de la *propriété* ; autrement dit, l'expression simple, naturelle et nette est la seule norme linguistique qu'il prône. C'est pourquoi il revendique l'usage populaire, puisque c'est dans "la xente de mediana i menor talla, en quien mas se conserva la lengua i propiedad" (Correas 1625:144), ce qui explique son intérêt pour les adages et proverbes, compilés dans son ouvrage monumental *Vokabulario de Rrefranes i Frases Proverbiales*, attitude qui rappelle celle de Juan de Valdés et qui a été interprétée comme la persistance pendant tout le XVIIe siècle des idées d'Erasme (v. Padley 1988:188).

Finalement, Correas n'a pas pour dessein l'imposition d'un modèle de correction idiomatique en tant que patrimoine exclusif d'un groupe social déterminé. Au contraire, par sa profonde connaissance des variétés de la langue et sa grande capacité d'observation, il admet même la multiplicité de normes, à condition qu'elles soient subordonnées à son idéal de propriété.

Ce qui étonne dans le long texte — que je transcris dans son intégralité — c'est sa coïncidence avec certains postulats de la linguistique moderne : il établit sa conception de la langue comme un grand ensemble de dialectes, de niveaux sociaux et de styles, et c'est la raison pour laquelle on a considéré qu'il "se anticipó en más de tres siglos a la sociolingüística de nuestro tiempo" (Lope Blanch 1986:44) :

> Ase de advertir que una lengua tiene algunas diferenzias, fuera de dialectos particulares de provinzias, conforme á las edades, calidades, i estados de sus naturales, de rrusticos, de vulgo, de ziudad, de la xente mas granada, i de la corte, del istoriador, del anziano, i predicador, i aun de la menor edad, de muxeres, i varones: i que todas estas abraza la lengua universal debaxo de su propiedad, niervo, i frase: i á cada uno le esta bien su lenguaxe, i al artesano no le esta mal escoxer lo que parece mexor á su proposito como en el traxe: mas no por eso se á de entender que su estilo particular es toda la lengua entera, i xeneral, sino una parte, porque muchas cosas que él desecha, son mui buenas i elegantes para el istoriador, anziano, i predicador, i los otros (Correas 1625:144).

On peut observer dans le texte la distinction que Correas établit entre variantes diatopiques ou de lieu ("dialectos particulares de provinzias"), variantes diaphasiques ou de style ("de la corte, del istoriador ... i predicador") et variantes diastratiques ou d'état social ("conforme á las edades, calidades, i estados de sus naturales"). Plus encore, il détermine en toute netteté les facteurs ou variables dont se sert la sociolinguistique de nos jours : l'âge ("del anziano ... i de la menor edad"), le niveau social ("de vulgo" et "de la xente mas granada"), le milieu urbain ou rural ("de rrusticos" et "de ziudad") et le sexe ("de muxeres, i varones").

Correas ne considère pas qu'une des ces variétés soit supérieure aux autres et ne pose pas entre elles une hiérarchie. Finalement, la *propriété* reste le seul critère d'évaluation qu'il introduit. "A cada uno le esta bien su lenguaxe" — affirme l'auteur —, ce qui prouve son attitude ouverte devant les phénomènes linguistiques, si éloignée de la rigidité du critère sélectif de la grammaire normative. La position de Correas sur le rôle de la grammaire et des types d'usage à codifier constitue une grande nouveauté pour les études linguistiques, non seulement en Espagne mais aussi par rapport au reste des traditions vernaculaires européennes. Au XVIIe siècle, aussi bien en France qu'en Italie, la grammaire, favorisée par les académies, dont le dessein principal consistait à préserver la pureté de la langue, s'engage dans la correction idiomatique. Tandis que l'usage des gens cultivés et celui des écrivains s'érige en principe d'autorité, l'usage commun est généralement considéré comme source de fautes et d'erreurs.

L'italien Buonmattei, non plus, n'a pas l'ampleur de critère de Correas. Son monumental *De la lingua toscana* (Venise 1643) a été conçu comme un ouvrage analogue à l'*Arte de la lengua* de Correas par sa tendance à lier les préceptes de la grammaire générale à l'observation minutieuse de la langue vulgaire[1]. Bien que Buonmattei, à l'exemple de Correas, conçoit le peuple comme "autor e padrone" de l'usage linguistique, il affirme cependant que ce sont les écrivains qui fournissent les règles de la science du langage (apud Padley 1988:152).

[1] V. Padley (1988:150 et 189). Pour un analyse des exposés universalistes de Buonmattei, v. Padley (1985:254–268) et Brekle (1975:324–329).

Il ne se tient pas à l'écart de la tradition puriste de l'Accademia della Crusca, dont il fut le secrétaire, raison pour laquelle il adhère à la tendance qui prône le toscan archaïsant des auteurs du *Trecento*. Alors que Correas fait de l'usage commun le fondement de l'activité grammaticale, Buonmattei s'en sert seulement occasionnellement et comme si c'était une simple vérification additionnelle.

Le traité de Juan Villar est tout à fait opposé à l'ouvrage de Correas. Villar, poussé par le désir de "ver nuestra lengua castellana ajustada a el rigor de reglas y preceptos de la gramatica suya" (Villar 1651 : *A El lector*), adopte, dans la période étudiée, une position normativiste, ce que l'on déduit du titre même de son ouvrage : *Arte de la lengua española. Reducida a reglas y preceptos de rigurosa gramática* (Valence 1651). Villar admet l'existence de catégories grammaticales communes à toutes les langues, ce qui, en dernier ressort, lui permet de justifier l'utilité de sa grammaire comme accès à la grammaire latine, ce qui coïncide donc avec la position de Correas sur ce point-là. Mais c'est le seul point de cette analogie, parce qu'il ne révèle pas une mise au point universaliste ; puisque les aspects qui sont communs aux langues, étant stabilisés et privés de toute modification, n'ont pas besoin d'un critère normatif ou correcteur, ils ne font pas partie de son projet.

Villar observe à ce propos que ce sont justement les caractéristiques spécifiques et particulières aux langues qui sont les plus propices à *alteraciones* et *mudanças* et celles qui portent atteinte à la pureté de la langue :

> Enseñado à la experiencia de tiempo largo, que la lengua vulgar de qualesquiera naciones, adquirida con sola imitacion de el comun uso, no ayudada de arte, o reglas, con lo que de nuevo se va en ella introduciendo, se corrija, y ajuste, padece frequentes alteraciones y mudanças, no en el número de las partes de la gramatica, ni de la oracion; concordancias, y otras qualesquiera cosas, que a todas las lenguas son comunes; pero si, en lo que a cada qual es particular y propio.
>
> Esto es lo que està mas espuesto a yerros, y por tanto, en quien la ambicion de viciosas novedades, mas facil se disimula ... De aquí es,

> que en nuestra lengua Castellana no ay palabra, o dicion ... que de tales mudanças estê segura (Villar 1651 : *A El Lector*).

Tel que le montre le texte ci-dessus, l'attitude adoptée par Villar sur les relations entre l'usage et la norme est opposée à celle de Correas : alors que pour celui-ci l'usage est "mas poderoso que los prezetos i rreglas", Villar considère que l'usage commun, sans avoir pour support l'art grammatical, permet l'introduction de *viciosas novedades*, qui perturbent et menacent la pureté de la langue et qu'il faut corriger et ajuster. Par conséquent, le rôle attribué à la grammaire par les deux auteurs sera aussi différent : dans la conception descriptive de Correas, l'art grammatical dérive de l'usage (ou art naturel), c'est à dire que l'usage est systématisé. Dans l'orientation normative de Villar, l'art est superposé à l'usage : l'usage doit se soumettre à l'art. Pour Villar la fonction de la grammaire consiste à agir comme facteur de stabilisation idiomatique. C'est dans cette optique qu'est conçu son ouvrage, avec lequel il prétend accorder à la grammaire espagnole la même fermeté et stabilité que l'art grammatical avait attribuées à la langue latine. Tout cela est possible à partir de règles et de préceptes, de normes de correction sorties de l'usage des savants[1], et que le grammairien impose au sujet parlant afin de fixer les usages hésitants.

L'attitude puriste et normative de Villar coïncide avec les tendances qui dominent en France et en Italie à la même époque. Cependant, sa tentative a été un cas isolé et, à l'exemple de la *Gramática de la lengua castellana* de Nebrija, il lui a manqué la protection d'une institution telle que la Real Academia Española, dont Villar lui-même a été un incontestable précurseur. Toutefois, un siècle devra encore passer pour que la grammaire académique voie le jour, poussée par les mêmes idéaux de pureté et de perfection que Nebrija et Villar avaient montrés bien longtemps auparavant.

1 Ainsi, au sujet de l'emploi du relatif invariable *que* au lieu de *el cual* ou *la cual*, il considère que "no parece bien fundado el uso que algunos van introduciendo, diziendo siempre *que* en semejantes noticias, y olvidandose de la claridad, o perspecuidad de todos los doctos y cuerdos, siempre tan encomendada" (Villar 1651:71).

REFERENCES

Aldrete, Bernardo José. éd. 1972–75. *Del origen y principio de la lengua castellana o romance que oi se usa en España* (Rome 1606). Éd. facs. et étude de L. Nieto Jiménez. Madrid : C.S.I.C. 2 vols..

Brekle, Herbert Ernst 1975. "The Seventeenth Century". *Historiography of Linguistics,* éd. par Th. A. Sebeok, 277–382. La Haye/Paris : Mouton.

Correas, Gonzalo. 1625. *Arte de la lengua española castellana*. Éd. et étude de E. Alarcos García. Madrid : C.S.I.C, 1954.

Kukenheim, Louis 1974. *Contributions à l'histoire de la grammaire italienne, espagnole et française à l'époque de la Renaissance*. Utrecht : H&S Publishers (Réimpression de la première édition, Amsterdam, 1932.)

Lope Blanch, Juan Manuel 1986. "La lingüística española del Siglo de Oro". *Actas del VIII Congreso de la Asociación Internacional de Hispanistas*. Vol. I.37–58. Madrid : Istmo.

Nebrija, Antonio 1492. *Gramática de la lengua castellana*. Salamanque : chez l'auteur. (Éd. et étude de A. Quilis. Madrid : Editora Nacional, 1980.)

Padley, G.Arthur 1985. *Grammatical Theory in Western Europe. 1500–1700. Trends in Vernacular Grammar. I*. Cambridge : University Press.

— . 1988. *Grammatical Theory in Western Europe. 1500–1700. Trends in Vernacular Grammar. II*. Cambridge : University Press.

Pozuelo Yvancos, José María. 1986. "Norma, uso y autoridad en la teoría lingüística del siglo XVI". A. Quilis & H.-J. Niederehe (éds.). *The History of Linguistics in Spain,* 77–94. Amsterdam/Philadelphie : John Benjamins.

Sánchez de las Brozas, Francisco. 1587. *Minerva o De la propiedad de la lengua Latina*. Éd. de F. Rivera Cárdenas. Madrid : Cátedra, 1976.

Valdés, Juan de. 1535. *Diálogo de la lengua*. Éd. de J.M. Lope Blanch. Madrid : Castalia, 1969.

Villalón, Cristóbal de. 1558. *Gramatica Castellana*. Éd., facs. et étude de C. García. Madrid : CSIC, 1971.

Villar, Juan. 1651. *Arte de la lengua española*. Valence : Francisco Verengel.

Yllera, Alicia. 1983. "La gramática racional castellana en el siglo XVII: la herencia del Brocense en España". *Serta Philologica F. Lázaro Carreter natalem diem sexagesimum celebranti dedicata*. I.649–666. Madrid : Cátedra.

How to "Improve" a Language: The Case of Eighteenth Century Descriptions of Greenlandic

ELKE NOWAK
Universität Stuttgart

1. GRAMMARS TEND to have a strong impact on the languages they describe. Grammars are not merely descriptions of languages but ways of representation and interpretation. These interpretations tend to gain a remarkable amount of prescriptive capacity. Grammars offer explanations of how a certain language works, these explanations are taken over and used, and finally they will be taken for granted.

Grammars make use of concepts, categories and a certain terminology, all of which were not developed with regard of just the one language to be described. Grammars are used as tools; they are means of describing the ways of the functioning of languages.

The prescriptive capacity of Latin grammar and its impact on European languages is well known and needs no further explanation. It is easy to imagine that this impact was even stronger on a language like Greenlandic, a language entirely different from Indo-European languages.[1] While the most obvious shortcomings and misunderstandings are overcome today, there still remain essential difficulties, most of which are due to the polysynthetic nature of the language and its syntactic structure. In syntax the traditional notions subject, object and transitivity as well as the sentence pattern linked to them play an im-

[1] Greenlandic (Kalaallisut) represents the eastern most branch of the Eskimo language group. It is closely related to the languages spoken by the Inuit (Eskimo) of the Canadian Eastern Arctic, Northern Quebec and Labrador. Greenlandic is spoken by approximately 50.000 people. In Greenland it is the language of every day life as well as the official language and the language of education. Today Greenlandic looks back on a tradition as a literary language of at least 140 years.

portant but not very fortunate role. The notion ergativity does not add much of an improvement to the problem.

2. Missionary work in Greenland started in 1721 when the Norwegian minister Hans Povelsøn Egede (1686–1751) arrived and founded a permanent mission close to the present capital Nuuk. He was in search of the descendants of the vikings, who had first settled in Greenland as early as the year 1000. Later these people had adopted the Christian belief and even had had a bishop. At the beginning of the eighteenth century the contact with the colony had been lost for more than 200 years, yet it had not been completely forgotten. But Egede could not find a trace of the old settlements, he only met Greenlanders who had no knowledge of Christianity.

The earliest grammar on an "Eskimo language" is Paul Egede's *Grammatica Grönlandico–Danico–Latina* which was published in Copenhagen in 1760. Paul Egede (1708–?) was the son of Hans Egede, and had come to Greenland as a child. In the years between 1721 and 1760 a number of manuscripts on the Greenlandic language were written, and Paul Egede's grammar is likely to be not only the result of his own linguistic work. His father had tried to delve into the language from the very beginning; when he first came to Greenland he was not only provided with the word list published by Olearius (1656) but yet another one to be found in Resen's Atlas Danicus of 1680.[1] The necessity to communicate with the Greenlanders was demanding and consequently the linguistic work gained such importance that in 1723 an assistant, Albert Top (1697–1742[?]), was sent to help Egede. Egede and Top started collecting words, inflectional paradigms as well as single phrases. In the edition by Bergsland/Rischel 1986 their work has received elaborate comments and is now easily accessible. It should be

[1] The complete Atlas Danicus is unpublished; it consists of several manuscripts. The part on the Faeroe Islands was published in 1972 by Jørgen Rischel and Povl Skårup. According to Bergsland/Rischel (1986:10) the word list which is part of the section on Greenland was published in the journal *Grønland* in 1985: vol. 33, issue 5–6–7, pp. 156–192.

Concerning the different manuscripts see the introduction by Rischel/Skårup to the 1972 edition, esp. pp. V–VI and VIII–IX; concerning the sources of the *Atlas Danicus* see pp. XVIII ff, esp. XX and XXX.

pointed out that Bergsland/Rischel state explicitly the influence of traditional Latin grammar on Hans Egede's and Albert Top's work. A brief glance shows us that the same is true of Paul Egede's grammar of 1760.

In 1733 the first Moravian Brethren, Christian David (1690–1751) and Matthäus and Christian Stach arrived in Greenland. Actually they had been sent to support the Danish mission, but soon conflicts arose between Egede and David and subsequently a second mission was established. The linguistic work of the Moravians is of considerable interest. In fact they laid the groundwork of a long tradition of grammar-writing not only in Greenland but in Labrador and other places of the Arctic as well. While the later works, especially the famous grammar by Samuel Petrus Kleinschmidt (1814–1886) and the Labrador grammar by Bourquin are well known, the early manuscripts are virtually unkown.[1]

According to the guidelines of the Moravian Society the brethren were all lay brothers or lay priests. Most of them had no or hardly any formal education but were workers or craftsmen. Christian David, for example, had never attended school, and was a carpenter. The brethren were trained for their missionary task only on religious behalf and had strict instructions as regards their behaviour towards the native population. Of course they had not received any linguistic training. In later years the missionaries who had returned to Europe gave advice and worked as instructors. The manuscripts written down in Greenland were revised and used for this purpose too.

The foremost interest in linguistic work was, naturally enough, the acquisition of the language, communicating with the people and translating the bible and other religious texts into Greenlandic. Exegesis of the bible was essential for the Moravians and so literacy was regarded as necessary for everyone. As early as 1738 the Moravians established their first school in Greenland.

[1] These manuscripts are to be found in the archives of the Moravian Society in Herrnhut. They are written in the old German writing system, which is of a somewhat different appearance than the Roman alphabet and shows different characters and specific signs suitable for the German sound system.

Though Egede and David were not in agreement as to religious questions, Egede helped the Moravians during their first, extremely difficult years in Greenland. He provided them with the material on the language he had gathered, and it is no surprise if Bergsland/Rischel point out the remarkable conformity of Egede's and Top's word lists and the one given by David (Bergsland/Rischel 1986:25, 26). David's notes and his diary clearly reveal the enormous difficulties he had with tackling the language. The "manuscript by brother Christian David, how he strove to improve the Greenlandic language, together with dispersed reflections on Scriptural conversations"[1] is not really more than a private note book, but its title is revealing: it was necessary to "improve the language" because its lack of so many important European and Christian features, names and terms as well as of words for things and animals not in existance in Greenland. Of course this lack was taken as an intellectual deficiency which had to be overcome. Moreover, this "improvement" was absolutely necessary for any translation into Greenlandic. While the missionaries gathered knowledge of the language by pointing at things and asking for their "names", they simply turned that precedure round and "named" all these concepts they were in want of. Especially during the first decades this was accomplished by taking the German words, adjusting them more or less to Greenlandic pronunciation and giving them a Greenlandic ending. In his letters to Bourquin Kleinschmidt mocks that attitude,[2] but he himself takes great pains to create acceptable Greenlandic versions for biblical names, geographical places and so on. The first comprehensive grammar written by a Moravian brother was "a grammatical introduction into the learning of the Greenlandic

[1] "ein manuscript vom bruder Christian David, wie er sich bemüht hat, die grönländische sprache zu verbessern, nebst dazwischen kommenden betrachtungen über biblische gespräche", 14.Dec. 1733. All translations given in this text are mine.

[2] Kleinschmidt wrote to Bourquin: "The older spelling books contain several pages with the most awful syllables, all of which are utterly impossible in the Greenlandic tongue *(baurng, beirng* and so on). In the Labrador spelling book (1812, 20 and 42) there are syllables *(zug, zal, zom, jeing, urng, irng* and so on) which are probably as different from true Eskimo as, for example, Chinese is from German." (See Holtved 1964:22,23)

language" (1755) by Johann Beck (1706–1777). Beck had come to Greenland in 1734 and was to stay there until his death in 1777. In spite of the fact that he had never gone to school, he not only composed this treatise, but also did nearly all of the early translation work and was known as the one who had mastered the language. His writings were used extensively and copied several times. Again, the similarities with Egede's grammar are striking, and it is very likely that Beck just took over at least the outline of that grammar.

He starts off with the "letters" ("de literis") and then proceeds to "words". His unfamiliarity with grammatical categories and terminology becomes quite obvious when he writes: "adjective nouns are expressed by past tense, which is used by means of the participle, i.e. *-tok and -pok"*.[1] Interestingly enough, Beck has serious problems to distinguish nouns from verbs, but he clearly recognizes the fundamental differences between stems and affixes, which he calls "augments". The cases he distinguishes correspond to those of Latin and are given as nominative, which is the unmarked absolutive, genitive, which is the ergative *(-up),* dative, accusative, ablative and vocative. It is not surprising that there is no discussion of sentence structure or the relation indicating verbal endings.[2] Beck arranges verbal paradigms according to phonetic variations[3] and tries to establish tenses: present, past and future. Quite clearly he recognizes the different moods. Beck provides a wealth of examples and lists of words, so that the manuscript sometimes resembles more of a dictionary.

[1] "Nomen Adjektivum werden gemeiniglich durch Präteritum ausgesprochen, welches participialiter i.e. mit *-tok* und *-pok* gebraucht wird." The pagination of Beck's manuscript is incomplete.

[2] Verbal inflection in Greenlandic expresses mood, person, number and transitivity or intransitivity. The transitive forms relate to two persons and indicate the relation of these persons as well: for example *takuvakkit* "I see you (sgl)" as opposed to *takuvaannga* "they see me" or *takuvavut* "we see them". All possible relations can thus be expressed. Reflexives are not included in that paradigm so that all of these forms are non-reflexive.

[3] He gives *-kpok; -rpok; -pok; -ok and -rok;* the first three variations are of no importance at all. As can easily be seen they just indicate the final consonant of the preceeding stem.The last two forms are harder to understand. The first probably tries to catch the variation due to a preceeding vowel; in Beck's orthography this should be *-vok*. The last ending is enigmatic, as are the forms *gau, -kau and -rau.*

Four years before Beck's death, Christof Michael Königseer (1723–1786) arrived in Greenland, the next in a succession of grammar writers and the first with a decent education, the first who was familiar with Latin grammar. Königseer had worked on Greenlandic texts even before he had come to Greenland, probably he had used or even revised Beck's extensive materials. His task was to improve the *Grammar of the* Greenlandic *language,* which is Beck's *Introduction.* This improvement consisted of a more professional arrangement, the elimination of terminological inconsistencies and didactic adjustments such as the explanation of Greenlandic examples, which were contrasted with their German counter parts. The greater professionality had the effect that the generally expected grammatical frames and features were imposed on the language with much more intensity than in Beck's case, who had never had real command of them. Königseer's grammar provides striking examples of the discrepancies between the frameworks and categories introduced by the grammarians and the properties of the language. Königseer noticed that there is no inflectional marking of the various tenses, but nevertheless he arranged different paradigms according to the familiar tense system. The same is true of active and passive: he states explicitly that there is no difference in inflection between active and passive, but again he fulfils the requirements of Latin grammar and gives two sets, which turn out to be the same. Later he states that passive is expressed by means of affixes, but he is unable to merge the two aspects. Auxiliaries, he states, are never used with verbs, but with nouns as verbalizers.

What is most remarkable is his attempt at syntax. It primarily deals with cases and clearly reveals the descriptive and terminological difficulties which today are an essential part in the discussion of ergativity.

3. Königseer's grammar was copied at least twice and used widely not only by the missionaries for their own purposes, but it also very likely provided the background for the lessons given to Greenlandic pupils. They had to overcome two enormous obstacles to understanding what the missionaries were talking about: the newly invented words and concepts and the whole world of ideas connected with them as well as the way their language was handled by the Europeans. The confusion

of concepts and categories shown above, let alone their appropriateness for the language, must have had devastating effects. Nevertheless in 1825 nearly all people living within the range of the missions were able to read.

The biggest problem was the orthography set up by the missionaries. Their only means of investigation had been their untrained ears, used to listening to German or Danish sounds; the only means of preserving and categorizing the Greenlandic sounds were the Roman letters. Luckily enough the Greenlandic sound pattern is not altogether different from German, but nevertheless all idiosyncratic sounds were omitted or changed. Prominent examples are of course /k/ and /q/, which only Kleinschmidt distinguished as different phonemes and introduced ĸ for discrimination of /q/ in writing. Without any doubt it was assumed that there must be five vowels and again it was Kleinschmidt who understood that there are only three vowels, /i/e/ and /o/u/ being allophones (Kleinschmidt 1851:1; Holtved 1964:22). One of the few compromises he made however was just to keep on with the familiar writing of five instead of three vowels only; he agreed at last for the sake of his fellow missionaries.

When Kleinschmidt started his linguistic work in 1845 he had the strong feeling that it would be best to make a new start. He thought very little of the existing grammars, the only exceptions being Egede's grammar which he held in high esteem as pioneering work, and the work of Otho Fabricius. Kleinschmidt changed the orthography completely and fought hard to establish it as a standard. In his letters to Labrador missionary Theodor Bourquin he points out the shortcomings of the traditional orthography and over and over again emphasizes the need for an adequate writing system:

> It is a pity that the orthography of the Eskimo words (in the [Labrador-] lexicon and elsewhere) does not represent the correct pronunciation, as far as I understand it. The situation seems to be similar to the one we have had and still have here [in Greenland, E.N.]: nobody was able to give a rule for the pronunciation of the letters used. One had to understand the word and its composition to be able to read it correctly. Consequently people got used so much to more or less wrong

> pronunciations that in the end they did not realize it anymore, even when they finally understood the words. This was fostered further by the fact that usually the language was not learned from the native people, but from older collegues and out of books. On top of it they themselves thought to understand the language better than the Greenlanders do. (Holtved 1964:28).

He sharpsightedly states the interplay between a distracted spelling and wrong pronunciation by the teachers and the pupils' efforts to understand and their readiness to immitate:

> I once asked Brother Kruth, ..., if the Eskimos really talked the way indicated by the spelling in the books or the way he himself talked. He answered: "yes, all who were brought up here or who have attended school speak just the way we do" (Holtved 1964:57).

Kleinschmidt tried very hard to make Bourquin change the old writing system, but he did not succeed. The Labrador grammars were largely based on the already existing Greenlandic ones and Bourquin's task was to revise them. While he took up the outline of Kleinschmidt's grammar, he did not do so with the orthography, although he admitted the shortcomings of the old one freely and even refers to Kleinschmidt and his criticisms in his own grammar (Bourquin 1891). But the resistance against any such change was extreme. The other missionaries felt strongly that a traditional system, how misleading and deficient it ever may be should not be abandoned — especially if they themselves had had to go through all the pains of adopting it. Another reason was an already printed stock of bibles. While Bourquin at last gave up the idea of a revision, Kleinschmidt had already left the Moravian Society in 1859.

Today Inuit languages are written in two different writing systems, Roman letters and syllabic, and in at least six different orthographies. These do not represent primarily phonetic differences between the languages but the history of missionary work as well as economic and political influences. In Greenland a revision of Kleinschmidt's orthography was accomplished in the early 1970s; in Labrador such a revision failed again and here the pre-Kleinschmidt Moravian orthography is still in use. In the Canadian Northwest Territories the syllabic system is cherished by the people of the Eastern Arctic, while the Western Arctic writes in Roman letters, just as the Alaskan Inuit do.

4. To return to grammatical issues, Kleinschmidt's grammar stands again for major improvements. Unfortunately he was not as successful in upholding his concept of grammar as he had been with his orthography. While the dominant role of wordformation was widely accepted, his interpretation of the Greenlandic sentence structure was set aside by later grammarians or they simply took no notice of it. Today's grammars of Inuit languages mostly exhibit the traditional pattern of subject – object – predicate, and subsequently all the confusion caused by it. The whole discussion on ergativity is due to that pattern which is not suited at all for the phenomenon. The term 'ergativity' refers to the deviant arrangement of subject and object in certain languages as well as to the distribution of thematic roles. It exhibits clearly an inclination to Latin grammar, more precisely to the typical sentence pattern, which is rearranged in a kind of mirror image interpretation, turning objects into subjects and vice versa. This interpretation not only utilizes the old concepts and categories but the whole range of connotations and expectations attached to them. These expectations inevitably obscure even strong counter-evidence. A closer look shows that the whole problem is not a matter of re-arranging subject and object. It is more likely that there are two external arguments to the transitive verbal phrase. Ergativity in Inuit languages thus is not an exotic re-arrangement of a familiar sentence structure but a phenomenon which can only be described adequately if the traditional outline of possible sentence patterns as well as traditional terminology are at least partly abandoned. Again it should be kept in mind that grammars, their concepts, categories and ways of arrangement are the product of philosophical, cultural and scientific traditions — and not neutral frameworks, which can be applied just as successfully to any language. The early manuscripts and grammars on Greenlandic provide striking examples of this inadequacy of the traditional grammatical framework. Grammars, once written, tend to influence the language, they will fix it and give an abstract and theoretical status to it. Grammars are

interpretations with the strong tendency to dominate all further investigation. Of course a generally accepted terminology will ensure scientific discourse and will make a preliminary represention of a yet little known language possible. But grammars or the generally accepted outline of grammars, the theories of grammar, categories and concepts are not a natural growth and as such necessary or unchangeable. It is important to understand their historical relativity and thus their identity as revisable constructions.

REFERENCES

Beck, Johann. 1755. *Eine grammaticalische Einleitung zur Erlernung der grönländischen Sprache, nebst derer Nomina et verb. Flexion und unterschiedenen grönländischen mit Fleiß zusammengetragen zum Gebrauch.* Herrnhut: Ms.

Bergsland, Knut & Jørgen Rischel, eds. 1986. *Pioneers of Eskimo Grammar.* (= *Travaux du Cercle Linguistique de Copenhague* 21) Copenhagen: Reitzel.

Bourquin, Theodor. 1891. *Grammatik der Eskimosprache wie sie im Bereich der Missions-Nieder-Lassungen der Brüdergemeine an der Labradorküste gesprochen wird.* Nain: Distributed by Moravian Mission Agency, London and Universitätsbuchhandlung, Gnadau.

David, Christian. 1733. *Ein Manuskript vom bruder Christian David, wie er sich bemüht hat, die grönländische Sprache zu verbessern, nebst dazwischen kommenden Betrachtungen über biblische Gespräche.* Herrnhut: Ms. 14.Dec. 1733.

Egede, Paul. 1736. *Grönländische Grammatica.* Herrnhut: Ms 8.10.1736.

—. 1750: *Dictionarium Grönlandico-Danico-Latinum.* Copenhagen: Royal Library.

—. 1760: *Grammatica Grönlandico-Danico-Latina edita a Paulo Egede.* Copenhagen: Royal Library.

Fabricius, Otho. 1791. *Forsøg til en forbedret Grønlandsk Grammatica.* Copenhagen: Royal Library

Holtved, Erik, ed. 1964. *Kleinschmidts Briefe an Theodor Bourquin.* (= *Meddelelser om Grønland,* 140/3.) Copenhagen: Reitzel.

Kleinschmidt, Samuel. 1851. *Grammatik der grönländischen sprache mit theilweisem einschluss des Labradordialects.* Berlin: Reimer. (Repr., Hildesheim: Olms, 1968.)

Königseer, Christof Michael. 1777. *Verbesserte grönländische Grammatica*. Herrnhut: Ms 1.8.1777; 215 pp.

Olearius, Adam. 1656: *Vermehrte Newe Beschreibung Der Muscowitischen und Persischen Reyse*. Schleswig (Repr. Dieter Lohmeyer, ed. Tübingen: Narr, 1971.)

Resen, Peder Hansen. 1680. *Atlas Danicus, Faerøerne*. Edited by Jørgen Rischel and P. Skårup. *Faerensia,* vol. IX.

Lichtenberg on Language and Reason: One Aspect of the Crisis in German Enlightenment*

JOHANNES ROGGENHOFER
Universität Regensburg

THE EMINENT GERMAN physicist, man of letters and philosopher Georg Christoph Lichtenberg, known today mainly for his satiric and aphoristic writings, was born in Darmstadt on 1 July, 1742. Following his two sojourns in England in 1770 and in 1774/75 — which laid the foundation for his lifelong curiosity and openmindedness as well as his lifelong anglophilia — he was given the Chair of Experimental Physics at the then leading German university in natural studies, the Georgia-Augusta in Göttingen. After having been appointed Privy Councillor (Hofrat) by George III in 1788 and elected a member of the Royal Society in 1793 (among other distinctions), he died in Göttingen on 24 February, 1799 as one of the most accomplished natural scientists and renowned authors of almanacs of his time.

What his contemporaries could not know, since he kept his remarks to himself, was that he was also perhaps the most able aphoristic writer ever to whet his quill on the German tongue. In the more than 8000 aphorisms still extant he deals with almost every subject imaginable, but most subtly and interestingly with psychology, epistemology and the philosophy of language.

His linguistic remarks have won him a special reputation ever since Wittgenstein proclaimed their philosophical merit. This has led many people to consider Lichtenberg a forerunner to the "later" Wittgenstein. In my opinion, this view is untenable and rests solely on the superficial

* I wish to thank my dear friend and colleague Steve Uppendahl for untiringly correcting my non-native English.

similarity of several of Lichtenbergs's aphorisms to some of Wittgenstein's.

If one attempts to compare their respective theories, there remain no substantial parallels whatsoever, because Lichtenberg failed to realize the importance of the process of the "making up" of rules as the central problem in the philosophy of language or any theory of meaning in particular. However, I shall not dwell on this topic, as a thorough examination would take much more time and space than I am allowed here.[1]

Let me, instead, consider Lichtenberg's own attempts to build a theory of language, scientific truth (or validity) and meaning, paying special attention to the relationship of these attempts to the general development of philosophical attitudes during the second half of the eighteenth century. It is most useful to look at Lichtenberg's language philosophy as the product of a critical analysis of mainstream Enlightenment ideas.

When reading Lichtenberg or any other thinker of the Enlightenment, one thing must never be forgotten: all their efforts in whatever field of work were unified by the common zeal to further the self-determination of man. Self-determination presupposes freedom of external oppression, where external oppression is taken to mean both mental oppression resulting from such things as superstition, ignorance, censorship and social control, and physical oppression, running the gamut from military and civil violence, punishment and persecution to physical annihilation. All of which can collectively be called terror, and it was against terror that the Enlightenment had set out to fight on its crusade. (Ironically, the Enlightenment itself ended up with nothing else but terror, *la Terreur.)*

Yet, the motto of this crusade and the credo of the crusaders had well been formulated many centuries before the Age of Enlightenment. In the first century B.C., the Roman poet Lucretius had already cast it into lucid Latin hexameters:

1 An in-depth examination of this topic is provided in the second chapter of my dissertation, cf. Roggenhofer 1992.

> Hunc igitur terrorem animi tenebrasque necessest
> non radii solis neque lucida tela diei
> discutiant, sed naturae species ratioque
> *(De rer. nat.* I 146–8).

> "This terror then and darkness of the mind must needs be
> smitten not by the rays of sun nor by the lightening
> shafts of day, but by nature's observation and reason."

Empirical observation and reason were chosen to be the weapons to fight terror and oppression and the tools to build a better world.

This program could also be found in the works of Francis Bacon, who was most highly esteemed by Lichtenberg, as can be seen from the numerous excerpts Lichtenberg wrote in his wastebooks ["Sudelbücher" — his private notebooks, containing his aphorisms, L. himself used the English commercial term "wastebooks" to define their use as a collection of materials and notes, cf. E 46).

He generally adds a few words of praise for Bacon's ingenuity in the excerpts, cf. J 1067:[1]

> Es gibt auch ein Wort Gottes zum besseren Nachdenken und sicherer Erforschung der Natur. Baco's Novum Organum ist einer der besten Kommentatoren darüber.

> "There is also a word of the Lord for a better meditation on and a more certain investigation into nature. B.'s N.O. is one of the best commentators on that."

or J 1109:

> Baco ein Magazin von Licht

> "B. a storehouse of light"

Note the use of the light metaphor in the latter remark.

[1] This notation refers to the numbering of Lichtenberg's aphorisms according to the Promies-edition.

Of course, the idea of basing philosophy (in the broad sense of the eighteenth century, still including natural sciences) on empirical investigation and reason — as postulated by thinkers like Lucretius and Bacon — was commonplace among Enlightenment philosophers and is most prominently exemplified in the works of the French encyclopedists.[1]

But the idea of a reconciliation of empiricism and rationalism, which would have put an end to the schisma of Western philosphy, had some intrinsic problems which could not possibly pass the sharp eye of Lichtenberg unnoticed, the astronomer and minute surveyor that he was.

The problem that immediately comes to mind is the following: if knowledge and the achievement of knowledge is the main purpose of Enlightenment, a concept of knowledge must be given. But empiricismand rationalism offer entirely different solutions to this problem, solutions that are so antithetical that no easy compromise can be found at all.

Both may hold true that knowledge is the adequacy of the intellect to the thing to be known. Empiricism believes the way to obtain this state of the intellect is through empirical, inductive investigation; but rationalism finds true knowledge only in the deduction of phenomena from abstract principles and eternal laws. The achievement of knowledge consists either of a vision of some kind of Platonic idea, or of reaching a degree of certainty equivalent to that with which we know of our own existence.

The recourse to Platonic ideas was prevented by their non-empirical status which excluded them by definition from scientific investigation. And everything excluded from possible scientific investigation

[1] Cf. Diderot's Prospectus (1750) for the *Encyclopédie* and d'Alembert's *Discours préliminaire* (of 1751, esp. pp. 63–65), where Bacon is honoured as a godfather to the enterprise of constructing an encompassing tree of human knowledge: "Si nous en [constructing the tree, J.R.] sommes sortis avec succès, nous en aurons principalement obligation au chancelier Bacon, qui jetait le plan d'un dictionnaire universel des sciences et des arts, en un temps où il n'y avait, pour ainsi dire, ni sciences ni arts. Ce génie extraordinaire, dans l'impossibilité de faire l'histoire de ce qu'on savait, faisait celle de ce qu'il fallait apprendre" (Diderot 1750:286).

automatically presents itself as an idol in the sense of Bacon, i.e. something that has to be overcome. Remember that Bacon himself counted the deficiencies of ordinary language to be among the *idola* fori, the Idols of the Market Place, cf. *Novum Organum* (1620; ed. Spedding/Ellis I 170):

> At idola fori omnium molestissima sunt, quae ex foedere verborum et nominum se insinuarunt in intellectum.
>
> "But the Idols of the Market Place are the most molesting of them all, which insinuate themselves into the intellect out of the union of verbs and nouns [or: of predicates and subjects]".

The belief in the absolute certainty given by the immediate feeling of one's own existence was overturned by Lichtenberg himself, because he could show an essential weakness in Descartes' argument. The *cogito* already presupposes some kind of ego, but this needs not to be so. Lichtenberg in a wellknown remark says that

> ... *Es denkt,* sollte man sagen, so wie man sagt: *es blitzt*. Zu sagen cogito, ist schon zu viel, so bald man es durch *Ich denke* übersetzt. Das *Ich* anzunehmen, zu postulieren, ist praktisches Bedürfnis" (K 76).
>
> "*It thinks,* one should say, as one says: *it thunders*. To say *cogito* is already too much, as soon as you translate it by *I think*. To assume, to postulate the *ego* is practical need" (K 76).

The problem that fuels the rationalism versus empiricism debate can be restated in linguistic terms and can be summed up by way of the following three questions:

Firstly, what is the nature of linguistic universals?
Secondly, what is the nature of consciousness?
Thirdly, what is the nature of a true scientific language?

It is easy to see how these questions overlap: every scientific language must use universals, because it must allow for generalisations, and every language is by its very nature intimately connected with consciousness.

The problem was even greater for eighteenth-century-thinkers, because they had but little notion of non-linguistic knowledge. I venture to say that, in this respect, Lichtenberg perfectly reflects the development of the philosophy of language during the eighteenth century, albeit with some delay.

For the rationalistic philosophers of the sixteenth and seventeenth centuries, the relation between language and knowledge was not problematic, because they conceived them to be nearly identical. This language-knowledge relation can be clearly seen in Spinoza and Leibniz. Knowledge was supposed to be organised in a way similar to Euclidean geometry, i.e. deducible from first principles. Once these first principles had been moulded into a perfect order, a perfect language would result and vice versa. This is why rationalists were so inclined toward the idea of a universal language.[1]

But the rise of empiricism and empirical science soon cast doubt upon this conception, and Newton's famous dictum *Hypotheses non fingo* discredited all purely deductive systems. Now, language was no longer conceived to be a carrier of perfect knowledge, but only a means to talk *about* knowledge, to spread it and to enlighten people by way of it.

Therefore, it was not an ideal, universal language that had to be constructed, but instead everyday-language had to be properly defined; and scientific terminologies had to be devised capable of expressing the empirically won knowledge. This is, what the project of the Encyclopédie and the works of Linné and Lavoisier were concerned with.

[1] But not Descartes, who was always sceptical about universal languages, because these would treat all kinds of problems and all kinds of knowledge exactly alike and not each question "iuxta suam naturam" (as he indicates in a letter to Beeckman — Adam/Tannery X 157, 4) — in strong contrast to his own "méthode", which supposedly treats different questions according to their nature. It is obvious that Descartes' method is — at least without further specification — indeed liable to the same criticism of uniformly treating things not necessarily uniform. But I shall not tackle this subject here.

If ordinary language could be made precise in its notions in accordance with scientific standard, all people could equally participate in the knowledge of the time. Thus, a democracy of knowledge could be achieved which sooner or later would lead to a democracy in politics.

But again hopes proved premature and, ultimately, in vain. The idea of setting ordinary language in a proper state presupposes that language is a passive medium which does not exert any influence of its own on minds and knowledge. Already Bacon had admitted some doubt as to whether the idols of language could really be purged, because in order to arrive at better definitions one again has to resort to words, cf. *De augmentis scientiarum* (1623; ed. Spedding/Ellis I:645):

> Quod vero hujus remedium est (definitiones scilicet) in plurimis huic malo mederi nequit; quoniam et ipsae definitiones ex verbis consistent, et verba gignant verba.
>
> "But what is the remedy of this (namely, definitions) mostly can not remedy this evil, because definitions themselves are made up of words, thus words do words beget".

Philosophers like Lichtenberg could not help recognizing that language on its own might guide and even determine the minds of men and that in the end any willful effort to reform language and terminology would tend to produce — at least at first — a worse state of affairs than before.

When he was young (in his first wastebook [1765–1770]), Lichtenberg still found the idea of a universal language appealing, cf. A 3, A 12, where he approvingly cites Leibniz. But soon he became suspicious of the feasibility and usefulness of such a project. In Book E (1775–1776) he already jokes about universal languages, when he writes the following concerning the *ars magna:*

> Er war der eigentliche Besitzer von Lullys Kunst, denn er konnte stundenlang über eine Materie disputieren ohne ein Wort davon zu verstehen (E 32).

"He was truely in possession of Lully's art, because he was able to discuss a subject matter for hours and hours without having the least understanding of it" (E 32).[1]

In Book F (1776–1779) he can be seen agreeing with the concept of ordinary language as a "melting pot of knowledge", common among Enlightenment philosophers, cf. F 474:

Man findet Spuren aller Wissenschaften in den Sprachen und umgekehrt vieles in den Sprachen, das in den Wissenschaften nützen kann.

"You can find traces of all sciences in the languages, and vice versa, there is much in the languages that can be of use to the sciences".

Later, he indulged in the problem of adequate terminologies and language reform in general, probably stimulated by his work on the revised editions of Erxleben's physical compendium and his own plan of writing a general course or handbook of physics.

[1] Prof. McMahon has suggested that this might be a paraphrase of Descartes'. The story Descartes tells in a letter to Isaac Beeckman (dated 29th April, 1619) indeed has some similarity to Lichtenberg's phrase:

'Repperi nudius tertius eruditum virum in diversorio Dordracensi, cum quo de Lulli *arte parvâ* sum loquutus: quâ se vti posse gloriabatur, idque tam feliciter, vt de materiâ quâlibet vnam horam dicendo posset implere; ac deinde, si per aliam horam de eâdem re agendum foret, se plane diversa à praecedentibus reperturum, & sic per horas viginti consequenter. Vtrum credas, ipse vederis. Senex erat, aliquantulum loquax, & cuius eruditio vtpote à libris hausta, in extremis labris potius quam in cerebro versabatur" (Adam/Tannery X 164,15–165,6).

But I am not sure whether Lichtenberg knew one of the early editions of this letter. Perhaps a more likely candidate is a passage in the Discours de la Méthode, also bearing some similarity to E 32:

"... ie pris garde que, pour la Logique, ses syllogismes & la pluspart de ses autres instructions seruent plustost a expliquer a autruy les choses qu'on sçait, ou mesme, comme l'art de Lulle, a parler, sans iugement, de celles qu'on ignore, qu'a les apprendre" (Adam/Tannery VI 17, 16–20).

On the other hand, it could also have been Bacon who inspired Lichtenberg, cf. De augmentis scientiarum VI, II:

"... Talis fuit Ars Lullii; ... quae nihil aliud fuerunt quam vocabulorum artis cujusque massa et acervus; ad hoc, ut qui voces artis habeant in promptu, etiam artes ipsas perdidicisse existimentur" (Spedding/Ellis I:669).

Yet in all three cases, there is no direct irony turned against the ars Lullii, whereas Lichtenberg's irony is clear enough.

But by the printing of the 6th edition of the Erxleben in 1794, he had become thoroughly sceptical about the whole idea, and recommended changing as little as possible. The clearest statement of his arguments is to be found in K 19–21, where he says:

> Man schreibt sehr viel jetzt über Nomenklatur und richtige Benennungen, es ist auch ganz recht, es muß alles bearbeitet und auf das Beste gebracht werden. ... Der unermeßliche Vorteil den die Sprache dem Denken bringt besteht dünkt mich mehr darin, daß sie [die Namen oder Wörter, J.R.] überhaupt Zeichen für die Sache, als daß sie Definitionen sind. ... Was die Dinge sind, dieses auszumachen ist das Werk der Philosphie. Das Wort soll keine Definition sein, sondern ein bloßes Zeichen für die Definition, die immer das veränderliche Resultat des gesamten Fleißes der Forscher ist, ... so ist es fast besser gar keines derselben [der Zeichen, J.R.] eine Definition sein zu lassen, als auf das Ansehen einiger Zeichen hin, die richtige Definitionen sind, so vielen anderen die es nicht sind einen falschen Kredit zu verschaffen. Das würde eine Herrschaft der Sprache über die Meinungen bewirken die alle den Vorteil wieder raubte den die Zeichen uns verstatten. ... Das beste Wort ist das das jedermann gleich versteht. ... Was kann es schaden die Kometen Kometen das ist Haarsterne zu nennen, und was würde es nutzen sie Brand- oder Dampf-Sterne zu nennen? (Sternschnuppe.) ... Der Dispüt hat wirklich etwas Ähnliches mit den puristischen Bemühungen der Sprachmelioristen, und Orthographen. Man hofft zu viel von guten und fürchtet zu viel von schlechten Wörtern. ..."
> (K 19)
>
> "Now, very much is being written about nomenclature [terminology] and proper namings, it is allright anyway, everything has to be worked on and brought up to its best. ... Methinks the immense advantage that language offers to thinking is altogether constituted by [names] being the signs of things rather than their definitions. ... To find out what things are really like is the work of philosophy. The word should not be a definition, but a mere sign of the definition, which is always the result of the joint industry of researchers, ... thus it is almost better to let no sign be a definition, than to give false credit to so many signs which are no true definitions on the mere reputation of some that are. That would

lead to a rule over opinions by language which would take away all the advantage that we are granted by the signs. ... The best word is the one that everybody understands at once. ... What harm can it do, if comets are called comets, i.e. "Haarsterne" [(long-) haired stars], and what would be the good of it, if they were called burning or steaming stars? (shooting star). ... The dispute is really somewhat similar to the puristic efforts of the language meliorists [reformers], and orthographers. They hope for too much from good words, and they stand too much in awe of bad words. ..." (K 19)

Nomenklatur. Auch hier ist die eingeschränkte Monarchie der Aristokratie vorzuziehen. Wenn man bloß vernünftig gewählte Ausdrücke gelten machen will, so gibts eine Aristokratie, und dann welche sind dann die vernünftigsten und wer soll darüber entscheiden? Es können ja viele gleich gut und gleich vernünftig gewählt sein. Ich halte auch hier einen geschnitzten Monarchen für den besten; geschnitzte Heiligen richten mehr aus als die beseelten. ... Hypothesen sind Gutachten, Nomenklaturen sind Mandate (K 20).

"Nomenclature. Here also constitutional monarchy is to be preferred over aristocracy. If only reasonably chosen expressions are to be made valid, an aristocracy is to result, and then which are the most reasonable and who is to decide? Many can equally well and equally reasonably be chosen. Here as well, I consider a carved monarch to be the best; carved saints accomplish more than breathing ones. ... Hypotheses are advisory, nomenclatures are mandatory" (K 20).

Nomenklatur. Ich glaube immer ist es am besten gar nicht zu reformieren. Es erweckt Erbitterung und Neid und Verachtung, auch wird zuviel über Namen geschrieben, das doch eigentlich nichts ist. Das Unsinnige verliert sich von selbst, und das was gleichsam die Natur abstößt, wächst nicht wieder (K 21).

Nomenclature. I believe it is always best not to reform at all. It wakens embitterment and envy and despise, also too much is written about names, which, virtually, is all nothing. Nonsense wanes out by itself, and that which is repulsed by nature, does not come up again" (K 21).

So, linguistic universals are to be understood as the result of the "joint industry of researchers", an idea somewhat reminiscent of Putnam, which minimally implies that the meaning of the signs denoting these universals may change in time.

On the other hand, if language is not allowed to be used with its normal vagueness and inexplicity of meaning, it may even prevent minds from further "advancement of learning" (and knowledge).

Lichtenberg seems to have developed a notion of the possible influence of language on the mind similar to Orwell's idea of the workings of Newspeak. Orwell, too, was firmly convinced that a rigidly defined language would be absolutely mandatory over human thinking.

The fatalistic and even bitter tone of K 21, given above, is almost certainly a reflection of the disappointment Lichtenberg felt about the development of the French Revolution. Here he was again quite enthusiastic in the beginning, but deeply disappointed and shocked by its practical outcome.

So, the man who early in 1796 wrote:

> Ich kann freilich nicht sagen, ob es besser werden wird, wenn es anders wird; aber so viel kann ich sagen, es muß anders werden, wenn es gut werden soll (K 293)
>
> "I really cannot say whether things will get better, once they change; but this much I can say, they have to change, if they are to turn out all right" (K 293)

and who still in the fall of 1796 acknowledged the French Revolution as being something that was irreversible by saying:

> Die Französische Revolution hat durch die allgemeine Sprache, zu der es mit ihr gekommen ist, nun ein gewisses Wissen unter die Leute gebracht, das nicht leicht wieder zerstört werden wird ... (L 25)

> "The French Revolution, by the common language it produced, has distributed a certain kind of knowledge among people that will not easily be destroyed again ..." (L 25)[1]

writes quite resignedly in 1798:

> Man spricht viel von Aufklärung, und wünscht mehr Licht. Mein Gott was hilft aber alles Licht, wenn die Leute entweder keine Augen haben, oder die, die sie haben, vorsätzlich verschließen (L 472).

> "There is a lot of talk about Enlightenment, and one wishes for more light. Lord, of what use is all [this] light, if people either have no eyes, or deliberately close those they have" (L 472).

I believe that at the end of his life Lichtenberg felt that he had failed in two important respects and that he shared these personal failures with his whole Age. The first failure was the inability to turn the ideas of the Enlightenment into real politics. There was not a single ideal of the *philosophes* that was not soiled in the course of the French Revolution. The second failure was the inability to give a clear definition of a truely scientific language that would be able to express the results of empirical science adequately and in a manner understandable to all citizens. These failures are related to each other by the fact that according to the view of the *philosophers* the democratic participation in all knowledge at hand was the necessary (and perhaps also sufficient) prerequisite for a more democratic society. The construction of a language capable of serving these demands was correctly understood to be a problem of linguistics and the philosophy of language.

Concerning Lichtenberg, I have shown the reasons why the construction of such a language proved not only unattainable, but even incompatible with the strive for man's self-determination.

As, up to now, no satisfactory theory of linguistic universals and the relation between knowledge and language has been found, linguists

[1] L 25 is clear evidence for the powerful social and political impact Lichtenberg attributes to language. The lasting merit of the French Revolution is seen in the creation of a language containing the ideas of freedom and human rights.

continue to have special reason to be doubtful about the possibility of true enlightenment, desirable as it may be, and yet for linguistic reasons, Lichtenberg's remark still holds true:

> Quaesivi lucem ingemuique reperta (L 284)
>
> "Light I sought, and I wept when I had found it."

REFERENCES

D'Alembert, Jean-(Baptiste-)le-Rond. 1751. *Discours préliminaire de l'Encyclopédie.* (Oeuvres complètes. Tome I.13–114, 1967).

Bacon, Francis. 1857–74. *The Works of Francis Bacon.* Collected and edited by James Spedding, Robert Leslie Ellis, Douglas Denon Heath. XIV vols. London: Longman & al. (Facsimile-Neudruck. Stuttgart-Bad Cannstatt : Frommann - Holzboog, 1963).

Descartes, René. 1964–74. *Oeuvres de Descartes.* Publiées par Charles Adam & Paul Tannery. Nouvelle présentation, en co-édition avec le C.N.R.S. XI tomes. Paris: Librairie Philosophique J. Vrin.

Diderot, Denis. 1750. *Encyclopédie ou Dictionnaire raisonné des sciences, des arts et des métiers. Prospectus.* (Oeuvres complètes. Edition chronologique. Tome II.281–320, 1969.)

Erxleben, Johann Polycarp. ^{6}1794. *Anfangsgründe der Naturlehre.* Mit Verbesserungen und vielen Zusätzen von G. C. Lichtenberg. Göttingen: Dieterich.

Lichtenberg, Georg Christoph. ^{2}1973. *Schriften und Briefe.* Herausgegeben von Wolfgang Promies. Bd. I: Sudelbücher I. Munich: Hanser.

— . ^{2}1975. Schriften und Briefe. Herausgegeben von Wolfgang Promies. Bd. II: *Sudelbücher II, Materialhefte, Tagebücher.* Munich: Hanser.

Roggenhofer, Johannes. 1992. *Zum Sprachdenken Georg Christoph* Lichtenbergs. Tübingen: Niemeyer.

John Wallis' *Grammatica Linguae Anglicanae* (1653): The New Science and English Grammar

JOSEPH L. SUBBIONDO
University of the Pacific

BECAUSE THE NEW science inspired by Francis Bacon (1561–1626) and Rene Descartes (1596–1650) dominated the intellectual landscape of seventeenth-century England, most historians of English linguistics have focused their attention on what they have considered the most representative, if not the only, response by the grammarians of that century to the new science — namely, the philosophical language movement. Consequently, much has been written about the leading practitioners of that movement: grammarians such as John Wilkins (1614–1672), George Dalgarno (1626–1687), and Francis Lodwick (1619–1694).

While historians of English linguistics have commented on the seventeenth-century particular grammarians (those who specialized in descriptions of English), they have generally considered their works antithetical to the goals of the new science. Most seventeenth-century particular grammarians were influenced by William Lily (c.1468–1522) and merely transferred Latin grammar to English. However, such was not the case for John Wallis (1616–1703), the most celebrated English grammarian of his time: his work reflected Cartesian empiricism in theory and practice. A study of his *Grammatica Linguae Anglicanae* (1653), the first structural grammar of English, reveals that if we are to appreciate fully the new science's impact on seventeenth-century English linguistics, we need to recognize that particular and philosophical grammars can be two sides of the same coin.

I should admit from the outset that this paper has challenged my scholarly objectivity. Having published a paper (Subbiondo 1978) on William Holder (1616–1698), I regard Wallis an incorrigibly arrogant and self-serving opportunist. Let me explain — Holder (1668) taught a deaf-mute Alexander Popham to speak and reported his work to the Royal Society; and Wallis, who worked with Popham years later, claimed sole credit for Popham's success. In his published letter to Robert Boyle (1627–1691), Wallis (1670) never mentioned Holder's work with Popham. Even when Holder protested in his rebuttal to the Royal Society (1678), Wallis (1678) still held his ground. The Holder incident was typical as throughout Wallis' life, he continually embroiled himself in disputes with scholars as prominent as Thomas Hobbes (1588–1679) and Seth Ward (1617–1689). Kemp's (1972) accounts of these controversies in the excellent introduction to his translation of the sixth edition of the *Grammatica* (all references are to this translation) will support an unsavory image of Wallis.

Yet despite his character flaws, Wallis contributed a great deal to the scientific movement. A principal founder of the Royal Society, he was widely and justifiably acclaimed for his scholarly activities in astronomy, geometry, linguistics, mathematics, philosophy, and theology. Although his extraordinary work in English phonology has been duly noted (e.g. Cohen 1977, Lehnert 1937–8, Robins 1967, Sundby 1952, and Zachrisson 1914), Wallis' English grammar, when it has been noticed, has been generally criticized for what it was not — a philosophical grammar — rather than valued for what it was — the first particular grammar constructed according to the principles of the new science.

Wallis argued that his *Grammatica* was derived from "a completely new method, which has its basis not, as is customary, in the structure of the Latin language but in the characteristic structure of ... [its] own" (p. 111). Thus unlike the school grammarians who imposed Latin grammar on English, and unlike the philosophical grammarians who designed a general grammar on what they perceived to be the conceptual structure of the mind, Wallis was the first to analyze English grammar by framing and testing hypotheses which were based on formal criteria derived from his observations of English structure. His generalizations about English grammar, arrived at through rigorous empirical inquiry, were the results of evidence and proof. Consequently, his assertions were scientifically vulnerable because they could be tested for verification.

This paper is organized around the two themes from Wallis' preceding statement on method: "characteristic structure of ... [its] own" and "a completely new method". These phrases capture the essence and the originality of Wallis' contribution to the history of English grammatical theory because they indicate the *what* and *how* of his work: *what* he understood to be the subject matter of English grammar and *how* it should be studied.

In his broad history of the English language sketched in the "Preface" (this extensive version of the "Preface" was first published in the fifth edition, 1699), Wallis delineated the subject matter of his grammar. Certainly, most readers will be impressed by his references to enough sources to provide a state-of-the-art seventeenth-century bibliography of the history of the English language (for example, he cited the works of Joseph Scaliger (1540–1609), John Davies (c.1567–1644) and Samuel Bochart (1599–1667) among many others). His history showed the range and depth of his reading as well as his talent to weave diverse sources of scholarship into a coherent history. More important than the quality and sophistication of his history of English, was his use of that history to differentiate English from other languages. He argued that since seventeenth-century English, like all natural languages, was the product of its own history, he needed to develop a grammar which would describe the unique structural characteristics of English.

Wallis' neutral acceptance of the history of English set him apart from the philosophical grammarians — after all, they invented languages because they thought that seventeenth-century English had become less communicative than earlier forms of itself or of ancient languages. To many of them, the perfect language was the first language and the linguistic consequences of the Tower of Babel could not be overcome by "improving" extant languages. On the other hand, Wallis did not consider seventeenth-century English inferior or superior to earlier versions of itself or to other languages, natural or artificial. Rather he recognized that "as a result of borrowing, and partly too just through time passing, which causes significant changes in other languages as well, the Anglo-Saxon language has slowly changed into the present English language" (p. 103). He then showed how a variety of historical factors such as migrations, politics, and dialects changed, not reduced, English lexicon, meaning, sounds, and syntax. Because he knew that English, like everything in the universe, was in a state of change, Wallis never believed that historical processes diminished the efficacy of the language. Rather, English adjusted to change and, as illustration of this, Wallis pointed out that English relied on word order to compensate for its gradual loss of inflectional and conjugational forms. In short, Wallis understood that history neither improved nor ruined language, it only changed it.

Arguing that English grammar should take into account the language's unique structure, he charged his predecessors Alexander Gil (1565–1635), Ben Jonson (1574–1637) and Henry Hexham with failing to devise

> the method which is best suited to the task. They all forced English too rigidly into the mould of Latin (a mistake which nearly everyone makes in descriptions of other modern languages too), giving many useless rules about the cases, genders, and declensions of nouns, the tenses, moods, and conjugations of verbs, the government of nouns and ... verbs, and other things of that kind, which have no bearing on our language, and which confuse and obscure matters instead of elucidating them. (pp. 109–111)

Just as in his *Tractus de Loquela,* which he later incorporated into his *Grammatica* and in which he provided the most exhaustive description of English sounds written in the seventeenth century; in his grammar, his subject matter — "the structure of the English language as a whole" (p. 277) — determined his study of it. Rather than relying on earlier studies of English grammar, Wallis offered a perspective as if he were studying the language for the first time. To see this, we need only look at his grammatical terminology: he recognized that much of the traditional nomenclature was simply inappropriate to describe English structure. Thus, he used only those Latin terms such as "noun", "pronoun", "transitive", and "mood", which were still applicable to English. He wrote: "Do not expect ... that everything in our language will be exactly equivalent to something in Latin. English, in common with nearly all modern languages, differs enormously in syntax from Greek and Latin." (p. 279). Accordingly, he invented a metalanguage to describe English grammar such as "respective adjectives" which "express nearly all relationships other than those expressed by the possessive adjective" (p. 311) as in "*sea*-fish", "*home*-made", and "*man*-slaughter"; "material adjectives" which "signify a material" (p. 315) as in "*golden* ring", "*leaden* pipe", and "*woolen* cloth"; "rect pronouns" which appear before verbs as "*I*" and "*thou*"; "oblique pronouns" which appear after verbs or prepositions as in "*us*" and "*thee*"; and "defective auxiliary verbs" which "have no participles and cannot be preceded by auxiliary verbs" (p. 337) as in "*shall*" and "*will*".

In addition to creating English-specific grammatical terms, Wallis framed his grammar around what he considered to be the most characteristic feature of English structure — word order. For example, in his treatment of prepositions, he broke from the traditional case grammar by noting that "When you have learnt the meanings of these few small words [prepositions], you can immediately understand the whole syntax of nouns" (p. 291). He explained: "When a preposition is prefixed to a substantive governed by another word, it shows what relationship exists between the substantive and the word by which it is governed, whether it is a verb, a noun or another part of speech. For the main function of prepositions is to indicate logical connections ..." (p. 291). He then listed all the English prepositions, indicating the governing relationships they had with nouns and verbs. In describing the adjective, he observed that they were "put immediately before the substantive" (p. 303) as in *a good man*. Thus Wallis' definitions of the parts of speech and his descriptions of syntactic relationships in English, like those for preposition and adjective, were based primarily, if not solely, on word order.

Insisting that "the whole of its [English] structure can be contained in a very small number of rules" (p. 277), he pointed out that the task of describing English grammar had been made "more complicated than it need be" (p. 279) by those who had not understood the patterns of English structure. Along with the philosophical grammarians and the Port Royalists (whom he cited in his work), he agreed that a finite set of rules could generate all the sentences in a language; however, he held that the nature of rules for each language should be different because they were drawn from the structure of the target language.

Unlike the philosophical grammarians whose grammatical rules were drawn from their views of an ideal language, Wallis based his English grammar on common usage. In short, he described the way speakers of English spoke their language rather than prescribe how they ought to speak their language. For example, in his discussion of the accusative, he noted: "The accusative word usually follows transitive verbs nowadays, for example, he burneth me. At one time it often preceded the verb, *he me burneth, me he burneth;* this is still a regular construction in German and and sometimes in English as well, especially in poetry" (p. 353). Here Wallis not only recognized historical changes at work in the language, but he also realized that the standard dialect consisted of registers. Moreover, he accepted variant usages as legitimate alternatives of the standard as he observed *"That* is often used instead of the relative *which*" (p. 329). In attempting to reduce English grammar to a series of rules, Wallis stressed that a theory of syntax should be systematic. With the enthusiasm of the "young grammarians" of two centuries later, he argued that English structure consisted of a series of regularities and that there were even patterns for the irregularities. When faced with the glaring inconsistencies of English as in the case of the irregular verbs, he sought a pattern of regularity to account for the irregularity. He pointed out that "All the irregularities which follow concern only the formation of the imperfect tense past tense and the passive participle" (p. 357); and he concluded "There is nothing else irregular about these irregular verbs" (p. 357). He added: "All the irregularities, whether small or great , are confined to words of native origin and hardly affect imported words at all". Moreover, Wallis pointed out that analogy would level most of the irregularities: he wrote: "Verbs which possess ... irregular or contracted form mostly have a regular form as well which is no less acceptable than the contracted one, for example, *placed, fished, ... bereaved, girded,* and *burned,* etc.. "(pp. 361, 363). Again, note his acceptance of alternate forms in the standard dialect.

Wallis not only viewed grammar as a syntactic system, but as a system in which phonology and syntax were integrated. It would not be unreasonable to argue that he understood the concepts of morphemic and morphophonemic structures. For example in analyzing the formation of noun plurals, he recognized {s} as the plural morpheme and that morphophonemic rules determined the appropriate allomorph of the verb morpheme. Moreover, he generalized that "Singular substantives are made plural by adding *s;* sometimes, this is preceded by *e,* when the pronunciation makes it necessary, for example when *s* immediately follows *s, z, x ,sh,* or *c, q, ch,* when they have their softer sound" (p. 281). He then listed examples, and concluded that "This is the only regular way (nowadays) of forming the plural number" (p. 281).

Certainly Kemp's (1972:34) assessment of Wallis' *Grammatica* is accurate: "… his Grammar," he writes, "taken in the context of his day, marked a turning point..." Within the practical limits that he set for himself he succeeded handsomely and deserves credit for removing some of the blinkers that had been obscuring the view of grammarians of English prior to his time". However, I would go farther in my appreciation of Wallis' *Grammatica.* In every detail of his "completely new method", he exemplified the Cartesian spirit of the new science in that he accepted nothing as true unless demonstrated as such, he resisted all prejudgments about English grammar, he systematically classified the object of his study into its constituent parts, and he built his generalizations inductively. Lastly, since his generalizations were arrived at from his observations of the language, they were verifiable in that they could be tested for completeness. Thus, drawing on the new science as no other English grammarian before him, Wallis analyzed English structure so differently that he produced a new genre of particular grammar.

REFERENCES

Cohen, Murray. 1977. *Sensible Words: Linquistic Practice in England 1640–1785*. Baltimore: Johns Hopkins University Press.

Holder, William. 1668. "An Experiment concerning Deafness", *Philosophical Transactions of the Royal Society*. London: Royal Society.

— . 1678. "A Supplement to the Philosophical Transaction of July, 1970, with some reflexions on Dr. John Wallis, his letter there inserted". London: Royal Society.

Kemp, John. 1972. *John Wallis's Grammar of English*. London: Longman. (A translation of the 6th edition (1765) of *Tractus de Loquela and Grammatica Linguae Anglicanae* with commentary.)

Lehnert Martin. 1937–8 "Die Abhängigkeit frühneuenglischer Grammatiken", *Englische Studien* 72.192–206.

Robins, R[obert] H[enry] 1967. *A Short History of Linguistics*. London: Longmans and Indianapolis: Indiana University Press.

Subbiondo, Joseph L. 1978. "William Holder's *Elements of Speech* (1669): A study of applied English phonetics and speech therapy". *Lingua* 46.169–184.

Sundby, Bertil. 1952. "A Case of Seventeenth-Century Plagiarism", English *Studies* 33.209–213.

Wallis, John. 1670. "Letter to Robert Boyle", *Philosophical Transactions of the Royal Society*. London: Royal Society.

— . 1678. *A Defence of the Royal Society and Philosophical Transactions in Answer to the Cavils of Dr. William* Holder. London: Royal Society.

Zachrisson, Robert E. 1914. "Notes on the Relation ... of Some Early Grammars", *Anglia Beiblatt* 25.247–253.

Theory and Description in the Dutch Grammatical Tradition: The Case of the Passive

MARIJKE J. VAN DER WAL
Rijksuniversiteit Leiden

1. INTRODUCTION

THE AUTHORS OF early grammars in Western Europe were faced with the problem of how to describe the analytic passive in the vernaculars within the available, well-known framework of Latin grammar. First of all, the definition of passive was connected with the morphological, synthetic Latin passive, although an analytic passive pattern arose after the classical period, in Vulgar Latin. How did the grammarians solve this problem? Were the language data of the vernacular taken seriously or not? We shall concentrate on the solution of the passive description problem in the Dutch grammatical tradition and go therefore into two questions. First, I would like to take stock of what was derived from Latin grammar. I shall pay attention, in this respect, to verb classifications and the definition of the concept 'passive'. Secondly, the value of the descriptions will be assessed by comparing them with the passive data in the early stages of the Dutch language. I shall begin with a short survey of the available data.

2. DATA FOR THE PASSIVE AND A COMPARISON WITH THE ENGLISH AND GERMAN DATA

The early stages of Germanic languages often show similarities which no longer exist in the modern Germanic languages due to different patterns of development. In Middle Dutch (Dutch before 1500) the uncompleted passive event can be expressed by two past participle combinations: either *werden + past participle* or *sijn + past participle* (henceforth p.p.). The variation in expressing an uncompleted event can be shown by the following examples:

(1) *hi wart gedragen* "he was carried"
(2) *een sward was gegeven* "a sword was given"

An identical situation is to be found in the early stages of English and German. All three languages originally had the possibility of using two auxiliaries in the imperfect tenses.[1]

	early Dutch	early German	early English
uncompleted event	*sijn*	*wesan*	*wesan*
(imperfect tense)	*werden*	*werdan*	*weorþan*

This situation does not continue in any of the three West Germanic languages. English lost the verb *weorþan* in the course of time, as we know; only the verb *wesan* "to be" remained to indicate the uncompleted event. German and Dutch kept the equivalents of *weorþan* to fulfil the same role, while the earlier possibility of using German *wesan* or *sein* and Dutch *sijn* was no longer available. Nowadays, Dutch and German have *worden* and *werden,* respectively, as passive auxiliaries for the imperfect tenses. English, on the other hand, has the auxiliary *to be.* The periphrastic combinations of the past participle with *zijn, sein worden* and *have been* indicate the perfect tenses (or the completed event) in Dutch, German and English. The use of the auxiliaries may be presented as follows:

	Dutch	German	English
uncompleted event (imperfect tenses)	*worden*	*werden*	*to be*
completed event (perfect tenses)	*zijn*	*sein worden*	*have been*

[1] These striking similarities have by no means always been recognised. For a further description of the facts and changes with respect to the passive in the three cognate languages the reader is referred to Van der Wal 1986.

In Dutch and German the perfect tenses were originally more alike than the present difference would suggest. The passive consisted of *sijn + p.p.* in Dutch and *sein + p.p.* in German. The so-called tripartite construction *(sein worden + p.p.)* arose as a more recent phenomenon in the Middle High German period. This development was consolidated in German and ousted the original combination.

The change in favour of *worden* to indicate the uncompleted event can be observed very clearly in the Middle Dutch period: the incidence of the *sijn/werden* variation decreases more and more. The line of development is from a more frequent occurrence of *sijn + p.p.* as compared with *werden + p.p.*, through an increase of *werden + p.p.*, to a higher incidence of *werden + p.p.*, expressing the uncompleted event, in fifteenth century texts. The *sijn*-pattern however remains current for a long time: examples are still to be found in sixteenth and seventeenth century texts, although they are not frequent. Apart from the variation under discussion, there is another interesting variation phenomenon which came into being during the late Middle Dutch period. Beside the usual combination *sijn + p.p.* which indicates the completed event, tripartite *sijn/hebben...gheweest* and *sijn/hebben...gheworden* forms arise. In one and the same text one can find:[1]

(3) *...seyden dat dit slot* ***verbrant was*** *van viere*
"they said that this castle had been burnt down by fire"

(4) *en* ***hadde*** *dat duvelse slot niet* ***verbrant geworden***
had that devilish castle not been burnt down
"if that devilish castle had not been burnt down"

[1] The examples are to be found in Jehan Froissart, *Cronyke van Vlaenderen* (ed. N. de Pauw, vol. I, Gent 1898), page 34, lines 20–2 (example 3), page 35, lines 30–2 (example 4), page 77, lines 19–21 (example 5).

(5) *dair die scipperen, poirteren van Ghendt*
where the members of the crew, citizens of Gent,
*so **mishandelt hadden geweest***
so ill-treated had been
"the place where the members of the crew, citizens of Gent, had been so ill-treated"

The tripartite forms are also present in the Dutch language of the sixteenth and seventeenth century. They are more frequent than in Middle Dutch, but *zijn + p.p.* remains the form in general use. The tripartite forms did not take the place of *zijn + p.p.* as happened in German (cf. van der Wal 1986:194–201; van der Wal 1988).

The short overview shows us what the passive system of Dutch is like in different periods. General practice from the sixteenth century on is clear; in addition to this usage we come across two cases of variation. The question to be answered in this paper is whether these facts are adequately presented in the contemporary grammars.

3. The Dutch grammatical tradition

After this short introductory survey, I would like to concentrate on the following questions: 1. What are the ideas on passive in the Dutch grammatical tradition, and 2. How are the passive facts — including the two variations — described within that tradition. Apart from a wide variety of orthographic writings, the Dutch grammatical tradition starts in the second half of the sixteenth century with the *Voorreden vanden noodich ende nutticheit der Nederduytscher taelkunste* (1568), a grammar fragment in manuscript. The earliest complete printed grammar is the *Twe-spraack vande Nederduitsche letterkunst* (1584). In these two grammatical works a definition of the verb is to be found, but no attention is paid to the passive. Christiaen van Heule is the first grammarian who deals with the passive in his (1625:37–8) and (1633:56–8) grammars. Van Heule, who had some influence[1] on other

[1] For example, F. Hillenius (1664), a grammar for foreign language learning, was strongly influenced by Van Heule.

Twe-spraack
vande
Nederduitsche
Letterkunst/
ófte
Vant spellen ende eyghenst
des Nederduitschen taals,
uytghegheven by de Kamer
IN LIEFD BLOEYENE
t'Amstelredam.

TÓT LEYDEN,
By Christoffel Plantyn
M. D. LXXXIV.

De Nederduytsche
SPRAEC-KONST
Ofte
Tael-beschrijvinghe/
Waer in alle gemeyne veranderingen der Woorden, ende Spreuken grondelic vertoont ende geleert worden, door
CHRISTIAEN van HEULE
Mathematicus.
De tweede Druc verbetert.

'ot Leyden/ by Jacob Roels Boec-verkoper
wonende over 't Weeshuys, Anno 1633.

(By courtesy of Leiden University Library)

grammars, the observant Petrus Leupenius (1653) and the authoritative grammarian Arnold Moonen (1706) represent the grammatical tradition of the seventeenth and eighteenth centuries, which I propose to investigate in what follows. Additionally, other publications will occasionally be taken into consideration, including A.L. Kok's 1649 grammar.

4. BORROWING FROM THE LATIN GRAMMATICAL TRADITION: THE DEFINITION AND CLASSIFICATION OF THE VERB

In the definitions of the verb, starting from the Voorreden (1568), a tripartition is present: a verb expresses working or doing *(werken, doen)*, suffering *(lijden)* or something that is alternately described as an event *(geschieden)* or a state *(een zijn)*.[1] Compare the following quotations from Van Heule and Leupenius:

> Een werc-woort beteykent eene werkinge/ die gedaen of geleden wort/ of geschiet/ als *Ic beminne, Ic worde bemint,* ende *Het regent.*
> "A verb signifies a working which is done or suffered or which happens such as *I love, I am loved* and *it rains.*" (Van Heule 1633:56).

> ..de *werkwoorden,* dat syn sulke woorden die eenig *werk, lyden* of *weesen* beteekenen.
> "..the *verbs* are words that signify a *work,* a *suffering,* or a *state.*" (Leupenius 1653:40).

The three characteristics are also found in contemporary English and German grammars, where the third characteristic usually is described by means of *to be* (compare Michael 1970:364–5; Jellinek 1913–4:II,92–3). It is well-known that the Latin tradition has been decisive in this respect.[2] Compare Donatus:

> Verbum est pars orationis cum tempore et persona sine casu aut agere aliquid aut pati aut neutrum significans.
> "The verb is a part of speech with tense and person indications but without case, signifying the doing of something, or the suffering or neither of them.".

[1] Cf. Voorreden 1568:46; Twe-spraack 1584:217; Kok 1649:22; Moonen 1706:138.

[2] Donatus added the third characteristic *neuter* (neither of them) to *doing* and *suffering,* the two characteristics which are to be found in the Greek tradition, in the work of Dionysius Thrax (cf. Keil 1855–74 IV:381).

Three different kinds of verbs correspond with the three characteristics: active verbs, passive verbs, neither active nor passive (neuter) verbs or three genera (kinds of voices), the active voice, the passive voice and the third voice. This tripartition can be found in many seventeenth century and eighteenth century Dutch grammars. It is self-evident that the formal characteristics by which the Latin active, passive and neuter genus were defined, could not be used in the vernacular grammars. According to Donatus those verbs are active which end in *-o* and become passive when an *-r* is added to it *(lego – legor);* those verbs are passive that end in *-r* and become active when the *-r* is deleted; those verbs are neuter which end in *-o,* but cannot become passive *(sto, curro).* The semantic characteristics, however, which are found together with the formal distinctions in the classical grammatical tradition, were adopted: working or doing, suffering, neither of them. The important verbum substantivum *(esse)* was considered to belong to the class of neuter verbs. That is why the semantic criterium "to be" *(zijn)* is used for this category of verb. It is important to note that active and passive were not considered to be syntactic patterns. On the contrary, there were active verbs *(beminnen – to love),* passive verbs *(bemind worden – to be loved)* and neuter verbs. Translations of Latin neuter verbs *(staan – to stand; lopen, wandelen – to walk; leven – to live* etc.), belong to the last category. In Latin they lacked one formal characteristic: they could not become passive *(sto, curro, vivo, ambulo).* In the grammars of the vernaculars the reason why these verbs have to be considered as neuter verbs is the assumption that they signify a state or neither a working nor a suffering. We note that this semantic characterization of the neuter verbs does not seem to cover examples as *lopen, wandelen (to walk)* without certain problems.

5. DESCRIPTION OF THE PASSIVE DATA

The semantically defined category of passive verbs also has one formal characteristic in the grammars of the vernacular: the auxiliary, a new concept arising in the vernacular grammars, unknown in the Latin grammatical tradition. The grammarian Van Heule (1633:58) states that such an auxiliary is necessary in Dutch because of the lack of verbs which indicate a suffering on their own. The verbs *zijn* and *worden,* which are both mentioned with the classical label substantival verb (verbum substantivum), fulfil this role. Our review of evidence from the grammars chosen reveals that the general rules concerning the passive and the two possible variations are not always completely described by the seventeenth and eighteenth century grammarians. Van Heule (1633:58) for instance confines himself to *worden* examples in his description of the passive verbs. Compare:

> De lijdende Werc-woorden worden altijt met een zelfstandich Werc-woort uytgedrukt/ als *Ic worde geslagen, Ic wiert onderwezen,* zo dat de lijdende Werc-woorden altyt by haer hebben Het woordeken/ *Worden, Werde, Wiert* etc. "The passive verbs are always expressed with a substantival verb such as *I am beaten, I was taught,* so it happens that the passive verbs are always accompanied by the little word *Worden, Werde, Wiert* etc."

Van Heule is an exception in this respect. Leupenius and Moonen are at one to mention both *worden + p.p.* used to indicate the imperfect tenses, and *zijn + p.p.* used to refer to a perfect tense event. In the seventeenth century grammars no attention at all is paid to the infrequent *zijn*-pattern, expressing the uncompleted event. Neither is the variation of the tripartite forms described by van Heule or Leupenius, although it is to be found in another contemporary grammar. The regular combination with the verb *zijn* and past participle as well as the tripartite forms *zijn/hebben geweest + p.p.* are mentioned in the grammar of A.L. Kok, where the verb is dealt with extensively (cf. Kok 1649:49–53). Since no comment is given on this variation, the reader of the grammar gets no indication as to how it is used. Nearly sixty years later, Arnold Moonen not only sums up the facts, but also mentions the possibility of a tripartite *gheweest* and a tripartite *gheworden* combination *(Ik Ben Gehoort Geworden* or *Geweest, Ik Was Gehoort Geworden* or *Geweest;* cf. Moonen 1706:140; 174). He adds the following remark:

> hoewel het beter en aengenamer is, gelyk ook in de dagelyksche samenspraeke geschiedt, dat men zonder het verdubbelen zegge, *Ik Ben Gehoort, Ik Was Gehoort.*

"although it is better and more pleasing, as it happens in common speech, that one says without duplication, *I am heard* (= I have been heard), *I was heard* (= I had been heard)" (Moonen 1706:140).

This appears to be a constraint on the paradigms presented earlier in his work: as a matter of fact the tripartite forms are redundant. Moreover important information is given about usage: in everyday speech the tripartite forms are not being used.

6. CONCLUSIONS

In the Dutch grammatical tradition the passive is dealt with within the framework of a semantically motivated tripartition of the verbs. The passive is one of three kinds of verbs (active, passive and neuter), the distinction being borrowed from Latin grammar. That distinction remains present in seventeenth and eighteenth century grammars, but new characteristics are sometimes added. Now and then *transitivity* is mentioned as a characteristic connected with active verbs, *intransitivity* as a feature of neuter verbs.[1] Moreover, a *transformation idea* is put forward: active verbs can be transformed into passive, but neuter verbs cannot (Séwel 1712:241). The idea of a morphological transformation was already to be found in the Latin grammatical tradition (cf. section 4). In the vernacular grammars it is a matter of syntactical transformation in which the auxiliary plays a crucial role. In the nineteenth century a further development of these two ideas, transitivity/intransitivity and transformation, lead to a break from the classical inheritance. The unsuitable tripartition (active, passive and neuter verbs) was rejected and the passive – active distinction became a characteristic of the transitive verbs. In the view of many nineteenth-century grammarians two kinds of verbs, transitive and intransitive verbs, have to be distinguished (cf. Weiland 1805, Brill 1846 and Terwey 1878. Transitive verbs can manifest themselves in two ways: in an active or in a passive syntactic pattern. This grammatical move, however, is not

[1] One has to pay attention to the fact that transitivity and intransitivity are not always considered to be syntactic notions. In the view of several pre-nineteenth-century grammarians transitivity and intransitivity are part of the meaning of a verb.

without problem. In Dutch, as opposed to English, a so-called impersonal passive is a restricted possibility. Some intransitive verbs can be passivized, as in the following examples:

(6) er wordt gewandeld
there is walked
"there is some walking"

(7) er wordt gevoetbald
there is played football
"playing football is done"

These examples do not fit into the clear-cut division between transitive and intransitive verbs and that is why the nineteenth-century grammarians point to them as exceptional. These data, which are not exceptional at all in the Dutch language, are a problem for the nineteenth-century grammars and for several twentieth-century grammatical theories as well.

The ideas on the passive and how the phenomenon of passive was to be dealt with — which were both influenced by Latin grammar — changed in the course of time. Ultimately we can ask what descriptive value did the works selected, which used the Latin framework, have. The relation between theory and description has been examined for one particular construction, the passive, in some representative grammars. Our conclusion must be that the definition of the concept passive and the classification of the Dutch data were determined by the example of Latin in the sixteenth, seventeenth and eighteenth centuries. That is not at all surprising; it is the usual way of doing it in the vernacular grammars of the time. This does not mean, however, that accurate observations on the data are altogether absent. The general passive pattern and sometimes even the variation possible are described. Several authors pay attention to natural language practice and take their data seriously. Moonen's comment on the tripartite forms is a good example of this. Also the famous eighteenth century comparative linguist avant la lettre, Lambert ten Kate, points out that, for instance, a passive imperative form is artificial (cf. ten Kate 1723 I:532).

There is a long way to go before all artificial language distinctions which were introduced into the vernacular grammar have disappeared. The way in which the Latin grammatical system influenced the vernacular grammars in several countries is an interesting subject for the practitioner of the history of linguistics (cf. Michael 1970 and Padley 1976, 1985). The same sources, however, are also important for the historical linguist. Contemporary observations can reveal important information about the language use of a native speaker of the time. Several more detailed studies can be done in the field of different languages. I hope that my contribution for Dutch may provoke future investigations with respect to the interesting relationship between theory and description in the past.

REFERENCES

Brill, W[illem] G[erard] 1846. *Hollandsche spraakleer*. Leiden: S. & J. Luchtmans.

Heule, Christiaen van. 1625. *De Nederduytsche grammatica ofte spraec--konst*. Leyden: Daniel Roels. Ed. by W. J. H. Caron. Groningen-Djakarta: J. B. Wolters, 1953. (Trivium.)

—. 1633. *De Nederduytsche spraec-konst ofte tael-beschrijvinghe*. Leyden: Jacob Roels. Ed. by W. J. H. Caron. Groningen-Djakarta: J. B. Wolters, 1953. (Trivium.)

Hillenius, François. 1664. *Den Engelschen ende Ne'erduitschen onderrichter*. Rotterdam: Bastiaan Wagens.

Jellinek, M.H. 1913–1914. *Geschichte der neuhochdeutschen Grammatik von den Anfängen bis auf Adelung*. 2 vols. Heidelberg: Winter.

Kate Hermansz., Lambert ten. 1723. *Aenleiding tot de kennisse van het verhevene deel der Nederduitsche sprake*. 2 vols. Amsterdam: Rudolph & Gerard Wetstein.

Keil, H. 1855–1874. *Grammatici Latini*. 6 vols. Leipzig: Teubner.

Kok, A[llardus] L[odewijk]. 1649. *Ont-werp der Neder-duitsche letter-konst*. Amsterdam: Johannes Troost. Ed. G.R.W. Dibbets. Assen: Van Gorcum, 1981.

Leupenius, Petrus. 1653. *Aanmerkingen op de Neederduitsche taale*. Amsterdam: Hendryk Donker. Ed. W.J.H. Caron. Groningen: J. B. Wolters, 1958. (Trivium.)

Michael, Ian. 1970. *English Grammatical Categories and the Tradition to 1800*. Cambridge: University Press.

Moonen, A[rnold]. 1706. *Nederduitsche spraekkunst*. Amsterdam: François Halma.

Padley, G. A[rthur]. 1976. *Grammatical Theory in Western Europe 1500–1700: the Latin Tradition*. Cambridge: University Press.

—. 1985. *Grammatical Theory in Western Europe 1500–1700: Trends in Vernacular Grammar*. Cambridge: University Press.

Séwel, Willem. 1712. *Nederduytsche spraakkonst*. Amsterdam: Robert Blókland.

Terwey, T. 1878. *Nederlandsche spraakkunst*. Groningen: J. B. Wolters.

Twe-spraack vande Nederduitsche letterkunst, 1584. Leyden: Christoffel Plantyn, Ed. G.R.W. Dibbets. Assen/Maastricht: Van Gorcum, 1985.

Voorreden vanden noodich ende nutticheit der Nederduytscher taelkunste . 1568. Ed. K. Bostoen, *Kaars en bril: de oudste Nederlandse grammatica* Middelburg: Koninklijk Zeeuwsch Genootschap der Wetenschappen, 1985.

Wal, M[aria] J[acoba] van der. 1982. "Opvattingen over het werkwoord en meer in het bijzonder over het passief in de nederlandse grammatikale traditie van de 17de t/m de 19de eeuw". *Studies op het gebied van de geschiedenis van de taalkunde*, ed. L. van Driel & J. Noordegraaf, 52–80. Kloosterzande: Grafische Industrie Duerinck-Krachten.

—. 1986. *Passiefproblemen in oudere taalfasen, middelnederlands* sijn / werden + *participium praeteriti en de pendanten in het gotisch, het engels en het duits*. Dordrecht: ICG Printing. (with English summary).

—. 1988. "De drieledige vormen in taal en taalbeschouwing". *De Nieuwe Taalgids* 81.383–400.

Weiland, P[etrus]. 1805. *Nederduitsche spraakkunst*. Amsterdam: Johannes Allart.

Animal Language: a Chapter from the Controversy between Rationalism and Sensualism

HELMUT WEIß
Universität Regensburg

I. INTRODUCTION

SINCE Aristotle — or even earlier — it has been a commonplace in philosophy that language is a mental faculty belonging only to human beings but not to animals. For Aristotle "man alone of all animals is furnished with the faculty of language", whereas beasts could only "indicate pleasure and pain" (Aristotle 1961:6). He based this distinction on the human ability to have moral knowledge, which, according to him, animals lacked completely. Though Aristotle did not reject the view that they had some mental functions, he did not ascribe them reason.

In the further history of philosophy the question of animals and language was a problem of high interest for philosophers, as Tabarroni (1989) and Eco et al. (1989) have shown. Ancient grammarians and dialecticians discussed the Aristotelian statements and even medieval thinkers treated the status of animal language in various ways. For more detailed informations on these periods see the works just mentioned.

In the seventeenth and eighteenth century philosophers were again concerned with this issue discussing the Cartesian thesis, that animals were mere automata without mind. In the following I shall sketch this background, which forms the basis of my interpretation of the works of Meier and Plitt concerning animal language. I shall confine myself to the epistemological and the linguistic aspects, neglecting others like the biological or the theological ones. It is clear that the semiotic approach which is successfully applied by Eco et al. (1989) for medieval philosophy is not adequate for a investigation of the discussion of the

Cartesian tenet. In the context of this discussion linguistic and (hence semiotic) arguments played an eminent role, but these cannot be understood without the epistemological background. Pure classifications of signs never appeared in this discussion.

II. The Context of the Meier–Plitt Debate

II.1 *The Epistemological Context*

The animal-machine hypothesis, which René Descartes developed in the *Discours de la méthode* (1637), is founded on his mind-matter dualism (cf. Descartes 1986:79–81). Only men are granted mind, while beasts are pure machines — with quasi-mental functions like sensation, imagination and so on — but these are mere corporeal phenomena, functioning only in a mechanical way. Intellectual faculties, especially higher ones like reasoning could not be attributed to beasts. One of the main arguments for denying mind to animals was the obvious lack of language: they could not "indicate either by voice or signs that which could be accounted solely by thought and not by natural impulse", so Descartes wrote in a letter to Henry Moore (Young 1967:122).

This doctrine became a crucial issue in the controversy between rationalism and sensualism. As is well-known, John Locke attacked the Cartesian position, and in Leibniz's examination of Locke's *Essay concerning Human Understanding* "the problem of the status of animals occupies an important place" (Jolley 1986:119). The epistemological aspects of the issue had wide-ranging implications for the status of men. For this reason Leibniz rejected Locke's ascription of reason to animals, because it would reduce the essential difference between man and animals to a mere gradual one. Leibniz himself didn't deny certain kinds of reasoning to brutes, "conceived in an almost Humean way" (Jolley 1984:120), that is inductive reasoning by experience. Men are characterised "by their capacity for non-inductive reasoning" (l.c.). In the Locke–Leibniz debate these aspects which constituted the epistemological background were of special interest.

II.2 *The Linguistic Context*

As mentioned above, for Descartes the lack of language was the main reason for denying mind to animals. Linguistic aspects were relevant in the epistemological background, and vice versa epistemological criteria were important with regard to what I call the linguistic background of the issue. This is the question of the origin of human speech, a debate which reached its climax in the eighteenth century. In this discussion animal language was a basic element in many theories: by contrasting the "natural" expressions of animals with human speech the special features of the latter were illustrated.

The possibility of animals having language had been accepted by the second half of the eighteenth century, furthermore it was agreed on that language served as an instrument for communication. Johann Georg Hamann, for instance, has claimed: "Die Stimme der Thiere komt uns für ihren gemeinschaftlichen Wechsel eingeschränkter vor, als sie seyn mag, weil unsere Sinnen unendlich stumpfer sind" (Hamann 1967:91). This quotation shows a general agreement within sensualism on this issue (Weiß 1990:60).

The distinction between "natural" and "artificial" signs was of importance in the context of the origin-debate. Etienne Bonnot de Condillac based his explication of the genesis of human understanding on the conviction that sensations were at the beginning of human understanding which, in turn, developed by means of arbitrary signs, a capacity which animals lacked. Animals use only natural signs to indicate their feelings, ideas and so on. At an early stage in history men and some kinds of beasts had the same language, the so-called "langage d'action", consisting of unarticulated cries and actions (cf. Condillac 1947:361), being, of course, natural signs. Their denoting power results from the constant, nature-given connection between the signifier and the signified. In his *Essai sur l'origine des connaissance humaine* Condillac considers the absence of memory in animals to be the reason of why they cannot communicate with arbitrary signs. The nature of artificial signs is based on an arbitrary connection between signum and signatum imposed by men. A similar distinction is made by Johann Gottfried Herder in his *Abhandlung über den Ursprung der Sprache,* when he distinguishes the "Natursprache", being common to men and animal, from human speech. The latter constitutes the special feature of human beings. It is responsible for the development of man and without it man would not be man but merely an animal.

Though both Condillac and Herder emphasized the fundamental difference between animal language and human speech, they didn't completely deny the capacity of communication to beasts. The main reason for this was the obvious existence of some kind of knowledge and understanding in animals and the fact that beasts were social beings capable of communicating with each other. For Herder the difference between animal and human language is in some sense a result of the different complexity in the social community.

III. THE MEIER-PLITT DEBATE

Next I shall examine two almost unknown monographies on this issue, namely Georg Friedrich Meier's *Versuch eines neuen Lehrgebäudes von den Seelen der Thiere* (1749) and Johann Jakob Plitt's *Prüfung* of Meier's opinions dating from the same year. Both authors belong to the German tradition which intends to overcome the Cartesian dualism within the theory of knowledge.

III.1 *Georg Friedrich Meier*

First I shall give a few data about the life of Meier to supply the necessary historical information (cf. Brekle et al.). Born in 1718, he studied at the University of Halle, attending theological and philosophical lectures by the famous Siegmund Jakob and Alexander Gottlieb Baumgarten. The latter was the founder of the philosophical discipline we call aesthetics today. Later Meier became professor of philosophy in Halle. He died there in 1777. In many of his works he tried to popularize the philosophy of Wolff and Baumgarten, e.g. his *Anfangsgründe aller schönen Künste und Wissenschaften.* His *Commentatio de soloecismis hebraicis* (1739) and his *Betrachtung über die Natur der gelehrten Sprache,* dating from 1763, are of some interest tor linguists. The work which will be examined in this section, his "essay on a new system of animal souls" appeared in two editions in 1749 and in 1750, when the French translation was published as well.

The importance of the work may be illustrated by means of an external fact. In his famous *Allgemeinen Betrachtungen über die Triebe der Thiere* (1760) Hermann Samuel Reimarus devoted 17 pages to the discussion of Meier's opinions, no other work on the issue was reflected so extensively — except for Condillac's *Traité des animaux,* which was certainly the major work before Reimarus.

Meier's little book can be charactarised in one word as anti-Cartesian. His explicit claim is to reject the Cartesian tenet that animals are mere automata without mind, a tenet following from the mind-matter dualism of Descartes. For Meier this strict dualism does not exist, because mind must not necessarily be similar to unmaterial substance, when more than one sort of knowledge or understanding is assumed. On the basis of the theories of knowledge of Leibniz, Wolff and Baumgarten Meier develops his own epistemological theory, in which he distinguishes several degrees of knowledge. The faculty of knowledge, in German called "Erkenntnisvermögen", has a sensitive (sinnlich) and a rational component (Verstand), the first of which produces obscure ("dunkle") and clear-confused representations ("klar-verworrene Vorstellungen"), the latter clear-distinct ones ("klar-deutliche"). This is the well-known Wolffian classification of ideas (cf. Wellberry 1977:14–7). The intellect (Verstand) is the faculty to produce clear-distinct representations, reason (Vernunft) is a special kind of intellect which Meier defines as "Vermögen den Zusammenhang der Dinge deutlich zu erkennen" (Meier 1749:73). Both mental faculties, intellect and reason, are differentiated according to the complexity of the representations: there are e.g. two degrees of reason with regard to the connection of single things and the connection of what Meier called "allgemeine Sätze" (Meier 1749:74) which means ratiocination, "Schlüsse nach der Vernunftlehre" (Meier 1749:74).

For Meier the anti-Cartesian result concerning the animal-thought-problem is that beasts possess mind, what they lack only is an "allgemeine deutliche Erkenntniß" (Meier 1749:107), i.e. the second degree of reason and some kinds of intellect. But they are capable of obscure, clear-confused and even clear-distinct representations. The final reason for ascribing thought to animals is a metaphysical or ontological one: "Nirgends ist in dieser Welt ein Sprung, oder eine unausgefüllte Leere anzutreffen" (Meier 1749:107). Gaps and leaps would conflict with his construal of the best of all worlds.

Meier even rejects the Cartesian doctrine that animals do not possess language. His rejection is based on two arguments, a negative and a positive one:

1. Deficiency of human language does not necessarily indicate a lack of mind. Meier defines language as an "Hülfsmittel des Gebrauchs der Vernunft" (Meier 1749:101) which gives duration to abstract ideas, when these are fixed on words (an "die sinnlichen Begriffe der Wörter ... geheftet"). Speech has no constitutive function with regard to thought, only a communicative and an auxiliary one. But even these are not confined to the phonetic language of human beings. This can be shown by means of mathematics operating with certain kinds of signs obviously distinct from words. Not even the totality of all human languages would contain all conceivable arbitrary signs of ideas:

> Es können also vernünftige Wesen seyn, welche von keiner eintzigen menschlichen Sprache einen Begriff haben; und demohnerachtet durch Hülfe anderer Zeichen vernünftig dencken (Meier 1749:102).

Thus, the argument of Descartes that deficiency of language indicates lack of mind is reduced to absurdity. It is worth noting that Meier's argumentation lies almost completely within the boundaries of the rationalistic theory of speech: rationalism too denies a constitutive function of language for thinking, only an auxiliary and a communicative one is attributed to speech.

2. In his second argument against Descartes Meier defines language as a system of arbitrary signs denoting ideas. The material signs consist of, is irrelevant for their nature of being signs, just as it is of no consequence how many signs a language has. Meier supposed that there is no evidence which could lead one to assume that beasts do not possess language — construed in this almost structuralist sense.

III.2 *Johann Jakob Plitt*

A refutation of Meier's explanations appeared in the same year. The author was Johann Jakob Plitt, born in 1727 near Marburg. Plitt studied in Halle for two years, attending lectures by Wolff, among others. Later he became Professor for theology in Rinteln and Frankfurt/M. He died in 1773. He published about 60 books, most of them being theological and philosophical treatises or sermons. Beside the book which will be examined in this section his *Betrachtung über die Weisheit Gottes bei den Sprachen* (1756) is of some linguistic interest: there he describes for instance the terrible consequences of a speechless world and he praises the wisdom of God who gave language to man (all bio-bibliographical data are from Brekle et al.).

The full title of Plitt's work against Meier is: *Prüfung derer Gründe, womit Herr Georg Friedrich Meier ... die Vernunft der Tiere in diesem und jenem Leben erweisen will.* Plitt does not only attack Meier, Descartes' mechanical explanation of animals is rejected too. Therefore he uses above all the epistemology of Alexander Gottlieb Baumgarten, the teacher of Meier, and applies it to this special issue.

Similar to Meier Plitt assumes that animals possess the faculty of knowledge, but contrary to him he does not ascribe them complex representations, that is "zusammenhängende Vorstellungen" (Plitt 1749:75) which are formed only by reason. Animals, then, have neither reason nor language, because language is defined as the faculty to communicate complex representations, that is propositions. It is clear that Plitt's definition of language can only mean human speech. As to the question, whether animals have reason and language, Plitt agrees with Descartes.

Nevertheless he does not think that beasts are pure machines. He attributes to animals what is called in the epistemology of Wolff and Baumgarten the "analogon rationis" or "das Vernunftähnliche" (Plitt 1749:51). That is — roughly speaking — the faculty to perceive and to represent external things in the mind, in other words it embraces nearly all mental processes below the level of abstract thinking. Even mental faculties which Meier would regard as parts of the intellect and reason belong to the "analogon rationis", e.g. the faculty of the soul to recognize the similarities and dissimilarities between things (cf. Plitt 1749:54), and a further faculty called "das untere und sinnliche Vermögen zu urtheilen" (Plitt 1749:55). Part of the "analogon rationis" is furthermore the "facultas characteristica sensitiva" or in German "das sinnliche Bezeichnungsvermögen" (Plitt 1749:55) which allows animals to communicate their sensitive representations ("sinnlichen

Vorstellungen"). Plitt, then, summarizes his ideas in the following statement:

> Daß sie aber gewisse Zeichen haben müssen, wodurch sie die Vorstellungen ihrer Sele an den Tag legen können, solches erhellet der Möglichkeit nach aus der Beschaffenheit ihrer Sele und ihres organischen Körpers; der Nothwendigkeit nach, aus ihrem gesellschaftlichen Leben, und der Würklichkeit nach, aus der täglichen Erfahrung (Plitt 1749:76f.).

Plitt too attributes the faculty of language to animals, but for him language is not the same as for Meier. At the end of our research we'd like to point out that though both Meier and Plitt agreed on ascribing language to beasts their definition of language differed in many respects, especially with regard to the position of language within the theory of knowledge. And this is the central point which explains the diversity of possible answers (at least within sensualism).

IV. CONCLUSION

Plitt's conclusion quoted above shows the final state of discussion in the eighteenth century before Reimarus.

Surely, from the viewpoint of present-day linguistics the topic of animal language — without taking into account the philosophical background — is of little interest. But it is a topic that shows paradigmatically the connections between different philosophical disciplines. As shown above, the interrelations between epistemological and linguistic aspects are central in this debate, these connections being typical for the Enlightenment, especially for sensualism. Sensualists like Condillac can be characterized as epistemologists, whose theory of knowledge is based on a theory of language, or vice versa. Even in the German tradition of epistemology, i.e. of Leibniz and Wolff, the term "signs" is of great importance: the so-called "cognitio symbolica" is defined as the understanding operating with signs, normally with words (Weiß 1990:123–126).

The investigation of the Meier–Plitt-debate has also shown that the eighteenth century discussion of animal language was not a semiotic one. The question of the status of animals gained new dimensions (and on the other hand lost one). Firstly, it was chiefly a problem of epistemology, in this context linguistic arguments were of great importance. But the crucial point is that they were integrated in this background and one could not explore this issue without taking the essential interrelation of epistemology and linguistic into account (I do not want to deny the importance of semiotic aspects at all for this debate or for the philosophy of this period, for the semiotics of the eighteenth century philosophy in Germany cf. Roeder's (1927) fundamental and still modern monograph).

More important for an adequate understanding of the controversy initiated by the Cartesian animal-machine hypothesis are the ontological implications. Only the consequences for the status of man can explain why the problem of animal thought and language became a crucial point in the controversy between Rationalism and Sensualism.

REFERENCES

Aristotle. *The Politics*. Translated with an Introduction, Notes and Appendixes by Ernest Baker. Oxford: Clarendon Press (1961.)

Brekle, Herbert Ernst, Edeltraud Dobnig-Jülch, Hans Jürgen Höller, Helmut Weiß (forthcoming). *Bio-bibliographisches Handbuch der Grammatiker, Sprachtheoretiker und Lexikographen des 18. Jahrhunderts im deutschsprachigen Raum mit Werkbeschreibungen ihrer sprachwissenschaftlichen Arbeiten.*

Condillac, Etienne Bonnot de. 1947. *Oeuvre philosophiques*. Vol.I. *(=Corpus Général des Philosophes Français. Auteurs Modernes,* Tome 33.) Paris: Presses Universitaires de France.

Descartes, René. 1986. *Ausgewählte Schriften. Ausgewählt und mit einer Einleitung versehen von Ivo Frenzel*. Frankfurt/M.: Fischer Taschenbuch Verlag.

Eco, Umberto, Roberto Lambertini, Constantino Marmo, Andrea Tabarroni. 1989. "On Animal Language in the Medieval Classifications of Signs". *On the Medieval Theory of Signs*. Ed. by U. Eco and C. Marmo. Amsterdam & Philadelphia: John Benjamins.

Hamann, Johann Georg. 1967. *Schriften zur Sprache*. Einleitung und Anmerkungen von Josef Simon. Frankfurt/M.: Suhrkamp.

Herder, Johann Gottfried. o.J. *Abhandlung über den Ursprung der Sprache*. Text, Materialien, Kommentar von Wolfgang Proß. München: Carl Hanser.

Jolley, Nicholas. 1986. *Leibniz and Locke: A Study of the New Essays on Human Understanding*. Oxford: Clarendon Press.

Meier, Georg Friedrich. 1749. *Versuch eines neuen Lehrgebäudes von den Seelen der Thiere*. Halle: Carl Herrmann Hemmerde.

Plitt, Johann Jakob. 1749. *Prüfung derer Gründe, womit der HERR Hr. Georg Friedrich Meier [...] Die Vernunft der Thiere in diesem und jenem Leben erweisen will*. Kassel: Johann Bertram Cramer.

Reimarus, Hermann Samuel. 1762. *Allgemeine Betrachtungen über die Triebe der Thiere*. 2. Auflage. Hamburg: Johann Carl Bohn. (Reprint Göttingen: Vandenhoeck & Ruprecht, 1982.)

Roeder, Werner. 1927. *Beiträge zur Lehre vom Zeichen in der deutschen Philosophie des 18. Jahrhunderts*. Berlin: Adolph Fürst & Sohn.

Tabarroni, Andrea. 1989. "On Articulation and Animal Language in Ancient Linguistic Theory". *Versus* 50/51.103–121.

Weiß, Helmut. 1990. *Johann Georg Hamanns Ansichten zur Sprache: Versuch einer Rekonstruktion aus dem Frühwerk*. Münster: Nodus Publikationen.

Wellberry, David Edward. 1977. *Aesthetics and Semiotic in the German Enlightenment*. Yale University Diss.

Young, Robert M. 1967. "Animal Soul". *The Encyclopedia of Philosophy*, Vol. I 122–127. New York: The Macmillan Company & The Free Press; London: Collier-Macmillan.

The "Poznań School" of Structural Linguistics

WIESŁAW AWEDYK & CAMIEL HAMANS
Adam Mickiewicz University, Poznań

THE "KAZAŃ SCHOOL", in which two Poles — Jan Baudouin de Courtenay and Mikołaj Kruszewski — played the most eminent role, is generally acknowledged (cf. Jakobson 1971). The "Poznań School" on the other hand, has not received due attention yet. Here two researchers, namely, Mikołaj Rudnicki (1881–1978) and Ludwik Zabrocki (1907–1977) deserve special recognition for their scholarly achievements. The accomplishments of these two linguists in the theory of sound change, distinctive morphology, structural phonetics, general and diachronic phonology as well as in Indo-European, Germanic and Slavic linguistics were well ahead of their times (cf. Bańczerowski 1980, 1981).

This article discusses Zabrocki's contribution to the theory of sound change and his theory of distinctive morphology. In the first part of this article sound change will be discussed, in the second part distinctive morphology.

SOUND CHANGE

Zabrocki introduced three dichotomies of diachronic phonology:

(1) phonetic : phonological process
(2) surface : deep process
(3) phonetic : substitution process (cf. Zabrocki 1958, 1961, 1962)

The first two dichotomies will only be presented briefly and the third one will be analysed in more detail.

THE PHONETIC : PHONOLOGICAL PROCESS

Phonetic processes are primary and their causes are largely unknown. Phonological processes are secondary and they are entailed by primary phonetic processes. Zabrocki illustrates this difference with High German vowel changes. In Old High German Proto-Germanic diphthongs *ai* and *au* were monophthongized to *e:* and *o:* in some contexts. It was a primary phonetic process.

In order to avoid merger the original *e:* and *o:* (from PG *e:* and *o:)* became *ie* and *uo,* respectively. It was a secondary phonological process, i.e., the diphthongization of *e:* and *o:* was entailed by the monophthongization of *ai* and *au*. Later the newly created diphthongs *ie* and *uo* were monophthongized to *i:* and *u:*, respectively (primary phonetic process). This change caused the diphthongization of the original *i:* and *u:,* which became finally *ai* and *au* (phonological process).

Thus, Zabrocki explains the shift in High High German by a chain of primary phonetic monophthongization and secondary phonological diphthongization processes. This dichotomy proved to be very useful in the analysis of similar shifts in other Germanic languages (cf. Awedyk and Hamans 1989).

THE SURFACE : DEEP PROCESS

Terms like devoicing, spirantization, aspiration refer to the result of a process. They do not explain the change as these terms are labels for surface processes. The aim of a diachronic linguist is to discover deep (or underlying) processes, i.e., to discover the mechanism of the change. For example, the change from *t* to *th* (surface process = spirantization) may be due to two different and, in fact, opposite, processes, namely, (1) fortition (reinforcement) of the subglottal pressure and of the supraglottal closure, and (2) lenition (weakening) of the supraglottal closure. Naturally, in order to discover the mechanism of a process it is essential to analyse the shifts of the whole systems and not changes of segments in isolation. This approach allowed Zabrocki to account for the second consonant shift in some Armenian dialects (cf. Zabrocki 1951:162–169).

THE PHONETIC : SUBSTITUTION PROCESS

More than a quarter of a century ago Zabrocki (1961) made a successful attempt at resolving the Neogrammarian controversy. According to Zabrocki a sound change may be either lexically abrupt, as Neogrammarians claimed, or lexically gradual as dialect geographers, Neolinguists, and "Teleologen" postulated (recently also lexical diffusionists).

Zabrocki distinguishes between a phonetic process, which is lexically abrupt, and a substitution process, which is lexically gradual. A phonetic process is exceptionless and affects all relevant lexical items, e.g., the diphthongization of *u:* in some High German dialects like Bavarian. The process may spread to a neighboring dialect, whose speakers adopt their pronunciation to the pronunciation of speakers of another dialect. This, however, is not a phonetic process. The speakers of the borrowing dialect substitute their pronunciation for another one. The substitution will occur first in those lexical items which are used by the speakers of both dialects. Due to its nature the substitution process is not exceptionless. Therefore, it is not surprising to find forms with the original and new (borrowed) pronunciation, for example, one may find forms like *u:s* and *haus* existing side by side in one dialect.

This is the first stage of the substitution process. Secondly the speakers of the borrowing dialect may borrow a rule like: *u:* > *au* and substitute *u:* for *au* also in those lexical items which occur only in their dialect. The second stage, i.e. rule borrowing, accounts for spreading the new pronunciation to a larger and larger part of the lexicon of the borrowing dialect. Rule borrowing also explains hypercorrect forms which may occur in the borrowing dialect.

There is still another difference between a phonetic and a substitution process. The phonetic process affects all the relevant lexical items, both common names and proper names, including the etymologically non-transparent ones. The substitution process, on the other hand affects first of all common names and may affect etymologically transparent proper names, too. The etymologically non-transparent proper names will, however, remain unchanged. Thus the analysis of onomastic data makes it possible to determine whether a phonetic or a substitution processprocess operated in a given dialect.

The distinction between a phonetic and a substitution process allowed for a new interpretation of English (cf. Awedyk in press) and (cf. Awedyk and Hamans in press) dialect data.

The voicing of initial fricatives is an interesting problem in English historical linguistics (cf. Fisiak 1984, for discussion and references). In Middle English voicing was recorded in the South, South-West, and also in the North-West Midlands. By the end of the second half of the 14th century voicing began to recede southwards, probably under the influence of Standard English. Modern English dialects in Kent, Surrey, and Sussex do not show initial voicing. There are, however, place names with initial voiced fricatives, e.g., *Vange* in Essex.

From the point of view of traditional dialectology the lack of reflexes of voicing in the North-West Midlands is puzzling. One would expect to find forms with initial voiced fricatives in those dialects since the influence of the London dialect must have been weaker than in the South. Zabrocki's dichotomy offers the following explanation: the voicing of initial fricatives started in the South and South-West as a phonetic process as evidenced by place names like *Vange* in Essex. Then voicing spread northwards as a substitution process. Later, under the influence of Standard English initial voiced fricatives were almost entirely eliminated in the South but preserved in the South-West. The elimination of voiced fricatives in the North-West Midlands was possible in spite of a weaker influence of the London dialect since in this area voicing operated as a substitution process.

The diphthongization of Middle Dutch *y:* ([y:] > [oey]) is one of the most often discussed problems in Dutch historical linguistics (cf. Awedyk and Hamans 1989; Awedyk and Hamans in press, for discussion and references). The followers of the 'expansionistic' and the 'autochthonous' theory seem to agree on one point, namely, that at a certain stage the Provinces of North and South Holland, or at least some parts of the provinces, were the first diphthongization area in the northern part of the Low Countries.

In Modern Dutch dialects the diphthong area also covers, apart from North and South Holland, the provinces in the centre and in the East, i.e., the Province of Utrecht and South-West Gelderland (De Betuwe). If the Provinces of North and South Holland were the first diphthongization area where diphthongization operated as a phonetic process and from there this change spread to the East as a substitution process, one would expect to find etymologically non-transparent place names with a monophthong [y:] west of the [y] : [oey] isogloss. No place name with a monophthong was recorded in the Province of Utrecht. However, a number of etymologically non-transparent names were found in De Betuwe, e.g., *Kule-* in Maurik, *Nude-* in Renen. In the same area etymologically transparent place names have a diphthong, e.g. *Buitentuin* in Maurik (cf. *buiten* "outside", *tuin* "garden"). West of De Betuwe even etymologically non-transparent place names have a diphthong, e.g., *Achterkuik* in Schalkwijk.

On the basis of the analysis of the dialect data presented above the following conclusion may be drawn: the diphthongization of Middle Dutch *y:* operated as a phonetic process not only in the Provinces of North and South Holland but also in the Province of Utrecht. In this whole area no instances of etymologically non-transparent place names with a monophthong were recorded. Diphthongization spread to De Betuwe as a substitution process: in De Betuwe etymologically transparent place names have a diphthong while etymologically non-transparent ones have a monophthong.

The aim of the first part of this article was to present Zabrocki's contribution to the theory of sound change. His analyses of a number of languages including German, Armenian, and Finno-Ugric as well as the application of his theoretical assumptions to the analysis of English, and German yielded interesting results.

Distinctive Morphology or Diacrisis

As early as 1911 Mikołaj Rudnicki, together with Ludwik Zabrocki, the founder of the "Poznań School", introduced a theory of diacrisis (cf. Bańczerowski 1981). The theory of diacrisis discussed here, also known under the name of distinctive morphology, was introduced by Zabrocki in the mid sixties (cf. Zabrocki 1980).

The starting point for Zabrocki's theory was a critical review of the "Prague School" concept of the phoneme, where it was mainly defined in terms of distinctive function. According to Zabrocki this distinctive function is performed in language by segments not necessarily corresponding to a single segment but to units which are sequences of such segments (Bańczerowski 1980:16–17).

An example will explain Zabrocki's criticism:

(1) m*an*
p*an*
br*an*
pl*an*

These words rhyme. They have a common ending *-an,* the so called confusivum. They differ by means of distinctive parts, the diffusiva. In the case of m*an* – p*an* the diffusiva are single sound segments: the phonemes *m* – *p*. In the examples br*an* – pl*an* the confusivum is still *-an,* but the diffusiva consist of sequences of sound segments, the clusters *br-* and *pl-*.

Confusiva as well as diffusiva may be minimal. In (2) the confusivum is underlined:

(2) ma*n*
so*n*
gu*n*
pi*n*

In (3) the diffusiva are minimal. The confusiva are in italics:

(3) *ma*n
*ma*p
*ma*m
*ma*t

A diffusivum may be zero as well:

(4) ever DØ + ever
never Dn + ever
sever Ds + ever
clever Dkl + ever

Confusiva may be zero, too:

(5) fat
knock
spur
wild

These words have nothing in common. So the diffusiva are maximal and as a consequence there are no confusiva.

Confusiva may be even discontinuous, as in:

(6) *brother*
breather

Not only the criticism of the "Prague School" gave Zabrocki the idea of distinctive morphology, but also the derivation of new suffixes from existing ones:

> Die Grenzen der Diffusiva und Konfusiva können zufällig mit den Grenzen der semantischen und der grammatikalischen Morpheme übereinstimmen, wie im Falle Viel*heit* : Krank*heit*. Das ist aber nur reiner Zufall, kein Prinzip! Die Grenzen zwischen den diffusiva und den konfusiven Elementen sind völlig unabhängig von den Morphemgrenzen der lexikalischen und grammatikalischen Morpheme. Die Grenzen zwischen den diffusiva und den Konfusiva können sich sogar stärker als die morphematischen Grenzen erweisen. Das beobachten wir beim Aufkommen von neuen Suffixen. In dieser Weise entwickelte sich z.B. im Deutschen das Suffix *-ling*. Nach dem Muster *edeling : wihseling* "filius suppositus" : *smerling,* wo wir ein Konfusivum *-ling* haben, das nicht mit dem morphematischen Suffix *-ing* übereinstimmt, entstand ein neues Suffix *-ling*. Die Grenze der distinktiven Morpheme erwies sich somit als stärker gegenüber der morphematischen Grenze.(Zabrocki 1980:107–108).

Let us consider a more recent example:

(7a)	philo*logy*	(7b)	music*ology*
	bio*logy*		dialect*ology*
	theo*logy*		snake*ology*
	neo*logy*		Egypt*ology*
	pharmaco*logy*		pest*ology*

The original suffix was *-logy,* but from (7a) it is clear that there was already a confusivum *-ology*. And so a new suffix *-ology* originated.

Another example from Latin shows the productivity of this process:

(8a)	cantare	can - tus
	quaerere	quaes - tus
	evenire	even - tus
	ornare	orna - tus
	armare	arma - tus

Next to the suffix *-tus* a confusivum *-atus,* as in *ornatus* and *armatus,* was recognized and so a new suffix *-atus* came up:

(8b)	magistratus	magister
	senatus	senex
	principatus	principis (gen.sg.)

In this way not only suffix reinterpretation can be explained but also the origin of complete new suffixes as for instance *-rama/-orama*.

In *panorama,* from Greek *pan + horama, horama* was not a suffix at all. *Georama* and *teleorama* were subsequently derived from *panorama*. The "suffix"like part is *-rama,* but the confusivum *-orama.* In this way new words and names with *-orama* were produced:

(9a)	Dutch	French	English
	panorama	panorama	panorama
	georama	myriorama	cosmorama
	lectorama	politicorama	cyclorama
	organorama	castorama	skiorama

In some of these examples, for instance in *georama, politicorama* and *cosmorama* the "suffix" could be *-rama* as well. No wonder that there are words and names ending solely in *-rama:*

(9b)	lecturama	loisirama	cinerama
	literama	cityrama	pleasurama group

Diacrisis is not only productive in suffix reinterpretation, but also operates in word formation processes and in the creation of new names. Diacrisis is highly productive in the world of commerce, marketing and advertisement.

After the introduction of *cafeteria,* speakers considered the part *-teria* as a kind of a suffix, since there is also a word *café*. So from *cafeteria, fruiteria* was formed. Even a name *snacketeria,* with *-eteria,* was created.

(10) cafeteria
fruiteria
snacketeria

In *intro,* the part *in-* was seen as an independent part or prefix. Compare for instance *intro* with *infix,* where there is a confusivum *in-*. At the moment *intro* was seen as consisting of two parts *in* and *tro,* the neologism *out-tro* became possible too.

(11) intro
in-fix
out-tro

A more common example is found in (12):

(12a) hotel
motel
botel

Hotel and *motel* share a confusivum *-otel*. *Motel* and *motor* have a confusivum *mot-*. So for every speaker who knows the meaning of *hotel* and *motor,* the meaning of *motel* will be clear. The middle part

-at- belongs to both possible confusiva and that is why the word *motel* is highly acceptable and semantically transparent.

Hotel, motel and *botel* share a confusivum *-otel*. That is why *-otel* itself could become productive, which it has:

(12b) aerotel (12c) aerodynamics

Aerotel contains the well known part *aero-*, cf. *aerodynamics*. So speakers could also consider the part *-tel* as a confusivum, may be even as a suffix. This confusivum *-tel* is used for coining names as:

(12d) sportel (sport hotel)
stutel (student hotel)

Sportel has a confusivum *sport* with sport, *stutel* a confusivum *stu-* with *student*. Therefore, the meaning of *sportel* and *stutel* becomes clear immediately.

Diacrisis also explains why speakers of a language feel a meaning relation between formally, semantically and etymologically unrelated words like:

(13) *sl*ender or *sl*ander
*sl*ight *sl*ang
*sl*inky *sl*attern
*sl*im *sl*ogger
*sl*anting *sl*oppy

In the first list the confusivum *sl* seems to symbolize small, whereas in the second list it has a negative meaning. This type of sound symbolism cannot be explained formally. In the theory of diacrisis it is quite clear why speakers feel a semantic relation between the words of these lists. This does not mean that the cluster *sl-* has a meaning "small" or "negative" or both, but at the moment speakers reflect upon such lists they get the impression that the words have something in common. This is the confusivum, which has an intuitive semantic load.

Diacrisis also offers a way out for the classical *cranberry – strawberry* problem (cf. Awedykowa 1981). *Cran-* is not an independent word or word part. *Cran-* does not have a meaning on its own, either.

So, it is impossible to consider *cran-* as a morpheme. On the other hand *cran-* must be a morpheme, since *berry* is one. The semi-solution classical linguistics offered for this problem was to consider *cran-* as a special kind of morpheme, a morpheme without an independent meaning.

In distinctive morphology the status of *cran-* is clear:

(14) strawberry
raspberry
cranberry

The parts *straw-, rasp-* and *cran-* are the diffusiva. So it is not necessary to suppose that *cran-* has morpheme status or a distinct semantic character.

In 1988 Beatrice Warren, who works in the school of natural morphology, presented a paper "The Importance of Combining Forms", in which she discussed "certain morphemes which linguists feel are neither proper roots, nor proper affixes". She discussed combining forms such as *psycho-, bio-, -crat, -nik* and *-athon.*

Her main conclusion was that "there is no standard account of these elements", which is true. Warren then concluded "that the most interesting aspect of these combining forms is the ad hoc manner in which they can be formed", which is not true as may be concluded from the examples given before. Warren and the school of natural morphology appear not to be aware of Zabrocki's work and the solution his theory of distinctive morphology offers for classical morphological problems.

The aim of the second part of this article was to present Zabrocki's contribution to morphological theory. His analysis of suffix reinterpretation, sound symbolism and neologisms has yielded interesting results. Moreover, his theory of diacrisis appeared to be useful for the analysis of new suffixes or suffix-like parts. Zabrocki's theory of distinctive morphology is an important contribution to both general and historical linguistics.

The three dichotomies discussed in the first part and the analysis of suffix reinterpretation discussed in the second part are only some of Zabrocki's achievements in diachronic linguistics. The theory of speech communities, perhaps the first integrated theory of sociolinguistics, allowed Zabrocki to present a new dynamic theory of the development of the West Germanic speech community (cf. Zabrocki 1963). Zabrocki was also one of the first linguists to apply cybernetic models to language analysis (cf. Zabrocki 1970). It will not be, perhaps, an exaggeration to repeat what Saussure remarked about J. Baudouin de Courtenay and M. Kruszewski (cf. Godel 1957:51) — one can only regret that those ideas are little known to Western linguists.

REFERENCES

Awedyk, Wiesław. (in press). "Lexical Diffusion and Sound Change". *Phonological Explorations*. Ed. by J. Fisiak and S. Puppel.

Awedyk, Wiesław & Camiel Hamans. 1989. "Vowel Shifts in English and Dutch: Formal or Genetic Relation?". *Folia Linguistica Historica* 8.99–114.

—. (in press). "'Hollandse expansie' revisited".

Awedykowa, Sława. (1981). *Untersuchungen zur sprachlichen Diakrise des Einsilber im Polnischen und Norwegischen*. Poznań: Wydawnictwo Uniwersytetu im. Adama Mickiewicza.

Bańczerowski, Jerzy. 1980. "Ludwik Zabrocki as a Theorist of Language".. Zabrocki 1980:9–22.

—. 1981. "On Mikołaj Rudnicki's General Linguistic Conceptions". *Lingua Posnaniensis* 24.7–27.

Fisiak, Jacek. 1984. "The Voicing of Fricatives in Middle English". *Studia Anglica Posnaniensia* 17.3–16.

Godel, Roman. 1957. *Les sources manuscrites du Cours de linguistique générale de Ferdinand de Saussure*. Geneva: Droz.

Hamans, Camiel. 1988. "De overeenkomst tussen literama en actreutel". *Spektator* 17.289–299.

Jakobson, Roman. 1971. "The 'Kazań School' of Polish Linguistics and its Place in the International Development of Phonology". *Selected Writings. Vol II. Word and language*, 394–428. The Hague: Mouton.

Warren, Beatrice. 1988. "The Importance of Combining Forms". *Abstracts for the Sixth International Phonology and Third International Morphology Meeting*, 87. Krems.

Zabrocki, Ludwik. 1951. *Usilnienie i lenicja w językach indoeuropejskich i w ugrofinskim* ["Fortition and lenition in Indo-European languages and in Finno-Ugric"]. (Résumé in French, 257–89). Poznań: Poznańska Drukarnia Naukowa.

—. 1958. "Zagadnienia fonetyki strukturalnej [Foundations of structural phonetics]". *Sprawozdania Poznańskiego Towarzystwa Przyjaciół Nauk* 53.165–185.

—. 1961. "Prawa głosowe, procesy głosowe, onomastyka [Sound laws, sound changes, and onomastics]". *Onomastica* 7.1–20.

—. 1962. "Zur diachronischen strukturellen Phonetik". *Proceedings of the Fourth International Congress of Phonetic Sciences,* 805–815. The Hague: Mouton.

—. 1963. *Wspólnoty komunikatywne w genezie i rozwoju języka niemieckiego* ["Speech communities in the genesis and the development of the German language"]. Wrocław: Ossolineum.

—. 1970. "Kybernetische Sprechmodelle". *Proceedings of the Sixth International Congress of Phonetic Sciences,* 1047–1050. Prague: Academia Publishing House.

—. 1980. "Phon, Phonem und distinctives Morphem". (1962); "Aufbau und Funktion der phonologischer Einheiten". (1964/65). "Phonologie und distinktive Morphologie". (1967/69). *U podstaw struktury i rozwoju języka* ["At the Foundation of Language Structure and Development"], 75/112. Ed. by Jerzy Bańczerowski, 75–112. Warsaw: Państwowe Wydawnictwo Naukowe.

Salomon Stricker's Motor Theory of Language

T. CRAIG CHRISTY
University of North Alabama

OVER A CENTURY AGO, in his *Studien über die Sprachvorstellungen* of 1880, Salomon Stricker (1834–1898) gave a detailed, introspective account of sensations he routinely experienced in his organs of articulation during silent thinking. As Stricker allowed, "An das stille Denken in Worten ... knüpfe sich die Wahrnehmung oder das Gefühl, als ob ich mitreden würde" (p. 3). What Stricker experienced was not simply the perception of simultaneous articulation, but actual impulses in the muscles of his articulators. This "ghosting" phenomenon seemed, moreover, not to be restricted to the realm of words. Stricker claimed, for instance, that whenever he let a wordless melody pass through his memory he experienced a peculiar sensation in his larynx: "...es kommt mir vor, als ob ich (gleichsam innerlich) mitsingen würde" (p. 2), an observation sustained by numerous others he consulted. Meanwhile, pianists and players of other string instruments were more inclined to experience such sensations in their hands, while those playing wind instruments reported sensations in their lips. In each case, the thought process appears to evoke the sensation of that particular motor activity most closely associated, in a given individual, with the content of thought.

Stricker's observations found seeming corroboration in ongoing studies of aphasia patients, for here, too, the central issue was the localization of sensorimotor activity. As a professor of general and experimental pathology at the University of Vienna with training in phonetics from his studies under Ernst Brücke (1819–1892), Stricker was well qualified to interpret the findings of Paul Broca (1824–1880) and Carl Wernicke (1848–1905) regarding the specific areas of the brain connected with speech production and comprehension. To augment and confirm such anatomical evidence, Stricker turned, once again, to his own subjective experience to throw light on the issue of the localization of language ability:

> Nachdem ich mich mehrere Jahre hindurch mit der Frage der Localisation der Gedanken beschäftigt hatte, fiel es mir plötzlich auf, dass ich beim Denken in Worten vornehmlich ein Gefühl in der linken Stirn- und Scheitelgegend habe. (p. 101)

Even if we allow, as William James (1842–1910) has, that "Professor Stricker of Vienna [...] seems to be a 'motile' or to have this form of imagination developed in unusual strength" (1892:307), it is difficult to avoid concluding that, in this instance, the power of suggestion, if not sheer overzealousness, has gotten the best of him.

James's remarks appear in his chapter on "Imagination" where, as was customary in the psychology of this period, the mental correlates of sensations were categorized in terms of ideational type, that is, on the basis of whether thought takes place in visual, auditory, or tactile images, or, as in Stricker's case, in motor images — that is, in images of muscular sensations. This line of research is perhaps most strongly associated with the work of Francis Galton (1822–1911), Charles Darwin's cousin, who, in his *Inquiries into Human Faculty* (1883), concluded, most importantly, that there was not simply one faculty of imagination common to all human minds, but rather a variety of imaginations. While the large-scale statistical inquiry Galton conducted clearly points to this conclusion, it should be emphasized that subjective analysis, in the absence of any objective control, is frequently compromised by inaccuracies. As James points outs:

> Most persons, on being asked *in what sort of terms they imagine words,* will say, "In terms of hearing." It is not until their attention is expressly drawn to the point that they find it difficult to say whether auditory images or motor images connected with the organs of articulation predominate. A good way of bringing the difficulty to consciousness is that proposed by Stricker: Partly open your mouth and then imagine any word with labials or dentals in it, such as "bubble," "toddle." Is your image under these conditions distinct? To most people the image is at first "thick," as the sound of the word would be if they tried to

> pronounce it with the lips parted. Many can never imagine the words clearly with the mouth open; others succeed after a few preliminary trials. The experiment proves how dependent our verbal imagination is on actual feelings in lips, tongue, throat, larynx, etc. (1891:307–308)

While Stricker maintains that no auditory images whatsoever are present in the words in which he thinks, surveys such as Galton's suggest that most people in fact make use of the full spectrum of ideational types in varying degrees and in step with their diverse nonpathological and pathological idiosyncrasies. As James relates:

> The study of Aphasia has of late years shown how unexpectedly individuals differ in the use of their imagination. In some the habitual "thought-stuff," ... is visual; in others it is auditory, articulatory, or motor; in most, perhaps, it is evenly mixed. (pp. 308–309)

Of course the beauty of Stricker's account — to a pathologist, at any rate — was that it enabled the strict correlation of mental with neurophysiological functions, a goal earlier prosecuted by Gustav Fechner (1801–1887) under the rubric "psychophysics" and, more particularly to the present point, by the Scottish philosopher and psychologist Alexander Bain (1818–1903), who, in his work *Mind and Body: The Theories of their Relation* of 1873,[1] claimed that "a suppressed articulation is in fact the material of our recollection, the intellectual manifestation, the idea of speech" (James 1892:308).

This reductionist approach in interpreting manifestations of the mind, in conscious emulation of categorization and quantification techniques so successfully deployed in the physical sciences, runs throughout the study of psychology as practiced during this period. James, for instance, declares that "All consciousness is motor" and "... that every possible feeling produces a movement, and that the movement is a movement of the entire organism, and of each and all its parts" (1892:370). For psychology, neurology in particular was, of course, the passport to liberation from the precincts of philosophy and physiology, its "certificate of majority", as it were, and so it is scarcely surprising

[1] See also his *The Senses and the Intellect* (1855).

that the deliberations of the day were awash in such terms as "neural process", "nervous discharge" and the like.

Stricker's claims are, once again, that there is a feeling, nerve-bound, in the articulatory organs which is inseparably associated with the mental image of every sound, that these feelings are based in the muscles, and that they resemble those feelings which accompany the actual articulation of sounds (p. 15). As a composite of sounds, a word is, most essentially, a gestural complex, and not, as per the view prevalent at the time, simply a "Schallbild" — an image in sound or sonic image. To support his claim that we do not in fact remember only "Schallbilder" when we think in words, Stricker points out that the information conveyed through speech is in fact independent of such phonetic features as the speaker's voice. He claims, for instance, that, whereas the words spoken by a stranger are, at first, recalled along with the stranger's voice, the memory of the voice itself gradually recedes leaving only that of the words, that is, the actual content of the message (p. 19). Naturally, the voices of those with whom verbal intercourse has been sustained over a period of time are not so perishable. Yet even in this case Stricker argues that the memory of the voice is not permanently connected to the memory of the words "Beim Auftauchen des ersten Wortes pflegen zwar Stimme und Worte an einander zu haften. Im weiteren Verlaufe aber merke ich, dass die Worte so in mir aufleben, als wenn ich sie unabhängig von der Erinnerung an Gehörtes denken würde" (p. 19). Nor do his images of words contain any visual images such as the memory of written characters. After all, Stricker reasons, no one, in remembering an article previously read, for example, remembers it in terms of the letters on the page (1884:687).

After briefly reviewing developments in the study of the relation between brain and language pathologies chronicled by Adolf Kussmaul (1822–1902) in his (1877) account "Ueber die Störungen der menschlichen Sprache",[1] Stricker concludes that all "Sprachvorstellungen", or mental images in language, must accordingly be mediated by regions of the brain in which no sensory perceptions arise. For, he notes, both studies of living aphasia patients and evidence from

[1] Cf. Stricker 1880:21.

autopsies repeatedly showed that the seat of their affliction was restricted to the motor regions, that is, to regions not connected with sensory perception: "Die motorischen Gebiete der Hirnrinde können also unmöglich auch der Sinneswahrnehmung dienen" (p. 26). In the findings of research into aphasia Stricker thus claims to find confirmation of his conclusion, arrived at through introspection, that "Sprachvorstellungen" must consist of something other than sensory images.

For Stricker this "something" is the memory of a specific muscular movement or sequence of movements — nothing more, nothing less. After defining as *pure word images* "reine Wortvorstellungen" words in an unknown language which, though he can repeat them, are meaningless and devoid of sensory perceptions (p. 20), Stricker concludes: "Die reine Wortvorstellung besteht also bei mir aus nichts Anderem, als aus dem Wissen, dass in den Sprachmuskeln etwas vorgeht" (p. 28). And this, in turn, can result only from nerve impulses travelling from the cortex to the muscles. That is, it is from the motor regions of the brain that the speech muscles receive their impulses. Thus "Wortvorstellungen", or mental images of words, are, in fact, *motor images* "motorische Vorstellungen", more commonly referred to in the technical literature, Stricker points out, as "Bewegungs-Vorstellungen" (p. 29). Stricker reasons, moreover, that mental images of words — that is, motor images — consist of consciousness of the impulses sent out to the muscles of articulation from the language center (p. 30, 33). It is, then, in the transmission of an impulse that we are to find the characteristic feature of a given sound's mental image, and, by extension, the features of a given "Wortvorstellung". The observation that any attempt to prolong articulation of a given sound inevitably leads simply to sending out its characteristic impulse over and again is adduced by Stricker as yet further corroboration of his claim (p. 30–31). And, just as the impulse to innervation awakens the motor image, so this motor image, as word image, must awaken other mental images attached to it to make possible understanding, to yield meanings:

> Wenn also in meinem Sprachcentrum das Wortzeichen "Pferd" auftaucht, so muss von hier aus die Erregung auf jenes Gebiet des

> Gehirns übertragen werden, in welchem die Erinnerung an ein gesehenes Pferd auftauchen kann. (p. 53)

From this statement it is clear that, in effecting a connection between the bare motor image and meaning, Stricker is pressing the localization-of-brain-functions construct to its logical, or illogical, extreme. Wilhelm Wundt (1832–1920), who, in his voluminous treatise *Die Sprache* (³1911) finds the excessive claims of the localization hypothesis unsettlingly evocative of those earlier advanced by phrenology,[1] identifies, as a major shortcoming, the neglect, in the localization scheme, of the multifarious functional interrelations manifest in every linguistic event. As Wundt puts it:

> Die Erkenntnis dringt durch, daß sich jeder noch so einfach erscheinende sprachliche Vorgang aus einer Fülle elementarer psychophysischer Funktionen verschiedener Art zusammensetzt und regelmäßig zugleich bestimmte Hilfsfunktionen in Anspruch nimmt, so daß es völlig unmöglich erscheint, ihn an ein eng begrenztes Hirngebiet oder gar an eine einzelne Hirnzelle binden zu wollen. (p. 549)

In short, what began as a set of encouraging correlations between specific cortical areas and specific language behaviors, particularly pathological, ended as a veritable 'localization mania' with every category of mental image — motor, sound, memory, visual, and so on — being assigned to its own self-contained area in the brain. And, whereas this line of research was initially propelled to prominence by studies involved with the localization of certain types of aphasic dysfunction, it was eventually overtaxed, as a theoretical matrix, to account for a variety of other language pathologies. As Wundt points out, "Die üblichen Lokalisationshypothesen pflegen ... schon an der Tatsache zu scheitern, daß mit tieferen Störungen des Wortgedächtnisses beinahe regelmäßig Störungen der Artikulationsfähigkeit verbunden sind" (p.

[1] As conceived by the Viennese physician Franz Joseph Gall (1758–1828) and later developed by his disciple Johann Kaspar Spurzheim (1776–1832), phrenology purported to enable determination, through study of skull contours, of a person's character and mental capacity.

562). While Wundt is thus alert to the limitations of explanations within the framework of localization, he nevertheless acknowledges the role, in speech and thought, of what Stricker calls "motor images", though he makes no reference here to Stricker:

> Das Denken in Worten ist zugleich leises Sprechen, und auch wenn die sichtbaren Bewegungen der Sprachorgane unterdrückt werden, bleibt es dies in dem Sinne, daß schwache Impulse zu denselben samt den sie begleitenden leisen Empfindungen zurückbleiben. (p. 562)

The idea that language is encoded in thought as a series of subvocal responses surfaces again within the framework of John B. Watson's (1878–1958) behaviorist psychology, where it conveniently facilitates his stimulus-response model of speech production and perception. Beyond that, it is something of a curiosity with respect to his overall behavioristic paradigm since, as conceived by Stricker at any rate, these sub-vocal responses are insignificant in the absence of consciousness (cf. Pillsbury 1929:294–295).

More recent studies in which Stricker's motor theory or close clones thereof figure prominently are, in the main, clinical approaches cast in terms of feedback mechanisms. While it is a commonplace that the speaker, in a given exchange, is simultaneously also hearer, the reverse — that the hearer is simultaneously also speaker — is perhaps most readily cogent only if, with Stricker, we assume that the hearer is, as it were, empathetically generating a map of the speaker's articulatory gestures, which, moreover, may at times actually cross the innervation threshold with results ranging from tentative articulatory movements of a similar type to outright synchronous lip movements ("lipsync"). Put another way, the hearer, in effect, transforms exteroceptor into proprioceptor sensations which are rooted in kinesthetic memories. He becomes, so to speak, the vicarious speaker. As David Abercrombie notes in his *Elements of General Phonetics* (1967), "Speech rhythm[,] ... essentially a muscular rhythm, ... is experienced as a rhythm of movement. ... We talk, for convenience, about 'hearing' rhythm, but in fact we *feel* it, entering empathetically into the movements of the speaker, to which the sounds we hear are clues" (p. 96–97). Thus rhythmic pulses become correlated with rhythmic impulses.

A. M. Liberman and his colleagues have done a great deal of work in which, like Stricker, they attempt to show that speech is perceived by reference to its production. In their article "Perception of the Speech Code" (1967), for instance, they argue that the speaker uses the inconstant sounds of speech simply as a means of finding his way back to the articulatory gestures which produced them, and that, accordingly, it is at the level of commands to the muscles that message units are recovered in the neuromotor system. In this way multidimensional acoustic signals are resolved,... from their encoded traces in the sound stream" (p. 455), into a series of significant articulatory events. Perceptual recognition routines must, of course, involve, in addition to the hearer's knowledge of articulatory gestures, his knowledge of grammar. Even Stricker, as pointed out, related his motor images to other memory images to account for understanding: "Jede motorische Wortvorstellung muss irgend eine psychisch fungirende Hirnregion in Erregung versetzen, wenn wir das Wort verstehen sollen" (1880:53). All the same, the simple fact that, on the one hand, speech must be produced in the vocal tract, and, on the other, must be transmitted through the air, guarantees that a given phonologic feature must have articulatory as well as acoustic correlates. As Philip Lieberman concludes in his book *Intonation, Perception and Language* (1967), "The 'motor theory of perception' ... simply describes one aspect of the listener's total linguistic competence that *may be invoked* in the perceptual recognition routine" (p. 167; emphasis added by TCC).

As for disagreement over the extent to which, or even whether, motor images should be accorded a place within the speech decoding mechanism, this seems to stem, on the one hand, from such related false starts as Sir Richard Paget's mouth-gesture theory of glottogenesis,[1] and, on the other, from discrepant opinions as to the relative primacy of articulatory versus acoustic representation in speech recognition.[2] In the end, whatever we make of Stricker's original

[1] See his *Human Speech* (1930), where he presents his 'oral-gesture theory', excerpted in Fromkin & Rodman (1983:25).

[2] Cf. for instance Jakobson's remarks in his 1966 paper (repr. 1979, see esp. 246–248).

theory, I think it fair to say that he has, in all events, given a new meaning to the phrase "I can't hear myself think."

REFERENCES

Abercrombie, David. 1967. *Elements of General Phonetics*. Chicago: Aldine.

Fromkin, Victoria, & Robert Rodman. [3]1983 ([1]1974). *An Introduction to Language*. New York: Holt, Rinehart & Winston.

Jakobson, Roman. 1979. "The Role of Phonic Elements in Speech Perception". Jakobson, Roman, and Linda R. Waugh, eds. *The Sound Shape of Language*, 239–248. Bloomington: Indiana University Press.

James, William. 1892. *Psychology*. New York: Henry Holt & Co.

Kussmaul, Adolf. 1877. *Die Störungen der Sprache. Versuch einer Pathologie der Sprache*. Leipzig: F. C. W. Vogel.

Liberman, A. M., F. S. Cooper, D. P. Shankweiler, & M. Studdert-Kennedy. 1967. "Perception of the Speech Code". *Psychological Review* 74.431–461.

Lieberman, Philip. 1967. *Intonation, Perception, and Language*. Cambridge, Mass.: M.I.T. Press.

Pillsbury, Walter B. 1929. *The History of Psychology*. London: George Allen & Unwin.

Stricker, Salomon. 1880. *Studien über die Sprachvorstellungen* Vienna: Wilhelm Braumüller.

—. 1884. "Notes sur les images motrices". *Revue Philosophique* 18:685–691.

Wundt, Wilhelm. 1911. *Völkerpsychologie*. Vol.I: *Die Sprache*. Part I. 3rd ed. Leipzig: Wilhelm Engelmann (First ed., 1900.)

Victor Henry et les lois phon(ét)iques*

PIET DESMET
Katholieke Universiteit Leuven

0. [ALEXANDRE-ANDRE-] VICTOR HENRY (°Colmar, le 17 août 1850 – † Sceaux, le 6 février 1907) est une des figures qui ont marqué le développement de la linguistique historique et générale en France à la fin du XIXe siècle. Il a été un des premiers à intégrer le modèle néogrammairien et peut être classé, avec Gaston Paris et Michel Bréal[1], parmi les fondateurs de la linguistique historico-comparative en France. On ne saurait réduire (Meillet 1907:230–231) son rôle à celui de vulgarisateur des résultats obtenus en grammaire historique. En dehors de ses nombreuses contributions à la grammaire comparée des langues indo-européennes et aux études védiques, Henry s'est également signalé dans les domaines de la linguistique générale et de la philosophie du langage. Ainsi, dans la controverse autour des lois phoniques[2], il défend une position originale par rapport aux néogrammairiens et à leurs critiques (surtout Hugo Schuchardt). De même, ses *Antinomies linguistiques* (1896) constituent une réflexion épistémologique sur les conditions de possibilité d'une science du langage, dont *Le Langage martien* (1901) apporte la confirmation

* Nous tenons à remercier les Professeurs L. Melis et P. Swiggers ainsi que notre collègue J. De Clercq pour leurs remarques judicieuses sur une version antérieure de cet article. Nous dédions ce travail au Lt-Col Van Hellemont, au 1Lt Vanhelmont et au Cpl Delvaux, sans la bienveillance desquels notre participation à ICHoLs V eût été impossible.

[1] Pour une esquisse du rôle institutionnel et scientifique de G. Paris, voir Desmet et Swiggers (1989; 1991). Sur la carrière et la position de Bréal, voir Desmet (1990).

[2] Nous préférons le terme neutre de "loi phonique" à celui de "loi phonétique" vu que l'action des lois ne se limite pas au domaine restreint de la phonétique tel qu'il a été défini par opposition à la phonologie au début du XXe siècle.

expérimentale. Notre analyse veut contribuer à une meilleure compréhension des conceptions théoriques de ce linguiste français du siècle dernier.

Nous nous baserons sur l'intégralité de la production linguistique de Henry. Celle-ci se compose non seulement d'une quarantaine de livres et de quelque soixante articles, mais aussi d'un peu plus de trois cents comptes rendus, publiés essentiellement dans la *Revue critique d'histoire et de littérature*. Notre documentation inclut aussi sa correspondance inédite avec Hugo Schuchardt, qui contient 45 lettres écrites entre 1885 et 1905.

Notre article est consacré plus particulièrement à la position de Henry dans la controverse autour des lois phoniques. Si ses premières publications s'inspirent clairement du modèle organiciste de Schleicher (1.), il s'oriente très vite vers le modèle néogrammairien (2.) qu'il soumet ensuite à quelques menues modifications, analogues à celles que H. Paul y avait apportées. Henry introduit en plus quelques innovations personnelles originales (3.). Vers la fin de sa vie, il entrevoit l'importance des propositions de Meillet pour un renouvellement méthodologique des sciences du langage (4.).

1. Dans ses premières publications, Henry se montre un adepte convaincu des idées schleichériennes. Ceci s'explique entre autres par le fait qu'il s'est initié à la linguistique avec l'aide des collaborateurs de la *Revue de linguistique et de philologie comparée*, l'organe de la linguistique évolutionniste en France[1]. Tant dans ses *Esquisses*

[1] Henry n'a pas le profil du linguiste comparatiste, tel que G. Paris, M. Bréal ou plus tard A. Meillet. Après sa licence en droit à Strasbourg, il est promu docteur en droit à Dijon en 1872 et nommé professeur de législation usuelle, d'économie politique et de géographie commerciale à l'Institut du Nord à Lille. Il ne sera amené à la linguistique que vers 1877 par le biais de l'américanisme. Son goût pour les langues amérindiennes le pousse à devenir collaborateur de la *Revue de linguistique*, dans laquelle il publie entre autres une grammaire de la langue innok et de l'aléoute. Nommé conservateur de la Bibliothèque de Lille en 1880, Henry se sent de plus en plus attiré vers la grammaire comparée des langues indo-européennes et décide de prendre la licence à Douai en 1880. Après avoir soutenu ses thèses de doctorat avec grand succès à la Faculté des lettres de Paris en 1883, il est nommé chargé de cours complémentaire de philologie classique à Douai pour devenir en 1886 professeur adjoint à la même Faculté des lettres, transférée à Lille

morphologiques (Henry 1882) que dans son *Etude sur l'analogie* (Henry 1883), Henry défend la conception organiciste de la langue en prenant la métaphore de la vie du langage au sens littéral. Selon lui, la linguistique historique relève des sciences naturelles et doit se consacrer à la reconstitution de la langue originelle (*Ursprache)* qui aurait été soumise à une longue et inéluctable dégénérescence (Henry 1883:64).

Cette dégénérescence se serait produite suivant des lois phoniques nécessaires et aveugles comparables aux lois physiologiques de la nature : "Oui, les lois phoniques sont aussi aveugles, aussi fatales dans leurs manifestations, que les lois physiques. A vrai dire, que sont-elles, sinon des lois physiques d'un ordre particulier?" (Henry 1883:63–64). Il attribue les éventuelles exceptions à l'action de plusieurs lois affectant un même mot et ne recourt à l'analogie que comme *ultimum refugium*, en la concevant comme une des sept causes perturbatrices possibles d'altération du langage[1].

Son attitude envers l'analogie est pourtant marquée par une certaine ambiguïté. Adoptant le point de vue de la langue comme organisme, il considère l'analogie comme une "forme hystérogène et anti-grammaticale [qui] s'introduit dans le langage, créée à l'image d'une autre forme primitive et régulière" (Henry 1883:14) et qui détruit la structure primitive. Adoptant, à d'autres moments, le point de vue de la langue comme expression de la pensée, il admet que l'analogie "rajeunit le langage et le met en harmonie avec le progrès incessant de la pensée humaine" (Henry 1883:13). L'analogie se limite d'ailleurs strictement au domaine de la morphologie, dans la mesure où son action ne s'exerce, selon lui, que sur le résultat de la transformation phonique (Henry 1883:34).

en 1887. Comme la mort d'Abel Bergaigne avait rendu vacante en août 1888 la chaire de sanskrit et de grammaire comparée de la Faculté des lettres de Paris, Henry est appelé en décembre 1888 à la Sorbonne où il est chargé d'un cours complémentaire de grammaire comparée. En 1894, il obtient sa nomination de professeur titulaire de sanskrit et de grammaire comparée.

[1] A côté de l'analogie grammaticale, Henry (1883:6–13) retient encore comme cause d'altération du langage la désuétude, l'atavisme ou la recherche d'archaïsme, l'écriture, le contact entre les langues, la loi du moindre effort et l'analogie lexicale qui crée des homophones.

Bien que ses premières publications aient en général été bien reçues en France, les critiques sont quasi unanimes à rejeter le point de vue naturaliste de V. Henry. Ainsi, lors de sa soutenance de thèse, Bergaigne (cf. Anonyme 1883:96) avait fait remarquer "qu'il a adopté les théories de la nouvelle école. Mais il avait eu antérieurement une autre éducation linguistique, et parfois le vieil homme reparaît : c'est alors un naturalisme à outrance qu'il professe".

2. Henry abandonnera très vite ce "naturalisme à outrance" pour s'orienter vers le modèle néogrammairien. Déjà à partir de 1884, il se distancie du naturalisme de Schleicher pour insister avant tout sur son apport méthodologique que les néogrammairiens ont retenu, par exemple dans la conception des lois phoniques, dans l'insistance sur la primauté de l'étude de la forme par rapport à celle de la fonction ou dans la volonté de bannir l'arbitraire de toute explication phonétique.

Il présente Schleicher plutôt comme un précurseur immédiat des néogrammairiens qui en aurait fait partie s'il n'était pas mort prématurément. Ainsi, dans le manuscrit[1] qu'il a joint à sa lettre à Schuchardt du 13 mai 1886, il propose de ranger parmi les néogrammairiens tous

> ceux qui suspendent leur jugement, plutôt que d'avancer une conjecture qui contredise une loi phonétique constatée, ou que de supposer une mutation sporadique qui concilie tout. Tel est mon critérium, et à ce point de vue je me croirais autorisé, je l'ai déjà dit, à comprendre dans l'école nouvelle Schleicher lui-même, mort avant la séparation des deux tendances.

Henry défend avec vigueur la constance des lois phoniques, conçues comme des phénomènes essentiellement physiologiques. S'inspirant directement des critères de scientificité en vigueur dans les sciences naturelles, il considère que la linguistique n'est scientifique que si elle se base sur des lois nécessaires et absolues :

> Qui dit science entend par là présentement la recherche du fond général et permanent qui se cache sous l'amoncellement des manifestations

[1] Conservé dans le "Schuchardt-Nachlass", à Graz.

> sporadiques et des irrégularités apparentes, et la linguistique ne mériterait jamais ce nom, si elle ne savait faire le départ de ses constantes et de ses variables. (Henry 1886:222–223)

Même après avoir pris connaissance des critiques du modèle néogrammairien que Schuchardt (1885) avait formulées dans son *Ueber die Lautgesetze*, Henry reste convaincu de la nécessité de maintenir le principe de la constance des lois phoniques. Dans son compte rendu de Schuchardt, il continue à défendre la supériorité méthodologique de la "nouvelle école" (Henry 1886:226). Les seules mutations dont il veut accepter qu'elles ne se laissent pas ramener à des lois sont celles qui touchent les *vocabula usu trita,* les mots d'emploi quotidien, qui ne constituent pour lui qu'une minorité infime de cas exceptionnels.

Henry n'arrive pas à réfuter un argument essentiel de Schuchardt, à savoir que la distinction rigoureuse des facteurs physiologiques et des facteurs psychiques est imaginaire. Henry (1886:223) le considère comme l'argument "le plus redoutable qu'ait jusqu'à présent rencontré le principe des néogrammairiens". En effet, le seul argument pour défendre que l'analogie n'intervient qu'après une mutation phonique est que l'analogie est de nature psychologique alors que les lois phoniques sont de nature physiologique. Si on admet toutefois que la distinction du physiologique et du psychique est loin d'être évidente, l'hypothèse de Schuchardt qu'une mutation phonique est le résultat d'une diffusion à travers le lexique basée sur le mécanisme de l'analogie phonétique[1] devient alors théoriquement tout aussi valable que celle de la constance des lois phoniques. Seul un repli dogmatique permet encore à Henry (1886:225) de sauver le principe de l'infaillibilité des lois.

La *Revue critique* publie aussitôt une réplique de Schuchardt, qui s'en prend avant tout au dogmatisme de Henry auquel il veut substituer le scepticisme critique (Schuchardt 1886:295). Il se demande quelles sont les "marques distinctives" qui permettent aux néogrammairiens de considérer des conformités phoniques comme absolues :

[1] Pour une présentation critique de l'hypothèse de l'analogie phonétique afin de rendre compte de la diffusion d'une innovation à travers le lexique, voir Desmet & Van Hoecke (1989:7–10).

> Les connexions causales sont les seuls faits vraiment acquis à la science. Il est absolument inadmissible de revêtir d'un caractère absolu des conformités phonétiques qui ne sont constatées qu'empiriquement ; elles représentent des probabilités qui s'approchent plus ou moins de la certitude, et c'est comme telles qu'elles doivent entrer dans nos calculs. (Schuchardt 1886:297)

Il critique Henry de ne pas toujours avoir bien saisi le point essentiel de son argumentation, d'avoir laissé son jugement en suspens sur l'hypothèse de l'analogie phonétique et de considérer les lois phoniques comme des entités essentiellement physiologiques, là où les néo-grammairiens eux-mêmes ont évolué vers une conception psycho-physiologique des lois.

Henry envoie à son tour une réplique à la *Revue critique*, mais la direction de la revue l'invite à renoncer à la publication, comme nous l'apprend la chronique du 10 mai 1886. Heureusement, ce texte est conservé dans le "Schuchardt-Nachlass" à Graz. Après avoir précisé ses critères pour qualifier un linguiste de néogrammairien, Henry s'oppose à l'idée qu'il serait impossible de démontrer la constance des lois phoniques. Il invoque non seulement le principe logique qui veut qu'une même cause, dans les mêmes conditions d'action, produise les mêmes effets mais mentionne aussi les cas du rhotacisme en latin et de la loi de Verner comme preuves empiriques de l'existence de lois phoniques absolues. Il admet toutefois que l'hypothèse de l'analogie phonétique permettrait elle aussi de rendre compte de ces évolutions. Mais comme il est convaincu que toute science doit s'élever des faits mieux connus à des lois organiques immuables, il se déclare partisan de la constance des lois phoniques : "Il y a des maladies et il y a des monstres: cela ne prouve rien contre la constance des lois qui président au fonctionnement ou au développement normal de nos organes".

De même, dans l'introduction à son *Précis de grammaire comparée du grec et du latin*, Henry (1888a:15) défend la nature avant tout physiologique des lois phoniques. Pour qualifier un changement phonique de loi, il faut pouvoir démontrer la possibilité physiologique de la transition, qui est conçue comme un processus graduel et imperceptible. Ici aussi, il justifie son recours au principe de l'infaillibilité des lois phoniques par son souci de sauvegarder le caractère scientifique de la discipline (Henry 1888a:16).

3. A partir de 1887, la position de V. Henry subit quelques légères modifications, analogues à celles que Paul (1880) avait apportées au modèle tel qu'il avait été conçu dans les premières publications d'Osthoff et Brugmann (Osthoff et Brugmann 1878, Brugmann 1879)[1]. Rejetant explicitement le naturalisme (Henry 1887b:282), il commence à prendre en considération la composante psychologique et reconnaît le rôle créateur du sujet parlant dans l'évolution linguistique. Ainsi, dans son compte rendu des *Principien* (Paul 1880, [2]1886), Henry (1887a:11) loue Paul pour avoir affirmé qu'il n'y a dans le langage qu'une seule réalité objective, à savoir le sujet parlant.

Les lois phoniques ne sont plus conçues par Henry comme des entités essentiellement physiologiques mais comme des généralisations *a posteriori* d'un fait observé, comme il appert de son compte rendu de Regnaud :

> Les lois physiques sont la généralisation d'un fait qui se produit constamment de la même façon, dans des conditions identiques ; une loi phonétique est la généralisation d'un fait observé, pendant une certaine période de temps, dans l'étendue restreinte d'une petite unité linguistique. (Henry 1888b:184)

Quant à l'analogie, Henry (1888a:103) ne la conçoit plus comme un facteur perturbateur, mais la considère comme un agent indispensable de la formation des mots et même comme l'essence du parler humain. Dans son compte rendu du *Précis,* Havet (1889:46–47) insiste à juste titre sur ce changement de position qu'il approuve.

Henry s'oppose aussi, comme l'avaient d'ailleurs fait les néogrammairiens dès leurs premières publications, aux tentatives "glottogoniques" qui visent la reconstitution de la langue-mère (Henry 1894a:

[1] Ces modifications ne sont pas encore intégrées à l'introduction au *Précis de grammaire comparée du grec et du latin* (1888a). Comme la préface date du 5 juin 1887, tout porte à croire que le texte de base a été rédigé au plus tard au début de 1887.

1895). Selon lui, les racines sont le résidu dernier et insoluble de l'analyse linguistique et ne sauraient être considérées comme des réalités objectives qui expriment un concept élémentaire (Henry 1888b ; 1888c). Il rejette l'idée d'une dégénérescence de la langue primitive (Henry 1894b) pour défendre, au contraire, que toutes les langues se valent (Henry 1900). Les études linguistiques devraient se concentrer avant tout sur les patois et les langues vivantes dans la mesure où seules les langues des populations illettrées et rurales ont gardé leur pureté originelle (Henry 1906a).

L'originalité de la position de Henry réside dans le fait qu'il n'hésitera pas à apporter d'autres modifications à son modèle sans s'inspirer d'une évolution dans la pensée des néogrammairiens eux-mêmes. Ainsi, dans sa lettre à Schuchardt du 31 janvier 1890, il introduit une distinction entre trois niveaux d'application, qu'il appelle des "couches phonétiques", à savoir les *vocabula usu trita,* le langage transmis et le langage appris. Le langage transmis constitue le fond même de la langue et contient les mots nécessaires et primordiaux, appris en général entre 2 et 6 ans. C'est uniquement à ces mots-ci que s'appliquent les lois phoniques. Les *vocabula usu trita* comprennent les mots et locutions constamment répétés et entendus avant que l'enfant soit capable de les répéter. Déjà en 1886, Henry avait concédé qu'ils échappent à la rigidité des lois phoniques. Le langage appris regroupe tous les termes techniques, les emprunts et les mots savants qui ne sont appris qu'à un âge plus ou moins avancé et qui demeurent étrangers à notre vie mentale. Ces éléments surérogatoires se soustraient également à l'action des lois phoniques. Dans ses *Antinomies linguistiques,* Henry (1896:63) reprend cette distinction pour résoudre l'antinomie de la constance de l'évolution linguistique en affirmant que seul le langage transmis est soumis à l'action des lois phoniques constantes :

> Thèse: Si la science du langage est vraiment une science, elle doit aboutir à la constatation de lois fixes, constantes et invariables dans leurs effets — Antithèse : Usus, quem penes arbitrium est et jus et norma loquendi. — Synthèse: Les deux propositions sont vraies, respectivement, du langage transmis et du langage appris.

Une autre originalité de V. Henry est que dès 1888 il reconnaît l'hétérogénéité de la communauté linguistique et admet que seule la langue individuelle peut être absolument pure (Henry 1888d:336). C'est pourquoi, dans son introduction au *Précis de grammaire comparée de l'anglais et de l'allemand* (Henry 1893:18), il restreint l'existence de lois phoniques constantes aux langues idéalement pures[1]. Henry réduit alors les lois phoniques à des principes purement méthodologiques vu l'impossibilité de les constater empiriquement. Henry a donc substitué le "méthodologisme" au "réalisme", qu'il avait défendu dans l'introduction à son *Précis de grammaire comparée du grec et du latin* (Henry 1888a).

Finalement, Henry sera aussi parmi les premiers pour insister, avec Saussure, sur la nature systémique des changements phoniques. Ainsi, il critique Wright de ne pas avoir suffisamment indiqué les liens et les connexions entre les différents changements phoniques (Henry 1892:466). De même, dans son compte rendu de Bühlbring, il énonce le principe général que "il n'importe pas moins, partout où cela est possible, de lui [= à l'élève] faire comprendre qu'une langue est un ensemble, qu'elle évolue d'ensemble, et non point par fragments isolés" (Henry 1902a:188).

Si sur tous ces points l'opinion de Henry a connu une certaine évolution, il subsiste toutefois certains points pour lesquels il reste attaché à ses idées premières. Ainsi, il a toujours été pénétré de la nécessité de séparer strictement la forme et la fonction et défend même la primauté de l'étude de la forme sur celle du sens. Selon Henry (1894a:31), une telle position se justifie par le fait que "tout est mécanisme dans l'acte de la parole, et [que] c'est postérieurement que la pensée attache une valeur dynamique et significative à ce qui ne fut à l'origine qu'une inconsciente succession de réflexes". Ceci explique aussi que le modèle descriptif qu'il adopte dans ses deux *Précis* privilégie la phonétique et la morphologie, qui subsume l'étude de la

1 Ceci ne l'amène toutefois pas à intégrer les phénomènes variationnels et hétérogènes dans son modèle explicatif, comme le feront entre autres Hugo Schuchardt et Antoine Meillet. Il préfère au contraire se concentrer sur un objet homogène idéalisé, tout en reconnaissant qu'il fait par là abstraction de l'hétérogénéité de toute communauté linguistique existante.

formation des mots, de la déclinaison et de la conjugaison, au détriment de la syntaxe, qui n'est que marginalement traitée[1].

De plus, Henry est convaincu du caractère inconscient des phénomènes linguistiques et s'oppose à toute tentative d'explication finaliste de l'évolution du langage. La dernière partie de ses *Antinomies linguistiques* est intégralement consacrée au problème de l'inconscience du sujet parlant à l'égard des conditions de ses activités langagières :

> Pour tout être qui pense et qui parle [...], le langage se confond absolument avec la pensée. Et cette illusion immanente, qui constitue l'antinomie essentielle du langage, celle qu'on pourrait nommer l'antinomie psychologique, se formulera brièvement en ces termes : le langage est le produit de l'activité inconsciente d'un sujet conscient. (Henry 1896:65)

4. A partir de 1894, Henry considère la grammaire comparée des langues indo-européennes de plus en plus comme une science toute faite, dont l'un des principaux acquis est le principe de la constance des lois phoniques et qui ne peut dès lors plus être remis en question :

> Je passe sur la question de la constance des lois phonétiques, que j'ai déjà trop souvent traitée pour en excéder encore le lecteur : tout en est dit, et, s'il y a quelque part des linguistes qui se plaisent à y voir autre chose qu'une règle de méthode, ou à la contester comme telle, ce n'est vraiment pas notre faute. (Henry 1895:469)

C'est sans doute la raison pour laquelle Henry (1896:63) a décidé de reléguer en note l'antinomie des lois phoniques dans ses *Antinomies*

[1] Les modèles descriptifs de ses deux *Précis* sont légèrement différents. Ainsi, le *Précis de grammaire comparée du grec et du latin* (Henry 1888a:11) aborde successivement la phonétique, ou l'étude des sons; l'étymologie, ou l'étude de la formation des mots et la morphologie ou l'étude des formes grammaticales (déclinaison, conjugaison). Dans le *Précis de grammaire comparée de l'anglais et de l'allemand*, par contre, Henry (1893:15) ne distingue plus que la phonétique et la morphologie, ou la comparaison des formes, à laquelle il intègre l'étymologie.

linguistiques pour se concentrer sur les antinomies de la nature et de l'origine du langage et sur celle du rapport entre langue et pensée.

Henry a vu encore la parution des premiers ouvrages de Meillet et de son "école linguistique". Il comprend très bien ce que leur méthode contient d'innovateur pour les études linguistiques. Selon Henry (1903:463), Meillet se distingue de ses prédécesseurs par son point de vue strictement inductif. Toutes ses conclusions générales sont basées sur des faits minutieusement observés et directement attestés, sans faire appel à des formes reconstruites. Dans cette nouvelle "école", la forme et la fonction sont considérées dans leur complémentarité. C'est pourquoi la grammaire historique ne saurait plus se concentrer exclusivement sur l'étude de la forme. Selon Meillet, l'étude de la fonction doit aller de pair avec celle de la forme :

> Maintenant que la forme et la fonction sont bien nettement tenues pour distinctes et que la linguistique ne court plus le risque de les confondre, elle peut sans inconvénient, elle doit, pour se former une idée adéquate du langage, renoncer à les séparer. Deux réseaux concordants, l'un de formes, l'autre de fonctions. (Henry 1903:464–465)

Evaluant la contribution de cette nouvelle génération de linguistes[1], Henry (1903:462) n'hésite pas à affirmer : "Si schleichérien qu'on soit d'éducation ou de tempérament, il faudra bien qu'on s'accommode de ce nouveau point de vue. C'est le vrai et le définitif". D'ailleurs, il conçoit cette évolution non comme un échec pour le modèle néogrammairien mais comme la preuve de son succès (Henry 1906b:265–266). Malheureusement, Henry n'a pu participer activement à la réalisation de ce renouveau méthodologique qui constituait pour lui le couronnement du mouvement néogrammairien.

Nous espérons avoir démontré que la contribution de Henry dépasse largement celle d'un simple vulgarisateur vu l'importance de son rôle dans le débat de la constance des lois phoniques, qui a dominé les

[1] D'autres innovations, dont Meillet est l'auteur, comme la distinction entre les lois générales et possibles et les lois particulières et nécessaires (Henry 1902b:403) ou l'introduction de la composante sociale dans la description linguistique, ne sont traitées que marginalement par Henry.

discussions théoriques de la fin du XIXe siècle. Bien que Henry (1896: 63) lui-même prétende que "c'est là une doctrine sur laquelle, depuis mes premiers débuts, je n'ai point connu de variation", nous avons pu distinguer plusieurs phases dans l'évolution de sa position, qui correspondent au développement de la linguistique à la fin du XIXe siècle, évoluant du modèle organiciste de Schleicher au modèle historico-comparatif de Meillet. On comprend dès lors pourquoi Antoine Thomas (1907:328) considère la mort de Henry "comme une grande perte pour la linguistique générale".

REFERENCES

Anonyme. 1883. "Thèses de doctorat ès lettres. Soutenance de M. Victor Henry". *Revue critique* N.S. 16.93–98.

Brugmann, Karl. 1879. "Zur Geschichte des Nominalsuffixe *-as, -jas* und *-vas*". *KZ* 24.4–8.

Desmet, Piet. 1990. "The Role of Semantics in the Development of Historical Linguistics in France". *BJL* 5.133–158.

Desmet, Piet & Pierre Swiggers. 1989. "Gaston Paris : aspects linguistiques d'une oeuvre philologique". K.U.Leuven : Dep. Linguïstiek (preprint n° 125, 34 pp.). (A paraître dans les *Actes du XIXe Congrès International de Linguistique et de Philologie Romanes. Saint-Jacques de Compostelle, 4–9 septembre 1989).*

— . 1991. "Diachronie et continuité : les vues de Gaston Paris sur la grammaire historique du français". *FLH* 11 (à paraître).

Desmet, Piet & Willy Van Hoecke. 1989. "Le caractère graduel ou discret du changement phonique : un faux problème". (preprint n° 126, 23 pp.). K.U. Leuven : Dep. Linguïstiek (A paraître dans les *Actes du XIXe Congrès International de Linguistique et de Philologie Romanes. Saint-Jacques de Compostelle, 4–9 septembre 1989.)*

Havet, Louis. 1889. Compte rendu de Henry (1888a, ^{2}1889). *Revue critique N.S.* 27.41–50.

Henry, Victor. 1882. *Esquisses morphologiques, considérations générales sur la nature et l'origine de la flexion indo-européenne*. Lille : Quarré. (Extrait du *Muséon* 1.427–437, 477–493.)

— . 1883. *Etude sur l'analogie en général et sur les formations analogiques de la langue grecque*. Paris : Maisonneuve.

— . 1886. Compte rendu de *Cenni sullo stato presente della Grammatica Ariana istorica e preistorica* de Pietro Merlo (Turin 1885) et de *Ueber die Lautgesetze,*

gegen die Junggrammatiker de Hugo Schuchardt (Berlin : Oppenheim, 1885.). *Revue critique* N.S. 21.221–226.
—. 1887a. Compte rendu de Paul (1880, ²1886). *Revue critique* N.S. 23.6–11.
—. 1887b. Compte rendu de *La Vie des Mots, étudiée dans leurs significations* d'Arsène Darmesteter (Paris : Delagrave, 1887.) *Revue critique* N.S. 23.282–285.
—. 1888a. *Précis de grammaire comparée du grec et du latin*. Paris : Hachette. (Rééditions ²1889, ³1890, ⁴1892, ⁵1894.)
—. 1888b. Compte rendu de *Origine et Philosophie du Langage, ou Principes de Linguistique Indo-européenne* de Paul Regnaud (Paris : Delagrave, 1888.). *Revue critique* N.S. 25.181–186.
—. 1888c. Compte rendu de *Origin of the Greek, Latin and Gothic Roots* de James Byrne (Londres : Trübner, 1888.), *Revue critique* N.S. 25.475–477.
—. 1888d. Compte rendu de *Quelques observations sur la Phonétique des patois et leur influence sur les langues communes* (Extrait de la *Revue des Patois Gallo-Romans)* de Jean Psichari (Paris : Leroux, 1888.) et de *Observations phonétiques sur quelques phénomènes néo-grecs* (Extrait des *Mémoires de la S.L.P.*) de Jean Psichari (Paris : Imprimerie Nationale, 1888). *Revue critique* N.S. 26.335–337.
—. 1892. Compte rendu de *A Primer of the Gothic Language, Notes and Glossary* de Joseph Wright (Londres : Clarendon, 1892.). *Revue critique* N.S. 33.466.
—. 1893. *Précis de grammaire comparée de l'anglais et de l'allemand rapportés à leur commune origine et rapprochés des langues classiques*. Paris : Hachette. (Réédition ²1906.)
—. 1894a. Compte rendu de *Die Entstehung der Dehnstufe* de Wilhelm Streitberg (Strasbourg : Trübner, 1894.) *Revue critique* N.S. 38.27–32.
—. 1894b. Compte rendu de *Progress in Language, with special reference to English* d'Otto Jespersen (Londres : Swan Sonnenschein, 1894.) *Revue critique N.S.* 38.501–504.
—. 1895. Compte rendu de *Agglutination und Adaptation* d'Edwin W. Fay (Baltimore : Friedenwald, 1895.) *Revue critique* N.S. 40.469–471.
—. 1896. *Antinomies linguistiques. (Bibliothèque de la Faculté des lettres de Paris*. 2). Paris : Alcan.
—. 1900. Compte rendu de *The Practical Study of Languages, a Guide for Teachers and Learners de Henry Sweet* (Londres : Dent, 1899.) *Revue critique* N.S. 49.78–80.
—. 1901. *Le Langage martien: Etude analytique de la genèse d'une langue dans un cas de glossolalie somnambulique*. Paris : Maisonneuve. (Extrait de la *Revue de linguistique et de philologie comparée* 33(1900)317–371, 34(1901)1–43, 125–178.
—. 1902a. Compte rendu de *Altenglisches Elementarbuch* de Karl D. Bühlbring (Heidelberg : Winter, 1902) *Revue critique N.S.* 53.187–189.
—. 1902b. Compte rendu des *Mélanges linguistiques offerts à M. Antoine Meillet par ses élèves, D. Barbelenet, G. Dottin, R. Gauthiot, M. Grammont, A. Laronde,*

M. Niedermann, J. Vendryes, avec un avant-propos par P. Boyer (Paris : Klincksieck, 1902.) *Revue critique N.S.* 54.401–403.

—. 1903. Compte rendu de *Introduction à l'étude comparative des langues indo-européennes* d'Antoine Meillet (Paris : Hachette, 1903.) *Revue critique N.S.* 55.461–466.

—. 1906a. Compte rendu de *A Grammar of the Dialect of Kendal (Westmoreland) descriptive and historical* de T. O. Hirst (Heidelberg : Winter, 1906.) *Revue critique N.S.* 61.174.

—. 1906b. Compte rendu de *Grundriss der vergleichenden Grammatik der indogermanischen Sprachen. Zweiter Band : Lehre von den Wortformen und ihrem Gebrauch. Erster Theil : Allgemeines, Zusammensetzung (Komposita), Nominalstämme* de Karl Brugmann (Strasbourg : Trübner, ²1906.) *Revue critique N.S.* 62.261–266.

Meillet, Antoine. 1907. "Victor Henry". *BSLP* 14.224–231.

Osthoff, Hermann & Karl Brugmann. 1878. *Morphologische Untersuchungen auf dem Gebiete der indogermanischen Sprachen. I.* Leipzig: Hirzel.

Paul, Hermann. 1880. *Principien der Sprachgeschichte.* Tübingen : Niemeyer. (Réédition utilisée ⁵1920.)

Schuchardt, Hugo. 1886. "Correspondance. Sur les lois phonétiques. Réponse à M. V. Henry. [Voir *Revue critique*, n° 12, art. 66]". *Revue critique N.S.* 21.294–300.

Thomas, Antoine. 1907. "Victor Henry". *Romania* 36.328.

The Role of Acoustics and Apperception in Franz Boas' Theory of Phonetics*

MICHAEL MACKERT
University of Delaware

HISTORIOGRAPHERS OF LINGUISTICS have not fully considered nineteenth-century work in acoustics and the concept of apperception in understanding the psycholinguistic theory underlying Franz Boas' (1858–1942) refutation of ethnocentric views of alternating sounds. Rulon Wells (1974:50), for example, dismisses Boas' views by maintaining that "Boas' psychological explanation of alternating sounds has little if any value". Similarly, Anderson (1985:208), who focuses on rules and representations, ignores the role of acoustics in Boas' views on alternating sounds and wrongly renders *apperception* as *perception*. However, it is my view that both acoustics and apperception are vital for a better understanding of Boas' account of alternating sounds. In what follows, I shall outline the theory underlying Boas' account by drawing on his texts in psychophysics and on a neglected draft of a letter by Boas (1888) to Horatio Hale (1817–1896) who, as a member of the Wilkes Expedition (1838–1842), had pioneered American ethnology. Boas' physiological views on speech-sounds and his essentialist ideas of the acoustical nature of sounds will be situated within the context of nineteenth-century work in acoustics, physiology, psychology, and psychophysics. I shall argue that Boas' theory presupposes a machine model of the mind in which the ear is seen as a mechanical extension and that Boas viewed speech-sound

* I would like to thank the American Philosophical Society for granting me permission to quote from Boas' professional correspondence. I would also like to thank Mark Amsler and Susan Braidi for their suggestions, which have led to a much improved paper.

recognition as a deterministic process governed by the law of differential thresholds and apperception.

In September 1888, after Boas had returned from his first field trip to the North-West coast of North America for the British Association for the Advancement of Science, he corresponded with his supervisor Horatio Hale about the format of his report. In their letters, Boas and Hale discussed the phonetic alphabets of Max Müller [1855], Lepsius [1863], Techmer [1884], and Powell [1880], and they worked out a printable phonetic alphabet adequately representing the sounds peculiar to Native American languages. In order to convince Hale of some new sound symbols, Boas drafted a letter containing a first sketch of his psycholinguistic theory of phonetics which supplements his views put forward in "On Alternating Sounds" (Boas 1889).

In his draft, Boas emphasized that from a physiological perspective speech-sounds form continuous series. In addition, in discussing the positions of the speech organs, Boas (1889:73) remarked that "it will be readily understood that these positions will not be exactly the same every time we attempt to produce a certain sound, but that they will vary slightly." For Boas, these variations were accidental or influenced by the phonetic environment of a sound. Hence, Boas (1888) maintained that from an acoustical perspective "there are no absolutely definite sounds in a language, but their physical character approaches a certain average."

Boas' views on the acoustical nature of speech sounds are further revealed in his phrase "certain groups of vibrations which are most prominent in our consonants giving them their [...] principal character [...]" (Boas 1888). Boas' notion of 'principal character' of consonants reflects widely held compositional views on speech-sounds in nineteenth-century phonetics and acoustics. In both fields, sounds were seen as combinations of more basic acoustic phenomena giving each sound its peculiar quality. Hermann Helmholtz (1821–1894), for instance, maintained that any regular periodic vibration producing the sensation of a clang (a musical sound or vowel) may be analyzed into different simple vibrations (Helmholtz 1877). Each simple vibration is equivalent to a group of oscillations and produces the sensation of a tone. The group of oscillations with the lowest frequency produces the sensation of the fundamental tone of the clang. Other groups standing in a simple numerical relationship to the frequency of the fundamental tone produce its harmonic overtones. For Helmholtz, the presence and number of the harmonic overtones were responsible for the 'Klangfarbe' (timbre) of musical sounds and vowels.

Boas' adherence to Helmholtz' compositional view of sounds is revealed in Boas' discussion of Helmholtz' theory of timbre. Boas (1882:372) stated, "die Klangfarbe eines Tones hängt bekanntlich von der Art seiner Zusammenfassung aus Partialtönen ab [as is well known, the timbre of a tone depends on the nature of its composition out of partial tones]". At the same time, Boas (1882:372) also expressed his belief in the compositional nature of vowels when he noted that simple tones may be combined to create different shades of timbre "wie die Versuche von Helmholtz über die künstlichen Vokale lehren [as Helmholtz' experiments on artificial vowels show]".

Boas' phrase 'vibrations which are most prominent in our consonants giving them their principal character' is also reminiscent of Wilhelm Wundt's (1832–1920) account of characteristic partial tones in consonants. Wundt proposed that irregular periodic vibrations producing sensations of noise such as consonants also contain simple vibrations, and he maintained that certain consonants were also characterized by specific overtones. For Wundt (1880:37), the presence of overtones in speech-sounds allowed for the latter's use as audible signs, and he claimed that each "konstante Klang- und Geräuschfärbung [constant timbre of a clang and a noise]" was an element "mannigfacher Vorstellungs- und Gefühlszeichen [of various signs of representation and feeling]" which serve as vehicles of expression.

Although Boas did not mention that characteristic overtones made it possible for speech sounds to be used as auditory signs, he must have had the identifying function of overtones in mind when he used the phrase 'principal character'. Furthermore, Boas' use of the term 'combination' and the phrase 'groups of oscillations' in his discussion of the human ear reveals his awareness of the pendulumlike nature of the sound waves causing the sensation of partial tones and shows that Boas presupposed a mechanical model of the analytic faculty of the ear as put forward by Helmholtz (1877) and Wundt (1880). According to

Boas (1888), the ear has the ability to pick out only "certain groups of oscillations from a [...] combination and to hear them more clearly than others which may be [...] from a purely physical standpoint just as much developed as" the selected ones. In both Helmholtz' and Wundt's models, the ear mechanically analyzes periodic vibrations into groups of oscillations producing the sensations of partial tones. Helmholtz (1877:209–250), for example, theorized that the fibres of the basilar membrane in the ear are tuned to specific frequencies like the strings of a piano. Each fibre of the membrane resounds with sympathetic vibration if stimulated by a group of oscillations with the corresponding frequency. When a complex vibration impinges on the ear, its component groups of oscillations simultaneously set into sympathetic vibration their corresponding fibers of the membrane and the connected Cortian arches. The arches are connected to specific nerve fibers each of which transmits different tonal sensations individually to the brain. For Helmholtz, the transmission of each sensation proceeded like the flow of the electric current in a telegraphic wire. From his perspective, each tonal sensation entered consciousness individually.

At first, Boas' (1888) ideas on the analytic faculty of the ear seem to contradict Wundt's and Helmholtz' views. For Boas, a choice is involved and only certain oscillations are selected and heard more clearly than others which are physically "just as much developed". By contrast, within Helmholtz' and Wundt's models, the ear cannot make a choice but only reacts passively with sympathetic vibration to all incoming oscillations of sufficient amplitude within its frequency range. What Boas' statement about the selective faculty of the ear suggests, however, is that he viewed the ear as a mechanical extension of the mind and that he used the term 'ear' as a synecdoche for 'mind', which alone may make a choice. The term 'select', on the other hand, referred to those mechanical operations of the mind which are involved in hearing. In this sense does Boas' remark that the ear selects only "certain groups of vibrations from combinations" become intelligible within the context of then current mechanical models of the ear.

Furthermore, Boas' deterministic view of the mechanical operations of the mind is also revealed in his remark that "this *choice* is not voluntary but affected by [...] the perceived sounds. That is, new, *unknown sounds are apperceived by means of known sounds* [...]" (Boas 1888; italics mine: M.M.). This last-mentioned statement in effect links his theory to ideas about the mechanics of mental representations and apperception as developed by Johann Friedrich Herbart (1776–1841) and his followers, while standing opposed to Helmholtz' and Wundt's views. Whereas Helmholtz considered apperception as a higher degree of consciousness at which complex sensations could be analyzed into individual component sensations, Wundt linked apperception to attention and will and used the term to refer to the subject's awareness of mental representations. By contrast, Herbartian psychologists viewed apperception as an interactive process between two mental representations. For Moritz Lazarus (1824–1903), for instance, perception designated the soul's 'Auffassung' (apprehension) of images provided by the senses (Lazarus 1878). Apperception, on the other hand, referred to the reproduction of older mental representations by a new representation given in perception and to the integration of the new representation into the group of the older representations. From Lazarus' perspective, perception and apperception accompany each other with the older representations supplementing new representations given in perception. Similarly, for Boas' teacher Benno Erdmann (1851–1921), apperception referred to the reproduction of a set of dispositions by a stimulus and their simultaneous amalgamation into an apperceived representation (Erdmann 1886). By contrast, Heymann Steinthal (1823–1899), Lazarus' friend and collaborator, viewed apperception as a process in which an apperceiving representational mass and an apperceived representational mass amalgamate, while perception referred to the result of this process (Steinthal 1881).[1]

Like the Herbartians, Boas viewed apperception as a process in which a new mental representation interacts with similar older representations. Boas (1889:74) made clear that "a new sensation is apperceived by means of similar sensations that form part of our knowledge". Within Boas' phonetic theory, the two elements of apperception were a representation of a sound given through the sense of hearing and

[1] For a more detailed account of the Herbartian framework underlying Boas' theory, see my dissertation (in progress).

a representation of a similar known sound already part of a speaker's phonetic system. Boas referred to the former component as the 'percept' of a sound while he seemed to employ the term 'concept of a sound' for the latter. According to Boas, a listener perceives a sound when appropriate vibrations stimulate the listener's tympanic membrane. Then, the listener will apperceive the sound by means of similar known sounds. Boas (1889: 70) further observed "that the vibrations producing the percept vary slightly, about a certain average; besides this, we have to consider that the concept of a sound is still more variable" .For Boas, the percept of a sound is produced by vibrations impinging on the ear and is then furnished to the mind. Although Boas did not mention the reproduction of concepts by percepts, one may assume that within the Herbartian context he took for granted the reproduction of concepts as prior to or simultaneous with the process of apperception. In either case, the percept of a sound amalgamates with a reproduced similar concept in the mind of a listener.

Boas' (1889:75) discussion of sound blindness shows how Boas conceived of apperception as a classifying process synonymous with 'involuntary assimilation'. For Boas, this process was involuntary because the direction of assimilation is determined by the sensation and not by the will of the subject. That is, a sensation will automatically reproduce a concept derived from similar sensations. As Boas (1888) put it, "this *choice* [the selection of oscillations by the mind] is not voluntary but affected by [...] the perceived sound."

The mental operation which chooses groups of oscillations from a combination and classifies them under similar concepts is the process of apperception. This choice is not voluntary but deterministic because, without any interference of the will, familiar component groups of oscillations characterizing a sound given in sensation automatically reproduce the concept of a sound containing the same or similar groups of oscillations.

Boas' deterministic view of the mechanical operations of the mind provided him with an explanation of combined or alternating sounds. In his letter to Hale, Boas stressed that these sounds did not really exist, and he maintained that they were "merely such sounds which we apperceive through two or more sounds to which they resemble, that is the vibrations of all are combined is the [...] vibrations" (Boas 1888). In his statement, he did not deny the phenomenon of combined or alternating sounds, but he rejected the views of scholars like Daniel G. Brinton (1837–1899), Max Müller (1823–1900), and Archibald H. Sayce (1845–1935) that these sounds were unstable and the hallmark of primitive languages. For Boas, alternating sounds were just as much averages moving within certain limits as the sounds of European languages. Acoustically, an alternating sound *a* of a Language 1 constitutes an average containing different groups of oscillations *x, y,* and *z* each of which characterizes the different sounds *b, c,* and *d* in a Language 2 respectively. For example, in Haida, a language spoken in the Queen Charlotte Islands in the Western part of Canada, the sound [d] combines groups of oscillations which occur separately in the different combinations of groups of oscillations characterizing the English voiced and voiceless alveolar stops [d] and [t] respectively.[1]Sapir For Boas (1889), the seemingly unstable character of the [d] sound of Haida was a result of different alternating apperceptions of the average variations of the sound by native speakers of English. If in the Haida sound, the groups of oscillations characterizing the English voiceless alveolar stop predominated, the percept of the Haida sound automatically reproduced the concept of the voiceless alveolar stop of English to which it assimilated. However, if the oscillations characterizing the English voiced alveolar stop were dominant in the percept, they reproduced and assimilated to the concept of the voiced stop.

Boas (1888) also maintained that students unfamiliar with Haida are "prejudiced by the *d* and *t* bias, and therefore psychologically the limits of the [...] apparent variation are extended (in accordance with a well known psychophysic law)". Hence, students will often hear the English stops instead of [d]. The coocurrence of the terms 'limit', 'extended', and 'well-known psychophysic law' in Boas' draft and his discussion of threshold phenomena in "On Alternating Sounds" suggest that Boas

[1] Sapir (1923:145) described the series of alternating or intermediate stops as "unaspirated 'voiceless lenes' ... ".

understood alternating apperceptions of combined sounds in terms of Fechner's law of thresholds. Gustav Theodor Fechner (1801–1887) had found that a difference in magnitude between two sensations became unnoticeable even though the value of the difference in magnitude between their two stimuli had not reached zero. Fechner referred to the value at which a difference between two sensations was not noticeable any longer as *differential threshold* (Fechner 1860). In his own psychophysical work, Boas (1881, 1882) investigated the influence of attention and practice on differential threshold values, and he demanded that research on thresholds investigate not only differences and similarities in the intensities of stimuli but also in their qualities.

Fechner's law and Boas' own observations supplemented his account of alternating sounds as being the result of alternating apperceptions. From this psychophysical view, alternating apperceptions depend on whether the threshold of similarity between a percept and a concept is exceeded or not. Depending on the predominant groups of oscillations in the acoustic stimulus, the actual 'limits of the apparent variation' of the Haida sound are psychologically extended to include either all of the groups of oscillations characterizing the voiced alveolar stop or the voiceless alveolar stop of English. That is, in apperception, oscillations not given in the stimulus are supplemented by the reproduced concept.

To sum up, Boas' theoretical explanation refuted positions which viewed alternating sounds as unstable. Boas believed that speech-sounds were averages whose component groups of oscillations give each sound its character. Boas' theory presupposed a view of mind as an agentless machine connected to the world through its mechanical extension, the ear. The ear analyzes speech-sounds into their component oscillations, and the resulting sensations are individually transmitted into consciousness. Apperception, the involuntary assimilation of a percept to a similar concept, and the law of differential thresholds produced the phenomenon of alternating sounds.

REFERENCES

Anderson, Stephen R. 1985. *Phonology in the Twentieth Century*. Chicago: University Press.

Boas, Franz. 1881. "Ueber eine neue Form des Gesetzes der Unterschiedsschwelle". *Pflüger's Archiv* 26.367–375.

— . 1882. "Ueber den Unterschiedsschwellenwerth als ein Maas der Intensität psychischer Vorgänge". *Philosophische Monatshefte* 18.367–375.

—. 1888. Letter to Horatio Hale, 24 Sept. 1888. Boas' Papers. Item # 130. 2 pp. Philadelphia: American Philosophical Society.

—. 1889. "On Alternating Sounds". *American Anthropologist* 2:47–53. (Repr. in *The Shaping of American Anthropology* ed. by George W. Stocking, 72–77. New York: Basic Books, 1974.)

Erdmann, Benno. 1886. "Zur Theorie der Apperception". *Vierteljahreszeitschrift für wissenschaftliche Philosophie* 10:4.391–418.

Fechner, Gustav T. 1860. *Elemente der Psychophysik.* 2 vols. Leipzig: Breitkopf & Härtel.

Helmholtz, Hermann. [4]1877 [[1]1863]. *Die Lehre von den Tonempfindungen.* Braunschweig: Friedrich Vieweg.

Lazarus, Moritz. [2]1878. *Das Leben der Seele.* Vol. II: *Geist und Sprache.* Berlin: Heinrich Schindler.

Lepsius, Richard. [2]1863. *Standard Alphabet.* London: Williams & Norgate. (Reprint ed. with an introduction by J. A. Kemp. Amsterdam: John Benjamins, 1981.)

Mackert, Michael (forthcoming). *Re-reading Franz Boas: Intertextuality, Discontinuities, and Strategies in the History of Modern Linguistics.* University of Delaware (Dissertation in progress.)

Müller, Friedrich Max. [2]1855. *The Languages of the Seat of War in the East.* London: William & Norgate.

Powell, John Wesley. [2]1880. *Introduction to the Study of Indian Languages.* Washington: Government Printing Office.

Sapir, Edward. 1923. "The Phonetics of Haida". *International Journal of American Linguistics* 2.143–158.

Steinthal, Heymann. [2]1881. *Abriss der Sprachwissenschaft.* Vol.I: *Einleitung in die Psychologie und Sprachwissenschaft.* Berlin: Ferdinand Dümmler.

Techmer, Friedrich. 1884. "Transkription mittels der lateinischen Kursivschrift." *Internationale Zeitschrift für Allgemeine Sprachwissenschaft* 1.171–192.

Wells, Rulon. 1974. "Phonemics in the Nineteenth Century, 1876–1900". *Studies in the History of Linguistics* ed. by Dell Hymes, 434–453. Bloomington: Indiana Univ. Press.

Wundt, Wilhelm. [2]1880. *Grundzüge der Physiologischen Psychologie.* 2 vols. Leipzig: Wilhelm Engelmann.

The Beginning and Development of Persian Syntactic Descriptions

MEHDI MESHKOT DINI
Ferdowsi University

I. INTRODUCTION

THERE IS NO INFORMATION available about the existence of any syntactic or morphological studies of Persian remaining from the Old or Middle Persian eras; although there is, for certain, enough evidence that scholars of the Middle Persian era had some precise knowledge of the Persian sound system. The fact that they transcribed Avestan texts into an alphabet system which they invented on the basis of the Middle Persian (Pahlavi) alphabet, indicates that they were efficient phoneticians who had some precise knowledge about the Avestan as well as the Middle Persian sound system (Reichelt 1968:93).

During the Islamic era, i.e., the Modern Persian period, there were a host of Iranian linguists, among whom Sibvayh (765–796) was the most outstanding, but they all studied Arabic only, as it was the language of religion, knowledge, education, politics and social prestige. They did not consider Persian at all as a subject of linguistic study and description, although many quite well known and outstanding poets and writers produced invaluable poetic and literary works in Persian. Nevertheless, in later centuries, sporadic references were made to Persian morphology within discussions about different subjects such as Persian prosody, Arabic grammar, or in introductions to Persian dictionaries compiled in India. Shamsuddin Mohammad Ibn Qais Razi (thirteenth century A.D.) was the first literary scholar who made some references to elements of Persian morphology in his work on Persian prosody, named *al-muʕjam fi maʕāyir-i ašʕār-ilʕajam*, "On Persian rhyme and rhythm, in Persian". Ibn-i Mohanna's work (fourteenth century, A.D.) was another one written in Arabic, on the morphology and syntax of three languages: Arabic, Mongolian, and Persian. The writer lived during the Mongolian reign, and thus, in his book, he explained that some knowledge of these three languages was necessary at the time. Abu Hayyan Nahvi's (1256–1344) work on Persian morphology and syntax (fourteenth century) was still another written in Arabic, but it is no longer available.

Since the seventeenth century, in the introductions to Persian dictionaries compiled in India, such as Jahangiri's Persian Dictionary, by Jamaluddin Hosain Inju Shirazi, and *Borhān-i Qātiʕ* "Strict reason", by Mohammad Husain Ibn Khalaf Tabrizi, famed as Borhan (seventeenth century), some references to Persian morphology are included, but nothing at all about Persian syntax. However, no serious studies of Persian morphology and syntax were produced before the nineteenth century, although Iranian grammarians provided detailed and precise works on Arabic morphology and syntax during the same period.

II. THE BEGINNING AND DEVELOPMENT OF PERSIAN TRADITIONAL GRAMMAR

During the late eighteenth century and early nineteenth century,studies and works on Persian grammar, were no more than partial translations of Arabic *Sarf-o nahv,* "morphology and syntax", as they called it in Arabic, into Persian language. During the same time, some copy translations of the grammar of Turkish as well as of some European languages were also produced as Persian grammars. This type of grammar, however, dealt mostly with morphology, while syntax was being neglected altogether.

The earliest Persian grammars appeared only late in the nineteenth century. *Qavāʕed-e Sarf va Nahv-e Fārsi,* "Persian morphological and syntactic rules", was the first Persian grammar written by Abdul-Karim Ibn Abil Qasim Irvani in Azarbayjan (north-west Iran). In writing his grammar, he explained in the introduction, he used previous studies of Persian morphology included in the introductions to Persian dictionaries, but he claimed that he added a lot to the knowledge. He gave evidence for his morphological and syntactic rules by citing verses from Persian poetry.

Next we come to Mohammad Karim Khan Kermani's (1847–1906) grammar of Persian, written about a decade after Irvani's Persian grammar. Kermani's main goal was Arabic grammar, but therein he included Persian grammar as well, to facilitate the learning of Arabic grammar. One of the most important syntactic points which he took notice of was the distinction between the two types of subject: subject, the actor and subject, the patient, which had not been introduced in this way into Arabic syntax before. *Tanbih as-sebyān* by Mohammad Hosain Masʕud Ansari (d. 1895) was another Persian grammar which appeared in the last decade of nineteeth century during Naser ad-Din Shah Ghajar's reign. In the introduction to his book, he explained that he used to study French in his leisure time while staying in Turkey. Then, he found out that it was not easy to learn French or Arabic grammar without having some knowledge about Persian grammar. That was why, he added, he began to describe and present Persian grammatical rules. Notice that the three Persian grammars mentioned above were the most outstanding ones, written in the late nineteenth century. Nevertheless there were some others of less importance.

At the same time, however, Mirza Habib Isfahani (d. 1898) wrote the first Persian grammar on the basis of parts-of-speech-framework, which he named *Dabestān-e Pārsi* "Persian primary school", published late in the nineteenth century (1890). In his grammar, he introduced the Persian term *dastur* meaning "grammar", for the first time. He wrote his grammar while living in Istanbul, Turkey, where he taught Persian language and grammar. He knew Persian, Turkish, Arabic and French well. He was also acquainted with some other European languages. In writing his Persian grammar, therefore, he used his knowledge about the grammars of European languages. In his Persian grammar, he introduced ten parts of speech: Noun, Adjective, Pronoun, Demonstrative, Verb, Verbal, Adverb, Preposition, Interrogative, Interjection. He emphasized that he followed previous grammarians in his proposed parts of speech. It should be noted that Mirza Habib had already written a former version of his Persian grammar, named *dastur-e Sokhan,* "a grammar of speech" nine years earlier (Homayi 1955:122–127).

Mirza Habib Isfahani's most important contribution to Persian grammar was the fact that he tried to present morphological and syntactic rules of Persian by relying on Persian language data, and not as it was practiced before, relying on a translation of Arabic rules only. Hence, we can consider his work as almost the first true grammar of Persian, although the fact that he used his knowledge about the grammars of European languages in writing his Persian grammar should, however, have given rise to some problems. *Lisān al-ʕajam* "Persian language", published early in the twentieth century, by Mirza Hasan Taleghani was another Persian grammar, presented again, just as a translation and a copy of Arabic morphology and syntax.

Dastur-e kashef, "Kashef's grammar" by Gholam-Hosain Kashef (1900) comes next. The writer copied Turkish rules into Persian. Thus, his Persian grammar became linguistically invalid. *Zabān-Āmuz-e Fārsi,* "A Handbook of Persian" (written almost at the same time) by Ali-Akbar Nazemul-Atebba (1847–1923) is yet another Persian grammar which, just like Kermani's Persian grammar previously mentioned, was originally written for the purpose of teaching Arabic grammar; however, it includes Persian grammatical descriptions to facilitate the teaching of Arabic grammar.

The most comprehensive Persian grammar was written in three books for high-school students by Abdul-Azim Gharib (1878–1965) in the first half of the twentieth century. Abdul-Azim Gharib was the most eminent grammarian whose Persian grammar books were published and then reprinted more than twenty times during his life. In writing his grammar, Gharib followed Mirza Habib Isfahani but supplied some improvements to Isfahani's descriptions. While Isfahani had presented ten parts of speech, Gharib recognized only nine: noun, adjective, pronoun, number, verb, adverb, preposition, conjunction, interjection (Homayi 1955:127).

Abdur-Rahim Homayun-Farrokh (1874–1959) also wrote a detailed and comprehensive grammar entitled *Comprehensive Persian Grammar* (1958) in seven volumes. He, too, adopted the parts-of-speech framework for writing his Persian grammar. Like all Persian traditional grammarians, he also cited a large number of verses from classical Persian poetry to indicate the validity of his grammatical statements (Homayun-Farrokh 1960).

Following Gharib's example a large number of Persian grammars were written during the second half of the present century, all based on the parts-of-speech framework. Obviously, the shortcomings of all traditional grammars are inherent in them, among these, imposing of the grammatical categories and structures of other languages on Persian, mixing of linguistic and nonlinguistic categories, taking into account language data from different stages of Persian — both from prose and poetry — and adopting the written instead of spoken language are the most outstanding ones (Bateni 1977:29). Yet, their efforts are most worthy of consideration, as they initiated and developed Persian grammar as a subject of study. Indeed, through their efforts syntactic structures of Persian were specifically dealt with and described in detail although not, however, in an entirely scholarly fashion. Among these the following are the most interesting: "Noun + Noun" as a genitive structure, "Noun + Adjective" patterns, direct and indirect objects, subclasses of the noun and the adjective, different types of sentence structure, (i.e. simple and compound,as well as main and subordinate clauses, and also statement,question and imperative sentences), verb conjugations, and finally, the morphological analysis of nouns, adjectives and verbals.

The most important characteristic to note in the traditional grammar of Persian is the semantic approach to the description of syntactic structures, while surface structures were mostly taken for granted. Accordingly, in many cases no clear representation of surface elements was given.

III. LINGUISTIC THEORIES AND PERSIAN GRAMMAR

During the 1940s and 1950s, a number of articles were published by Parviz Natel Khanlari (1913–1989), on various linguistic subjects, such as language origin, language change, and also on some of the earlier views on linguistics. These articles may possibly be considered as the beginning of modern linguistics in Iran.

Some years later, that is in 1964, Khanlari wrote an article on Persian grammar, which in some respects differed from the traditional view of the grammar of the language, even though it had much in common with traditional concepts. In 1967, Khanlari published his *Persian Grammar* which was originally designed for high school students. Later he revised and expanded it into the last edition published in 1972 and reprinted several times during subsequent years.

Khanlari's Persian *Grammar* may be considered as the first grammar in which the sentence is — partly, at any rate — analysed in terms of the framework of immediate constituents. Nevertheless, traditional notions are mixed into it in almost all parts. The definitions given are mostly based on meaning, although some formal relations are also considered. For example, subject and object are defined in terms both of their position in the sentence and of semantic considerations such as the doer or the recipient respectively (Khanlari 1972:13).

Since then, alongside introducing different linguistic theories in the universities in Iran, a number of Persian grammars were also written on the basis of newer linguistic theories, among which the following are the most important: Mohammad-Reza Bateni's *A Description of* Persian *Grammatical Structure* (1969), based on M.A.K. Halliday's Scale and Category model; Ali-Ashraf Sadeghi's and Aržang's *Grammar* (1976), based on André Martinet's functional framework, and Mehdi Meshkot Dini's *An Introductian to Persian Transformational Syntax* (1987), based on Noam Chomsky's Transformational-Generative model. During the last few years, X´ syntax and Government-Binding theory have also been being tried out onto Persian syntactic description by some scholars.

REFERENCES

Bateni, Mohammad-Reza. 1969. *Tousif-e Sāxtemān-e Dasturi-ye Zabān-e Fārsi [A Description of Persian Grammatical Structure]*. Tehran: Amir-Kabir.

—. 1977. *Negāhi Tāze be Dastur-e zabān [A New Approach to Grammar]*. Tehran: Agah.

Gharib, Abdul-Azim, et al. No date. *Dastur-e Zabān-e Fārsi [Persian Grammar]*. Tehran: Lithography.

Homayi, Jalalud-Din. 1955. *Dastur-e zabān-e Fārsi, [Persian grammar], Moghaddame-ye Loγat-nāme-ye Dehkhoda [Dehkhoda's Dictionary: Introduction]* Tehran: University Press.

Homayun-Farrokh, Abdur-Rahim. 1960. *Dastur-e jāmeʕ-e zabān-e Fārsi [A Comprehensive Persian Grammar]*. Tehran: Ali-Akbar Elmi.

Khanlari, Parviz Natel. 1972. *Dastur-e zabān-e Fārsi [Persian Grammar]*. Tehran: Bonyād-e Farhang-e Iran.

Mashkur, Mohammad-Javad. 1976. *Dastur-Nāme: dar Sarf va Nahv-e zabān-e Fārsi [A Grammar Book: on Persian Morphology and Syntax]*. Tehran: Shargh.

Meshkot Dini, Mehdi. 1987. *Dastur-e zabān-e Fārsi: bar pāye-ye Nazariyye-ye Gaštāri [An Introduction to Persian Transformational Syntax]*. Mashhad: Ferdowsi University Press.

Moʕin, Mohammad [1912–1971]. 1981. *Tarh-e Dastur-e zabān-e Fārsi [An Outline of Persian Grammar]*. Tehran: Amir-Kabir.

Najafi, Abul-Hasan. 1979. *Mabāni-ye zabānšenāsi va kārbord-e Ān dar Zabān-e Fārsi [Elements of Linguistics Applied to Persian]* Tehran: Azad University Press.

Reichelt, Hans. 1911. *Avesta Reader*. Strasburg: Karl J. Trübner. (Repr., Berlin 1968: Walter de Gruyter.)

Sadeghi, Ali-Ashraf and Gholam-Reza Aržang 1976. *Dastur [Grammar]*. Tehran: Sāzmān-e Ketābhā-ye Darsi Press.

Shoʕar, Jaʕfar, Esmail Hakemi, 1976. *Dastur-e zabān-e Fārsi-ye Emruz [Modern Persian Grammar]*. Tehran: Amir-Kabir.

Thirty-Five Years of English Auxiliaries: A Small History of Generative Grammar

STEPHEN J. NAGLE
University of South Carolina-Coastal

CHOMSKY'S NOTE that he has "not hesitated to propose a general principle of linguistic structure on the basis of observations of a single language" (1980:48) is a salient reminder that at least the early stages of transformational-generative research were linguicentric, with English offered as the test case for various notions on a purportedly universal cognitive entity called grammar. Orthodox generative grammar (roughly, that version endorsed by Chomsky) is now in a third or fourth phase, depending on the chronicler, and claims for universality have heightened as numerous languages have been analyzed.

A basic tenet from the start has been that tense, aspect, and, in English, modality as expressed lexically by modal auxiliaries (e.g., *may, would)* are in some way distinct from verbs.[1] In *Syntactic Structures* (Chomsky 1957), the node Aux was dominated by VP (1), but by the late 1960s it was granted autonomy as a discrete category under S:

(1) S > NP VP
VP > Aux V NP
Aux > C(M) (have+en) (be+ing) (be+en)[2]

[1] The modals do not show overt person or number; they do not have a gerund, participles, or a *to* infinitive; nor do they take direct objects.

[2] The English passive *(be + en)* was base-generated in Chomsky 1957, but was arrived at by transformation in the 1965 *Aspects of the Theory of Syntax* model. In current Goverment-Binding generative theory, passive is once again represented at deep structure for certain theory-specific reasons (cf. Sells 1985).

(2) S > NP Aux VP
Aux > T(M) (have-en) (be-ing)

Chomsky continues to view AUX (more recently INFL) as a package of tense and agreement features and auxiliaries, including *have* and *be* in addition to the modals. That English inverts subjects and auxiliaries, not subjects and verbs, as many other Indo-European languages do, at least partially motivated early ideas on AUX along with the disparate morphology of the English modals vis-à-vis verbs. Chomsky was perhaps intentionally elusive regarding the status of AUX in *Aspects of the Theory of Syntax* (1965), with AUX a sister of VP and dominated by S in three illustrations (1965:65, 69, 86), while again a sister of VP but dominated by 'Predicate-Phrase' in another (p. 108). At any rate the idea that there was an autonomous AUX node was prominent enough by the late 1960s to warrant a strong counterargument by Ross (1969).[1] This paper was seminal to the so-called 'main verb' analysis of auxiliaries, which persists in various forms in contemporary generative grammars. However, while the orthodox version has changed significantly over the years, it has retained an autonomous category for auxiliaries.

Within the linguistic wars of the late 1960s and 1970s, Ross's position reflected the philosophy of generative semantics, which could not tolerate a purely syntactic category such as AUX. Indeed, syntactic autonomy was anathema to a theory which sought to reduce sentences to their logical foundations (cf. Lakoff 1972). Regarding auxiliaries, the abtracting of syntax in generative semantics appeared in McCawley's (1971) revision of Ross, which proposed that Tense is an underlying verb. By the mid-1970s the battles over autonomous AUX were heated and frequent, and many generative grammarians were influenced enough by some of the main verb claims to propose that *have* and *be* are in fact base-generated under VP and then 'raised' or 'shifted' to AUX (Jackendoff 1972, Akmajian & Wasow 1975, Culicover 1976, Emonds 1976). Unlike the modals, these verbs can be transitive and are

[1] Ross's proposals built upon issues he raised in his 1967 [published 1968] dissertation.

clearly specified for tense and, especially in the case of *be,* agreement. Thus, rules such as shifting or raising have been proposed as grammatical devices based on differences in the behavior of various English auxiliaries.

Pullum & Wilson (1977) attempted to turn the tables on these analyses by arguing that raising applies to all auxiliaries, relying on the continued appeal of the grammatical simplicity metric to generativists. In their attempt to dismantle AUX, P&W drew attention to certain marginal modals such as *need* and *dare* which sometimes display morphological and syntactic characterisitics of main verbs (3a, b), while in other cases behaving like auxiliaries (3c, d):

(3) a. Does she need to leave early? *(do, to)*
b. She needs a new car. *(-s,* direct object)
c. Need she leave early? (inversion, lack of *-s)*
d. She need not leave early. (negative without *do)*

According to P&W, each of these verbs would have to be two lexically discrete items under the AUX approach; i.e., there would be a verb *need* and an auxiliary *need.* Akmajian, Steele, and Wasow (1979) quickly countered with an elaborate outline of AUX and VP, still widely cited, which retained a version of the earlier raising analysis of *have* and *be* and assigned the placement of marginal modals to a lexical rule. The appeal of this paper rested in part on its analysis of auxiliaries in Luiseno and Papago in addition to English; its clear purpose was to justify AUX as a universal category. But Pullum (1981) was not convinced, criticizing the AUX hypothesis with another look at data from Luiseno and English. Undaunted, AS&W joined forces with Demers, Jelinek, Kitagawa and Oehrle for *An Encyclopedia of AUX* (1981) in which Steele integrated work by the various authors on English, Egyptian Arabic, German (in an appendix), Japanese, Luiseno, and Lummi, noting in the preface the controversy over AS&W 1979 and Pullum's latest contribution (1981) to it.

An important contribution by AS&W was an analysis of VP based on X-bar syntax The X-bar convention (Chomsky 1970 and Jackendoff 1974, 1977) found its earliest appeal and motivation in explaining certain problems in English noun phrases, but in recent generative theory the notion of what constitutes a 'phrase' or a 'category' has changed (cf. Abney 1987 for the proposal of "determiner phrase": DP). Phrase structure rules have been replaced with endocentricity roughly based on X′′–X′–X° sentential and categorial structure, X° being the head which projects its features upward.[1] In "Government-Binding" generative theory, S has become I′′ (that is, IP or INFL Phrase) of which INFL is the head for English as in (4), adapted from Chomsky (1986):

(4)

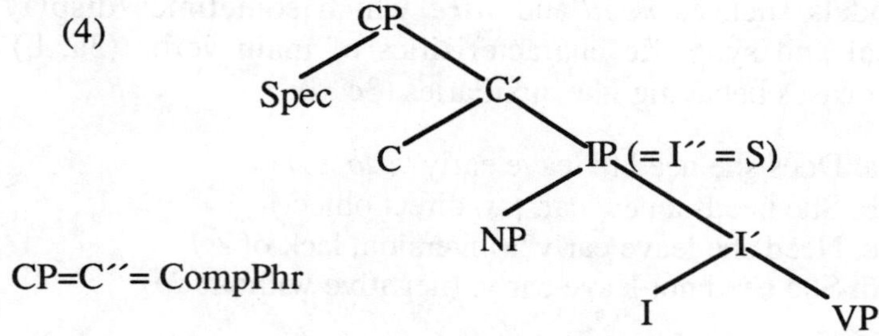

Thus, autonomous INFL/AUX in this variety of generative grammar has survived the challenges and has become a universal category, which in highly inflected languages contains tense and agreement morphology and in English (with relatively little of the latter) at least the modal auxiliaries. These parametric variations in INFL are held to underlie the surface grammar differences in forming questions between inflected and (again, relatively) uninflected Indo-European languages. In French, for example, the verb can invert with its subject after picking up agreement morphology from INFL, whereas in English INFL-generated auxiliaries invert. Both auxiliary and verb movement, then, are actually INFL movement.

As Government-Binding theory continues to evolve, once sacred AUX/INFL has come under attack from friendly quarters. Pollock

[1] There has been widespread disagreement over the maximal permissable number of levels/bars in a projection. A three-level scheme would often yield numerous "empty" levels in, say, a one-word NP. On the other hand, as Akmajian, Steele and Wasow showed, it offers certain advantages in describing the English VP, especially for an analysis of *have* and *be* as verbs which originate there. The three-level analysis is maintained in Lexical-Functional grammar (e.g. Falk 1984).

(1989) has proposed that tense, agreement, and negative are heads of their own phrases, this proposal drawing on the behavior of *have* and *be* (as well as problems in negation in French). In (5), Agr is an intermediate point in the raising of *have* and *be* from VP to Tense, from which they can undergo auxiliary movement in questions; the morphologically-odd modals, in contrast, are generated under Tense and never pick up agreement features from Agr:

(5)

```
CP
├── Spec
└── C′
    ├── C
    └── TP (= IP=S)
        ├── NP
        └── T′
            ├── T
            └── NegP
                ├── SpecNeg
                └── Neg′
                    ├── Neg
                    └── AgrP
                        ├── Agr
                        └── V
                            (have
```

Even assuming that this still-controversial revision displaces the earlier positions on INFL, the concept of a category for auxiliaries remains intact, despite differences on particulars. Given this rough unaninimity within the Chomskyan camp since the early 1980s, main verb advocates have incorporated their views in competing generative theories, e.g., Relational Grammar and Generalised Phrase Structure Grammar. From the latter framework Gazdar, Pullum & Sag (1982) presented an outline of the English verb system which was at the same time an important early polemic for their syntactic theory. Like Government-Binding theory, Generalised Phrase Structure Grammar is based on X-bar syntax, but with no discrete category for auxiliaries.

The different types of auxiliaries (modals, *have,* progressive *be,* passive *be)* are dominated by a respective V´. Falk (1984) has analyzed the English auxiliary system from the Lexical–Functional Grammar perspective, which also is X-bar based. Here there is a category M for the modals which "at least in English" (1984:492), is the head of M´´´, that is, the sentence. Both these proposals, differing regarding the categorial status of modal auxiliaxies; yet both within the generative tradition, profited from their appearance in *Language* to advance their syntactic theories through a novel analysis of English auxiliaries and refutation of previous arguments.

In historical linguistics developments in the modal auxiliaries have been at the heart of disputes over whether syntactic change is essentially gradual or rapid. Lightfoot's (1974, 1979) proposal that the modals' deep and surface changes illustrate a neat case of radical, abrupt syntactic restructuring in deep and surface grammar has survived controversy (with some revision), and many of his accompanying views on the methodology of historical syntax and the nature of language change have been influential. They have, however, been so controversial that in the 1980s criticism of his positions on the modals became a sort of linguistic cottage industry. In his 1979 book, Lightfoot offered the modals' reanalysis as a paradigm case of the operation of a Transparency Principle which would yield rapid deep change in an otherwise highly resistant grammar.

In his view the English modals in Middle English developed exceptional features independently, ultimately forcing their reanalysis as AUX items in Early Modern English.[1] His critics have pointed out flaws in his data (Plank 1984, Allan 1987), revised his interpretation of individual changes to support gradualism (Bennett 1981, Aitchison 1980, van Kemenade 1990), maintained some version of his reanalysis while revising certain theoretical or chronological specifics (Roberts 1985, Nagle 1989, 1990), or outright attacked the soundness of his

[1] Lightfoot took the position that the pre-modals' (his term) loss of direct objects, their failure to adopt a following *to* infinitive, and the loss of the non-modal members of the preterit-present paradigm (leaving only the modals) in Middle English were isolated, but in combination they built up opacity in the verb system, triggering the shift of the modals from VP to AUX.

theoretical approach (Romaine 1981). Nonetheless, or perhaps because of this response, any indepth historical treatment of auxiliaries or, to a lesser degree, syntactic reanalysis has to deal with Lightfoot's proposals. At the time, Lightfoot talked about the creation of AUX, but speculated that AUX might have existed all along, perhaps foreseeing the future universal claims regarding INFL.

The debates on English auxiliaries and their categorial status have thus been critical to the development of generative theory to its present state. The question which may then be asked, one which surfaces informally in my conversations with other linguists, is whether the universalist claims of recent Chomskyan linguistics are not a bit whimsical given the heavy reliance on English for data, at least in the earlier years of generative grammar. If Chinese (which has neither tense/agreement affixation nor auxiliary movement) had been the principal language of investigation or investigators, would autonomous AUX/INFL have been proposed? Would syntactic autonomy have become an acrimonious issue? Although generative grammar now studies a wide range of languages, today's thinking on phrase structure and categories reflects the years when English was a favorite battleground and autonomy for AUX and syntax became a standard of the royalists. If a grammatical theory based on one language can yield universally valid conclusions about human language in general, then the early preoccupation with English may have been felicitous.

The examination of numerous languages during the last 10 years has yielded some flexibility regarding what "universal" means, as reflected in the study of parametric variation within universal principles. This formalization of the sensible notion that languages, common in their cognitive foundation, differ in recurring, specifiable ways is refreshing. For even though generative grammar is open to criticism on many levels, in its various forms it has become a principal operating tool for syntactic investigation, and a philosophy of language as well. Theories sometimes tend to abstract away from their original empirical grounding, but they also often have a fortunate tendency to enrich themselves as their scope of inquiry widens. As a generative linguist, I would like the universalist claims to be true and the preoccupation with

English to have opened the door to the mind, not just English or languages like it.

REFERENCES

Abney, Steven. 1987. *The* English *Noun Phrase in its Sentential Aspect*. Ph. D. dissertation. Cambridge, Mass.: MIT.

Aitchison, Jean. 1980. Review of Lightfoot (1979). *Linguistics* 18.137–146.

Akmajian, Adrian and Thomas Wasow. 1975. "The Constituent Structure of VP and AUX and the Position of the Verb BE". *Linguistic Analysis* 1.205–245.

Akmajian, Adrian, Susan M. Steele, & Thomas Wasow. 1979. "The Category AUX in Universal Grammar". *Linguistic Inquiry* 10.1–64.

Allan, W. Scott. 1987. "Lightfoot noch einmal". *Diachronica* 4.123–157

Bennett, Paul A. 1981. "Is syntactic change gradual?". *Glossa* 15.115–135.

Chomsky, Noam. 1957. *Syntactic Structures*. (*=Janua Linguarum,* 4) The Hague: Mouton.

—. 1965. *Aspects of the Theory of Syntax*. Cambridge, Mass.: MIT Press.

—. 1970. "Remarks on Nominalization". *Readings in English Transformational. Grammar* ed. by Roderick A. Jacobs & Peter S. Rosenbaum, 184–221. Waltham (Mass.): Ginn & Co.

—. 1980 "On Cognitive Structures and their Development". *Language and Learning: The Debate between Jean Piaget and Noam Chomsky*. London: Routledge and Kegan Paul.

—. 1986. *Barriers*. (= *Linguistic Inquiry Monographs,* 13.) Cambridge, Mass.: MIT Press.

Culicover, Peter. 1976. *Syntax*. New York: Academic Press.

Emonds, Joseph. 1976. *A Transformational Approach to English Syntax*. New York: Academic Press.

Falk, Yehuda N. 1984. "The English Auxiliary System: A Lexical-Functional Analysis". *Language* 60.483–509.

Gazdar, Gerald, Geoffrey K. Pullum, & Ivan A. Sag. 1982. "Auxiliaries and Related Phenomena in a Restrictive Theory of Grammar". *Language* 58.591–638.

Jackendoff, Ray S. 1972. *Semantic Interpretation in Generative Grammar*. Cambridge: MIT Press.

—. 1974. *Introduction to the X-Bar Convention*. Bloomington: Indiana University Linguistics Club.

—. 1977. *X-Bar Syntax: A Study of Phrase Structure*. Cambridge, Mass.: MIT Press.

Kemenade, Ans van. 1990. "Structural Factors in the History of English Modals". Paper presented at the *Sixth International Conference on English Historical Linguistics,* University of Helsinki; to appear in conference proceedings.

Lakoff, George. 1972. "Linguistics and Natural logic". *Semantics and Natural Language,* ed. by Donald Davidson & Gilbert Harmon, 545–665. Dordrecht: D. Reidel.

Lightfoot, David W. 1974. "The Diachronic Analysis of English Modals". *Historical Linguistics I: Proceedings of the First International Conference on Historical Linguistics,* ed. by John M. Anderson & Charles Jones, 219–249. Amsterdam: North Holland.

—. 1979. *Principles of Diachronic Syntax.* Cambridge: University Press.

McCawley, James D. 1971. "Tense and Time Reference in English". *Studies in Linguistics and Semantics* ed. by Charles Fillmore & D. Terence Langendoen, 96–113. New York: Holt, Rinehart and Winston.

Nagle, Stephen J. 1989. *Inferential Change and Syntactic Modality in* English *(= Bamberger Beiträge zur Englischen Sprachwissenschaft,* 23) Frankfurt am Main: Peter Lang.

—. 1990. "Modes of Inference and the Gradual/Rapid Issue: Suggestions from the English Modal". *Historical Linguistics 1987: Papers from the Proceedings of the 8th International Conference on Historical Linguistics (= Current Issues in Linguistic Theory,* 66), ed. by Henning Andersen & Konrad Koerner, 353–362. Amsterdam: John Benjamins.

Plank, Frans. 1984. "The Modals Story Retold". *Studies in Language* 8.305–364.

Pollock, Jean-Ives. 1989. "Verb Movement, Universal Grammar, and the Structure of IP". *Linguistic Inquiry* 20.365–424.

Pullum, Geoffrey K. & Deirdre Wilson. 1977. "Autonomous Syntax and the Analysis of Auxiliaries". *Language* 53.741–788.

Roberts, Ian A. 1985. "Agreement Parameters and the Development of English Modal Auxiliaries". *Natural Language and Linguistic Theory* 3.21–58.

Romaine, Suzanne. 1981. "The Transparency Principle: What it is and Why it Doesn't Work". *Lingua* 55.277–300.

Ross, John R[obert]. 1968.*Constraints on Variables in Syntax.* Bloomington: Indiana University Linguistics Club.

—. 1969. "Auxiliaries as Main Verbs". *Studies in Philosophical Linguistics,* Series I, ed. by W. Todd, 77–102. Evanston, Ill.: Great Expectations.

Sells, Peter. 1985. *Lectures on Contemporary Syntactic Theories.* Stanford: Center for the Study of Language and Information.

Steele, Susan M., Adrian Akmajian et al. 1981. *An Encyclopedia of AUX: A Study in Cross-Linguistic Equivalence.* Cambridge, Mass.: MIT Press.

Dutch Linguists and the Origin of Language: Some Nineteenth-Century Views

JAN NOORDEGRAAF
Vrije Universiteit, Amsterdam

1. INTRODUCTION

ABOUT NINETY YEARS ago, it was remarked by the noted Dutch philologist Jan te Winkel (1847–1921) that nineteenth-century linguistic scholarship in Holland had produced only a few papers pertaining to the question of the origin of language (te Winkel 1905:58). Until some years ago I found it difficult to contradict him for, unfortunately, a comprehensive overview of the Dutch contribution to the debate concerning the origin of language is still lacking. Indeed, after browsing through the bulky two-volume *Theorien vom Ursprung der Sprache* (Gessinger & von Rahden 1989), one might feel inclined to agree with the conclusion of my distinguished nineteenth-century predecessor. I hasten to admit that in the Netherlands the subject in question has never caused such a great deal of controversy as it has in other countries. Nevertheless, some years ago a thorough search through a diversity of periodicals (cf. Visser 1985) brought to our notice more papers and books than previous scholarship seems to have discovered. It appeared that in particular the 1860s and the early 1870s saw the publication of a relatively large number of papers devoted to the question of the origin of language. As is well-known, this is the period in which Darwin's *The Origin of Species* (1859) and *The Descent of Man* (1871) were published. So what I would like to do now is try to relate a few of those papers to the reception of the Darwinian — in a broad sense — body of ideas in that period.

It is true to say that in the Netherlands evolutionary theory was accepted and integrated into the empirical sciences, modern theology and atheistic circles, whereas it was despised by orthodox Protestants and

Catholics. It has been concluded that evolutionary theory worked like a catalyst and caused polarisation, to use a political term: it sharpened long-standing controversies and brought to light the differences between the various positions (cf. Hegeman 1970). In general, Darwin's theory was regarded as an argument pro or contra current views, just because of the ideological conclusions that were drawn from it. What was the reaction in linguistic quarters?

In order to give a first tentative answer to that question I have singled out three different standpoints. First, that of the Utrecht professor of Dutch language Willem G. Brill, a Protestant origin theologian, who published papers on the question of the origin of language both before and after 'Darwin'. Second, that of the Roman Catholic chaplain Wessels, who defended an orthodox position in a number of papers published in the 1860s, concluding with the *lingua Adamica,* and third, that of Henri Moltzer, a linguist who embraced evolutionary theory in the early 1870s. Before considering their respective standpoints it might be relevant to make a general remark with regard to the context, the background of these papers. In the early 1850s, Matthijs de Vries (1820–1892), a devoted follower of Jacob Grimm and professor of Dutch language at Leiden University, had introduced the historical method to the study of Dutch. The "new school in linguistics", as it was later called, found a spokesman in de Vries, whose inaugural lecture of 1853 contained a plea for 'rigour' inspired by August Schleicher's *Linguistische Untersuchungen* (1850). de Vries was an influential man in scholarly circles. It was due to his influence that in 1865 Henri Moltzer was appointed to the chair for Dutch language and literature in Groningen. de Vries was a classicist by education. As a young student, he was on friendly terms with Brill, when the latter was working on his Dutch grammar of 1846 under the influence of the new German studies on language. His linguistic views were formed by way of his contacts with Brill during the 1840s. As to historical linguistics, both Brill and de Vries were self-educated men, and in their work we find traces of romanticism combined with the results of the new linguistic science. Thus, one could argue that the study of language in Holland at the time was still in a stage of transition, historical linguistics gaining more and more ground. A few years ago, I discussed one of the major contemporary Dutch debates concerning the foundations of linguistic study, a debate which reflects this transition very clearly (cf. Noordegraaf1990). The body of Dutch texts to be discussed here should also be seen as another grand debate pertaining to the fundamentals of linguistic science.

2. Willem Gerard Brill (1811–1896)

Two years before the publication of his influential *Hollandsche Spraakleer* ("Dutch grammar") of 1846, Brill published a brochure, which was intended to be an extensive introduction to the grammar. Here we find among other things, a discussion of several theories concerning the origin of language. Brill (1844:5–18) is of the opinion that reason provides man with a special place in creation; in using language man places himself at the pinnacle of creation. Brill mentions Herder's *Abhandlung über den Ursprung der Sprache* (1772) as a source of inspiration, but he seems to have been more inspired by mystical thought as was current in German Romanticism. According to Brill, language is not a conscious invention by man, nor a direct gift from God; neither are imitations of sounds, the expression of emotions or "Lautsymbolik" a source of language.

Like Herder, Brill argues that man is the sole creature that is free from nature. The essence, the idea of nature is inside him, man completely comprehends nature. Man looks around in creation, and when he finds the counterpart of something external in his internal nature then he has found a concept. He gives this concept a body, using his breath, the "natural body of the spirit". The whole of the sounds used by man to give account of his thinking is called language. Language is the external sign of human thinking, and thus the pledge of his high rank in creation. I would like to stress this characteristic of Brill's approach: he talks about an identification of what is externally perceptible, on the one hand, with the internal world of concepts which is already present in the mind, on the other hand; a sort of a priori complete knowledge of the world. Thus, Brill presupposes innate notions, but I would like to add that in his opinion the linguistic sign is arbitrary, it does not necessarily reflect mental knowledge. The communicative dimension of language is not based upon convention, but on love. In

Brill's opinion the love between the very first man and his consort is sufficient to explain the social side of language (cf. Brill 1851), but I cannot enlarge on that here. The stage is set now for the confrontation with Darwinian and Scheicherian ideas, although references to foreign opponents are conspicuous by their absence in Brill's papers.

From Brill's later publications I would like to highlight the following points. In 1861 he makes a sharp distinction in man between the physical and the spiritual side, of which language is a product, thus implicitely denying that anything spiritual could have developed from the material. Man can remain silent, which means he can free himself from nature. It is not the imitating animal in us that speaks, but the master of creation, the God in us, and that God is perfect in us. By speaking man creates a spiritual world of his own and he retains it by means of language. This principle is of an absolute validity, not of gradualness: it is present or it is not present. Thus, Brill concludes, our earliest ancestors must have been in the possesion of the same faculty, and thus of "the pledge of language".

Brill's paper of 1873 is a summa of his views on the origin of language. It is clear how the phenomenon of language is used as an argument against the idea of evolution. Referring approvingly to Max Müller's lecture *Über die Resultate der Sprachwissenschaft* (1872), Brill disputes Darwinian ideas, this time very explicitly. Brill states:

> as language shows, man is the judge of all creation. And man does not become so, he is so from the very beginning. We see him grow in knowledge; however, nothing is actually taught to the mind of man: what we call learning is nothing else than a gradual process of becoming acquainted with our own mind, a step-by-step discovery of what is already present there from the very beginning. Thus man, in respect to the mind, is an everlasting being, bearing the image of God, understanding good and evil. (Brill 1873:381–382)[1]

It is language that makes it impossible to see man as the result of an evolutionary process. I venture to conclude that Brill's ideas concern-

[1] Unless otherwise indicated, translations from Dutch are mine [J.N].

ing the origin of language show a remarkable continuity over the years. The debate about language and evolution in the 1860s simply prompted him to bring his ideas to the fore with more emphasis. His approach reminds us in several aspects of Max Müller; however, it is obvious that Brill developed his ideas independently.

3. Wilhelmus Wessels (1833–1900)

Without any doubt we may call Brill a religious man, but he should not be considered a representative of Protestant orthodoxy. He did not defend, for example, a literal interpretation of Adam's naming of the animals. This was done by the Roman Catholic priest Wilhelmus Wessels. How did he appear on the scene?

At the eighth Conference of Philologists at Rotterdam in September 1865, it was announced that professor Brill would present a paper under the title "How a correct understanding of the essence of language can terminate many a theory concerning the genesis of language and the development of mankind". Brill, however, decided to treat another topic; this subject, he said, he found too abstract for the occasion. Yet the subject was discussed at the conference, not by a linguist, but by the chaplain Wilhelmus Wessels. His paper on the theory of the genesis of language did not provoke any reaction. This was not at all surprising, noted a reporter of a Dutch weekly mockingly, for the honourable speaker had put forward views that were fully antiquated (Ising 1865). What had Wessels done to incur the wrath of the reporter?

He had argued against those who were of the opinion that human language had started with "a single word, or a single sound". No, Wessels (1865) said, as the first man must have been an adult person, fully-grown, both body and mind, he must have had a fully developed language from the very beginning. That language had been invented by man appeared to him to be impossible. In later publications (1866, 1869), Wessels elaborated his objections against the one-sided positivistic 'science of experience' — experience is not the sole source of knowledge —, and argued against the theories on language origin as supported by, among others, Grimm, and Schleicher. A major issue to him is that, historically, we cannot know anything about the origin of language — he rejects the validity of the uniformitarian principle —, and against Darwin he argues that the latter has failed to provide up conclusive evidence with regard to the "transsubstantiation" of brute minds, the transition from the brute world to the rational world. Language is part of man's nature, just like the other parts of his body; one cannot imagine early man with a half grown arm or foot ...

To be brief, Wessels generally follows a more or less defensive approach. Pointing out the weak spots in the theories of those who defended any form of the evolution of language, he argues for the divine origin of language, language as a gift from God. In his preface to Wessels' 1869 book *The Genesis of Language. A Contribution to the Evaluation of the Science of Experience,* the leading Roman Catholic man of letters and champion of Roman Catholic emancipation J.A. Alberdingk Thijm (1820–1889) warmly commended Wessels for his fight against Darwinism and 'the monkey theory'. "You have done a good job", Thijm remarked, "now you have launched an attack from the standpoint of philosophical linguistics against those theories which are so much a subject of discussion nowadays".

As I just said, Wessels does not develop a theory of his own, although in 1869 he does refer approvingly to Müller's views, because he considers them to be highly compatible with his own. However, in the same year — rather late, I think — he came across Kaulen's *Die Sprachverwirrung zu Babel* (1861). In his book Franz Philipp Kaulen (1827–1907), a pastor from Bonn, attacked all the new linguists as heretical and godless, and it was August Pott (1802–1887) who was singled out as candidate designate for the role of anti-Christ (for details cf. Leopold 1989). Wessels' studying Kaulen resulted in what we may call a 'shock of recognition': in Kaulen he found the most perfect expression of his own ideas. "Die Wahrheit hinsichtlich der Sprachentstehung ist die, daß die Sprache dem Menschen in der Schöpfung als ein Geschenk Gottes zu Theil geworden ist", he quotes the Bonn pastor with approval (Wessels 1869–70:253). Moreover, in an earlier paper Wessels has already expounded the idea that the linguistic sign is not arbitrary. Now, in his review of Kaulen's work, he agrees with Kaulen that the very first language was in fundamental conformity with nature, yes, words were themselves part of creation and nature. They were divine and natural, not human and conventional. That words and sounds are supposed to have a symbolic and organic meaning, means a return to the Adamic language doctrine in the form of 'Lautsymbolik', and Wessels fully embraces this.

There can be little doubt that the discussion concerning the pros and cons of the theories of Darwin and Schleicher strengthened Wessels in his own feeling that the whole debate could indeed be reduced to the question of the existence or non-existence of God. As far as I know, Wessels' biblicist views attracted no followers in professional Dutch linguistic circles around 1870.

3. H. E. Moltzer (1836–1895)

For a completely contrary opinion I would like to turn now to Henri Moltzer, who in 1865 was appointed professor of Dutch in Groningen. In his inaugural lecture Moltzer appears to depend heavily upon Max Müller's *Lectures on the Science of Language* (1861–64). Note that from the early 1860s on Müller was most popular in the Netherlands. Moltzer once characterized Max Müller as "the brilliant representative of the new school in linguistics" (1872:3).

From Moltzer's inaugural lecture (1865a) it becomes clear that the new school in linguistics, historical-comparative grammar, has made its decisive breakthrough. Moltzer pleads for a strict, inductive method taking its cues from the natural sciences. The methodological guidelines to be followed are those of unprejudiced observation, without any *a priori* assumptions. The linguist should follow the canons of the prestigious natural sciences. The subject of linguistics was not just grammar, but also the development of language, its genesis, its origin. Thus, he deemed the origin of language a legitimate subject of linguistic science, whose methods might solve the problem for ever (cf. Noordegraaf 1985:418–426).

In his first paper on the origin of language (1865b) Moltzer first gives an overview of current views. He rejects the possibility of a divine origin of language: language is not something innate nor is it the result of a direct revelation by God. He proceeds by criticizing various proponents of the human origin of language. Then he turns to Müller. Müller is perfectly right, he says: language and reason; these are the features by which man is distinguished from the brute. Summing up,

Moltzer concludes that man speaks because he thinks, just as he thinks because he speaks. “The word is the thought incarnate”, he quotes from Müller (1865b:12). Note that in his paper, completely written in a Müllerian vein, there is not a single reference to Darwin.

In 1871 Moltzer published a lenghty article under the title of “The Origin of Language and Darwin’s hypothesis”. This paper was based on public lectures given at meetings of the Society for Public Welfare, which means that the topic was fashionable enough to be discussed for a wider audience. It appeared in print not long after the publication of Darwin’s *The Descent of Man.* The content of this paper shows that Moltzer has changed his position completely. Reading both Darwin 1859 and 1871 and Schleicher’s well-known essays of 1863 and 1865 I assume he had his own ‘shock of recognition’. To put it briefly, Moltzer now concludes that whereas Müller claims an essential difference between man and brute, linguistic science supports Darwin’s hypothesis. Man and brute are of common descent. As Moltzer puts it:

> man has *more* to say than the brute and man can express what he has to say *much better,* that is the difference. … Thus, under no circumstances is the gift of language so distinctive a feature of man that it can be adduced as evidence against the thesis that mankind has sprung from any lower animal species (Moltzer 1871:256–257).

Moltzer’s standpoint is clear: both language and man are involved in a proces of evolution. Any idea of a ‘higher’ origin is mere phantasy. I think that Moltzer’s switch over to Darwin/Schleicher is a good example of ‘influence’ in linguistics.

5. Some final remarks

I have only been able to give a rough outline of three nineteenth-century positions concerning the question of language origin. However, I venture to conclude that the relatively large number of Dutch papers published in the 1860s and early 1870s on this problem should be seen as provoked by the publication of the works of Darwin.

The question was: “was man by origin a reasonable being, gifted with knowledge of the essence of things, and understanding of good and evil?". The answers greatly differed. Both Brill and Wessels said yes, and language was for them the ultimate evidence. No, Moltzer said, referring to Darwin and Schleicher: man has developed gradually, and language can be seen as proof of that.

What became of the question in later years? The era of the grand debates on this topic was over. Philosophically and metaphysically coloured approaches like those of Brill and Wessels had no follow-up at all. Wessels did not publish any more on linguistic themes, and in the early 1870s Brill said farewell to linguistics; he was to devote himself to what he called "more important studies". Moltzer concentrated on literary history. The new school in linguistics, hailed by Moltzer, preferred the empirical and detailed study of language to speculative theorizing. It was Karl Brugmann (1849–1919) who in the preface to the *Morphologische Untersuchungen* (1878) invited his fellow linguists to leave the "hypothesentrüben Dunstkreis der Werkstätte, in der man die indogermanische Grundformen schmiedet" for "die klare Luft der greifbaren Wirklichkeit" (cf. Pedersen 1931:293–294), and we owe a great deal to many of the specialized studies undertaken at that time. This abandoning of the question to other disciplines and to later generations may remind us of the fact that even prestigious nineteenth-century linguistics had its limitations.

REFERENCES

Alberdingk Thijm, Josephus Albertus. 1869."Voorrede". Wessels 1869b.i–iv.

Brill, Willem Gerard. 1844. *Over de taal als het pand van 's menschen hoogen rang in de schepping, en over het verband tusschen de meerdere of mindere intellectuële vatbaarheid eener natie, en de hoogere of lagere klasse, waartoe de taal door haar gesproken, behoort*. Zutphen: A. E. C. van Someren.

—. 1851. "Over den oorsprong der taal". *De Gids* 15:156–64.

—. 1861. "Over het beginsel bij de onderscheiding der woordsoorten in acht te nemen". *De taalgids* 3.257–269.

—. 1871. "Nogmaals over den oorsprong der taal". *Protestantsche Bijdragen tot bevordering van Christelijk leven en Christelijke Wetenschap* 2.325–338.

—. 1873. "De mensch, getuige de taal, rechter over het geschapene". *Handelingen van het twaalfde Nederlandsche taal- en letterkundig congres,* 381–382. Middelburg: J.C. & W. Altorffer.

Darwin, Charles. 1859. *The Origin of Species by Means of Natural Selection*. London: J. Murray.

—. 1871. *The Descent of Man*. 2 vols. London: J. Murray.

Gessinger, Joachim & Wolfert von Rahden, eds. 1989. *Theorien vom Ursprung der Sprache*. 2 vols. Berlin & New York: de Gruyter.

Hegeman, J.G. 1970. "Darwin en onze voorouders. Nederlandse reacties op de evolutieleer van 1860–1875. Een terreinverkenning". *Bijdragen en mededelingen betreffende de geschiedenis der Nederlanden* 85.261–314.

[Ising, A.]. 1865. "A propos van het kongres te Rotterdam/naar aanleiding van het congres te Rotterdam". *De Nederlandsche Spectator* 1865:39.309–311.

Leopold, Joan. 1989. "The Last Battle over the Tower of Babel: The controversy between August Friedrich Pott and Franz Kaulen". Gessinger & von Rahden, vol. I, 548–60.

Moltzer, Henri E. 1865a. *De nieuwe richting in de taalkunde*. Groningen: J. B. Wolters. (Inaugural address, University of Groningen.)

—. 1865b. "De oorsprong der taal". Offprint from *Kronijk voor Geschiedenis en Wetenschap* [MS dated 17 Oct. 1865].

—. 1871. "De oorsprong der taal en de hypothese van Darwin". *Taal- en Letterbode* 2.169–97, 237–61.

—. 1872. "Inleidend woord". *De uitkomsten van de wetenschap der taalkunde. Eene voorlezing gehouden aan de Keizerl. hoogeschool te Straatsburg 23 mei 1872* by F. Max Müller, 3–4. Groningen: P. Noordhoff & M. Smit. (Translation into Dutch by G. Penon of Friedrich Max Müller, *Über die Resultate der Sprachwissenschaft*. [Inaugural lecture as a Visiting Professor in Strasburg]. Strasburg: K.J. Trübner, 1872.)

Noordegraaf, Jan. 1985. *Norm, geest en geschiedenis. Nederlandse taalkunde in de negentiende eeuw*. Dordrecht: Foris.

— . 1990. "Trends in 19th-Century Linguistics and the Debate in the Royal Dutch Academy (1855–1858)". *History and Historiography: Proceedings of the Fourth International Conference on the History of Langage Sciences (ICHOLS IV), Trier, 24–28 August 1987* ed. by Hans-Josef Niederehe & Konrad Koerner, 715–728. Amsterdam: J. Benjamins.

Pedersen, Holger. 1931 [1924]. *The Discovery of Language: Linguistic Science in the 19th Century*. Cambnridge, Mass.: Harvard University Press.

Schleicher, August. 1850. *Linguistische Untersuchungen. II. Die Sprachen Europas in systematischer Übersicht*. Bonn: H. B. König.

— . 1863. *Die Darwinsche Theorie und die Sprachwissenschaft*. Weimar: H. Böhlau.

— . 1865. *Die Bedeutung der Sprache für die Naturgeschichte des Menschen*. Weimar: H. Böhlau.

Visser, Jitske. 1985. *Darwin en het woord. Een literatuurstudie naar het taaloorsprongsvraagstuk in de 19e eeuw.* Unpubl. ms., Dept. of Dutch, Vrije Universiteit Amsterdam.

Wessels, Wilhelmus. 1865a. "Over de theorie der taalwording". *Handelingen van het achtste Nederlandsch taal– en letterkundig congres, gehouden te Rotterdam, den 11, 12 en 13 September 1865,* 62–66. Rotterdam: M. Wijt & Zonen.

—. 1865b. "Nog iets dergelijks". *De Katholiek. Godsdienstig, geschied- en letterkundig Maandschrift* 48.314–316.

—. 1866. "Een nawoord over de theorie der taalwording". *De Taalgids* 8.81–107.

—. 1869a. "De wording der taal en der menschen. Eene bijdrage ter waardering van de wetenschap der ervaring". *De Katholiek* 55.281–316, 349–95.

—. 1869a. *De wording der taal. Eene bijdrage ter waardering van de wetenschap der ervaring.* The Hague: J. A. Fentrop.

—. 1869–70. Review of *Die Sprachverwirrung zu Babel (Linguistisch-Theologische Untersuchungen über Gen. XI,1–9* von Franz Kaulen (Mainz 1861). *De Katholiek* 56.205–258, 58.65–115.

te Winkel, Jan. 1905. *Inleiding tot de geschiedenis van Nederlandsche taal.* Culemborg: Blom & Olivierse.

"Maschine" vs. "Organismus". Einige Überlegungen zur Geistes- und Sprachwissenschaftsgeschichte im 18. und 19. Jahrhundert

PETER SCHMITTER
Westfälische Wilhelms-Universität Münster

1. BACK TO THE FUTURE — ODER: VOM 3:SYSTEMBEGRIFF ZURÜCK ZUM ORGANISMUS?

AN DEN ANFANG meiner Ausführungen möchte ich zwei Beobachtungen stellen, die auf den ersten Blick weder mit meinem Thema noch etwas miteinander zu tun zu haben scheinen. Die erste Beobachtung ist folgende: Im Dezember 1989 berichtete die *Deutsche Universitäts-Zeitung* in relativ großer Aufmachung davon, daß eine neue Theorie der Erde "die reduktionistischen Tendenzen" der heutigen Wissenschaft "stoppen" soll. Diese neue Theorie heißt nach der altgriechischen 'Mutter Erde', der Spenderin und Trägerin des Lebens, "Gaia". Sie wird von James Lovelock, einem Professor für Meeresbiologie, vertreten, und ihre Besonderheit besteht in der Forderung, die Erde nicht mehr unter den zahlreichen divergierenden Aspekten der verschiedenen spezialisierten Einzelwissenschaften zu betrachten und so in unzusammenhängende Einzelteile zu zerlegen, sondern die Erde insgesamt "als lebenden Organismus", als "Superorganismus", anzusehen. Dies ist an sich schon ein bemerkenswertes Faktum, doch das Interessanteste an Lovelocks Ausführungen ist für uns, daß er bei der Entwicklung seiner Theorie auf die Konzeption des schottischen Geologen James Hutton, der von 1726 bis 1797 lebte und 1795 seine *Theory of the Earth* der Öffentlichkeit übergab, zurückgreift und explizit nach einer Wissenschaft verlangt, die "zur Naturphilosophie" "zurückkehrt" (Lovelock 1989:11).

Die zweite Beobachtung, die ich voranstellen will, ist einer jüngeren Humboldtinterpretation entnommen. In dem 1986 publizierten Buch mit dem Obertitel *Apeliotes* plädiert Jürgen Trabant im Zuge seiner an

Orwell (1903–1950) *1984* anknüpfenden Auseinandersetzung mit dem Phänomen des "newspeak" dafür, die Sprache in den Umweltschutz einzubeziehen, und er fordert deshalb einen "Sprachschutz", bei dem es gilt, "lebensrettende romantische Tradition zu beleben" (Trabant 1986:125). Als ein wichtiger Faktor dieser Tradition wird dabei u.a. die Vorstellung genannt, daß es sich bei der Sprache "um etwas 'Lebendiges' und damit 'Natürliches'" handelt.

Betrachten wir die wesentlichen Aussagen dieser beiden Texte ein wenig genauer, dann zeigt sich, daß es entgegen dem ersten Anschein doch eine tiefgreifende Verbindung zwischen ihnen gibt. Denn von zwei verschiedenen Wissenschaften aus, nämlich der Biologie einerseits und der Sprachwissenschaft andererseits, wird hier übereinstimmend ein Umdenken gefordert, und zwar ein Umdenken, das in einer Rückbesinnung auf ältere Wissenschaftskonzepte besteht und sich an biologistisch-vitalistischen Modellvorstellungen des späten 18. und frühen 19. Jahrhunderts orientieren soll. Die entscheidenden Begriffe oder Schlagworte, die hier eingebracht werden, sind 'Ganzheitlichkeit', 'Lebendigkeit', 'Natur' sowie der alle diese Aspekte in sich vereinigende Begriff des *Organismus.*

Ich will nicht weiter darauf eingehen, daß dies ganz offensichtlich dem allgemeinen Trend unserer Zeit entspricht, und zwar nicht nur ihrer Tendenz zur Glorifizierung, wenn nicht sogar Deifikation der Natur und des Natürlichen, sondern auch ihrer Tendenz, das zukünftige Heil aus der Wiederbelebung alter Traditionen zu gewinnen, was man in Anlehnung an den Titel einer bekannten Filmserie auch mit dem Schlagwort "Back to the Future" bezeichnen kann. Auf solche übergreifenden Zusammenhänge sei hier aber nur *en passant* verwiesen. Statt dabei zu verweilen, möchte ich vielmehr eine weitere Beobachtung anschließen, die direkt in das Zentrum unserer Thematik führt und die Relevanz unserer historischen Überlegungen für die gegenwärtige bzw. zukünftige Linguistik deutlich macht[1].

[1] Zur damit angesprochenen Thematik des Verhältnisses von gegenwärtiger Sprachtheorie und Historiographie der Linguistik vgl. ausführlicher Schmitter (1990).

Im Zuge der immer stärker werdenden Kritik an der Systemlinguistik und der ihr zugrundeliegenden strukturalistischen Sprachauffassung scheint auch der Systemgedanke — oder besser: das Systemmodell — in Mißkredit zu geraten. Vor allem die verbreitete Auffassung von System als etwas Statischem, Nicht-Dynamischem, sowie die Ausklammerung der Größen 'Mensch' und 'Welt' und die damit verbundene Reduktion der Sprachbetrachtung auf rein innersprachliche Relationsphänomene werden dem Systemmodell gern vorgeworfen[1];. Gerät damit aber die Modellvorstellung von Sprache als 'System' insgesamt ins Kreuzfeuer der Kritik, dann liegt es nahe, die Systemmetapher zu verabschieden und sich nach anderen Begriffen bzw. Modellvorstellungen umzusehen, mit deren Hilfe man das Untersuchungsobjekt 'Sprache' adäquater charakterisieren kann.

Wenn ich richtig sehe, hat ein solcher Modellwechsel bisher zwar noch nicht stattgefunden, doch lassen Zeugnisse wie die beiden o.g. von Lovelock und Trabant vermuten, daß er zu erwarten ist und daß als einer der möglichen 'Ersatzkandidaten' für den Systembegriff der Organismusbegriff in Frage kommt, wie er in der Wissenschaft des 18. und 19. Jahrhunderts entwickelt worden ist. Somit ist es auch aus gegenwartsbezogener Perspektive ratsam, sich mit dem Organismusbegriff genauer zu befassen und seine historische Genese und Diversifikation zu untersuchen. Wenn ich nun im folgenden, soweit es das für diese Tagung vorgeschriebene Zeitlimit erlaubt, auf diese Problematik eingehe, dann soll es vor allem darum gehen, drei Punkte skizzenhaft herauszustellen: nämlich erstens, welche vorausliegende Modellvorstellung der Organismusbegriff selbst ersetzt hat und aus welchen Gründen dies geschah, zweitens, welche Inhaltskomponenten für den Begriff des Organismus in seinen beiden für die Sprachwissenschaft des 19. Jh.s wichtigsten Ausprägungen signifikativ sind, und drittens schließlich, weshalb das Organismusmodell dann zu Beginn des 20. Jh.s an Anziehungskraft verlor und vom Systemmodell abgelöst wurde. Die Ergebnisse dieser Überlegungen können dann zugleich auch

[1] Besonders auffällig ist dieses Phänomen im Bereich der sprachtheoretisch äußerst sensiblen Semantik, worüber beispielsweise der Sammelband von Schwarze & Wunderlich (1985) gut informiert.

Hinweise für die Beantwortung der Frage geben, ob es in der Tat geraten ist, den Begriff des Organismus für eine zukünftige Sprachwissenschaft zu reaktivieren.

2. DAS *MACHINA*-MODELL UND SEINE IMPLIKATIONEN

Mit vollem Recht hat Percival (1987:8) vor kurzem noch in impliziter Wendung gegen Thomas Samuel Kuhn und dessen Anhänger hervorgehoben, daß "nothing ever completely revolutionizes a discipline"[1]. Folgerichtig fährt Percival dann fort: "If we want to understand the result of a conceptual revolution, we are well advised to investigate the system that preceded it."

Diese Überlegungen gelten selbstverständlich auch für die Konzeption des Organismus. Und wenn man sich nun der Frage zuwendet, welches Modell der Organismusauffassung, die in der ersten Hälfte des 19. Jh.s ihren Höhepunkt erreicht, vorausliegt, dann stellt man erstens fest, daß dies das Modell der Maschine war[2], und zweitens, daß Maschine- und Organismuskonzeption sich nicht so radikal voneinander unterscheiden, wie man auf den ersten Blick vermuten kann. Es gibt vielmehr einerseits fließende Übergänge zwischen beiden, und andererseits zeigt sich auch, daß das Maschinenmodell, das seine Wurzeln in der spätmittelalterlichen kosmologischen Uhrenmetapher und dann im neuzeitlichen Begriff der *machina mundi* hat[3], in etlichen

[1] Zur irrtümlichen Interpretation Kuhns als eines Vertreters eines reinen Revolutionsmodells vgl. Schmitter (1982:171ff.), Thilo (1989:90ff.)

[2] Daneben gibt es auch im 18. Jh. bereits die Systemmetapher bzw. das Systemmodell wie beispielsweise bei James Harris (1709–1780), der in der 2. Aufl. des *Hermes* von 1765 Wort und Sprache wie folgt definiert: "It appears from hence, that a WORD may be defined *a Voice articulate, and significant by Compact* — and that LANGUAGE may be defined *a System of such voices, so significant*" (Harris 1976:329 (Buch III, Kap. 3); Hervorh. im Original). Dominant war in der Wissenschaftsgeschichte dieser Zeit jedoch nicht das System-, sondern das Maschinenmodell.

[3] Zur Entwicklung des Begriffs der *machina mundi,* der schon bei Nicolaus Kopernikus *(De revolutionibus orbium coelestium libri VI,* 1543, Widmungsbrief an Papst Paul III.) erscheint, und überhaupt zur Verdrängung der Uhrenmetapher durch das Maschinenmodell vgl. etwa Schmidt-Biggemann (1980) sowie zum Vorgang der "Mechanisierung des Weltbildes" insgesamt Dijksterhuis (1956).

Ausprägungen auch organizistische Komponenten in sich einschließt und das Organismusmodell vice versa auch mechanizistische Komponenten enthält. Letzteres macht übrigens auch die Tatsache erklärlich, daß mit dem Organismusmodell, wie etwa bei Bopp (1791–1867) geschehen, eine rein positivistisch orientierte Methodologie verbunden werden konnte. Doch dazu später. Vorerst wollen wir nur festhalten, daß der scharfe Gegensatz zwischen Maschine und Organismus[1], wie schon Judith E. Schlanger (1971:47ff.) hervorgehoben hat, über weite Strecken der Geschichte hin "une fausse antithèse" ist.

Wichtiger Ausgangspunkt für die Entwicklung der Maschinenkonzeption und ihre Anwendung über die Mechanik im engeren Sinn hinaus, d.h. ihre Anwendung auf die Natur, den Menschen, den Staat, die Sprache usw., war die von René Descartes (1596–1650) vorgenommene methodische Trennung von "res cogitans" (Geist) und "res extensa" (Materie), die die Voraussetzung dafür schuf, die Materie "als unabhängige Einheit mit mechanischen und geometrischen Mitteln zu beschreiben" (Schmidt-Biggemann 1980:792). An einer zentralen Stelle der 1644 publizierten *Principia philosophiae,* an der zugleich noch in traditioneller Weise die ältere Uhrenmetapher aufgegriffen wird, heißt es beispielsweise:

> Es gibt wirklich keine Grundsätze in der Mechanik, die sich nicht auch auf die Physik [= Lehre von der Natur, P.S.] ... erstrecken; und eine Uhr, die aus irgendwelchen Rädern zusammengesetzt ist, um die Zeit anzuzeigen, ist nicht weniger natürlich als ein Baum, der aus irgendeinem Samen entstanden ist, um bestimmte Früchte hervorzubringen. (Zitiert nach Schmidt-Biggemann 1980:792)

Die der mechanizistischen Beschreibung der Natur zugrundeliegende Geist-Materie-Dichotomie findet dann im sprachwissenschaftlichen Bereich z.B. ihren Niederschlag bei Gérauld de Cordemoy (1628–

[1] Da es sich hierbei um eine Erscheinung handelt, die nicht nur die Linguistik, sondern den gesamten wissenschaftlichen Bereich betrifft, sei hier vor allem auf die ausführlicheren Darstellungen von Klaus/Buhr (1971:812–813, s.v. Organismus), Ballauf/Scheerer/Meyer (1984), Röd (1984), Kondylis (1986) und Erpenbeck/Röseberg (1988) verwiesen.

1684), der in der 2. Aufl. des *Discours physique de la parole* von 1677 den Körper strikt von der Seele des Menschen trennt, ausschließlich den Körper als 'méchaniquement' arrangiert bezeichnet und dementsprechend auch in seiner Sprachreflexion zwei getrennte Bereiche unterscheidet: nämlich die Sprache, die dem Körperlichen zugeordnet wird, und das Denken, das zum Geistigen gehört. So hebt Cordemoy nach einer längeren Erörterung darüber, daß die Tiere, ohne eine Seele zu haben, aufgrund der 'disposition méchanique' ihrer Organe dazu in der Lage sind, Laute von sich zu geben, bezüglich der menschlichen Sprache die beiden folgenden distinkten Ebenen voneinander ab: erstens "la formation de la voix, qui ne peut venir que du corps", und zweitens "la signification ou l'idée qu'on y [sc. der Stimme, P.S.] joint, qui ne peut estre que de la part de l'Ame"[1].

Die hier manifeste Trennung von Lautlichem und Geistigem, von Mechanischem und Nicht-Mechanischem, innerhalb der Sprachbetrachtung wird sich dann später als ein Kernproblem der mechanizistischen Sprachauffassung (aber nicht nur dieser) erweisen. Genau 90 Jahre nach Cordemoys *Discours physique* versucht etwa Nicolas Beauzée (1717–1789) diese Dichotomie ansatzweise zu überwinden, indem er das Geistige als einen mit den Mitteln der Logik analysierbaren "méchanisme intellectuel" definiert und diesen geistigen Mechanismus als die 'Grundlage' der 'langage' bezeichnet[2]. Mit einer solchen Tendenz zur engeren Verknüpfung des Geistigen mit dem Materiellen als dessen regierendes Prinzip nähert sich Beauzées Auffassung dem avancierten Mechanizismus, wie er sich in Julien Offroy de La Mettries (1709–1751) *L'homme machine* von 1748 findet. La Mettrie geht nämlich in dieser Schrift nicht mehr im Sinne des Cartesianismus von einem äußeren geistigen Beweger aus, der die Materie bewegt, vielmehr spricht er der Materie eine Selbstbewegung zu, die von einem in ihr liegenden "principe moteur" ausgeht[3].

[1] Das erste Zitat ist Cordemoy (1970:14) entnommen, das zweite findet sich ebd. S. 122.

[2] Vgl. Beauzées *Grammaire générale, ou exposition raisonnée des éléments nécessaires du langage* (Paris 1767), préface, viij (Nachdruck Beauzée 1974).

[3] Vgl. dazu ausführlich Kondylis (1986:280ff.)

Die Hineinnahme des "principe moteur" in das anthropologische Maschinenmodell von La Mettrie und der damit verknüpfte Gedanke der Eigendynamik von Naturkörpern weisen deutlich auf eins der Kernprobleme des Maschinenmodells hin, nämlich auf die in ihm enthaltene Implikation, daß dieses Modell im Grunde eine außerhalb der Maschine existierende Bewegungskraft voraussetzt. Dies widerspricht aber den Erkenntnissen der sich damals vehement entwickelnden Wissenschaften von organischen Körpern, d.h. der Biologie, Anatomie etc., die bald eine Leitfunktion für alle Wissenschaften übernahmen. Aber nicht nur diese Komponente des Maschinenmodells wurde zum Problem, vielmehr läßt sich, was hier nicht im einzelnen geschehen kann, aufzeigen, daß auch die übrigen theoretischen Implikationen des *machina*-Modells nicht mehr mit den neueren naturwissenschaftlichen Erkenntnissen vereinbar waren und zu dessen allmählicher Ablösung durch den Organismusbegriff führten. Diese Komponenten lassen sich idealtypisch wie folgt rekonstruieren:

Implikationen des *machina*-Modells:

— Auffassung der als Maschine begriffenen Entität als *Instrument*

— Voraussetzung eines außerhalb der Maschine anzusetzenden *Erzeugers*

— Voraussetzung einer außerhalb der Maschine anzusetzenden *bewegenden Kraft*

— Annahme einer *mechanischen Kausalität der Abläufe* und damit der Berechenbarkeit des Zusammenspiels der Einzelteile

— Annahme eines *vorherbestimmten, vorgängig von außen festgelegten und unabänderlichen Zwecks*

— Annahme der *Wiederholung prinzipiell immer gleicher Abläufe*

Hinzu kommt als konstituierendes Merkmal noch

— die Auffassung der Maschine als ein *Ganzes,*

doch ist diese Komponente in gewisser Weise abzuheben, weil sie ebenfalls dem Organismusbegriff eigen ist und damit zugleich den Punkt darstellt, an dem das Organismusmodell anknüpfen konnte. Insofern haben wir es dann auch beim Wechsel der Modellvorstellungen nicht mit einem absoluten Bruch zu tun, sondern mit einem Ersatz bestimmter Inhaltskomponenten bei gleichzeitiger Beibehaltung der sowohl für das Maschinen- als auch das Organismusmodell überaus wichtigen Komponente der Ganzheit. Man könnte auch, um die Überlegungen Percivals wieder aufzugreifen, sagen, daß bei aller Diskontinuität eine bestimmte Kontinuität gewahrt bleibt.

3. Das Organismusmodell

Während Johann Georg Hamann (1730–1788) sich im Prinzip noch auf dem Standpunkt des vorhin erwähnten und Hamann auch bekannten[1] Cordemoy befindet und das Denken von der auf das Lautliche reduzierten Sprache trennt, wobei die Sprache dann nach Hamann der als "Maschiene" apostrophierten menschlichen Natur entspringt[2], ist die eigentlich menschliche Sprache für Johann Gottfried Herder (1744–1803) schon gar nicht mehr unter den Maschinenbegriff subsumierbar. Genauer gesagt trennt Herder in seiner Sprachursprungsschrift von 1772 bezüglich der menschlichen Sprache nicht mehr zwischen einer maschinenhaften Sprach- und einer geistigen Denkebene, vielmehr behält er, wie etwa H. Schmidt (1986:45ff.) gezeigt hat, den Begriff 'mechanisch' ausschließlich der tierischen Sprache und der ihr gleichzusetzenden 'Sprache der Empfindung', der 'Natursprache', vor. Lediglich diese 'Natursprache', nicht aber die auf Besonnenheit und Reflexion beruhende menschliche Sprache im eigentlichen Sinn, ist nach Herder tierischen Ursprungs und folgt, wie er sagt, dem Naturgesetz "einer empfindsamen Maschine"[3].

Soweit ich sehe — und zu demselben Ergebnis kommt auch Schmidt (1986) — findet sich bei Herder aber noch nicht der Gegenbegriff des Organismus zur Kennzeichnung der menschlichen Sprache verwendet. Dieser begegnet uns dann bei den Schlegel-Brüdern, bei W. v. Humboldt (1767–1835), bei Bopp usw., und seine Verbreitung hängt wohl eng mit den Aktivitäten des Jenaer und Weimarer Kreises am Ende des 18. Jahrhunderts zusammen.[4] Eine ganz entscheidende Rolle für die

[1] Vgl. Weiß (1990:28).

[2] Vgl. z.B. Hamann (1967:93 mit 139) sowie Weiß (1990:49–50).

[3] Vgl. Herder (1966:6ff.); Zitat ebd. S. 16.

[4] Natürlich ist der Begriff des Organismus selbst keineswegs neu, sondern läßt sich wortgeschichtlich bis in die Antike zurückverfolgen (vgl. z.B. Ballauf/Scheerer/Meyer 1984). Neu ist aber, daß er den Charakter eines wissenschafts-

Durchsetzung des Organismusbegriffs spielt aber Immanuel Kant (1724–1804), der in der *Kritik der Urteilskraft* von 1790 ausführlich auf den Begriff "organisierte Wesen" eingeht. Hierzu dürfte Kant u.a. durch den Anatomen und Physiologen Johann Friedrich Blumenbach (1752–1840) angeregt worden sein, der in seinem *Handbuch der Naturgeschichte* (1. Aufl. 1779/80; 6. Aufl. 1799:5) Tiere und Mensch als "belebte und beseelte organisirte Körper" bezeichnet. Kants Begriff der "organisierten Wesen" führt, wie in einer langen Deduktion KdU § 63ff. bewiesen wird und Kant § 66 selbst ausdrücklich sagt, "die Vernunft in eine ganz andere Ordnung der Dinge, als die eines bloßen Mechanismus der Natur" (Kant 1975b:489). Die bestimmenden Merkmale dieses Begriffs sind etwa folgende:

— (statt instrumentalistischer Auffassung) Auffassung der als Organismus bezeichneten Entitäten als *organisierte Wesen* (KdU § 65ff.)
— (statt Voraussetzung eines externen Erzeugers) Bestimmung als *Produkt der Natur* selbst (KdU § 63ff., bes. 66)
— (statt Voraussetzung einer (externen) bewegenden Kraft) Annahme eines inneren Bildungstriebes, einer *"bildenden* [= hervorbringenden, P.S.] *Kraft"* (KdU § 65; Kant 1975b:486)
— (statt Annahme mechanischer Kausalität) Annahme eines *"Naturzweck[s]"*, d.h. Annahme, daß etwas von "sich selbst wechselseitig" "Ursache und Wirkung" ist (KdU § 64ff.; Zitat 1975b:483f.)[1]
— (statt Annahme eines vorgängig von außen festgelegten unabänderlichen Zwecks) Annahme *"innerer Zweckmäßigkeit"* (KdU §

theoretischen Modells gewinnt und als ein solches in zahlreiche Wissensbereiche Eingang findet.

[1] Die Annahme eines Naturzwecks kann nach Kant nicht aus der Kausalität, aus mechanischen Gesetzen, abgeleitet werden, denn das Ding als Naturzweck ist kein konstruktiver Begriff für Verstand oder Vernunft, sondern ein regulativer Begriff für die reflektierende (teleologische) Urteilskraft, die "unter einem Gesetze subsumieren" soll, "welches noch nicht gegeben und also in der Tat nur ein Prinzip der Reflexion über Gegenstände ist, für die es uns objektiv gänzlich an einem Gesetze mangelt" (Zitat KdU § 69, Kant 1975b:498f.; zum Gedankengang vgl. KdU § 65 – 68 u.).

63) mit der Kraft, sich an gegebene Umstände anzupassen (KdU § 65, Kant 1975b:486; alle Kursivierungen von mir).

Hinzu kommt das entscheidende Merkmal der Bestimmung des Organismus als ein Ganzes, das das Organismusmodell mit der *machina*-Konzeption teilt, das aber innerhalb der Organismuskonzeption in besonderer Weise definiert wird. Denn hier wird der Organismus bestimmt

— als ein Ganzes, bei dem "die Teile (ihrem Dasein und der Form nach) nur durch ihre Beziehung auf das Ganze möglich sind" (KdU § 65, Kant 1987b:484), bei dem sich die Teile "zur Einheit eines Ganzen verbinden" und "umgekehrt (wechselseitig) die Idee des Ganzen wiederum die Form und Verbindung aller Teile" bestimmt (ebd. 485).

Diese Konzeption wird dann nicht nur in der Naturphilosophie (z.B. Schelling [1775–1854]) und in den weiten Bereichen der Naturkunde (z.B. Goethe [1749–1832]), Anthropologie und Staatstheorie (so etwa bei Georg Forster [1754–1794][1] und W. v. Humboldt) aufgegriffen, sondern auch in der sich nun als wissenschaftliche Disziplin konstituierenden Sprachkunde. Bekanntlich kommt hier sowohl den Brüdern Schlegel, als auch Wilhelm v. Humboldt eine besondere Bedeutung zu, und mit diesen beiden Namen sind auch schon zugleich zwei divergierende Richtungen angesprochen, in die sich der Organismusbegriff innerhalb der Linguistik entwickeln wird. Die eine Richtung kann man, grob gesagt, als die Schlegel-Bopp-Schleicher-Richtung bezeichnen, die andere ist die Humboldttradition[2], die über Steinthal (1823–1899) und Pott (1802–1887) verläuft.

Da der Begriff des Organismus sukzessive entwickelt und angeeignet wird, ist es äußerst schwierig, seine Genese bei den einzelnen Autoren

[1] Aufschlußreich ist in bezug auf Forster, daß er in seiner an Buffons (1707–1788) *Histoire naturelle, générale et particulière* (Bd. 12 u. 13, Paris 1764/65) orientierten Vorlesung *Ein Blick in das Ganze der Natur* (Fassung von 1783) noch von der "Weltmaschine" spricht (AA 8, 92), während er in seiner Einleitung zu *Cooks dritter Reise* (Manuskript von 1787, Druck 1789) den Organismusbegriff verwendet und ihn als "Gleichniß" auf den Staatskörper überträgt (Forster AA 5, 287–288.).

[2] Hierzu vgl. Haßler (1985).

chronologisch genau zu fixieren. Es scheint aber festzustehen, daß dieser Begriff sowohl von den beiden Schlegels als auch von Humboldt zum ersten Mal im Jahre 1795 (also 5 Jahre nach Kant) in bezug auf die Sprache verwendet wird[1]. Was Humboldt betrifft, so scheint man zwar mit Haßler (1986:171) annehmen zu können, daß der Organismusbegriff bei ihm in der Tat erstmals im Jahre 1795 auf die *Sprache* angewendet wird, doch weist Schmidt (1986:62–63) mit Recht darauf hin, daß die Organismuskonzeption als solche schon ab 1791 in Humboldts *staatstheoretischen* Schriften erscheint. Diese Linie läßt sich jedoch noch weiter zurückverfolgen, und zwar bis ins Jahr 1789, wo Humboldt unter dem Datum vom 27.–30. Oktober 1789 in seinen *Tagebüchern* das Konzept einer *Anthropologie* entwirft, in der der Mensch "in der that als ein ganzes anzusehn" ist (Humboldt GS 14, 211)[2].

Dies bestätigt nicht nur die weite Verbreitung und fruchtbare Anwendung des Organismusmodells in zahlreichen Wissensbereichen, sondern ist zugleich ein Beispiel dafür, daß die Organismuskonzeption auch schon vor Kants *Kritik der Urteilskraft* begonnen hatte, ihren Siegeszug anzutreten. Speziell auf Humboldt bezogen ist hier auf die

1 Bei den Schlegels ist hier ein Brief von Friedrich an seinen Bruder August Wilhelm vom 23. Dez. 1795 zu nennen, in dem es heißt: "Woher endlich die so auffallende und so große Verschiedenheit der Grundgesetze der Sprachbildung in verschiedenen Sprachen, wenn sie nicht aus der Organisation herrühren?" (zitiert nach Schmidt 1986:65). In bezug auf Humboldt ist hier ein Brief an Schiller (1759–1805) vom 14. Sept. 1795, anzuführen, in dem Humboldt (1900:136) schreibt: "Nicht bloß daß die Sprache selbst ein organisches Ganze ist, so hängt sie auch mit der Individualität derer, die sie sprechen, so genau zusammen, daß dieser Zusammenhang schlechterdings nicht vernachlässigt werden darf". Ohne näher präzisiert zu werden, erscheint der Begriff des organischen Ganzen in diesem Humboldtbrief bereits wie eine übliche Redeweise, und das scheint mir auch insofern leicht erklärlich, als die Organismuskonzeption schon in früheren Schriften Humboldts nachgewiesen werden kann (siehe dazu die weitere Argumentation im obigen Text).

2 Weiter ausgeführt werden die organizistischen Überlegungen im Bereich der Anthropologie dann z.B. in Humboldts Fragment *Über die Gesetze der Entwicklung der menschlichen Kräfte* von 1791 (vgl. bes. GS 1, 87–106), von wo sie dann in die staatstheoretischen Schriften übernommen werden. Vgl. etwa *Ideen zu einem Versuch, die Gränzen der Wirksamkeit des Staats* zu bestimmen (1791; bes. GS 1, 106).

Bedeutung hinzuweisen, die Humboldts intensive Bekanntschaft mit dem 'Weltreisenden' und 'Naturkundigen' Georg Forster für Humboldts damalige geistige Entwicklung hatte[1].

Betrachten wir Humboldts Konzeption etwas genauer, so sind für ihn m.A.n. drei Dinge bezeichnend: erstens, daß er das Organismuskonzept auf den gesamten 'Bau' der Sprache mit allen seinen Teilbereichen bezieht[2] und den Organismus des Baus der Sprache mit dem Organismus des Denkens in eine enge Verbindung bringt. Zweitens, daß Humboldt eine spezifische Methodologie für die Untersuchung des Sprachorganismus fordert, und drittens daß er im Laufe seiner geistigen Entwicklung der organizistischen Metaphorik immer kritischer gegenüberzustehen scheint und sich auf die Erörterung methodischer Vorgehensweisen konzentriert, die nicht mehr so stark an den Organismusbegriff gekoppelt sind[3]. Als Stichworte möchte ich hier zu Punkt 2 nur Humboldts Abgrenzung von 'anatomischer' und 'physiologischer' Sprachbetrachtung nennen, die mit seiner Ablehnung der instrumentellen Sprachauffassung zusammenhängt und auf seiner Auffassung der Sprache als eines dynamischen 'geistigen Prozesses' und eben nicht eines toten 'daliegenden Stoffs' basiert[4]. Zu Punkt 3 ist zu erwähnen, daß Humboldt dann selbst die 'physiologische' Betrachtung der Sprache als im Grunde inadäquat erscheint, weil die Sprache "ganz eigentlich dem Geistigen" im Menschen angehört (GS 6, 345). Daher zieht er schließlich den Begriffen *anatomisch/physiologisch* das Begriffspaar *statisch* und *dynamisch* vor.

Kommen wir zu Friedrich Schlegel (1772–1829), so verwendet er entgegen seiner früheren Auffassung, wo er den Organismusbegriff auf die Sprache insgesamt bezogen hatte[5], im Jahre 1808 in seiner wirkungsmächtigen Schrift *Ueber die Sprache und Weisheit der Indier*

[1] Vgl. dazu Schmitter (1991) und Sauter (1989:192ff.).

[2] Abgegrenzt hiervon wird jedoch die Untersuchung des 'Charakters' der Sprachen. Vgl. dazu ausführlich Trabant (1986: bes. 173ff.)

[3] Zu letzterem vgl. bes. Borsche (1981:219ff.)

[4] Vgl. etwa Humboldt GS V, 369; VI 146; VII 97 und zu dieser Problematik insgesamt vorläufig noch Schmitter (1987b).

[5] Vgl. etwa das Zitat in S. 301 Anm. 1 sowie insgesamt zu Schlegel Schmidt (1986:64–69) und Schmitter (1987b).

den Begriff des Organischen nur noch zur Kennzeichnung der flektierenden Sprachen, während er die übrigen 'mechanisch' nennt. Diese Reduktion in der Verwendung des Begriffs lediglich für ein ganz bestimmtes als 'lebendig' angesehenes morphologisches Verfahren erlaubt es dann später Bopp, die Sprachen zwar als einen Organismus zu betrachten, aber die von Humboldt betonte geistige Seite der Sprache aus seinen Betrachtungen weitgehend auszuklammern und nur die Sprache 'an und für sich' zu untersuchen[1]. Dies führt bei Bopp einerseits zu einer rein positivistischen Analysemethode, die er explizit als "eine anatomische Zerlegung oder chemische Zersetzung des Sprachkörpers" bezeichnet (Bopp 1833–1852:133). Andererseits führt das dazu, daß Bopp unter Organismus nur die Sprachen als "organische Naturkörper" versteht, die "nach bestimmten Gesetzen sich bilden, ein inneres Lebensprinzip in sich tragend sich entwickeln, und nach und nach absterben"[2]. Von hier aus ist es dann kein weiter Schritt zu Schleicher (1821–1868) und den evolutionistischen Sprachtheorien mehr, wo die biologistische Komponente noch stärker in den Vordergrund tritt. Und es ist auch nur noch ein kurzer Schritt zu einem historizistisch geprägten Positivismus, der sich in der Analyse von Einzelerscheinungen verliert, was dann alles insgesamt schließlich zur Kritik an der organizistischen Sprachauffassung führt und deren Ablösung zur Folge hat.

4. Und noch einmal die Frage: Vom "Organismus" über das "System" zurück zum "Organismus"?

Am Ende dieses sehr gerafften Überblicks[3] können wir uns erneut die Ausgangsfrage stellen, ob es denn sinnvoll ist, vom heutigen umstrit-

[1] Zu Bopps wenig präzisem Organismusbegriff und seiner Konzentration auf die Ausarbeitung von Analyseprozeduren vgl. vor allem die detailreiche Studie von Davies (1987).

[2] F. Bopp, [Rezension zu J. Grimm, *Deutsche Grammatik], Jahrbücher für Wissenschaftliche Kritik,* Nr. 31/32, Februar 1827, 251–252

[3] Eine ausführlichere Analyse hoffe ich in absehbarer Zeit in monographischer Form in der Schrift *Vom Mechanismus zum Organizismus. Eine modellgeschichtliche Untersuchung zur Entwicklung der (Sprach-)Wissenschaft um 1800* (Münster: Nodus Publikationen) vorlegen zu können.

tenen Systembegriff zur Organismuskonzeption zurückzukehren. Wie wir gesehen haben, sind für den Übergang vom Maschinenmodell zum Modell des Organismus zwei allgemeinere entwicklungsgeschichtliche Faktoren besonders charakteristisch: nämlich einerseits der Umstand, daß beide Modelle in einer gewissen Kontinuität zueinander stehen, und andererseits, daß das Maschinenmodell insofern überwunden wird, als diejenigen Komponenten ausgeschaltet werden, die mit dem neueren Erkenntnisstand nicht mehr vereinbar sind. Man kann diesen Vorgang auch ganz einfach mit einem heute in weiten Kreisen obsolet gewordenen Begriff 'wissenschaftlichen Fortschritt' nennen[1].

Wie wir wissen, hat sich das wissenschaftstheoretische Modell des Organismus als äußerst fruchtbar erwiesen und zum enormen Aufschwung der Sprachwissenschaft im 19. Jahrhundert beigetragen. Das gilt sowohl für die Humboldtrichtung der allgemeinen Sprachkunde als auch für die dominierende Richtung der vergleichenden und historischen Sprachwissenschaft. Trotzdem ist aber auch das Organismusmodell im Zuge der Konzentration auf neue linguistische Fragestellungen abgelöst worden, und zwar durch den Systembegriff. Ohne hier auf Details einzugehen, kann man mit Fug und Recht behaupten, daß sich bei dem erneuten Wechsel ähnliches vollzogen hat, wie beim Übergang vom *machina*-Modell zur Organismuskonzeption. Auch im Systemmodell wurden bestimmte Komponenten des älteren Organismusmodells beibehalten, vor allem der Gedanke des gegliederten Ganzen und der wechselseitigen Abhängigkeit und gegenseitigen Bestimmung seiner Einzelteile. Zugleich aber wurden andere Faktoren eliminiert, die sich als unzutreffend oder mißleitend erwiesen hatten. Dies war vor allem die biologistische Komponente, die leicht dazu verführte, die Sprache als ein autonomes, sich selbst steuerndes und entwickelndes Wesen anzusehen, wie wir es bei Bopp schon vorgebildet finden und was Schleicher u.a. noch stärker pointieren.

Auch dieser Wechsel ist also als ein Bemühen um ein besseres, d.h. adäquateres Modell zur Charakterisierung der Sprache zu verstehen.

[1] Zur Fortschrittsproblematik und dem trotz aller gegenteiligen Behauptungen möglichen 'empirischen' Umgang mit der Fortschrittskategorie vgl. ausführlicher Schmitter (1987a).

Und wenn wir nun feststellen, daß auch das Systemmodell gravierende Mängel hat, dann müssen diese Mängel zwar beseitigt werden, doch würde eine Wiederbelebung des historisch überwundenen Modells des Organismus einen Rückfall hinter eine bereits errungene Position bedeuten. Im besten Falle müßte sich der Versuch, den Organismusbegriff zu reaktivieren, als naiv erweisen, doch vor einem solch naiven Vorgehen kann uns die Auseinandersetzung mit der Geschichte der Linguistik schützen. Dies anzudeuten, war der eigentliche Sinn meines heutigen Vortrags.

LITERATUR

Ballauf, Th., Scheerer, E. & A. Meyer. 1984. "Organismus". *Historisches Wörterbuch der Philosophie,* hrsg. v. J. Ritter & K. Gründer, Bd. 6.1330–1358. Basel/Stuttgart: Schwabe.

Beauzée, Nicolas. 1974. *Grammaire générale ou exposition raisonnée des éléments nécessaires du langage, pour servir de fondement à l'étude de toutes les langues.* Nouvelle impression en facsimile de l'édition de 1767 avec une introduction par Barrie E. Bartlett Stuttgart-Bad Cannstatt: Frommann.

Bopp, Franz. 1833–1852. *Vergleichende Grammatik des Sanskrit, Zend, Griechischen, Lateinischen, Litthauischen, (Altslawischen), Gothischen und Deutschen.* 6 Lfgg. Berlin: Dümmler.

Borsche, Tilman. 1981. *Sprachansichten. Der Begriff der menschlichen Rede in der Sprachphilosophie Wilhelm von Humboldts.* Stuttgart: Klett-Cotta.

Cordemoy, Gerauld de. 1677. *Discours physique de la parole.* 2. Aufl. Paris: Estienne Michallet. (Nachdruck "avec un commentaire par Herbert E. Brekle" Stuttgart-Bad Cannstatt: Frommann ,1970.)

Davies Anna Morpurgo. 1987. "'Organic' and 'Organism' in Franz Bopp". Hoenigswald/Wiener 1987, 81–107.

Dijksterhuis, E[duard] J[an]. 1956. *Die Mechanisierung des Weltbildes.* Berlin & New York: Springer.

Erpenbeck, John & Ulrich Röseberg. 1988. "Naturwissenschaftliche Entwicklung und spätbürgerliche Philosophie: Physik, Biologie, Psychologie". *Enzyklopädie zur bürgerlichen Philosophie im 19. und 20. Jahrhundert,* hrsg. v. Manfred Buhr, 477–507. Leipzig: VEB Bibliographisches Institut; Köln: Pahl-Rugenstein.

Forster, Georg. 1958ff. *Werke. Sämtliche Schriften, Tagebücher, Briefe.* Hrsg. v. der Akademie der Wissenschaften der DDR, bearb. v. Gerhard Steiner u.a. Berlin: Akademie-Verlag [zitiert als AA].

Hamann, Johann Georg. 1967. *Schriften zur Sprache*. Einleitung und Anmerkungen von Josef Simon. Frankfurt a.M.: Suhrkamp.

Harris, James. 1765. *Hermes, or a Philosophical Inquiry concerning Universal Grammar*. 2nd ed. London: Nourse & Vaillant. (Nachdruck Hildesheim/New York: Olms, 1976)

Haßler, Gerda. 1985. "Zur Auffassung der Sprache als eines organischen Ganzen bei Wilhelm von Humboldt und zu ihren Umdeutungen im 19. Jahrhundert". *ZPSK* 38.564–575.

— . 1986. "Die These der Sprachrelativität des Denkens in der Aufklärung und bei Wilhelm von Humboldt". *Sprache-Bewußtsein-Tätigkeit,* hrsg. v. Klaus Welke, 154–177. Berlin: Akademie-Verlag.

Herder, Johann Gottfried. 1966. *Abhandlung über den Ursprung der Sprache*. Hrsg.v. D. Irmscher. Stuttgart: Reclam.

Hoenigswald, Henry M. & Linda F. Wiener, eds. 1987. *Biological Metaphor and Cladistic Classification. An Interdisciplinary Perspective*. London: Pinter.

Humboldt, Wilhelm von. 1900. *Briefwechsel zwischen Schiller und Wilhelm von Humboldt*. 3. verm. Ausg. mit Anm. von Albert Leitzmann. Stuttgart: Cotta.

— . 1903–1936. *Gesammelte Schriften*. Hrsg.v. Albert Leitzmann u.a. 17 Bde. Berlin: Behr. (Nachdruck Berlin: de Gruyter, 1968.) [zitiert als GS]

Kant, Immanuel. 1975a. *Werke in zehn Bänden,* hrsg. v. Wilhelm Weischedel. Bd. 3: *Kritik der reinen Vernunft*. Darmstadt: Wiss. Buchgesellschaft.

— . 1975b. *Werke in zehn Bänden* hrsg. v. Wilhelm Weischedel. Bd. 8: *Kritik der Urteilskraft und Schriften zur Naturphilsophie*. Darmstadt: Wiss. Buchgesellschaft.

Klaus, Georg & Manfred Buhr, Hrsg. 1971. *Philosophisches Wörterbuch*. 8. Aufl., 2 Bde. Leipzig: VEB Verlag Enzyklopädie / Berlin: das europäische buch.

Kondylis, Panajotis. 1986. *Die Aufklärung im Rahmen des neuzeitlichen Rationalismus*. München: Deutscher Taschenbuch Verlag.

Lovelock, James. 1989. "Die Erde ist ein Superorganismus". *Deutsche Universitäts-Zeitung* Nr. 24.11–14.

Neumann, Werner. 1984. "Zeichen und Organismus: Beobachtungen zum Wechsel eines Denkmusters in der deutschen Sprachwissenschaft des 19. Jahrhunderts". *Beiträge zur Erforschung der Deutschen Sprache* 4.5–38.

Percival, W. Keith. 1987. "Biological Analogy in the Study of Language before the Advent of Comparative Grammar". Hoenigswald & Wiener 1987, 3–38.

Röd, Wolfgang. 1984. *Die Philosophie der Neuzeit 2*. München: Beck.

Sauter, Christina M. 1989. *Wilhelm von Humboldt und die deutsche Aufklärung*. Berlin: Duncker & Humblot.

Schlanger, Judith E. 1971. *Les métaphores de l'organisme*. Paris: Vrin.

Schmidt, Hartmut. 1986. *Die lebendige Sprache: Zur Entstehung des Organismuskonzepts*. Berlin: Akademie der Wissenschaften der DDR, Zentralinstitut für Sprachwissenschaft.

Schmidt-Biggemann, W. 1980. "Maschine". *Historisches Wörterbuch der Philosophie,* hrsg. v. J. Ritter & K. Gründer, Bd. 5.790–802. Basel/Stuttgart: Schwabe.

Schmitter, Peter. 1982. *Untersuchungen zur Historiographie der Linguistik. Struktur — Methodik — theoretische Fundierung*. Tübingen: Narr.

— . 1987a. "Fortschritt: Zu einer umstrittenen Interpretationskategorie in der Geschichtsschreibung der Linguistik und der Semiotik". *Geschichte der Sprachtheorie*. Bd. 1: *Zur Theorie und Methode der Geschichtsschreibung der Linguistik,* hrsg. v. P. Schmitter, 93–124. Tübingen: Narr.

— . 1987b. "Le savoir romantique". *Histoire des idées linguistique,* dir. par Sylvain Auroux. Vol. 3 (à paraître). Liège/Bruxelles: Mardaga.

— . 1990. "Historiographie und Metahistoriographie". *Understanding the Historiography of Linguistics,* ed. by Werner Hüllen, 35–48. Münster: Nodus Publikationen.

— . 1991. "Zur Wissenschaftskonzeption Georg Forsters und dessen biographischen Bezügen zu den Brüdern Humboldt". *Language and Earth. Elective Affinities between the Emerging Sciences of Linguistics and Geology,* ed. by Gottfried Hofbauer, Bernd Naumann & Frans Plank, 91–124. Amsterdam/Philadelphia: Benjamins (im Druck).

Schwarze, Christoph & Dieter Wunderlich;, Hrsg. 1985. *Handbuch der Lexikologie*. Königstein/Ts.: Athenäum.

Thilo, Ulrich Ch. M. 1989. *Rezeption und Wirkung des Cours de linguistique générale: Überlegungen zu Geschichte und Historiographie der Sprachwissenschaft*. Tübingen: Narr.

Trabant, Jürgen. 1986. *Apeliotes oder Der Sinn der Sprache. Wilhelm von Humboldts Sprach-Bild*. München: Fink.

Weiß, Helmut. 1990. *Johann Georg Hamanns Ansichten zur Sprache: Versuch einer Rekonstruktion aus dem Frühwerk*. Münster: Nodus Publikationen.

Zur Geschichtsschreibung der Sprechakttheorie: der Fall Reinach*

FRANK J. M. VONK;
Staatsuniversität Utrecht

1. METHODOLOGISCHE VORÜBERLEGUNGEN ZUM THEMA SPRECHHANDLUNGSTHEORIE

IN DIESEM BEITRAG möchte ich anhand eines Beispiels aus der 'Geschichte der Sprechakttheorie', der sogenannten Theorie der sozialen Akte von Adolf Reinach[1], zeigen, daß *erstens* eine bereichsspezifische, fast traditionell subjektiv-sprachtheoretische Bestimmung der Sprechakttheorien John L. Austins (1911–1960) und John R. Searles den Blick auf bereichsüberschreitende Ansätze in der Geschichte der (Sprech-)Akttheorien von vornherein ausschalten muß und tatsächlich auch ausgeschaltet hat. *Zweitens* setzt die Objektivierung von Sprechakten

* Diese Studie entstand im Rahmen eines Forschungsprojektes (Projekt 300-162-011) der durch die Niederländische Organisation für wissenschaftliche Forschung (NWO) unterstützte "Stichting Taalwetenschap".

1 Adolf Bernhard Philipp Reinach wurde am 23.12.1883 in Mainz geboren und fiel im Ersten Weltkrieg, am 16.11.1917, an der Front in Flandern. Reinach studierte Philosophie (Edmund Husserl [1859–1938], Theodor Lipps [1851–1914]), Psychologie (Georg Elias Müller [1850–1934]) und Jura (Hermann Kantorowicz [1877–1940], Ernst Beling [1866–1932]). 1904 promovierte er mit der Arbeit *Über den Ursachenbegriff im geltenden Strafrecht* zum Dr.phil. Zwischen 1905 und 1909 studierte er u.a. bei Husserl in Göttingen; Reinach habilitierte sich 1909 u.a. mit der Arbeit *Wesen und Systematic des Urteils* (Probevorlesung: "Probleme und Methoden der Ethik"). Von 1909 bis 1914 war Reinach Privatdozent für Philosophie in Göttingen. Er las u.a. über Themen aus der Geschichte der Philosophie (Platon, René Descartes' *Meditationes,* Immanuel Kants *Kritik der reinen Vernunft,* David Humes Kausalitätsbegriff), über Rechtsphilosophie und Ethik. Seit September 1914 war Reinach als Kriegsfreiwilliger an der Westfront. Während des Krieges arbeitete Reinach vor allem an religionsphilosophischen Themen. Diese Fragmente wurden erst 1989 in der textkritischen Ausgabe herausgegeben.

logische Strukturen voraus, die gerade nicht bereichsspezifisch, das heißt zum Beispiel nicht nur sprach- oder rechtswissenschaftlich konstituiert, wohl aber grundlegend sind für eine allgemeine Theorie der Sprechakte und, so meine ich, in den Gegenstandsbereich der Geschichtsschreibung der Sprechakttheorie gehören.

In seiner *philosophischen* Dissertation schreibt Rudolf Kamp (1977: 77ff.), daß die Sprachwissenschaftler methodisch, im Anschluß an die Dreiteilung des Sprachbegriffs bei Ferdinand de Saussure (1857–1913) und Karl Bühler (1879–1963), einen allgemeinen, einen subjektiven und einen objektiven Begriff unterscheiden. Für die Sprachbetrachtung, den bereichsspezifischen Einstieg, bedeutet diese methodische Einteilung, daß Sprache im engeren Sinne (vgl. Kamp 1977:68ff.), der nur die natürliche menschliche Lautsprache betreffende Sprachbegriff, ebenfalls allgemein, subjektiv und objektiv betrachtet werden kann.

Für unsere Darstellung ist vor allem die objektive Sprachbetrachtung, Sprach*theorie*begriff$_3$ bei Kamp, von Bedeutung. Dieses das "spezifische[...] Gesamt bzw. System theoretischer Aussagen über Sprache" thematisierende Betrachtungskonzept erlaubt ebenfalls eine Ausdifferenzierung nach den "verschiedenen Konzeptionsmöglichkeiten von 'Sprache' im engeren Sinne" (Kamp 1977:78), und zwar nach der "Bedeutungsvariation" von Sprache (in engerem Sinne). Kamp (1977:77ff.) unterscheidet demnach eine *Sprachwesenstheorie,* der "der allgemeine Sprachbegriff zugrunde[liegt]", "subjektive Sprachtheorien", die man als *Sprechtheorien,* die "auf irgendeinen Modus des Sprechens als subjektiven Tuns" bezogen sind, charakterisieren kann und schließlich eine "*objektive* Sprachtheorie", die sich "auf *Sprache* qua Objektivgebilde, qua System" bezieht.

Für die Sprechhandlungs- oder Sprechakttheorie reserviert Kamp (1977:81ff.) in seiner Einteilung einen Platz im Bereich der subjektiven Sprachtheorien, neben biologischen, soziologischen und psychologischen Sprechtheorien. Der von ihm "pragmatisch-analytische Sprechtheorie" genannte Teilbereich der subjektiven Sprachtheorie wird durch "Ergebnisse der modernen Linguistik, die pragmatische Denktradition des englischsprachigen Kulturraums und die neuere Strömung der Analytischen Philosophie" (Kamp 1977:83) charakterisiert. Sie wird dann mit der "Theorie der Sprechakte" von Austin und Searle in Zusammenhang gebracht, die zunächst ganz unproblematisch in Kamps Charakterisierung untergebracht werden kann.

Probleme tauchen dann auf, wenn man die bereichsspezifische Abgrenzung der pragmatisch-analytischen Sprachtheorie von anderen in Kamps Darstellung besprochenen Sprechtheorien wie zum Beispiel "linguistischen-" oder "Sprechsituationstheorien" näher betrachtet. So zum Beispiel, wenn man die logische Struktur von Sprechakten im Sinne Reinachs thematisiert. Meine Kritik gilt hier also dem Seziermesserverfahren Kamps, das in bestehenden bereichsspezifischen Einsichten in die 'pragmatisch-analytische', sprachwissenschaftlich orientierte Forschungstradition begründet ist.

2. Zur Geschichtsschreibung der Sprechhandlungstheorie: Reinachs Theorie der sozialen Akte

Reinach veröffentlichte seine Theorie der sozialen Akte im Jahre 1913 in dem ersten Band des von Edmund Husserl herausgegebenen *Jahrbuch für Philosophie und phänomenologische Forschung*, und zwar als erstes Kapitel einer umfangreicheren Studie zu "Den apriorischen Grundlagen des bürgerlichen Rechtes" mit dem Titel "Anspruch, Verbindlichkeit und Versprechen". Diese Theorie hatte er bereits 1911 in zwei Vorlesungen in Göttingen vorgetragen. In diesen 1989 aus Nachschriften von Studenten rekonstruierten und veröffentlichten Vorlesungen entwickelt Reinach im Anschluß an die intentionale Aktlehre von Franz Brentano (1838–1917) und die Leib-Seele-Lehre von René Descartes (1596–1650) einen Aktbegriff ganz eigener Art: den auf ein anderes Subjekt gerichteten (sozialen) Akt. Bereits in diesen Vorlesungen weist Reinach darauf hin, daß

> [f]ür soziale Akte wesentlich ist die Voraussetzung eines anderen Subjekts, dem sie sich kundgeben wollen. Die Person, an die sie gerichtet sind, soll Kenntnis davon erhalten. Eine Verbindung zwischen Menschen ist aber nicht direkt möglich. Ausdrücke sind hier also nötig; die sozialen Akte müssen Ausdruck finden zur Mitteilung an den andern. Verschiedene Formen stehen hier zur Verfügung: Worte, Gesten usw. Ein Adressat ist also bei den sozialen Akten nötig. Die Richtung auf den Adressaten liegt im Wesen dieser Akte, ist ihre Seele. Ein

> Zweites, die Erscheinungsform, liegt nicht in ihrem Wesen und ist ihr Leib. Sie gibt es nur, weil es unter uns Menschen so ist, daß wir unsere inneren Akte nur an ihren Erscheinungsformen erkennen können (Reinach 1911:357).

2.1 *Das Versprechen*

Das Musterbeispiel eines sozialen Akts ist für Reinach das Versprechen als "ein Einzelproblem aus dem großen Gebiete der apriorischen Rechtslehre"[1] (Reinach 1913:147). Dieses Einzelproblem wird nach Husserls formalontologischem Strukturmodell der 3. logischen Untersuchung ausgearbeitet. Das Versprechen hat demnach verschiedene selbständige und unselbständige Teile und Momente, die unterschiedliche ein- oder zweiseitig fundierte Abhängigkeitsbeziehungen (vgl. das Versprechensmodell unten) aufweisen. Auf jeden Fall hat es mehrere Träger, von denen einer "der phänomenale Urheber des Aktes" (1913:158) ist. Das ist deshalb von Bedeutung, weil jeder soziale Akt ein einseitig fundiertes Wollen eines Subjekts oder Ichs als Quelle der Spontaneität braucht. Wäre dies nicht der Fall, so könnten die weiteren Aktmomente, die Folge(n) oder das Produkt (Reinach, S. 147) keinen Bestand haben. So zum Beispiel, wenn ich von jemandem dazu

[1] Vgl. Reinach (1989b:669), wo die Herausgeber die juridischen Kenntnisse Reinachs als eine der Grundlagen der Theorie der sozialen Akte herausarbeiten: "Reinachs spezifischer Beitrag [zur] Münchener Sprechakttheorie dürfte u.a. von seinen juridischen Kenntnissen, insbesondere vom römischen Recht inspiriert gewesen sein. Neben den entsprechenden Teilen der *Institutiones* (3,13ff. und 4,1ff.) sind hier vor allem die Bücher 44–46 der *Digesten* mit ihrer reichen Materialsammlung zu erwähnen. D44,7 handelt von Obligationen und Aktionen, d.h. den juridischen Schritten zur Eintreibung von Verbindlichkeiten, D45,1 von den Obligationen durch Worte (mündlich zustande gekommene Verbindlichkeiten), D46,1 und 2 von der Stellvertretung (durch Fideiussor, Mandat und Delegation). Noch im Rechtsbuch bezieht Reinach sich ausdrücklich auf Inst. 3,13 und auf D46,2. Im römischen Recht nehmen zwar die durch Delikt entstandenen Verbindlichkeiten — z.B. die *aus der Wegnahme einer Sache* erwachsen — einen relativ breiten Raum ein. Aber es wird z.B. auch festgestellt, daß keine Verbindlichkeit entsteht, wofern die Worte "ich verspreche" ohne den Willen sich zu verpflichten ausgesprochen werden (Paulus D44,7,3,2; vgl. die Lehre von Täuschungsvorbehalt, der *doli mali clausula,* Paulus D45,1,22). Dies erinnert an Reinachs Darstellung des Scheinversprechens. Weiter ist von Verbindlichkeit keine Rede bei Abwesenheit einer Person, 'denn sie müssen einander hören' (Ulpian D45,1,1 princ.), da sonst das Versprechen nicht trifft".

gezwungen worden bin, einem etwas zu versprechen, und faktisch nicht mehr selber das Versprechen erteile. Der Sachverhalt oder die Sachverhältnisse, auf die sich der eine Träger des Versprechens bezieht, besteht in der Verbindlichkeit, das Versprechen zu einer bestimmten Zeit einzulösen. Der Wille, das innere oder nicht-soziale Erlebnis des Verbindlichkeitsträgers, etwas selbst auszuführen oder zu tun und es nicht den Andern, dem man etwas versprechen will, tun zu lassen, ist nur eins der Strukturmomente des Versprechens, nicht selber schon, wie vor Reinach u.a. Hume und Lipps (vgl. Burkhardt 1986:91–92) behauptet haben, das Versprechen als sozialer Akt. Zu diesem Akt gehört notwendig eine äußere Seite. Der Originalitätsanspruch Reinachs in bezug auf die Analyse des Versprechens besteht, Hume und Lipps gegenüber, gerade in der Berücksichtigung und Betonung dieser äußeren Seite[1]. Denn nur sie ermöglicht es einem Versprechensempfänger, einen Anspruch auf die Leistung dessen zu erheben, was vom Versprechenden versprochen worden ist: der Versprechensinhalt. Irrelevant ist hier, in welcher Form soziale Akte erscheinen, nur daß sie "von [einem zweiten Subjekt] vernommen werden müssen" (Schuhmann 1988: 159). Die verschiedenen Strukturmomente des Versprechens bilden ein einfaches Ganzes, das in zwei existentiell unabhängigen Trägern, dem Versprechensträger und -empfänger, fundiert ist.

[1] Vgl. aber Reid (1788:438): "Between the operations of the mind, which, for want of a more proper name, I have called solitary, and those I have called social, there is this very remarkable distinction, that, in the solitary, the expression of them by words, or any other sensible sign, is accidental. They may exist, and be complete, without being expressed, without being known to any other person. But, in the social operations, the expression is essential. They cannot exist without being expressed by words or signs, and known to the other party." Etwas früher, um 1650, hat sich auch Thomas Hobbes über das Versprechen geäußert, und zwar im Rahmen der Vertragslehre (vgl. dazu Isermsnn 1991:246 ff.). Hobbes gewinnt die Bedingungen für den erfolgreichen Vollzug von Versprechens — als Vertragshandlungen aus den Faktoren, "die ein Versprechen als kommunikative Handlung mißlingen lassen können" (Isermann 1991:248).

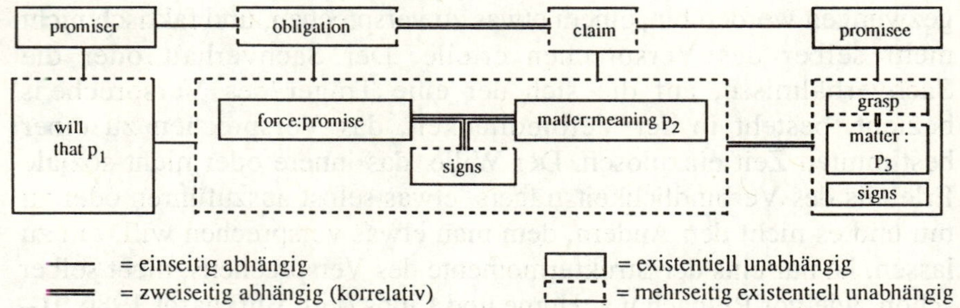

(ABBILDUNG; aus: Mulligan 1987b:60)

Obwohl es sich hier um ein 'Musterbeispiel' handelt, ist es möglich, modifizierte Strukturen und Abhängigkeitsbeziehungen darzustellen, die dann zum Beispiel als 'Unglücksfälle' im Sinne Austins (1962:40) betrachtet werden können — z.B. stellvertretendes Versprechen. Reinach faßt diese Struktur des Versprechens wie folgt zusammen:

> Das Versprechen ist weder Wille, noch Äußerung des Willens, sondern es ist ein selbständiger spontaner Akt, der, nach außen sich wendend, in äußere Erscheinung tritt (Reinach 1913:166).

> Anspruch und Verbindlichkeit setzen allgemein und notwendig einen *Träger* voraus, eine Person, deren Ansprüche und Verbindlichkeiten sie sind. Und ebenso ist ihnen ein bestimmter Inhalt wesentlich, auf den sie sich beziehen und dessen Verschiedenheit verschiedenartige Ansprüche und Verbindlichkeiten voneinander unterscheidet (S. 150–151).

> Der gleiche Anspruch und die gleiche Verbindlichkeit können aus sehr verschiedenen Quellen [Reinach nennt diese Sachverhalte oder Sachverhaltsgruppen — F.V.] entspringen. So kann ich meinen Anspruch auf die Rückgabe einer mir gehörigen Sache einmal ableiten aus dem Versprechen der Rückgabe, welches der gegenwärtige Inhaber der Sache mir gemacht hat. Oder ich kann ihn ableiten aus dem eigenartigen

Verhältnisse, in dem ich zu der Sache stehe, daraus, daß die Sache mir gehört (S. 156).

Es genügt [...] nicht, daß der Adressat die äußeren Erscheinungen wahrnimmt, daß er z.B. die Worte hört, ohne sie zu verstehen. Er muß durch sie hindurch das erfassen, dessen Erscheinung sie sind, er muß Kenntnis nehmen von dem Versprechen selbst, er muß, wie wir etwas genauer sagen wollen, des Versprechens innewerden (S. 169).

2.2 *Die Wesensmerkmale sozialer Akte*

Aus diesen Überlegungen zur Aktstruktur: des Versprechens entwickelt Reinach einen Katalog von Wesensmerkmalen, die jeweils eigene Aktstrukturen konstituieren. Für soziale Akte sind absolut wesentlich 'Spontaneität', 'Intentionalität', 'Fremdpersonalität' und 'Vernehmungsbedürftigkeit'. Beispielsweise ist dem Akt des 'Sich-Entschließens' wesentlich, daß er spontan und intentional ist, nicht aber die Vernehmungsbedürftigkeit; für das 'Verzeihen', daß er spontan, intentional und fremdpersonal ist, nicht aber vernehmungsbedürftig; für das 'Befehlen' ist dann wieder die Vernehmungsbedürftigkeit notwendig, sind aber auch bestimmte soziale Akte vorausgesetzt, zum Beispiel der der Unterwerfung. Bei sozialen Akten ermöglichen also erst die genannten vier Wesensmerkmale Anspruch und Verbindlichkeit, denn ohne das Vernehmen des Versprechens und des Versprechensinhalts gibt es keine Ansprüche und ohne vernommen worden zu sein, gibt es keine Verbindlichkeiten — beide, Anspruch und Verbindlichkeit, sind korrelativ oder zweiseitig fundiert. Weiter ist bei sozialen Akten jeweils eine Gemeinschaft von Personen als möglichen Trägern von Ansprüchen und Verbindlichkeiten vorausgesetzt und, für die meisten sozialen Akte, eine 'physische Grundlage', aufgrund derer die psychischen, nicht sozialen Erlebnisse erfaßt werden können (Reinach 1913:161).

Reinach faßt seine Theorie der sozialen Akte schließlich wie folgt zusammen:

Bitten, Ermahnen, Fragen, Mitteilen, Antworten und noch vieles andere [...] sind [alle] soziale Akte, welche von dem, der sie vollzieht, im

> Vollzuge selbst einem anderen zugeworfen werden, um sich in seine Seele einzuhaken (1913:160).

3. SCHLUßBEMERKUNGEN

Aus diesem Beitrag ist, hoffe ich, klar geworden, daß die bereichsüberschreitende Beschäftigung mit Akt- und Handlungsaspekten von Sprache keineswegs bereichsspezifische Betrachtungen ausschließt, daß aber eine prinzipiell bereichsneutrale, vorwissenschaftliche Strukturanalyse von Konzepten wie 'Versprechen', 'Befehlen' u. dgl. bestimmten 'pragmatisch-analystischen' Selbstverständlichkeiten eine neue Dimension verleiht, neue Fragestellungen hervorruft, die aus dem klassifikatorischen Blickfeld pragmatisch-analytischer Verfahren verschwunden waren. Ich weise hier auf das Handlungsmoment hin, das meistens (aber nicht immer) sprachlich zum Ausdruck gebracht wird, und das nicht unbedingt bereichsspezifisch ist. Die Handlung eröffnet ein eigenes Gegenstandsgebiet, das je nach sozialem Akt eigene Strukturmerkmale aufweist, die zunächst unabhängig von gesellschaftlichen (auch: wissenschaftlichen) Konventionen und Regeln einer Analyse unterzogen werden können. Auch wenn Armin Burkhardt (1987:159) in seinem Beitrag zu Mulligans *Speech Act and Sachverhalt* (1987) glaubt, daß die Begründung für die verbindliche Kraft des Versprechens darin liegt, "daß die Verwendung einer konventionellen Versprechensform [die Reinach also auch vorfindet - F.V.] nicht nur den Willen zu seiner Erfüllung, sondern auch den zur Selbstverbindlichung des Sprechers impliziert", und diese konventionelle Versprechensform der Grund dafür ist, daß "sich der Adressat auf die Erfüllung [des Versprechens] verlassen [kann]", so interessiert dieses Problem doch vor allem Burkhardt, wie er selber feststellt — "Uns mag [...] diese weitergehende Frage erlaubt sein" (Burkhardt 1987:160) —, nicht aber Reinach, der sich als Phänomenologe nicht mit Erklärungen, sondern mit "in sich selbst einsichtlichen Wesensgesetzlichkeiten" beschäftigt hat.

Außerdem glaube ich, daß in einer Zeit, in der die Sprechakttheorie Austins und Searles zum eisernen Bestand der sprachwissenschaftlichen Ausbildung gehört, auch die historische Seite, ihre konzeptuelle Entwicklung, innerhalb dieses eng begrenzten Bereichs inter- oder vielleicht besser: vordisziplinär zugänglich gemacht werden soll. Denn es muß den 'linguistischen Sprechakttheoretiker' wohl stutzig machen, wenn Reinach (1911:360) behauptet, daß es für "das, was im Wesen des sozialen Aktes liegt, [...] gleichgültig [ist], wie man ihn gewahr wird" — wenn auch mancher Reinach-Forscher, wie Burkhardt, darauf hinweist, daß die Abgrenzung der Sachverhältnisse sozialer Akte von denen anderer (intentionaler Akte) und das "Warum", der Grund der Verbindlichkeit (Konventionalität oder Handlungsstruktur) bei Reinach nicht ausführlich genug ausgearbeitet worden sind (vgl. Burkhardt 1987:159).

Auf meine letzte Frage, ob nicht doch die ontologischen Strukturen Reinachs durch einen bestimmten Bereich, hier: die Rechtswissenschaften, konstituiert werden, kann ich nur antworten, daß ich vermute, daß sie rhetorisch gemeint ist.

LITERATUR

Austin, John L[angshaw]. 1962. *How to Do Things with Words.* Edited by James O[pie] Urmson. London: Oxford University Press. (Von Eike von Savigny bearbeitet und ins Deutsche übersetzt als *Zur Theorie der Sprechakte (How to Do Things with Words.)* Stuttgart: Reclam Verlag, 1976.)

Burkhardt, Armin. 1986. *Soziale Akte, Sprechakte und Textillokutionen. A.* Reinachs *Rechtsphilosophie und die moderne Linguistik.* Tübingen: Max Niemeyer.

— . 1987. "Verpflichtung und Verbindlichkeit. Ethische Aspekte in der Rechtsphilosophie Adolf Reinachs". Mulligan 1987a:155–174.

Husserl, Edmund. 1900/01. *Logische Untersuchungen.* 2 Bde. Tübingen: Max Niemeyer (6. Aufl.,1980.)

Isermann, Michael. 1991 *Die Sprachtheorie im Werk von Thomas Hobbes.* Münster: Nodus.

Kamp, Rudolf. 1977. *Axiomatische Sprachtheorie: Wissenschaftstheoretische Untersuchungen zum Konstitutionsproblem der Einzelwissenschaften am Beispiel der Sprachwissenschaftstheorie Karl Bühlers.* Berlin: Duncker und Humblot.

Mulligan, Kevin, ed. 1987a. *Speech Act and Sachverhalt: Reinach and the Foundations of Realist Phenomenology.* Dordrecht & Boston: Martinus Nijhoff.

— . 1987b. "Promising and other Social Acts: Their Constituents and Structure". Mulligan 1987a:29–90.

Nuchelmans, Gabriël. 1969. *Overzicht van de analytische wijsbegeerte.* Utrecht, Antwerpen: Aula. (4. Aufl., 1978.)

Reid, Thomas. 1788. *Essays on the Active Powers of the Human Mind.* Edinburgh: James Thin ([8]1895) (Nachdr., Cambridge, Mass., London: M.I.T. Press, 1969.)

Reinach, Adolf. 1911. "Nichtsoziale und soziale Akte". *Sämtliche Werke,* 355–360.

—. 1913. "Die apriorischen Grundlagen des bürgerlichen Rechtes". *Sämtliche Werke,* 141–278.

—. 1989a. *Sämtliche Werke. Textkritische Ausgabe. Werke 1.* Herausgegeben von Karl Schuhmann & Barry Smith. München & Wien: Philosophia.

—. 1989b. *Sämtliche Werke. Textkritische Ausgabe. Kommentar und Textkritik 2.* Herausgegeben von Karl Schuhmann & Barry Smith. München & Wien: Philosophia.

Schuhmann, Karl, 1988: "Die Entwicklung der Sprechakttheorie in der Münchener Phänomenologie". *Phänomenologische Forschungen* 21.133–166.

Searle, John R. 1969. *Speech Acts. An Essay in the Philosophy of Language.* Cambridge: University Press. (ins Deutsche übersetzt von Rolf und R. Wiggershaus als *Sprechakte. Ein sprachphilosophischer Essay.* Frankfurt/M.: Suhrkamp, 1971.)

Smith, Barry. 1984a. "Ten Conditions on a Theory of Speech Acts". *Theoretical Linguistics* 11.311–330.

—. 1988: "Materials towards a History of Speech Act theory". *Karl Bühler's Theory of Language*, hrsg. von Achim Eschbach, 125–152. Amsterdam & Philadelphia: John Benjamins.

Linguistics vs. Philology in an 1864 Student Paper by Jan Baudouin de Courtenay

JOANNA RADWAŃSKA WILLIAMS
State University of New York, Stony Brook

THE POLISH LINGUIST Jan Baudouin de Courtenay (1845–1929) is recognized as an important figure not only in the history of Slavic linguistics. His long life and career span several periods in the history of linguistics as well as several countries. However, because of the scattered nature of his career, many of his works remain relatively inaccessible and little known. Among these is Baudouin's first work in linguistics, which is a student paper dating back to 1864.

This paper, entitled *Rozprawa mająca związek z kwestią językową,* "A Treatise in Connection with the Language Question" is significant for several reasons. It is indicative of the first intellectually formative period of Baudouin's career, as a student of Warsaw University or the Szkoła Główna ("Main School"). Secondly, it is Baudouin's first statement on general linguistics. Thirdly, Baudouin's paper is a reflection of the linguistics vs. philology debate in the 1860s.

The original manuscript of Baudouin's paper is preserved in the Special Collections of the Polish National Library (Biblioteka Narodowa) in Warsaw. The manuscript is dated 10 March 1864 (Baudouin 1864:61), and was therefore written when Baudouin was 19. It is 61 pages long, and contains extensive comments in the margins by Baudouin's professor, Henryk Struve, which are in red ink in the original manuscript. Pages 5 and 6 of the manuscript are missing. The last page, which is not numbered, consists entirely of Struve's commentary.

To my knowledge there have been two printed editions of the manuscript. One is a transcript in Polish in excerpted form published by Maria Chmura-Klekotowa in the journal *Poradnik Językowy,* in a 1976 issue of the journal devoted to Baudouin de Courtenay. The transcript reproduces approximately one half of the text of the original. The other edition is a translation of the entire text into French by Maria di Salvo, published in her anthology of Baudouin's works *Il pensiero linguistico di Jan* Baudouin de Courtenay (1975). di Salvo's translation is prefaced by a short commentary (77–78; cf. also 15–17).

On the last page of the manuscript, the comments by Henryk Struve are signed Struve, preceded by the capital letter D. Maria di Salvo interprets this to be the first initial of Struve's name but does not give any further identification. A much more likely interpretation is that the letter D signifies "Dr." Henryk Struve (1840–1912), who taught philosophy at Warsaw University from 1862 to 1903, was promoted to the rank of professor in November 1864 (Borzym 1975: 201), and thus in March 1864 would still have been titled Doctor. The comments by Henryk Struve are not rendered in either of the printed editions of the manuscript.

The topic for discussion, as given probably by Struve and quoted by Baudouin at the beginning of the paper, was formulated as follows:

> Can history and philology solve their task as disciplines without a strict connection with philosophy, namely the philosophy of history and the philosophy of language? If yes: which task do history and philology solve independently, without the aid of philosophy? If not: what does the independence of history and philology from philosophy consist in? (Baudouin 1864:1)[1]

In response, Baudouin at once asserts his intellectual independence by choosing to write, not on the relationship of philology and history to philosophy, but on the autonomy of linguistics as a scientific discipline:

> Since among the questions submitted for disputation, among the disciplines given, the discipline of language as an independent science was completely omitted, therefore I feel the obligation to come to the defense of its independence, its self-sufficiency. (Baudouin 1864:1–2)

[1] All translations are mine — J.R.W.

In Baudouin's argument there are strong echoes of Schleicher's (1850:1–5) distinction between linguistics and philology. As Koerner, (1981) has argued in "On the Historical Roots of the Philology vs. Linguistics Controversy", Schleicher's insistence that linguistics is a natural science played the polemical role in the 1850s and 1860s of establishing the autonomy of linguistics as a scientific discipline. Like Schleicher, Baudouin asserts that linguistics belongs to the domain of the natural sciences in distinction to philology as an historical science. Baudouin's term of choice is *lingwistyka* "linguistics", which he uses as synonymous with *językoznawstwo* (which may be rendered as "linguistics" or "science of language" and corresponds to the German term *Sprachwissenschaft)* and with *filologia porównawcza* "comparative philology", in distinction from classical philology. I quote excerpts from this discussion:

> It is well known that the entire edifice of human knowledge falls into 2 great divisions: the division of historical sciences and the division of natural sciences; the former have to do with the works of man, while the latter with the works of God [...]. Thus we firmly assert that the science of language or comparative philology is a physical science, and its method is the same as the method of Botany, Geology, Anatomy, Chemistry and other branches of the study of nature which successfully apply it [...]. It might seem that comparative philology is a science related to classical philology, i.e. a historical science, and that therefore its method is the method of history, history of art, law, politics and religion. [...] It is not difficult however to prove that although the science of language owes a great deal to classical philology, it nevertheless has almost nothing in common with classical philology and cannot be subordinated to it. (Baudouin 1864:2–3)

It is interesting to see at the outset of Baudouin's career such a strong assertion of Schleicherian naturalism, which seems to stand in opposition to the core of Baudouin's later linguistic thought, his search for a psychological explanation of linguistic phenomena.

A particularly striking passage in Baudouin's paper compares the natural growth of language, which Baudouin takes to be ahistorical in the sense that it proceeds independently of the will of man, with the growth of minerals in the earth's crust:

> The laws which operate during this infinite change of human speech are purely natural laws, physiological and psychological, but without the participation of the human will, and where there is no will, there is no history. We speak of "history" in the presence of the independent force of free will; while "growth" refers to the natural development of organic beings. We also speak however of the growth of the earth's crust, of the unrestrained growth of various crystals and we know very well what is understood by this; it is in this particular sense, not in the sense of the growth of a tree, that we have the right to refer to the growth of language. (Baudouin 1864:10–11)

The extreme nature of Baudouin's claim in favour of language as a natural phenomenon subject to the laws of nature and falling within the domain of the natural sciences, leads Maria di Salvo in her short commentary on Baudouin's paper to dismiss its contents as youthful and inconsistent with Baudouin's later thought on general linguistics:

> We are not concerned here with a work which is particularly original, and a good portion of its numerous contradictions can be explained exactly as an attempt to reconcile different doctrines; many of the tenets he defends here he would shortly abandon, above all the Schleicherian organicism which is adopted here without reservation. (Maria di Salvo 1975:77)

This dismissal however seems to me to give short shrift both to Baudouin's originality and to the significance of Schleicher's position. Interestingly, Baudouin does not explicitly mention Schleicher anywhere in his paper. The qualification "not in the sense of the growth of a tree" is indeed rather a disavowal than an adoption of organicism. Baudouin's lack of mention of Schleicher is in contrast to his explicit mention of Steinthal later in the paper, in reference to the relationship of linguistics to philosophy of language. Thus Baudouin's concern is not to support or refute Schleicher's views, but to present his own position on the nature of linguistics as an autonomous science. In this respect, for Baudouin as for Schleicher, the thrust of the argument for linguistics as a natural science is the difference in method between linguistics and philology. Philology is the study of the language of a nation within its historical context, and its method is critical and historical; while linguistics is the study of the nature of human language in general as part of the natural science of man, and its method is therefore the empirical method of the natural sciences. Baudouin gives the following characteristics of philology and of linguistics:

> The idea of philology is that of a historical discipline, and its task is to understand the spiritual states, strivings or aspirations, and spiritual fruits of a certain nation or several related nations during a specific epoch from the point of view of historical development. (Baudouin 1864:31) [...]
>
> Although philology takes language as the object of its study, it usually considers language as only a means through which it can penetrate the spiritual essence and life of one or several peoples. (Baudouin 1864:36) [...]
>
> In linguistics languages are not considered as a means, language itself is the only and exclusive object of scientific study. [...]
>
> We want to learn not languages, but speech; the view of the whole is fundamental here; we want to fathom and adequately investigate, what language is and how it can be the means or organ of our mutual communication of thought. We wish to understand its origin, its nature, its laws, and only in order to gain such knowledge we collect, order and classify all linguistic facts. (Baudouin 1864:37)

For Baudouin at this point there is not a contradiction between the claim that linguistics is a natural science and the psychological explanation of the phenomena of language. The natural laws of language are both physiological and psychological. Baudouin refers approvingly to the account of the psychological factor in the philosophy of language of Steinthal:

> The psychological factor plays a very important role here; it is the basis of the entire variety and logical unshapeliness of language; it explains certain forms in languages which cannot in any way be justified from the logical point of view. (Baudouin 1864:59–60)

In his discussion of the philosophy of language, Baudouin expresses the idea that language is the external manifestation of the internal human spirit. This does not for him contradict the idea of the law-governed nature of language and therefore of the applicability of the empirical method of the natural sciences to linguistics:

> Since the spirit is regularity and conceptuality itself, then how could language be unordered and nonconceptual. Language is the organ of the spirit, which it creates out of itself, in order to manifest itself, to show itself in the external world, in reality. (Baudouin 1864:51)

The philosophy of language, writes Baudouin, should take into account the special nature of language, and should therefore be distinct from the philosophy of nature in general:

> Since language belongs to the kingdom of nature, then the philosophy of nature should serve as the foundation [of linguistics]; since however despite the fundamental characteristics of natural life the internal, substantial essence of language is different than the essence of e.g., animals or plants, then the philosophy of nature which considers shapes, dimensions and weights cannot be the foundation of linguistics. These are all absent in language, which has a far more ideal nature, incomparably more spiritual. Therefore a different part of philosophy should serve as the base for linguistics, namely the philosophy of language. (Baudouin 1864:45)

While serving as the theoretical basis for linguistics, the philosophy of language should itself draw on the empirical data and general results of linguistic science. The philosophy of language, writes Baudouin (p. 53), is like "nerves which branch across the entire huge body of linguistics."

In his comments to Baudouin's paper, Henryk Struve approaches the relationship of linguistics and philosophy from a more traditional nineteenth century philosophical perspective. He does not recognize the distinctness of linguistics from philology as argued by Baudouin and the affiliation of linguistics with the natural sciences. His comments, however, do not directly challenge the autonomy of linguistics, but rather point out the weakness in Baudouin's argument. Struve accepts the division of academic disciplines into the historical sciences and the natural sciences. Within this division, the historical sciences deal with the domain of the human spirit and human affairs, while the natural sciences deal with the domain of matter. Language for Struve belongs exclusively in the former domain and thus any study of language, whether philology or linguistics, cannot be a natural science. The admission of the spiritual nature of language, according to Struve, necessitates the classification of the science of language as a historical science:

> One of the main reasons why linguistics cannot be included among the physical sciences is above all the view of language itself, of speech itself. He who considers language, speech, as the manifestation of the human spirit and not its physical nature, has to include linguistics among the spiritual historical sciences. The opposite view can only be supported with the proof that language, speech, is the result or manifestation of the physical or external nature of man. (Struve's note in the margin of Baudouin 1864:3)

The irreconcilability of Baudouin's and Struve's positions is due to their common assumption of a bipartite division of academic disciplines. While this is an understandable reflection of a mid nineteenth century conception, in the 1860s we already find ourselves at the juncture of the reconceptualization of the relationship of the disciplines into the modern tripartite division of the humanities, natural sciences and social sciences. It was in this context, with the rise of psychology and sociology, that linguistics was claiming its autonomy as a science. During this period of reconceptualization, the claim of the social sciences to scientific status rested on their alignment with the natural sciences. Hence the polemical nature of the linguistics vs. philology debate, which leads Baudouin in his paper to the strained argument that comparative philology is something altogether different from philology.

The source of the inconsistency within Baudouin's position, as Struve points out, is in his conception of the nature of language. On the one hand Baudouin maintains that language undergoes natural growth like a mineral, while on the other he points out that the nature of language is that of an ideal rather than a physical object. A later note added by Baudouin in the margin of the manuscript, shows that he accepted Struve's criticism. This note is in pencil in the original and is not legible in the microfilm copy (Baudouin 1864:59). The note appears next to Baudouin's mention of Steinthal's discussion of the psychological factor in language:

> Sprzeciwia się to zaliczaniu językoznawstwa do nauk przyrodzonych. [This contradicts the inclusion of linguistics among the natural sciences].

Thus Baudouin gained from his professor a valuable corrective against an overstated naturalism. Thereafter his thought on general linguistics was directed towards a theory of language based on a psychological conception of the nature of language. This is apparent already at the next stage of Baudouin's career, when as Schleicher's student he systematically applied the analogy principle in *Einige Fälle der Wirkung der Analogie in der polnischen Deklination* (1868).

I would like to conclude with a historical postscript to Baudouin's student paper. Henryk Struve (1903:364–365) in his work *Wstęp Krytyczny do Filozofii [A Critical Introduction to Philosophy]* gives credit to his former student as the best among Polish linguists ("najznakomitszy u nas badacz na polu językoznawstwa"). In summarizing Baudouin's thought Struve focuses on precisely the issues that were salient in Baudouin's student paper. Baudouin, writes Struve, makes a firm distinction between philology and linguistics. While the former consists in an erudite familiarity with concrete historical facts, the latter is a strictly defined science. Linguistics as a science is psychological-sociological in nature and draws upon the principles of psychology and sociology. Struve quotes Baudouin's statements on the nature of language:

> Those people are in error who consider language an organism and include linguistics among the natural sciences. (Baudouin 1889:92)
>
> The laws of language are fundamentally different from physical and chemical laws; they are different if only in that they have not yet been completely discovered and precisely defined. (Baudouin 1888–89:133)

While paying tribute to his former student, Struve must have felt a particular satisfaction and vindication in seeing this turnaround since Baudouin's student days at Warsaw University.

REFERENCES

Baudouin de Courtenay, Jan. 1864. *Rozprawa mającą związek z kwestią językową.* Manuscript. Rps BN II 5739, Warsaw: Polish National Library. [Catalogued under title: *Rozprawa o związkach historii i filologii z filozofią.* Reprinted in excerpted form, transcribed by Maria Chmura-Klekotowa in *Poradnik Językowy* 1976 no. 1.1–11. French translation in Maria di Salvo 1975:77–101.]

—.1868 "Einige Fälle der Wirkung der Analogie in der polnischen Deklination." *Beiträge zur vergleichende Sprachforschung* 6:1.19–88. (Polish translation, with restored preface, in Baudouin 1904:176–248).

—. 1888–89. "Mikołaj Kruszewski, jego życie i prace naukowe". *Prace Filologiczne* 2:3.837–849, 1888, 3:1.116–175, 1889. (Repr. in Baudouin 1904:96–175; Russian translation in Baudouin 1963, vol. 1:146–202.)

—. 1889. "O zadaniach językoznawstwa". *Prace Filologiczne* 3:1.92–115. (Repr. in Baudouin 1904: 24–49; English translation in Stankiewicz 1972: 125–143.)

—. 1904. *Szkice Językoznawcze.* Warsaw: Laskauer. (Repr. in Baudouin 1974.)

—. 1963. *Izbrannye trudy po obščemu jazykoznaniju.* 2 vols. Ed. by V. P. Grigor'ev and A. A. Leont'ev. Moscow: Izdatel'stvo Akademii Nauk SSSR.

—. 1974. *Dzieła Wybrane.* Vol. 1. Ed. by Witold Doroszewski. Warsaw: Państwowe Wydawnictwo Naukowe.

Borzym, Stanisław. 1974. *Poglądy Filozoficzne Henryka Struvego.* Wrocław/Warsaw/Kraków/Gdańsk: Zakład narodowy im. Ossolińskich.

—. 1975. "Henryk Struve". *Polska myśl filozoficzna i społeczna,* ed. by Barbara Skarga, Vol. 2, 201–230. Warsaw: Książka i Wiedza.

di Salvo, Maria. 1975. *Il Pensiero linguistico di Jan Baudouin de Courtenay: Lingua nazionale e individuale. Con un antologia di testi e un saggio inedito.* Venice & Padua: Marsilio Editori.

Koerner,, E.F. Konrad. 1982. "On the Historical Roots of the Philology vs. Linguistics Controversy." *Papers from the 5th International Conference on Historical*

Linguistics, ed. by Anders Ahlqvist; 233–42. Amsterdam: John Benjamins. (Repr., with an enlarged bibliography, in Koerner, 1989:233–244.)

—. 1989. *Practicing Linguistic Historiography*. Amsterdam & Philadelphia: John Benjamins.

Mugdan, Joachim. 1984. *Jan Baudouin de Courtenay (1845–1929): Leben und Werk*. Munich: Wilhelm Fink.

Schleicher, August. 1853. *Die Sprachen Europas in systematischer Uebersicht*. Bonn: H. B. König. (Repr. with an introd. by Konrad Koerner, Amsterdam & Philadelphia, 1983.)

Stankiewicz, Edward, ed. 1972. *A Baudouin de Courtenay Anthology: The Beginnings of Structural Linguistics*. Bloomington & London: Indiana University Press.

Struve, Henryk. 1903. *Wstęp Krytyczny do Filozofii, czyli rozbiór zasadniczych pojęć o filozofii*. 3rd revised. Warsaw: E. Wende.

Abstracts

Forms of Discourse, Linguistics, Literary Theory, and History Writing

MARK AMSLER

THE HISTORY writing of linguistics has been predominantly given as narratives (Schmitter). The history of linguistics is often distinguished from the practice of linguistics in the way that literary and and critical history has been differentiated from practical literary criticism. The history of the "past", including the prior existence of the sciences such as linguistics, presupposes the existence of the past. But the existence of the past is inscribed in discourse before it can be comprehended as "history". History writing, then, is structured as kinds of discourse which shape the events and concepts they call up.

Will there be a turn in linguistics similar to the recent turn in literary studies to historicism and hermeneutic criticism? There already has been such a turn in anthropological linguistics and cross-cultural sociolinguistics. But linguistics in general remains either theory-driven or empirical in a very explicit fashion, whereas literary studies have kept a distance from both "pure theory" and "raw facts", relying more on a belief in concrete poetic interpretation as "unencumbered reading".

Linguistic historiography and literary historicism have much more in common as narrative interpretations of the past. However, whereas literary historicism has cast its line into theoretical debates (in fact transforming the theoretical debate itself in literary studies), linguistic historiography has fished more gingerly in the pool of linguistic theory. In effect, linguistic history writing as currently practiced identifies and preserves itself by maintaining the distinction between science and history as a variant of that between theory and practice. Linguistic historiography presupposes the existence of the past which it claims the authority to present. Present linguistic history writing is linguistics' practical poetic criticism. Can linguistic historiography embrace its own discursivity and transform its marginal relation to linguistic science?

Skinner and Chomsky Thirty Years Later*

JULIE ANDRESEN

B. F. SKINNER'S *Verbal Behavior* (1957) achieved instant notoriety in linguistic circles as a result of Chomsky's excoriating review in *Language* (1959). Skinner's work subsequently sank into what seemed a well-deserved and permanent oblivion. Now, however, thirty years later, Skinner's book and Chomsky's review can be reread with an eye to determining the insufficiencies of Chomsky's approach.

First, I will argue that Skinner presents not some automaton-like account of verbal behavior but a richly nuanced and well-elaborated treatment of what is now called pragmatics — an approach that Chomsky's 1959 review might well be said to have programmatically exiled. Second, I will argue that in having fully integrated the study of the written language and literature into his account of verbal behavior Skinner anticipates the post-structuralist complaint that linguistics has unprofitably separated the spoken from the written. Third, advances in neurobiology in the past 30 years have rendered obsolete Chomsky's insistence in his 1959 review that "independent neurophysiological evidence is not available" for understanding the causes and organization of behavior, verbal and otherwise. With the evidence presented by such neurolinguistic studies as, e.g., M. Studdert-Kennedy along with the result of Parallel Distributed Processing models of language by D. Rumelhart and J. McClelland, it is now possible to reevaluate Skinner's approach to verbal behavior in a much more positive light.

B. H. Smart — a Nineteenth-Century Contribution to the Concept of Phrase-Structure Grammar

BARRIE E. BARTLETT

B. H. SMART was a mid-nineteenth-century scholar and teacher devoted to the "revival, correction, and exclusive establishment of Locke's Philosophy." Smart's corrections of Locke's views on the relation of thought and language can be seen as involving some elementary principle of binarity, of phrase-structure grammar, and of the syntagm. First, he rejects Locke's view that sensations may be equated with

* Published (1990) in *HL* 17.145–165.

simple ideas and that these may be constitutive of complex ideas. He argues that it is the relation of contrast between sentient states of being (where sensation A is contrasted with sensation B, or the presence of sensation A is contrasted with its absence) that gives rise to the "suggestive occasions" from which intellection derives knowledge and thought; *black* may therefore derive its existence and its value from a contrast with *white* while *warmth* achieves the same by its contrast with the *absence of warmth*.. Similarly, Smart rejects the view that words (parts of speech) are individually constitutive of the meaning of a sentence and claims that they are merely suggestive of it; the meaning of each individual lexical item is "suggested" by the lexical item to which it is joined, that is, by context. The meaning of a sentence is established as a 'rational consequence' — that is, as a result of the hearer's interpretation or decoding — of a linear surface structure involving a series of binary branchings. The branchings realize the hierarchical relations between the grammatical structures of which the sentence is composed and in which are imposed the lexical constraints that permit the "junction" of individual lexical items. Smart establishes that the nodes within the structure dominate grammatical groups that are themselves capable of being realized as sentences, syntagms or parts of speech which are then seen as being capable of various functions. Examples adduced from English and Latin lead Smart into some of the problems faced by IC analysis and into a recognition of the possibility of alternate analyses of utterances.

Anton Marty — Seine Stellung in der Sprachphilosophie der 19. Jarhrhunderts

BRIGITTE BARTSCHAT

ANTON MARTY (1846–1914) ist einer der führenden Sprahphilosophen des 19. Jh.'s. Er steht in der traditionslinie Wilhelm von Humboldts und Hajim Steinthals und hat zu den wichtigsten Fragen seiner Wisenschaft Stellung genommen. Im Beitrag wird insbesondere das Problem der "inneren Sprachform" und seine Ausdeutung und Präzisierung durch Marty behandelt. Dazu gehören die "figurative syntaktische innere Form" und die "konstruktive innere Form". Auf weitere Themen, zu denen Marty gearbeitet hat, so das Verhältnis zwischen Grammatik und Logik, die psychologischen Beziehungen im Satz (psychologisches Subjekt und Prädikat) und die Einteilung der Wortklassen in Autosemantika und Synsemantika wird nur kurz hingewiesen.

Laudes Hispaniae and the Renaissance Conception of Language

LUCIA BINOTTI

THE *LAUS*, a medieval rhetorical genre derived from the classical 'panegyrical discourse', was an encomiastic exercise dedicated to a given man, animal, plant, town, country, virtue or profession; *laudes* to towns and countries followed detailed precepts that required the enumeration of their artistic and scientific merits.

In Spain, Isidore of Seville initiated in his *Chronica* the long lasting tradition of the *laus Hispaniae*. After him, *laudes Hispaniae* develop into literary apologies for the nation that can be traced, by their topical structure, up to the Enlightenment.

During the Renaissance, with the establishment of Castilian as the language of official culture, the defense of the language becomes an essential element of every *laus Hispaniae*. The emphasis given to the language varies greatly and depends upon the political, religious and historical concerns of the author, but the arguments follow a common formal structure. Nonetheless, it is possible to distinguish a change of perspective within the *laudes*. The earliest apologists for the language serve only as an instrument to praise the political splendour and glory of the nation. Later, Castilian is emancipated, and the apologies center on the inner qualities of language itself, such as the complexity of its grammar, the richness of its lexicon, the elegance of its expression, and its facility in the adoption of borrowings from other languages.

This paper shows this change of perspective by examining a series of *laudes Hispaniae,* all of them composed within the first three decades of the XVII century. They all introduce a defense of Castilian whose common denominator is to confer great prestige on it by means of its babelic origin (the so-called 'theory of Primitive Castilian'). The first treatment of the theory, G. López Madera's *Discursos* (1601), and two subsequent treatises — L. de la Cueva's *Dialogos* (1603) and Bermúdez de Petraza's *Antiguedad* (1608) — present the antiquity and prestige of Castilian in service to the grandeur of Spain. The slow reorganization of the same material toward a less political and more linguistically technical treatment of the subject can be traced from F. de Quevedo's *España defendida* (1609), through G. Correas' *Apologia del Castellano* (1623) to Jiménez Patón's *Apologia Orada* (1626).

Special attention has been given to these works considering that linguistic theories of the origin of language with biblical or mythical foundation, similar to that of Primitive Castilian, were also common in the rest of Europe. Owing to their distance from the classical heritage, they inspired the development of technical analysis especially sensitive to the phenomenon of linguistic change, and consequently became precursor of diachronic and comparative Linguistics. In Spain, the assumption that Castilian preceded Latin initiated a significant change of focus in the same European direction, founding the basis for a more scientific analysis of the language.

Les Avatars de la grammaire dans le *Cours de linguistique générale* de Ferdinand de Saussure

SIMON BOUQUET

UNE ÉTUDE systématique des énoncés du *Cours de linguistique générale* se rapportant à la grammaire — ainsi que des sources manuscrites du *Cours* et des notes de Saussure sur la linguistique générale — fait apparaître que celle-ci occupe, dans l'édifice théorique saussurien, une position à la fois cruciale et mal assurée : que se soit à travers le jeu des oppositions où elle entre avec sa cousine, la comparée ; que se soit à travers l'emploi métaphorique du mot *grammaire,* emploi où ce dernier équivaut à *système* ; que se soit à travers la façon dont la grammaire s'articule avec les conceptions saussuriennes de *fait social* et de *fait individuel...* On trouve même cette phrase étonnante dans les sources manuscrites du *Cours* : "Nous avouons que c'est sur cette frontière seulement (la syntaxe) qu'on pourra trouver à redire à une séparation entre la langue et la parole".

Dans cette position qui est la sienne à la croisée de plusieurs problématiques, et en l'absence d'autres repères, on peut dire que, dans le *Cours de linguistique générale,* la question de la grammaire *laisse à désirer* — et soutenir, notamment, que c'est à partir de cette lacune au sein même du concept saussurien de *langue* que s'édifiera la théorie grammaticale de Chomsky.

The Oldest British Treatise upon Linguistics: Leonard Cox's *De erudienda iuventute**

ANDREW BREEZE

THE PAPER is a discussion of the humanist text *De erudienda iuventute*, published in 1526 at Kraków by Erasmus's Welsh friend, Leonard Cox (fl. 1512–47). The recent discovery of the only known copy of this text, in the library of the Rumanian Academy of Sciences, Bucharest, has shed considerable light on attitudes to linguistic matters in early sixteenth-century Britain and Poland.

As this text is effectively unknown outside Eastern Europe, the speaker has prepared an edition of it (with a translation into English) to be published by Toronto University Press in 1991. In his talk he outlines the main features of the text: its innovative suggestions regarding syllabus and the teaching of Latin and Greek; its recommendations on techniques of language acquisition; its attitude to the Greek language and to linguistic practice and purity in Europe of its time; its comments on Latin, and on such vernaculars as French, French, German and Hungarian; its response to such Italian writers on language as Vergeries, Guarino, Filelfo and Mancinelli; and its relation to the linguistic theories of Erasmus.

Reference is also made to Cox's friendship with Sir Thomas More, and to his studies with Henri Etienne at Paris and Philipp Melanchthon at Tübingen (as well as at the universities of Wittenberg and Prague). A brief account is given of Cox's extensive publications in Poland, including editions of St Jerome, Pontano, Adrian de Castello, Henry VIII, Martin Luther, Statius, Erasmus, Horace, and Cicero; and to his part there in various practical handbooks on language acquisition (grammars and dictionaries), including the first printed dictionary of Hungarian.

* Part of this paper has been published (1987–88) as "Leonard Cox, a Welsh Humanist in Poland and Hungary", *The National Library of Wales Journal* 25.399–410. The remainder has appeared (1991), with Jacqueline Glomski, as co-author as "An Early British Treatise on Education: Leonard Cox's *De erudienda iuvetute* (1526)", *Humanistica Lovaniensia* 40.112–167.

Current Historiographical Research Projects in West Germany. The 'Bio-Bibliographical Handbook of ... 18th Century' and Other Documentational Research Projects

HERBERT BREKLE & AL.

THREE HISTORIOGRAPHICAL aids with considerable claims as to quality and quantity are currently being worked on at three South German universities (Regensburg, Augsburg, Bamberg). Although there is some overlap, each work differs in structure and intention so that the needs of diverse user groups will be addressed after completion in the 1990s. Participants of ICHoLs V will certainly be anxious to get some insights into the concepts, methods, and problems, as well as the state of affairs of the projects themselves. Materials, drafts, preprints will be presented.

The following projects will be introduced in an exhaustive poster session:

a) 'Bio-Bibliographical Handbook of 18th-Century Grammarians, Philosophers of Language, and Lexicographers in German-Speaking Countries with Descriptions of their Linguistic Works" (Regensburg);

b) "Biographical and Bibliographical Dictionary of Foreign Language Teachers in German-Speaking Countries from the Late Middle Ages until 1800" (Augsburg);

c). Annotated Bibliography of German Theory of Orthography and Grammar the 16th to the 18th Century" (Bamberg).

The Regensburg Handbook offers articles on approximately 1600 authors who published works of linguistic interest in German-speaking countries between 1700 and 1800. Each article consists of a short biography, a description based on the review of all extant works of linguistic relevance, and a complete and exact bibliography (cf. *HL* VIII:1.171–190 (1981) — covering only the starting phase of the project). Projects b) and c) differ in the time periods covered as well as the contextual focus, but are similar in the structure of their articles.

Additionally, the usefulness of the work in answering questions of personal history and the history of ideas will be exemplified by members of the Regensburg project within the plenary sessions.

La *gramática general* (1847) de I. Nuñez de Arenas: un ejemplo de la influencia de J. Harris en España

Mª LUISA CALERO VAQUERA

DURANTE el siglo XIX, los gramáticos españoles se inspiran en gran medida en los principios de la gramática general tardíamente importada de Francia; la hegemonía política y cultural de Francia se traduce, pues, en una hegemonía de sus doctrinas gramaticales. Pero en la España del siglo XIX no sólo penetró, arrolladoramente, el pensamiento francés: también la influencia de la cultura inglesa comienza a ser un fenómeno creciente; así, es conocida la amplia difusión que, en el campo de las letras, hallaron las *Lectures on Rhetoric and Belles Lettres* (1783) de Hugh Blair. En cambio, nada o casi nada se ha dicho acerca de la influencia de los gramáticos ingleses en los españoles, como si tal influjo no hubiera existido. En nuestra comunicación pretendemos mostrar que la gramática inglese era conocida — si bien a través de conducto francés, al menos en el caso que estudiamos — en España; como muestra, la *Gramática general* (1847) de I. Nuñez de Arenas, autor que sigue — o mejor, plagia — el Hermes (1751) de J. Harris. Es aquélla, en la historia de la gramática española, una obra secundaria que intenta renovar la rutinaria enseñanza gramatical con las novedosas teorías de Harris, pero sin lograr librarse totalmente del peso de la tradición. Su exclusivo valor reside, por tanto, en ser una (quizá no la única) muestra del hasta ahora silenciado influjo de la gramática inglesa en la España del siglo XIX.

Le CNRS et le développement de la linguistique

JEAN-CLAUDE CHEVALIER

LE CENTRE national de la Recherche scientifique a été fondé en 1939, mais s'est surtout développé à partir de 1944 et a reçu un statut définitif en 1949. On étudiera cette époque 1944–1949 parce que les linguistes, particulièrement Mario Roques et Marcel Cohen ont joué un grand rôle dans le développement du CNRS, surtout pour les Sciences humaines. Epoque intéressante aussi parce qu'au travers des discussion et des décisions qui concernent de CNRS on voit s'esquisser une mutation assez considérable dans l'expansion relative de la linguistique et de la philologie, lesquelles conditionnent une réorganisation du champ de la linguistique en France.

Jacques Teyssier et la notion de cas dans les langues germaniques

JACQUES COULARDEAU

JACQUES TEYSSIER, avant de mourir en 1973, a consacré son dernier cours de maîtrise à l'étude de la déclinaison et des cas dans les langues germaniques. Ce cours, qui dévait être le point de départ, après mise forme, de publications, est resté à l'état brut.

Une étude attentive de notes extensives de ce cours (notes d'étudiant) révèle un fonctionnement intéressant au niveau de la constitution des hypothèses et des modèles proposés. Une pratique claire d'emprunts et de synthèse se révèle. Nous allons donc suivre à la trace ces emprunts et mesurer la part qu'il prennent dans les propositions finales.

Jacques Teyssier part de Fillmore, Sweet, Tesnière, Benveniste, Damourette et Pichon, Maratte et bien sûr Guillaume, puisqu'il se définit comme psychomécanicien. Il emprunte aux uns et aux autres certains concepts et modèles que nous allons tenter d'identifier. Sa matière d'analyse est vaste, et nous ne prévoyons pas de l'explorer. Nous en ferons seulement un inventaire rapide.

Nous allons d'abord étudier le système que Jacques Teyssier propose pour mettre en avant les emprunts et surtout les modifications des ces emprunts. Sa thèse principale est que le système des quatre cas germaniques peut être présenté selon le modèle d'un tenseur binaire radical où le Nominatif est l'entrée du nominal dans le verbal exprimant l'agence maximum par rapport au procés verbal, et l'Accusatif la position finale de la décroissance de l'agence du nom en rapport avec le procés verbal. Puis il y a franchissement d'un seuil avec le Datif qui remet en cause et transcende de premier mouvement en rendant de l'agence au nom objet, agence qui va croître jusqu'au Génitif qui retrouve un maximum d'agence, mais tout en restant dans l'objet du verbe, donc dans ce qui est causé et non ce qui cause. Mais avec le Génitif on peut franchir la limite du verbal pour ré-entrer dans le nominal.

Nous tenterons de montrer que cette approche dynamique est très riche par rapport aux autre grammaires de cas, mais n'atteint pas son objectif explicatif car elle réduit la langue à de la pensée, sémantique ou logique, et elle cantonne la syntaxe au nouveau du discours superficiel, linéarisé et réalisé en signifiant.

Jacques Teyssier est donc à la jointure entre Guillaume et les grammaires de cas structuralistes. Il dépasse bien celles-ci, mais, n'utilisant pas à fond les capacités de la psychomécanique, il manque l'explicativité qu'il aurait pu atteindre, et qui, aujourd'hui, est indispensable pour répondre à la demande de traitement mécanique et informatique de la langue : machines à traduire, traitement de texte formel, et toute utilisation d'informatique pour traiter des données linguistiques, sans oublier la didactique des langues.

Joachim Heinrich Campe Revisited: Some Corrections to the Stereotype of "German 18th-Century Purist"*

EDELTRAUD DOBNIG-JÜLCH

THROUGH WRITING the article on J. E. Campe for the Regensburg "Handbook-project" (introduced in the poster session) one is able to liberate a linguistically involved individual of the 18th century from his historiographical stereotype.

The Handbook offers materials both on the lives and works of authors and their cultural and philosophical backgrounds, giving authentic and exhaustive descriptions.

It is thus possible to differentiate Campe's current image as a puristic language reformer in such a way that more individual hues come to light, e.g. his insistence on leaving normative decisions to the "Gelehrtenpublik", or his life-long fixation on his "super-brother" Adelung. Arguments for this differentiation will be developed in the first part of the paper.

Campe's prevailing image as only a purist has effectively prevented researchers from seeing that Campe permeated his works with passages revealing him as a dedicated lexicographer, grammarian and even philosopher of language.

The second half of the paper attempts to reconstruct the model of grammar which is found in his "Versuch einer genauern Bestimmung und Verdeutschung der für unsere Sprachlehre gehörigen Kunstwörter" (1804). Furthermore, it is shown how Campe resolves the problem of scientific language, already virulent in the 18th century. Campe's theoretical and practical treatment of the problem is again taken as evidence for his many-sidedness.

* To appear (1993) as "Das letzte Gefecht. Zur Sprachkritik im 18. Jahrhundert", *Festschrift für Peter von Polenz*.

Having done away with Campe's stereotype, we conclude that an instrument like the Regensburg Handbook not only gives a more individual, and therefore, more accurate picture of each author, but also renders obsolete some historiographical stereotypes on 18th-century linguistics.

Le Profane et le religieux dans la genèse du comparatisme

DANIEL DROIXHE

LA TENDANCE naturelle, en histoire des sciences, est de lier la modernité à l'affranchissement par rapport aux schémas religieux. On présente ici quelques épisodes illustrant comment la pensée religieuse a développé des hypothèses, des règles explicatives, des conditions institutionnelles qui organiseront la genèse du comparatisme scientifique, dans le domaine indo-européen, mais aussi dans celui des langues sémitiques.

On envisagera surtout la fin du XVIIe siècle et le début du XVIIIe comme "laboratoire de paradigme", temporairement dissimulé par la montée conjointe des nationalismes et de la grammaire raisonnée. On comparera la crise des mythes bibliques relatifs au langage chez Richard Simon (source bien connue de la linguistique philosophique) et chez Basnage *(Antiquités judaïques,* 1713). On examinera cette crise dans le cadre d'un diffusionisme religieux qui plaçait la Révélation hébraïque à la source des cultures occidentales, en s'appuyant sur un "appareil comparatif" où les langues occupent une place importante : la théorie du phénicien chez Bochart sert l'hypothèse d'une transmission de la vérité juive au monde gréco-romain. On tâchera d'expliquer pourquoi Dom Calmet *(Commentaire littéral sur tous les livres de l'ancien et du nouveau Testament,* 1707–16), étiquetté comme un tenant de l'orthodoxie la plus rigoureuse sur le thème de Babel de l'hébreu langue-mère, a pu être aussi rangé au XVIIIe à côté de Simon, comme ayant banalisé le miracle.

Tout ceci conduira à voir dans l'œuvre de Frain de Tremblay — non seulement le *Traité des langues* (1703), mais aussi le *Discours sur l'origine de la poésie* (1713) — un modèle programmatique de la linguistique du siècle, en tant que conciliation entre religion, génétisme, primitivisme et histoire. On peut y reconnaître l'annonce d'un courant encore peu mis en valeur, aujourd'hui : celui élaborant en Grande-Bretagne l'idée de poésie sauvage (Blackwell, Warburton, Lowth, etc.). Si l'on a pu parler de "paradigme lockien", il faut expliquer comment celui-ci laisse entièrement échapper ce qu'annoncent Vico, Frain de Tremblay et une partie des biblistes, à savoir la conversion du génétisme sensualiste en primitivisme, et son rôle dans l'historicisation linguistique — en dehors des références habituelles à la "demande sociale" et à l'"horizon d'attente" constitué par le philosophisme des Lumières.

Paradigm Change and Paradigm Conflict in the Study of Contact Languages

MARKKU FILPPULA

THE TERM 'contact language' (also 'contact vernacular') is here used to refer to a form of language which has arisen through a (normally) long-standing contact between two languages, and which, being relatively well-established, is no longer dependent on bilingualism. A good example of a contact language is the variety of English spoken in Ireland, viz. Hiberno-English. Similarly, the form of Swedish spoken in Finland can be classified under the same heading. A third example is a whole group of varieties usually labelled as creoles.

The study of contact languages has traditionally operated with such concepts as **substratum**, **superstratum** and **adstratum**, and the principal aim of research has been to sort out the relative contributions of each of these elements in the given language contact situation. In the course of time, and depending on the contact language at issue, the focus of research has been on one or another of these factors — or researchers have argued for a combination of factors. The linguistic research on, e.g. Hiberno-English, has followed a path starting from subtsratum, with the superstratum emerging in the discussion only recently. A different chronological sequence can be attested in the study of creole languages.

Research carried out within the substratal/superstratal (/adstratal) framework can be said to constitute the **traditional** paradigm of research — traditional, first, because this type of research already has a long and honourable history; second, because it has in recent years been increasingly questioned and challenged by new approaches. Of these, perhaps the most influential has been one which emphasises the role of **general** and **universal constraints** on contact languages and on language acquisition in conditions of 'imperfect group learning' (or 'restricted input'). This line of research can be called the **universalist** paradigm.

Although the two paradigms have in some cases been in open conflict with each other, this may in the final analysis turn out to be a surface phenomenon only. In accordance with Thomason and Kaufman (1988), I shall argue in this paper that both competing paradigms in fact go back to a common, more general paradigm, which is the so-called **autonomous** (structural) linguistics in the Saussurean sense.

Attitudes to Language Change and Language History in Eighteenth-Century Scotland

†THOMAS FRANK

THERE WAS a great deal of writing and specualtion on language in Scotland in Scotland during the second half of the eighteenth century, so that it seems appropriate to treat Scottish writers on the subject apart from their English contemporaries, whose contribution to language studies is, with the exception of Harris's *Hermes*, largely of a practical and didactic nature. Writers such as Adam Smith, Monboddo, Elair and Beattie in their work wholly or partly devoted to language, all deal in one way or another with the phenomenon of language change, a subject of perennial interest to linguists. This paper intends to make a general survey of the ways these authors look at language change and subsequently to deal in greater detail with the anonymous article on "Language" in the first edition of the *Encyclopaedia Britannica* published in Edinburgh in 1771. This contains several points of interest, especially on the history of the modern European languages. The article probably represents one of the last "specualtive" histories of language before the rise of the German school of strictly scientific comparative linguistics in the early ninenteenth century.

One Distinctive Feature of French Linguistic Thought: The Metaphorical Nature of Human Languages

STEFANO GENSINI

In the last ten years historians of linguistics have emphasized the theoretical relevance of French linguistic thought. By doing so, the traditional view which reduces the so-called "questione della lingua" to a merely literary matter has been radically contradicted.

A crucial moment for the growth of philosophico-linguistic thought in Italy was the crysis of Renaissance in the Age of the "Principati". A large amount of theoretical reasons (namely, the development of neoplatonic tradition and on the other hand the study and comment of the great Aristotle's works such as *Poetica* and *Rhetorica)* and politico-cultural reasons (the conflict between French and Latin, between spoken and written language, the critical status of intellectuals) work together to produce a new idea of language. Some relevant thinkers of the Baroque Age introduced theories which finally considered language as an autonomous reality, no longer subordinated to extralinguistic perspectives: i.e. religious, political and so on.

Our paper focuses on a topic which becomes of the greatest relevance in the historical period under consideration: the role of metaphor in historical languages, a topic which is raised by philosophers like Giordano Bruno (1548–1600) and rhetoricians like Matteo Pellegrini (1595–1652) and Emanuele Tesauro (1591–1675). Tesauro's *Il Cannochiale aristotelico* (1655: usually seen as a *pendant* of Baltasar Gracian's *Agudeza y Arte de Ingenio)* will be the center of our attention.

The thinkers quoted develop the theory of metaphor discussed by Aristotle in *Rhet*. 1404b–1407a and *Poet*. 1457–1459a and raise objections concerning the significance given to it in the current rhetorical tradition. As a matter of fact, rhetoricians used to reduce metaphors and the other "figures of speech" to an *ornament* of language. On the contrary, Tesauro and others consider metaphors as a peculiar kind of knowledge. Metaphors not only "adorn" speech, they "create" a kind of truth, different from the one which is typical of science and history. Metaphors are therefore the real link between human gnosiological forces (especially *fancy)* and linguistic means.

We are confronted here with a consideration of historical languages which deeply differs from the rationalist one typical of the subsequent Enlightenment Age, especially in France. Metaphors and the other figures of speech are not only a mirror of human *imaginatio,* but also of needs, desires, material conditions of life. Here is a theoretical reason for the varieties of language both from a synchronic and a diachronic point of view. An Italian 'paradigm' for the philosophy of language is growing, that preludes Giambattista Vico's theories in his *Scienza Nuova seconda* (1744).

Gehirn und Sprache um die Wende vom 18. zum 19. Jahrhundert: Franz Joseph und der 'sens du langage'

JOACHIM GESSINGER

IN DER sprachphilosophischen und -psychologischen Diskussion der Spätaufklärung und bei den 'idéologues' galt der Zeichengebrauch des Menschen als Grundlage für seine stammesgeschichtliche wie individuelle Entwicklung, vor allem aber als Voraussetzung des Denkens. Im letzten Drittel des 18. Jahrhunderts wiesen Psychologen und Mediziner auf die organische Aspekte beobachteter Sprachstörungen hin, ohne aber diesen theoretischen Rahmen zu sprengen. Dies war erklärtermaßen das Ziel des Artztes und Anatoms Franz Joseph (1758–1828): Er wies die sensualistische Hypothese zurück, komplexe kognitive Fähigkeiten hätten sich aus sinnlichen Wahrnehmungen als Resultate eines Zeichengestützten Lernprozesses herausgebildet. Diese Fähigkeiten seien angeboren und in der Struktur des Gehirns festgeschrieben, sogar lokalisierbar.

Ich werde in meinem Beitrag zeigen, wie sich in diesem ersten ernstzunehmenden Theorieentwurf gegen das vorherrschende Paradigma Ergebnisse der vergleichenden Anatomie und historischen Morphologie des späten 18. Jahrhunderts mit älteren mentalistischen Annahmen vereinigten. Eine zentrale Rolle spielte dabei die von Buffon progressiv interpretierte Leibnizsche 'scala naturae'. machte (zusammen mit Spurheim) aus der metaphorischen Formulierung, Sprache sei ein intellektuelles 'Organ', ein Forschungsprogramm und sah im 'Sprach-Sinn' eine Gehirnfunktion, die sich nach dem allgemeinen Gesetz der organischen 'perfectibilité' gebildet habe. Er analogisierte organische Funktion und cerebrale Struktur und konnte auf diese Weise die verschiedenen Fähigkeiten des Menschen, mithin auch seine Sprachfähigkeit, im Gehirn des Menschen lokalisieren. Dabei setzte die Organisation des Schädelinnern mit einer äußeren Form in Beziehung und wurde so nicht nur zum 'point de référence' neuerer organologischer Konzepte der Cognitive Science, sondern auch zum Begründer der Phrenologie.

The Predominance of the Presence. A Plea for a Particular View on the History of Linguistics

ROLAND HEINE

ONE REASON for the increasing interest in the History of Linguistics — and related to it, in theoretical and methodological questions of the historiography of Linguistics — could be that nowadays Linguistics (as a scientific discipline) seems to be characterized by the dispersion of different tendencies which avoid dialogue (so that agreement about the objects themselves cannot be expected). Many people think that this is a typical phenomenon: it is often said that the history of a scientific discipline is consulted if there are opposing formulations of questions which seem to be incompatible On the one hand this is not astonishing because it is for the presence's sake that we are interested in history. But the consideration of history is used as a grounding of the present position too. Historiography is a dualistic and reciprocal concern because it has to promote our comprehension of the past in the light of the present and of the present in the light of the past. The valuations of history are never free of momentary interests, and they have an impact on the present. By using some results from the theory of action, and out of a pragmatic perspective, some of the problems which follow from this will be discussed in this paper. Considering a linguistic object like 'Modern Irish' some relevant applications of these considerations will be proposed.

Annotated Bibliography on German Theory of Orthography and Grammar from the 16th to the 18th Century

ASTRID JAHREIß

AT THE UNIVERSITY of Bamberg, the Department of Research on German Language History has been working on the project of "Annotated Bibliography on German Theory of Orthography and Grammar from the 16th to the 18th Century" since April 1985. This project provides the basis for judging the language-historical value and effect of those grammars and dictionaries of orthography of German which were published from the 16th to the 18th century.

The bibliography includes short biographies of the grammarians, comprehensive analytical data on all editions of their main works as well as comments on the contents of these works and an index of secondary literature.

The concept, methods, problems and the actual state of affairs — illustrated with abstracts from articles and copies of preprints — will be presented in the paper.

Rudolf von Raumer (1815–1876) and the Development of Sound Physiology

KURT R. JANKOWSKY

JACOB Grimm'S achievements in the field of sound description accounts to a significant extent for the great reputation he enjoyed among his contemporaries and has enjoyed ever since. It is, however, no secret that Grimm owes a great deal to other linguists who specialized, more than he did, in the exploration of the properties of language sounds. Grimm readily admitted his indebtedness to Rasmus Christian Rask, and he did not hesitate to also acknowledge that he had profited greatly from the reading of von Raumer's "Erstlingswerk" of 1837, entitled *Über die Aspiration und die Lautverschiebung*. This is the more remarkable as Rudolf von Raumer was barely 22 when he staged his scientific debut.

In the paper I intend to focus on v. Raumer's pioneering contribution to the development of the phonetic aspect in language analysis. His scorching criticism of Schlegel that he had offered nothing more than mere general ideas without giving much thought to supplying viable scientific proof (cf. v. Raumer, *Geschichte der Germanischen Philologie,* Munich 1870:361) was preceded by an activity of a different sort. Rudolf von Raumer discarded the idea of "Sprachgeist" as the mystical transformer of linguistic structures and replaced it with the notion of the individual as the sole originator of any and all linguistic changes. He provided an elaborate investigation of concrete linguistic data as to how sound changes occur and what the underlying causes might be. The paper will evaluate von Raumer's overall achievements and try to determine how they affected the work of his immediate successors and what they mean for us today.

Nabataean and North Arabian Writing Systems: History and New Approaches

WILLIAM JOBLING

THE HISTORY of the analysis of the North Arabian and Nabataean writing systems has for some scholars reached something of a quietus; the recent deaths of the Abbé Jean Starcky and Professor F. V. Winnett mark the end of an era of Nabataean and North Arabic epigraphic research which saw the establishment of both typologies and derived chronologies of these script systems. While both languages are still regarded as dialectally unrelated their co-existence in North Arabia, the Negev and Sinai in antiquity provides new theories concerning their nexus and sociolinguistic orientation to one another.

This study is concerned with an introductory review and discussion of the history of this scholarship with special attention being given to the typologies and script charts of Starcky and Winnett. In outlining and discussing their influence and the work of other scholars, attention is also drawn to the significance of the respective grammar and lexicons of Nabataean and North Arabian in the light of other research work, such as that of Dr Jay Levinson, Professor George Mendenhall and Professor Avraham Negev. These scholars have respectively argued for a wider consideration of Nabataean and North Arabian.

Finally the history of this research is discussed in terms of the application to the study of Nabataean and North Arabian writing systems of Principle Components and Correspondence Analysis in terms of micro-computer programs developed at the University of Sydney. The aim of these programs is to detect pattern in such epigraphic data with a view to defining distinctive differences by statistical analysis. This will assist a revision of the script charts and derived chronologies of Nabataean and North Arabian.

The Subconscious and Social in Saussure

JOHN E. JOSEPH

SAUSSURE'S interest in the psychological aspects of language are well documented, not so much with regard to the *CLG* but in his 'extracurricular' investigations into anagrams and glossolalia. These reveal a strong concern on his part with the level or levels of consciousness involved in linguistic production. The purpose of the present paper is to trace the effects of this concern upon Saussure's core linguistic theories as we know them from *CLG* and *CLG/E*.

Lest I be charged with reading yet another tenuous 'influence' onto Saussurean thought, I begin with the null hypothesis — that no differentiation of levels of consciousness is recoverable in Saussure's writings — and demonstrate that it is untenable; Saussure's system presupposes at least a dichotomy of conscious and subconscious, and possibly of unconscious thought.

The concept of levels of consciousness is itself a 19th-century creation that became part of the *Zeitgeist* of the last quarter of the century, to such an extent that we would in fact be more surprised to find Saussure uninfluenced by it than operating under its sway. But because he never makes it a central aspect of his linguistic system, the interconnection of consciousness with such key oppositions as arbitrary/motivated, *langue/parole/langage,* and especially social/individual, has not been sufficiently studied heretofore.

The two principal hypotheses put forth in this paper are: (1) that Saussure's thought conceals a consistent rejection of conscious thought from those aspects of linguistic production which are capable of being studied scientifically; (2) that Saussure's thought conceals a consistent conflation of the subconscious with the social. The latter hypothesis is particularly useful in demystifying certain confusing aspects of the Saussurean conception of *langue* as a 'social fact' that is nevertheless embodied in the mind of the individual speaker. As for the first hypothesis, I shall note that the alleged rejection likely does not originate with Saussure, but is inherited from both the Neogrammarian and Humboldtian traditions which his work (arguably) integrates. Nevertheless, the evidence of this personal fascination with subconscious aspects of language (anagrams and glossolalia) suggests that they may have played a hitherto unrecognized role in differentiating Saussure's thought from that of his immediate precursors and successors.

Reason, Usage and Development of Historical Linguistics in the 16th Century

DOUGLAS A. KIBBEE

IN THE SECOND half of the 16th century, French linguistic thought, as typified by the works of Louis Meigret, Abel Mathieu, Jacques Bourgoing, Honorat Rambaud, Léon Trippault and Henri Estienne, sought to sort out acceptable usage. The selection of one form over another might depend on appeals to *sociolinguistic criteria* (the form is preferred by a certain prestigious segment of the speech community), to *semantic identity* (one form distinguishes better between homonyms), or by appeal to to *historical logic* (either *etymological:* one form corresponds best to its Latin or Greek etymon; or *comparative:* one forms shows a clearer relationship with other members of the same family).

It is this last case which I shall consider most closely in this study, as it represents best the development of historical method over the course of the 18th century. The bizarre etymologies proposed to justify claims of linguistic glory concern me less than the attempts to create a logic of prescriptivism based on historical method. As an example, one can cite Meigrets selection of "liveau" over "niveau", citing historical development and related forms *(livre, libella* and *librare).* This logic battled, often unsuccessfully, with the more pragmatic criteria of sociolinguistic acceptability. Whatever its success or lack thereof, it represents a significant step towards the establishment of a method for historical linguistics, although still far from the scientific comparativism of the 19th century. In this paper, I shall present stages in the development of French historical linguistics in the authors cited above and the relationship between this method and the evolution of the prescriptivist method, both in morphology and in orthography.

On the Stoic Origin of the Grammatical Notion 'ABSOLUTIO'

C. H. KNEEPKENS

AT PRESENT the grammatical notion of "absolute" plays a marginal role in linguistic thought. However, from Late Latin Antiquity on it was a key term in linguistic thinking for many centuries. At first glance this notion seems to be of a simple structure, but a closer inspection shows that it actually covers different concepts which originally were not intermingled. For in the writings of the Latin grammarians two concepts which were current in the Greek grammatical tradition, viz. ἀπολυτός and αὐτοτελής have been merged into one concept of a more or less confused character, i.e. *absolutio/absolutus*. Already the Mediaeval grammarians appear to have been intuitively aware of this fact and tried to disentangle them, but, of course, they were at a loss for its reason.

L'Argument linguistique dans la *Methodus* de Jean Bodin (1566)

PIERRE LARDET

MÉTHODOLOGUE de l'histoire, Bodin procède selon un double mouvement de *circonscription* (qui découpe la spécificité d'une "histoire humaine", distincte d'une part de l'"histoire naturelle" et d'autre part de l'"histoire divine") et d'*extension* (qui refuse de privilégier le canon de la tradition gréco-romaine pour s'intéresser sans exclusive aux institutions de tous les peuples). Prudence et audace se conjuguent ici comme les préalables indispensables d'une démarche scientifique. Ne voulant ni s'appuyer sur les perspectives téléologiques qu'offrirait l'histoire divine ni s'en tenir aux inventaires d'une simple curiosité naturaliste, le comparatisme de Bodin trouve un terrain d'élection dans le domaine des variations linguistiques. Bien informé de recherches contemporaines (de Bovelles à Périon pour la France, de Münster à Lazius du côté germanique), Bodin se livre à une critique originale dont on verra comment elle mobilise toutes les ressources disponibles (étymologiques notamment) pour saper ces mêmes idéologies nationalistes qui avaient suscité ou stimulé nombre de travaux érudits en matière linguistique.

The Laurels of Linguistic Scholarship: The Prix Volney and its Contestants*

JOAN LEOPOLD

THIS PAPER will analyse the types of contestants who entered their published and unpublished works for the prestigious Prix Volney award of the Institut de France, from about 1822 to 1878. The Prix Volney was, at the time, the only international prize in general and comparative linguistics.

We shall discuss in summary and statistical form the contestants' backgrounds and degree of professionalism in linguistics. We shall also compare the overall contestants with the winners of prizes and honorable mentions in the Prix Volney competition, and characterize the nature of the works which were rewarded.

Roots and Implications of Cognitive Semantics

BARBARA LEWANDOWSKA-TOMASZCZYK

THE PAPER aims at providing the elucidation of the provenance of Cognitive Semantics in terms of its psychological, linguistic and philosophical roots. A discussion of relevant assumptions of *Gestalt*-psychology and the *mind-as-a-computer* model as well as that of prototype theories and recent connectionist frameworks is accompanied by the analysis of linguistic data which supports their cognitive explanation.

The discussion of the psychological and linguistic background of Cognitive Semantics together with the historical consideration of the debate between empiricism and rationalism will be shown to shed some light on the philosophical position of Cognitive Semantics with respect to basic epistemological issues such as the problems of nativism or modularity. An attempt is also made in this paper to show how Cognitive Semantics transcends some classical dichotomies such as the dichotomy between objectivism and anti-objectivism or that between universalism and relativism.

* Expected place of publication: *Prix Volney Essay Series,* vol. I. Dordrecht: Kluwer.

The Componential Semantics of Ramón Llull

WILLIAM E. McMAHON

PREVIOUSLY, I have argued that Aristotelian categorial theory, as understood by the medievals, was essentially a theory of componential semantics. An obstacle to this interpretation is that hardly anyone recognized the practical consequences of the theoretical outlook, i.e. that the "logical geography" of the conceptual fields represented by the categories should be mapped out, preferably in considerable detail. However, there was one notable individual, the Spanish Franciscan Ramon Llull (Lully), who for religious reasons did appreciate the task of providing a full-blown semantical theory. In addition to a set of categories he attempted to formulate combinatorial rules for generating complex senses from atomic ones. His approach was not especially influential at the time he was writing but later stimulated the semantical work of such thinkers as Wilkins, Dalgarno, and Leibniz. This paper thus explores the approach of Llull, which is not only of historical interest but also sheds light on current work in componential semantics.

The Study of the Paradigmatic Dimension of Language: An Attempt at Reconstruction

JAAP VAN MARLE

IN THIS PAPER I intend to discuss the Structuralist attempts to come to grips with the paradigmatic axis of language. As is well-known the discussion between paradigmatics and syntagmatics represent one of Saussure's famous dichotomies. In the *Cours* the relationships which have become known as paradigmatic (the term is Hjelmslev's) are characterized as 'rapports associatifs' bearing upon *elements in absentia*. That is, the paradigmatic dimension of language was, at least in part, characterized in *psychological* terms. In the case of syntagmatics, however, this is not so: there relationships were characterized in purely linguistic terms, i.e. as relationships holding between the elements constituting the 'chaîne de parole'. No doubt, this psychological orientation has contributed to the fact that Saussure's conception of the paradigmatic axis of language has often been criticized.

During the Structuralist enterprise several attempts have been made at a purely linguistically based conception of the paradigmatic relationships, while in

Saussure's *Cours* interesting initiatives in this direction can be found as well. In this paper, then, I will review these attempts to arrive at a purely linguistic concept of paradigmatic structure. In connection with this, I will discuss what other factors are at the root of the fact that the passages in the *Cours* dealing with the paradigmatic axis of language have been considered unsatisfactory by so many linguists.

Metalanguage in a Medieval Bilingual Dictionary

BRIAN MERRILEES

THE Latin-French *dictionarius* compiled from 1420 to 1440 by the Abbé Firmin le Ver of the Cartusian house of St. Honoré, Thuisson, near Abbeville in northern France, and preserved in MS Paris, BN n.a.fr. 1120, reveals a considerable sophistication in its metalexicographical structures. Not only does it have a visual presentation that reflects the advances in *ordinatio* and *compilatio* associated with the best of medieval manuscript layouts, its metalanguage indicates that its compiler was fully aware of the need for clarity and consistency in his task and could be said to anticipate many of the lexicographical advances of the Renaissance.

In this poster paper we shall show how Le Ver uses visual marks to enhance his presentation, how the metalanguage can be analysed into relational and attributional categories that enable the reader to work from a headword through Latin and French equivalents and definitions, to subheads organised in a coherent and logical order, creating a macro-entry structure that retains the etymological and derivational links that are important for medieval lexicography while using full alphabetisation that permits easy consultation. The visual marks include coloured capitals for headwords, ordinary capitals at the margin for subheads, grammatical notations in the right margin and various symbols within the text. The metalanguage used to mark definitional and derivational relationships will be examined along with the attributional terms that show grammatical features (morphology, phonology and orthography), language ties *(grece,* Latin*e, gallice)* and 'marques d'usage'.

The Early History of Romani Linguistics (1760 to 1799). Paulinus a Sancto Bartholomaeo and the Indian Origin of the Gypsy Language and People

JEAN-CLAUDE MULLER

WHILE groups of Gypsies appeared in Eastern Europe as early as the 14th century, their Indian ethnic and Linguistic origin remained unknown down to 1760, when a Hungarian student at Leiden (Valyi István) noticed similarities between the Sanskrit language — reported to him by three fellow students from India — and the language of the Gypsies near his home town of Györ. These resemblances between an Indian language and the dialects of European Romani, published in the *Gazette de Vienne* in 1763, were taken up Jacob Rüdiger in 1782, and formulated (independently?) by the Englishman Jacob Bryant in 1785.

At this juncture the paper addresses the theoretical issue of mutual influence versus independent discovery in the history of linguistics.

The historiographic thread is taken up again with the German Heinrich Grellman's 1783 study of language, customs and origins in *Die Zigeuner*, and influential book which was reprinted in an enlarged version in 1787 and simultaneously translated into French and English. Grellman developed the hypothesis that the European Gypsies originated in India as members of the lowest Hindu cast, the *sûdrah*.

The ground is thus prepared for a detailed analysis of a little noticed Latin text entitled *Anzeige, daß die Zigeuner Indianer sind, und Ihre Sprache ein Dialect ist, welcher aus der Sancritsprache entstehet* by the Austrian Carmelite Paulinus a Sancto Bartholomaeo (1748–1806) who is better known as the author of the first Sanskrit grammar printed in Europe *(Sidarubam,* Rome 1790) and the *Dissertatio historico-critica in linguam Samscrdamicam* (ibid.) of comparative vein.

Paulinus' intent, intended to further strengthen Grellman's hypothesis, is based on basic vocabulary lists of Romani and Sanskrit in the wake of Peter Simon Pallas' *Collection* of 1786. In fact the *Anzeige* ... was printed as an appendix to a 199-page study *(Über die Samsrkrdamische Sprache vulgo Sanskrit,* Wien 1799), in which Franz Carl Alter, a Vienna professor of Greek, printed data from Oriental languages belonging chiefly to the Indo-Iranian family for 273 items of basic vocabulary which were incompletely represented in Pallas' edition of 1786.

After putting Paulinus' contribution to the subject of Romani linguistics and ethnic origins in perspective, the paper will address more general issues like the use of basic vocabulary lists in early comparativism and the contemporary appearance of Sanskrit on the same scene (Sir William Jones 1786 etc.).

The paper chiefly aims at complementing a study by Ian Hancock ("The Development of Romani Linguistics", *Mélanges E. Polomé,* Berlin 1988:183–223), which is rather sketchy for this early period of Romani linguistics.

Schematism and Meaning

NUNO NABAIS

WE WILL analyse the role played by Greimas' semiotics in the hermeneutics of Paul Ricœur and in the morphological structuralism of Jean Petitot. Claiming that, in both cases, what is recognized as the main contribution of Greimas is the way in which he thinks the process of conversion in the deep grammar (paradigmatic) into the superficial one (syntagmatic), our aim will be:

1. to show how, in both cases, the adoption of Greimas' semiotics has been possible only through a return to the Kantian doctrine of transcendental schematism;

2. to analyse the epistemologic contribution to the problem of meaning of this return to Kant — not through pragmatics as proposed by Karl-Otto Apel — but through a structural approach.

Linguistic Dynamics: Expressivity and Semantic Change in Heinz Werner's Psychology of Language

BRIGITTE NERLICH

FOR SOME years now one can observe a "Bühler-revival" in the history and theory of the language sciences. This healthy tendency to look at European linguistics before the Second World War and all the deep changes that followed, will be continued in this paper by re-evaluating the psychology of language of Heinz Werner (1890–1964). Like Karl Bühler, Werner was forced to leave Germany when the Nazis came to power, but unlike Bühler, he did not stop his psycholinguistic production in the United States, he intensified it. Having always been interested in problems of 'aesthetics', from perception to expression, and especially in the developmental aspects of these phenomena, he came to focus on the acquisition and change of word meaning and the process of 'symbol-formation'. In all his works, he shows his dependency upon the German idealistic-romantic tradition (especially Kant, Herder, Humboldt and Cassirer). His theoretical background is otherwise eclectic, his writing a mixture of speculation and experiment — weaknesses that critics such as Bühler and Roger Brown for example were not slow to point out. On the other hand, Werner is one of the last psychologists who, building on a centenary tradition of thought about language, worked experimentally on phenomena such as semantic change, figurative language and linguistic dynamics. Hence, he provides us with a very different perspective upon psycholinguistic phenomena from that which was adopted in the 1960s with the advent of psycholinguistics properly speaking — a perspective that might counterbalance some of the shortcomings of the modern view. Werner was admired by philosophers, psychologists and linguists, such as Susanne K. Langer, Soloman Asch, Jerome S. Bruner, Roman Jakobson, Morris Halle and others.

In analysing a concrete example of early psycho-linguistics, this talk complements the general outlines provided in the paper given on the occasion of ICHoLS IV.

Sur la Formation de quelques catégories de la grammaire ancienne

RAFFAELLA PETRILLI

UNE NOUVELLE lecture des pages dédiées par Aristote au langage nous révèle l'importance d'une notion — celle d'ἀόριστον — qui va jouer un rôle décisif dans l'élaboration grammaticale des siècles suivants et qui a été cependant absolument méconnue. On peur saisir la véritable source des tentatives de classifier des entités linguistiques telles que la particule négative, certaines formes verbales, toutes sortes de pronoms, etc. ; il en est de même pour la formation des catégories générales de la description grammaticale telles que le couple *fini/infini*. En effet, les interprétations réservées à l'ἀόριστον par les grammairiens anciens proposent leurs effets sur un vaste secteur de la grammaire. Je voudrais esquisser l'histoire de la formation de ces concepts et notions grammaticales en partant de leur source aristotélicienne et en touchant au grand problème des rapports entre philosophie et grammaire.

Hobbes's Influence on the Leibnizian Project of a Universal Language

OLGA POMBO

THE AIM of this paper will be, not to evaluate the general influence that Hobbes' theory of language has exerted on Leibniz's linguistic thought, but to specify those Hobbesian theses which may have facilitated, prepared for or simply outlined the Leibnizian project of a Universal Language.

We will begin by the analysis of the systematic articulation of the Hobbesian conception of reason as a calculative activity and of his valuation of the mnemonic function of language above its communicative function — two aspects which are at the root of the decisive role Hobbes attributes to language in the constitution and progress of scientific knowledge and thus, even if indirectly, may have favoured the project of the construction of a Universal Language.

Special attention will then be given to Hobbes' refutation of the thesis of the regressive perfection of languages or original naturality of an Adamic language. In fact, it is by claiming the full human origin of the different languages that Hobbes opens up the possibility of asserting its arbitrary nature and it is by attempting to find a solid ground for that arbitrariness that — we will argue — Hobbes reaches his most powerful formulation of the thesis of the constitutive role of language.

We will see, at last, in which way Leibniz's project of a Universal Language presupposes the original and somehow convergent recovering of all these Hobbesian theses.

Some Features of Comenius' Conception of Language

JANA PŘÍVRATSKÁ

THE POSTER will introduce conference participants to to excerpts from the writings of Comenius, giving an idea of his views on language.

Besides illustrations of his main lines of thought — in particular the triads *res/mens/lingua* and *ratio/oratio/operatio* his attempts to perfect the use of language — will be demonstrated both by reference to his practical language textbooks and, principally, by the MSS of his *Panglottia* and *Novae harmonicae linguae tentamen primum,* in which he proposed a universal language.

Information on critical editions of the works of Comenius in the languages of the original editions will complete the poster.

Aristotle's Thoughts on Language — an Outgrowth of an "Intellectual Climate"*

HAIM B. ROSÉN

Reconnaissance et occultation à l'université : le cas de Georges Gougenheim

JACQUES-PHILIPPE SAINT-GÉRAND

ON A SOUVENT rappelé l'importance de l'institution universitaire dans le développement de la recherche française en linguistique. Un article de J.-C. Chevalier et P. Encrevé (*Langue* française 63 (1984) pp. 57–102) propose même un rapide survol de la question, au terme duquel la création de revues spécialisées et l'impulsion décisive donnée à la recherche paraissent émaner uniquement de personnalités en marge de l'Université (Meillet, Guillaume), ou fraîchement récupérées (Martinet, 1955), ou mal intégrées (Greimas, Guiraud, Quemada). Les autorités " scientifiques" sont essentiellement des philologues (Roques, Bruneau) qui répugnent à institutionnaliser en France la linguistique, sous quelle forme qu'elle se présente (générale : Saussure ; romane : von Wartburg ; anglo-saxonne : Bloomfield, Harris), en raison des connexions politiques inhérentes à cette nouvelle discipline. La stylistique textuelle — et non de la langue, comme l'eût voulu Bally —, qui est la seule matière tirant profit de ce refus, est elle-même en marge de la linguistique, à proprement parler.

Dans ce contexte, le cas de Georges Gougenheim (1900–1972), (qui ne paraît pas devoir figurer dans le futur *Lexicon Grammaticorum* de Stammerjohann), Professeur d'Université (Strasbourg, Sorbonne), mérite d'être étudié. Par sa formations, ses titres, mais aussi ses intérêts de philologue et linguiste, George Gougenheim, introducteur en syntaxe de la systématique — sinon du structuralisme — pragoise, couvre le champs entier des études classiques et modernes de

* This abstract is not available for publication.

l'université. Pourtant sa carrière et son influence resteront relativement discrètes. Les ouvrages qu'il a rédigés ont souvent été mal compris et accueillis (v. la condamnation lapidaire, par R.-L. Wagner, en 1947, du *Système Grammatical de la Langue française)* ; ses articles, diffusés dans de nombreuses revues, ne proposent pas de théorisation générale et brilliante ; ses recensions critiques portent, le plus souvent, sur des manuels de l'université la plus traditionnelle ; il pousse la provocation jusqu'à continuer de promouvoir l'histoire de la langue française, et apporte une riche documentation sur l'époque médiévale et la Renaissance, ainsi que sur la langue populaire du XIXe siècle. Son avancée dans le domaine contemporain suscite inquiétude, dérision, ou scepticisme : l'oralité du français *contemporain* n'est pas encore un phénomène entièrement reconnu et accepté ...

Je me propose d'examiner, dans cette communication, les méthodes et les acquis du travail linguistique de Georges Gougenheim ; leurs origines et leurs aboutissants ; d'analyser l'attitude ambigüe de l'Université française, et d'expliquer la prodigieuse récupération de son œuvre que la Sorbonne réalise après 1968, sous prétexte de lui offrir un volume d'hommage! Ce qui, d'une certaine manière, peut rendre compte du désintérêt dont l'œuvre de Georges Gougenhem est actuellement l'objet, tant dans les cercles de linguistique, que dans les équipes de recherche en histoire des sciences du langage — et ce n'est pas là le moindre paradoxe — dans l'enseignment universitaire lui-même.

Grammatica Illyrica, an 18th Century English Grammar from Bavaria

HANS SAUER

THIS GRAMMAR actually consists of two companion volumes, both in manuscript form, which have the titles *Principia Grammaticae Illyricae* and *Compendium Grammaticae Illyricae,* and are kept in the manuscript department of the Bayerische Staatsbibliothek in Munich. They have been largely ignored so far, although they are witnesses to the tradition of grammars of English written in Germany; they were probably the first English grammars to be written in Bavaria. They are also potential sources for the structure of English in the 18th century — although, of course, they have to be used with caution for the latter purpose. Despite their strange titles they are grammars of English, written in Latin, and intended for German learners of English, with the English examples translated into German.

The author is unknown; he just gives his initials (P.T.) and says that he is a Bavarian Capuchin. Presumably he used his grammar for teaching English in a grammar school, where pupils learnt Latin first. He wrote it in the second half of the 18th century, more precisely between 1762 and 1803 (he used R. Lowth's *A Short Introduction to English Grammar* [1762] as one of his sources). P.T. is fairly traditional in many respects; like most 18th and many 19th century grammarians, he is dominated by the model of Latin grammar, which is reflected, for example, in his insistence upon setting up inflexional paradigms, even where there is not much inflexion left in English, or in the divisions of his grammars, with sections about inflexion, syntax (limited to the syntax of word classes), pronunciation, and etymology (i.e. mainly word-formation).

But the unknown Capuchin also treats relatively new features and constructions peculiar to English such as the continuous form, the construction of questions and negations with *to do,* the group genitive, etc. His description of these is, however, often inadequate: he gives the forms, but does not make their function really clear. The pronunciation he provides contains a number of typically German mistakes, e.g. the inability to pronounce <th> correctly (he gives *s* for /θ/ and *d* for /ð/); it is nevertheless interesting because, among other things, it reflects the development of the English long vowels in the 18th century.

The Invisible Hand in the History of Language

RÜDIGER SCHREYER

IT IS ONE thing to describe the regularities of linguistic change and another to account for these regularities. Linguists have been fairly unsuccessful in doing the latter: a theory of linguistic change is still one of the desiderata of our science. One of the central problems is the explanation of the regularity of linguistic change. Linguistic regularity is evidently the result of the unconcerted linguistic activities of a large number of individuals. In this respect language is like any other structured social phenomena which can neither be classified as natural nor as artificial, which are neither to be understood as the result of mindless laws of nature, nor as the intended product of the human mind.

Karl Ferdinand Becker on When — and What Sort of — Grammar is Needful

†LESLIE SEIFFERT

K. F. BECKER, in the course of the his preface to the 1827 edition of his *Organism der Sprache,* comments on the circumstances under which a nation or people may need a grammar of their language. In the particular circumstances of Germany, he claims, provincials from Lower Saxony or the Upper Rhine need no grammar in order to speak the languages of their respective provinces, but they do need the aid of grammar when they want to speak (let alone write) High German.

This comment is set in a context in which Becker makes three points that bear on the issue:

(a) Grammar becomes the more needful once a language has come to co-exist with other dialects, and once culture has brought alien matter to bear upon it.

(b) Grammar, in helping users of a language to retain a clear sense of its identity under such circumstances as in (a), must proceed from the intrinsic import of the forms inherent in the organism of the language, or else it will only obscure the very clarity it purports to be fostering.

(c) When a language — as in the case of German, including High German — has maintained the fresh spirit of its organic life, then it is in the best position to allow its internal codification to proceed without the involvement of any legislative authority external to itself.

A close reading of this short passage can bring out the interconnectedness of these three themes in Becker's work.

William Sèwel and Thomas Dyche as Teachers of English

ROBIN D. SMITH

WILLIAM SEWEL and Thomas Dyche share considerable favour in elementary English language teaching in the eighteenth century. Although the impetus for teaching English as a foreign language on the basis of of grammars and dictionaries seems to have lessened in the Netherlands at the very time when teaching the English vernacular in England was become a desirable activity, Sèwel's English-Dutch, Dutch-English dictionary (1691, 1708 etc.) and his *Compendious Guide to the* English *Language* (1705) written in dominated the English teaching scene there for the whole of the century.

In particular the *Guide* was extensively reprinted and plagiarised. In England Thomas Dyche's elementary schoolbook, his *Guide to the English Tongue* (1709) appeared in some fifty editions and reprints before 1800. There were also multiple editions of the dictionary Dyche wrote with the otherwise unknown William Pardon, *A New General English Dictionary* (1735) which continued to be reprinted up till 1794.

The purpose of this paper is to provide a comparison of the working methods and linguistic insights of these two authors; of how they presented their material and which sources they depended on, with a view to making an assessment of their achievements within the linguistic and social contexts in which they worked.

Au revers de l'Histoire de la linguistique : la cryptographie

PIERRE SWIGGERS

LES HISTORIENS de la linguistique n'ont guère exploré jusqu'ici une documentation quelque peu marginale, mais très intéressante par ses côtés pratique **et** théorique : la cryptographie (encodage et décodage de messages politiquement importants). À partir d'un exemple concret *(L'Art de deschiffrer,* ms. Archives générales du Royaume [de Belgique], Bruxelles, Secrétairerie d'Etat et Guerre n° 3, on essaiera de montre la pertinence de ce type de document pour l'histoire de la linguistique. Les thèmes abordés seront:

(1) la cryptographie comme système sémiolinguistique tertiaire (déjà reconnu au XVIIe siècle!) ;

(2) l'algorithme de déchiffrement (surtout pour les systèmes à chiffres simples) ;

(3) les moyens de rendre un message indéchiffrable.

L'étude du document permettra de dégager quelques conclusions générales à propos de l'emploi de la cryptographie dans l'administration espagnole.

Latin Declensions and Conjugations: From Varro to Priscian

DANIEL J. TAYLOR

DECLENSIONS and conjugations are easily the most recognizable components of Latin grammar, and yet their evolution in ancient language science contains a number of significant discrepancies. This paper therefore attempts to determine in detail the development of declensions and conjugations in Latin from their origin in Varro (116–27 B.C.) to their ultimate articulation in Priscian. (fl. 5th–6th c. A.D.).

The earliest extant text to arrange nouns (including adjectives, of course) into what we nowadays call declensions is Varro's *De Lingua Latina,* but his schemes are not quite the same as those of his successors. Moreover, the linguistic analysis by which he distinguishes his morphological affiliations differs as well, and technical terminology is conspicuous by its absence. By the end of classical antiquity, however, the declensions and conjugations appear much the same as they do in a modern textbook or grammar; ditto for most of the linguistic analysis and terminology. In other words, declensions and conjugations do have a history. We can establish that history by answering three questions. Exactly how do the *grammatici Latini* broker out declensions and conjugations in Latin? What is their linguistic basis for doing so? What terms do they employ?

The answers to those questions are in some instances likely to prove surprising, and that is why it is important to set the historical record straight. For instance, Varro identifies five declensions, but they are not the same five which Priscian. has.Charisius (4th c. A.D.) says that there are four or five declensions, and in his text we find ourselves present, quite literally, at the creation of the fifth declension (though we cannot date the event precisely). Yet Diomedes (also 4th c. A. D.) enumerates seven declensions, or ten if borrowed Greek nouns are included. Then too, Varro's three conjugations turn into Priscian.'s four via the intermediate stage of a third *correpta* and a third *producta*. The linguistic basis for assigning declined and conjugated forms to particular classes and the terminology involved likewise vary and evolve in the course of the history of the Roman *ars grammatica*. Identifying those discrepancies in enumeration, analysis, and terminology is the major purpose of this paper.

In addition, however, this paper contains a hidden agenda or subtext. Ancient and modern scholars alike have always considered Varro the most independent and authoritative thinker in the Roman grammatical tradition, and yet his influence on that tradition has been, apparently, negligible. This study casts doubt on that latter assertion. Several idiosyncratic features of Varro's linguistic analysis and metalanguage seem to persist throughout the history of the Latin declensions and conjugations in classical antiquity. Put somewhat differently, the mistakes, if that is the proper word, which characterize Varro's original formulations and conjugations in Latin may account for the several discrepancies which occur throughout the later tradition.

In fine, the Roman *ars grammatica* is one of the most significant cultural artifacts transmitted from antiquity to modernity, and this paper seeks to understand exactly how its core, the declensions and conjugations of Latin, originates and develops.

Showing the Fly the Way Out of the Fly-Bottle (Or, why Theorists who Ignore the History of Linguistic Ideas do so at their Peril)*

TALBOT J. TAYLOR

GIVEN the recent growth of interest in the history of linguistic thought, some may want to ask: "Why?". Is it that, as some linguists would have it, linguistic theory has developed such complex analytic techniques that it has become too challenging a discipline for many of those with an interest in language, leading these dullards to take refuge in the less challenging arguments of pre-formal linguistics ("If you cannot do linguistics, do the historiography of linguistics!")? Does the study of the history of linguistic ideas yield only historical knowledge? Or does it have a contemporary relevance?

In this paper I will argue that, in contrast to what linguistic theorist swould have us believe, the study of the history of linguistic thought is not peripherally but *centrally* important to the contemporary study of the nature of language and communication and that those theorists who fail to study the history of linguistic ideas condemn themselves to a lack of self-awareness and to the endless repetition of the past.

At the same time my paper will suggest a new goal for those who work in the history of linguistic ideas, to go along with the historical and intellectual questions which already motivate it. Linguistic historiography needs to add to its repertoire

* Published (1991) in *HEL* 13/2.85–109.

the following questions: Why do linguists today continue to puzzle over those very same problems which our ancestors have been attempting to solve for over two thousand years? Is it that, as the progressivist ideology of contemporary theory maintains, we have not yet developed the instruments or the analytic techniques that will eventually reveal the final solutions to the great linguistic problems?

I will argue that such a view misunderstands the very nature of linguistic reflection and that a principal task of linguistic historiography should be that of accounting for the perenniality of linguistic theorizing and its constituent debates and puzzles. Such an account can only be provided by combining the task of inquiry into the conceptual foundations of linguistic reflection with that of historical investigation into the variety of forms which those reflections have assumed in different cultural, political and intellectual contexts. By discussing the theme of communicational scepticism in the Western linguistic tradition and its source in a descriptivist misinterpretation of the normative character of lay metalinguistic discourse, this paper will provide an example of the means by which we might begin to address these tasks. The relevance of linguistc historiography to contemporary theory may then be seen to lie in the ever-present need to recognize the source and fascination of the conceptual traditions within which linguists work. If we are to cure the disease we must first study its pathology.

Structuralism in the Early Works of Saussure

MÁRIA TSIAPERA

BENVENISTE, in *Esquisse d'une théorie de la racine,* incorporates many of Saussure's ideas in terms of his own theory of the PIE root. The root theory that Meillet considered as a prerequisite to etymological studies, Meillet in fact earlier attested that Saussure was the first to see the basic structure of the PIE root. Saussure realized that PIE phonology was far more complicated than previously thought, especially the sonants. In trying to fit the hypothetical syllabic nasals into his conception of the vocalic system of PIE, he dealt with the systematic structural aspects of languages rather than the phonetic reality of speech.

His essentially morphophonemic analysis of the PIE vocalic system was structural long before structuralism came to the foreground. He recognized as a functional entity the "voyelle indéterminée" with reflexes *i* in Sanskrit, *a* in Latin and ϵ, α, and ο in Greek. Comparing Latin *fēcī, faciō,* Greek τίθημι, θετός, from *dhe-*, **dha-* and then comparing roots such as **dhe-* with **pet-* and their respective weak grades **dha-* and **pt-*, Saussure concluded that vowel length is a 'systematic unit' (phoneme) that appeared in the weak grade as ə. This paralleled the sonants *r̥, l̥, m̥* and *n̥* and designated *A* and *Q* prehistoric phonemes as functional units in the underlying vocalic system of PIE. Unfortunately, he made this decision on the basis of comparative material rather than on the concept of system.

Saussure's contemporaries met the systematic analysis of PIE vocalism negatively with the exception of Hermann Møller who used *A* and *Q* as laryngeal consonants. Meillet dealt with the comparative evidence for the PIE sonants in light of Saussure's conception of systematic function and was able to describe the ablaut patterns of sonants clearly. It is this systematic function that is being re-examined.

Arab and Western Approaches to Syntax: The Conditional Clause

KEES VERSTEEGH

ONE OF THE MAJOR constraints in Arab linguistics is the one-to-one relationship between form and context. Although generally speaking the Arab grammarians did not concern themselves with the semantic side of linguistics, they did regard the transparency of the relationship between form and context as one of the important conditions for any linguistic analysis.

In the construction of the conditional clause in Arabic, the use of the verbal tenses differs from that in declarative clauses, since a past tense may be used for present conditions.

In this paper I study the solutions given in the Arab linguistic tradition for this discrepancy in view of the constraint mentioned above, both for early grammarians and for those grammarians who have tried to combine linguistics with semantics/stylistics such as al-Gurgani. Their approach to the problem is contrasted with the treatment given to the conditional clause in traditional Western grammars of Arabic. Modern transformational and functional theories on the Arabic conditional clause will be briefly mentioned.

General Linguistics in Poland between 1918 and 1939

ZDZISŁAW WĄSIK

BEFORE starting to review the development of general linguistics as a scientific discipline practised at the Polish universities in the period between the two World Wars one should discuss its notional scope and its methodological status among other subdisciplines of linguistics and, broadly taking, among other sciences of language.

In order to appreciate the contribution or the attitudes of Polish philologists towards the shifts of scientific paradigms in the theoretical thought on language as a definitional model it is necessary to take into account the intellectual climate of opinion that prevailed, at that time, in scientific research in general and in linguistics in particular, both in Poland and abroad.

Since developments in general linguistics have not only an intellectual dimension but also a personal and professional one, the next step in the historiographical analysis of the inter-war sciences of language, when it concerns periodization, is connected with the inquiry about the changes of generations, the educational background of linguists, as well as the institutional and professional contacts between particular scientists and schools of thought, from the point of view of the sociology of knowledge.

Index Linguarum

Adamic 280, 356
aléoute 238
allemand 50, 82, 131, 246
amérindien 238
anglais 131, 132, 245, 246, 249
Anglo-Saxon 17, 18, 20, 26, 68, 186
Arabic 103, 104, 105, 107, 108, 109, 110, 111, 261, 262, 263, 264, 365
    Egyptian Arabic 271
    North Arabian 346
    North Arabic 346
Aramaic 103, 104, 105, 107, 108
Armenian 104, 107
Avesta 261, 267
Canaanite 107
Castilian 332
    Primitive Castillan 333
    castillan 122, 145, 146, 148, 149, 150, 155
Chaldaean 105, 107, 109
Chimu 122
Chinese 106, 160, 275
Classical Languages 138
Danish 158, 163, 166
    danois 129
deutsch 57
Dutch 59, 71, 191, 192, 193, 194, 197, 199, 200, 201, 220, 224, 279, 280, 281, 285, 288, 289, 360
    early Dutch 192
    Middle Dutch 191, 193, 194, 216, 217
    Modern Dutch 216
English ix, xi, 3, 5, 20, 21, 22, 25, 26, 66, 68, 69, 71, 89, 95, 97, 99, 101, 107, 128, 132, 135, 138, 142, 171, 183, 184, 185, 186, 187, 188, 189, 190, 191, 192, 196, 200, 201, 202, 216, 217, 220, 224, 249, 257, 258, 269, 270, 271, 272, 273, 274, 275, 276, 277, 327, 331, 334, 336, 340, 341, 353, 358, 359, 360, 361
    Early Modern English 274
    frühneuenglisch 190
    Hiberno-English 340
    Middle English 224, 274
    Modern English 216
    Standard English 216
Eskimo 157, 158, 160, 163, 166
espagnol 131, 132, 145, 147, 148, 150, 155, 156
Ethiopic 104, 107, 108, 109, 110, 111
European 262
Finno-Ugric 217, 224
first language 106
flamand 126, 131, 132
français 54, 57, 74, 75, 76, 77, 78, 79, 80, 81, 82, 83, 123, 124, 125, 126, 127, 128, 129, 131, 132, 133, 136, 156, 248, 357, 358
    françois 49, 50, 57, 78, 80, 130, 132, 137, 142, 143
    französisch 57
    French ix, 20, 21, 25, 49, 50, 51, 54, 55, 56, 59, 127, 132, 133, 135, 137, 138, 141, 143, 206, 220, 224, 263, 272, 273, 320, 327, 334, 341, 342, 348, 352, 353
Frisian 59, 61, 62, 63, 64, 65, 66, 67, 68, 69, 70, 71
    Old Frisian 70, 71
German ix, 20, 25, 49, 50, 51, 59, 68, 106, 107, 131, 135, 138, 159, 160, 162, 163, 169, 188, 191, 192, 193, 194, 196, 206, 207, 209, 210, 217, 225, 271, 280, 321, 334, 335, 344, 358, 359, 360

Bavarian 215
High German 214, 215
Low German 63
Middle High German 69, 193
Old High German 69, 214
Germanic 69, 71, 191, 213, 214
Proto-Germanic 214
West Germanic 192, 224
germanique 337, 349
Germanisch 345
Gothic 249
grec 9, 10, 11, 131, 135, 143, 149, 242, 243, 245, 246, 248, 249, 352
Greek 9, 10, 11, 12, 13, 14, 30, 41, 67, 68, 104, 105, 106, 107, 135, 187, 220, 249, 334, 348, 349, 353, 362, 364
Greenlandic 157, 158, 159, 160, 161, 162, 163, 164, 165, 166
Gypsy 353
Haida 257, 258, 259
hébreu 339
Hebrew 103, 104, 105, 106, 107, 108, 109, 110
Illyric 358
Indian 353
Indo-European 110, 157, 213, 224, 270, 272
Proto-Indo-European 364, 365
indo-européen 238, 246, 250
Indo-Iranian 353
innok 238
Inuit 164, 165
Irish ix, 1, 3, 4, 5, 85, 87, 88, 91, 92, 93, 94, 95, 96, 97, 98, 99, 100, 101
Modern Irish 5, 344
Old Irish 1, 10
Italian 20
italien 131, 132, 145, 156
Japanese 271
Kalaallisut 157
Labrador 159, 163, 166
Latin 7, 8, 10, 11, 12, 13, 14, 15, 17, 18, 20, 21, 25, 28, 30, 31, 36, 37, 39, 41, 43, 45, 48, 60, 62, 64, 68, 73, 74, 75, 76, 77, 78, 79, 80, 81, 82, 83, 84, 88, 89, 90, 91, 92, 93, 95, 98, 99, 100, 101, 104, 105, 106, 107, 109, 115, 116, 117, 118, 119, 120, 121, 125, 126, 131, 135, 136, 137, 138, 141, 142, 143, 146, 148, 149, 150, 154, 155, 156, 157, 158, 159, 161, 162, 165, 166, 170, 183, 184, 186, 187, 191, 196, 197, 199, 200, 201, 220, 242, 243, 245, 246, 249, 331, 333, 334, 342, 348, 349, 352, 353, 358, 359, 362, 363, 364
Medieval Latin 13
Vulgar Latin 191
Luiseno 271
martien 237, 249
Mochica 113, 114, 115, 116, 117, 118, 119, 120
Mongolian 262
Muchik 122
Nabataean 346
Newspeak 179, 292
Norwegian 224
Oriental 104, 105, 107, 108, 353
Pahlavi 261
Papago 271
Persian 107, 108, 109, 261, 262, 263, 264, 265, 266, 267
Middle Persian 261
Modern Persian 261
Old Persian 261
Polish 224, 319, 327
polonais 126
Punic 107
Quechua 113, 115, 116, 121
sanskrit 238, 353, 364
Sclavonic 106
Semitic 103, 104, 105, 107, 108, 110, 111
Slavic 213, 319
Spanish 20, 113, 114, 115, 116, 118, 121, 135
Swedish 340
Syriac 104, 105, 107, 109, 111
Tartaric 106, 107
Turkish 107, 262, 263, 264
Universal Language 356
Welsh 87
Yankee 4, 5
Yunga 113, 122

Index Nominum

Aarsleff xxi, 48, 99, 101
Abbott 88, 99
Abercrombie 233, 235
Abney 272, 276
Adam 19, 83
Adam, Charles 174, 176, 181
Adam, Nicolas 79, 80
Adams 87, 99
Adelung 338
Adrian de Castello 334
Aelfric 17
Aelfric, abbot of Eynsham 17
Ahlqvist, Anders ii, iii, iv, v, ix, xiii, xxi, xxiii, xxvii, 1, 9, 14, 87, 100, 328
Ahlqvist, Jacob xii, xiii
Ahlqvist, Judith xiii
Aitchison 274, 276
Akmajian 270, 271, 272, 276, 277
al-Gurgani 365
al-Khalîl ibn Aḥmad 108
Alarcos García 156
Albareda 36
Alcuin 29, 31
Aldrete 147, 151, 156
Alfric 18
Allan 274, 276
Alter 353
Altieri 113, 114, 115, 118, 119, 120, 122
Alunno 22, 23, 25
Ambrogio 103
Amsler xiii, xxiii, 251, 329
Andersen 277
Anderson, John M. 277
Anderson, Stephen R. 251, 258
Andresen xiii, xxi, xxiii, 330
Ansari 263
Apel 354
Apollonius 41
Apollonius Dyscolus 39, 40, 41, 42, 43, 44, 45, 46, 48
Aristotle 29, 30, 33, 34, 36, 135, 137, 203, 211, 342, 351, 355, 357
Arnauld 54
Arntz 25
Aržang 266
Asch 355
Ascoli 14
Audax 30
Auroux ii, 110, 111, 124, 132, 143, 307
Austin 309, 310, 314, 316, 317
Awedyk vii, xiii, xxiii, xxvii, 213, 214, 216, 224
Awedykowa 222, 224
Ayres-Bennett 132
Bacon 171, 172, 173, 175, 176, 181, 183
Bain 229
Baker 211
Ball xiii, xxiv
Ballauf 295, 298, 305
Bally 357
Bańczerowski 213, 217, 218, 224, 225
Baratin 45, 48
Barbelenet, 249
Bartlett, Barrie E. xiii, xxvi, 305, 330
Bartlett, Marlène xiii
Bartschat xiii, xxiii, xxv, 331
Barwick 11, 14, 30, 36
Basnage 339
Bateni 266
Batteux 135, 136, 137, 138, 139, 140, 141, 142, 143
Baudouin de Courtenay 213, 319, 320, 321, 322, 323, 324, 325, 326, 327, 328
Baumgarten 206, 207, 209
Beattie 341

Beauzée 77, 80, 81, 82, 296, 305
Beck 161, 162, 166
Becker 360
Beeckman 174, 176
Bellot 21, 25
Bembo 25, 145
Bennett 274, 276
Benveniste 1, 337, 364
Bergaigne 238, 240
Bergin 87, 88, 92, 100
Bergsland 158, 159, 160, 166
Berlaimont 125, 132
Bermúdez de Petraza 332
Bibliander 104, 106
Binotti xiii, xxv, 332
Bischoff 29, 37
Blackwell 339
Blair 336
Blank 42, 48
Bloomfield 357
Blumenbach 299
Boas 251, 252, 253, 254, 255, 256, 257, 258, 259
Boccaccio 25, 145
Bochart 185, 339
Bodin 349
Boethius 29, 35, 37
Boileau 135
Bonfante 2
Bopp 110, 111, 295, 298, 300, 303, 304, 305
Borhan 262
Borsche 302, 305
Borzym 327
Bouhours 55
Bouquet xxvii, 333
Bourgoing 348
Bourquin 159, 160, 163, 164, 166
Bovelles 349
Boxhorn 107
Boyer 250
Boyle 184, 190
Bradley 25
Braidi 251
Bréal 143, 237, 238
Breeze xiii, xxiv, 334
Brekle v, xiii, xxi, xxiii, xxvi, 49, 50, 56, 153, 156, 206, 209, 211, 305, 335
Bremmer v, xiv, xxiii, 59, 63, 68, 71
Brendan (Father) 85
Brentano 311
Breuker 59, 61, 65, 66, 67, 69, 71
Brill 199, 201, 280, 281, 282, 283, 287
Brinton 257
Broca 227
Brouwer 64, 71
Brown 355
Brücke 227
Brugmann 243, 248, 250, 287
Bruneau 357
Bruner 355
Bruno 342
Bryant 353
Buchmann 104
Buffon 300, 343
Bugarski ii
Bühlbring 245, 249
Bühler 310, 317, 318, 354, 355
Buhr 295, 305, 306
Buonmattei 153, 154
Buridant 129, 130, 132
Burkhardt 313, 316, 317
Bursill-Hall, Geoffrey L. xiv, xxiv, 27, 37, 48, 124, 132
Bursill-Hall, Hilary xiv
Bynon 37
Byrne 249
Calepino 104
Calero Vaquera xiv, xxv, 336
Calmet 339
Campe 338
Canini 104
Carolingians 28, 30, 35, 36
Caron 201
Carrera 113, 114, 115, 116, 117, 118, 119, 120, 121, 122
Casas Homs 36
Cassiodorus 29, 30
Cassirer 355
Castell 106, 107, 108, 109, 111
Catullus 66
Caxton 21, 25

Chalmers 136, 143
Changeux 80
Charisius 11, 14, 30, 36, 362
Charlemagne 7, 28
Charles the Bald, 14
Chevalier xiv, xxiii, 336, 357
Chittenden 12, 14
Chmura-Klekotowa 319, 327
Chompré 80
Chomsky 27, 266, 269, 270, 271, 272, 273, 275, 276, 330, 333
Christmann ii
Christy vii, xiv, xxvi, 227
Cicero 140, 141, 142, 334
Clemens Scottus 32
Clyne xiv, xxiv
Cohen, Marcel 336
Cohen, Murray 184, 189
Colombat vi, xiv, xxiv, 73, 76
Comenius 21, 356
Condillac 53, 55, 137, 138, 143, 205, 206, 207, 210, 211
Conlan 86, 100
Conry 86
Cook 300
Cooper 235
Cordemoy 138, 143, 295, 296, 298, 305
Corneille 54
Correas 148, 149, 150, 151, 152, 153, 154, 155, 156, 332
Coulardeau xiv, xxiv, 337
Covington 40, 45, 48
Cox 334
Cram xiv
Culicover 270, 276
d'Alembert 53, 172, 181
Dalgarno 21, 183, 351
Damourette 337
Dante 25, 145
Darmesteter 249
Darwin 228, 279, 280, 282, 284, 285, 286, 287, 288, 289
David 159, 160, 166
Davidson 277
Davies, Anna Morpurgo 303, 305
Davies, John 185
De Buck 86, 100
de Clercq vi, xiv, xxiv, 85, 86, 100, 237
de Dieu 105
de la Cueva 332
De Launay 78, 80, 83
de Lusenet xi, xvii
de Mauro 111
de Quevedo 332
De Rijk 33, 37
de Saumur 74
de Saussure 224, 245, 307, 310, 333, 341, 346, 347, 351, 357, 364, 365
de Vries 280
Debrunner 2
Delesalle 143
Delvaux 237
Demers 271
Descartes 173, 174, 176, 181, 183, 189, 203, 204, 206, 207, 208, 209, 211, 295, 296, 309, 311
Desfontaines 55
Desmet vii, xiv, xxiv, 237, 241, 248
Despautère 73, 74
Devoto 1
di Salvo 320, 322, 327
Dibbets. 201
Diderot 53, 80, 83, 172, 181
Dietrich 17
Dijksterhuis 294, 305
Dillon 100
Diogenes Laertius 40, 48
Diomedes 30, 362
Dionysius of Halicarnassus 135, 136, 138
Dionysius Thrax 196
Dobnig-Jülch xiv, xxiii, 56, 211, 338
Donatus 7, 8, 10, 11, 12, 14, 15, 28, 31, 196, 197
Donatus Ortigraphus 12, 13, 14, 32
Dornseiff 20, 25
Doroszewski 1, 327
Dottin 249
Douay-Soublin 76, 83, 84
Draak 9, 14
Dreike xiv
Droixhe xiv, xxiii, 339
Du Marsais 76, 77, 78, 79, 80, 81, 83, 84

Duchosal 84
Duke Karl Eugen 51
Dumas 78, 79, 84
Duns Scotus 86
Dyche 360
Eco 203, 211
Egan 87, 88, 89, 90, 91, 92, 100
Egede, Hans 158, 159
Egede, Paul 158, 159, 160, 161, 163, 166
Elair 341
Ellis 173, 175, 176, 181
Emmius 68
Emonds 270, 276
Emperor Charles V 59
Encrevé 357
Engler ii
Erasmus 146, 152, 334
Erdmann 255, 259
Erondell 128, 132
Erpenbeck 295, 305
Erxleben 176, 177, 181
Eschbach 318
Estienne 348
Etienne 334
Eutyches 28
Fabricius 163, 166
Falk 272, 274, 276
Fay 249
Fechner 229, 258, 259
Feitsma 71
Filelfo 334
Fillmore 277, 337
Filppula xiv, xxvii, 340
Fisher 127, 132
Fisiak 216, 224
Formigari xv, 111
Forster 300, 302, 305, 307
Frain de Tremblay 339, 340
Frank x, 341
Frenze 211
Fréron 55
Froissart 193
Fromkin 234, 235
Furetière 55, 139, 143
Gabbema 59, 65, 66, 67, 69, 70
Gall 232, 343
Galton 228, 229
Gauthiot 249
Gazdar 273, 276
Gensini xv, xxv, 341
Geoffroi 55
George III 169
Gerbert of Aurillac 34
Gesner 69, 104
Gessinger xv, xxvi, 279, 288, 343
Gessler 127, 131
Ghajar 263
Gharib 264, 265, 266
Gibson 9, 14, 29, 37, 48
Gil 186
Gilbert 86, 100
Godel 224
Gougenheim 1, 357
Gough 51, 57
Gracian 342
Grammont 249
Greimas 354, 357
Grellman 353
Grigor'ev 327
Grimm 280, 283, 303, 345
Gründer 305, 307
Gruntfest vi, xv, xxv, 103
Guarino 334
Guichard 105
Guillaume 337, 338, 357
Guiraud 357
Gwynn 88, 99
Haastrup 129, 132
Hachette 54
Hale 251, 252, 256, 259
Haliday 91
Halle 355
Halliday 266
Hallig 22, 25
Hamann 205, 211, 212, 298, 306, 307
Hamans vii, xv, xxiii, xxvi, 213, 214, 216, 224
Hancock 354
Harmon 277
Harris, James 294, 306, 336, 341
Harris, Roy 20, 25
Harris, Zellig S. 357
Hartmann 25, 26
Haßler 300, 301, 306
Havet 243, 248

Hayden's Hotel xxiv
Heegslag 59
Hegeman 280, 288
Heine xv, xxvii, 344
Heine-Raab xv
Heiric of Auxerre 14
Helmholtz 252, 253, 254, 255, 259
Henry 237, 238, 239, 240, 241, 242, 243, 244, 245, 246, 247, 248, 250
Henry VIII 334
Herbart 255, 256
Herder 205, 206, 211, 281, 298, 306, 355
Herren 14
Hertz 9, 10, 12, 14, 48
Hexham 186
Hiberni 85
Hicks 48
Hilarides 71
Hillenius 194, 201
Hio xv
Hirst 250
Hjelmslev 1, 351
Hobbes 184, 317, 356
Hoenigswald 306
Hofbauer 307
Hoffmann 22, 24, 25
Hofman v, xv, xxv, 7, 9, 14
Holder 183, 184, 190
Höller 56, 211
Holtved 163, 164, 166
Holtz 7, 8, 9, 10, 11, 14, 27, 37
Holyband 124, 132
Homayi 263, 266
Homayun-Farrokh 264, 265, 267
Hopper 68
Horace 76, 135, 334
Hottinger 106, 108, 109, 111
Hovdhaugen vi, xv, xxv, 113
Hüllen v, xv, xxv, 17, 21, 22, 25, 133, 307
Humboldt 22, 111, 291, 298, 300, 301, 302, 303, 304, 305, 306, 307, 331, 347, 355
Hume 204, 309, 313
Hungarian 334
Husserl 309, 312, 317
Hussey 87, 88, 89, 90, 91, 92, 96, 97, 98, 99, 102
Hutton 291
Hymes 259
Ibn-i Mohanna 261
Ibrahim x, xv
Idris xv
Illyricus 69
Irish Tourist Board x, xxvi
Irmscher 306
Irvani 262
Isermann 317
Isfahani 263, 264
Isidore 12, 13, 29, 30, 34, 332
Isidore (Brother) 85
Ising 283, 288
Jaʕfar 267
Jackendoff 270, 271, 276
Jacobs 276
Jahangiri 262
Jahreiß xv, xxiii, 344
Jakob 206
Jakobson 1, 213, 224, 234, 235, 355
James, G. 25
James, William 228, 229, 235
Jankowsky xv, xxiv, 345
Japix 59, 65, 66, 67, 69, 70, 71
Jaucourt 55
Jean Scot 15
Jelinek 271
Jellinek 196, 201
Jennings 86, 100
Jerome 334
Jespersen 249
Jiménez Patón 332
Jobling xvi, xxiv, 346
Jones, Charles 277
Jones, Sir William 354
Jonson 186
Joseph xvi, xxvii, 346
Jouvency 76
Junius 20, 67, 69
Junius, 26
Kaltz vi, xvi, xxiv, 123
Kamp 310, 311, 317
Kant 299, 300, 301, 306, 309, 354, 355
Kantorowicz 309

Kärnä xvi, xxv
Kashef 264
Kaufman 341
Kaulen 284, 288, 289
Keil 36, 196, 201
Kelly vi, xvi, xxv, xxvii, 135, 143
Kemp 184, 189, 190, 259
Kenny's Bookshops x, xxiv
Kenny, Desmond xi
Kermani 263, 264
Khanlari 265, 266, 267
Kibbee xvi, xxiv, 123, 126
Kiparsky 1
Kitagawa 271
Klaus 295, 306
Kleinschmidt, E. 25
Kleinschmidt, Samuel 159, 160, 163, 164, 165, 166
Kneepkens xvi, xxiv, 40, 41, 44, 48, 348
Koerner ii, iii, iv, ix, xi, xii, xvi, xxi, xxiv, 100, 101, 277, 288, 321, 327, 328
Kok 195, 196, 198, 201
Kondylis 295, 296, 306
Königseer 162, 167
Kopernikus 294
Kruszewski 213, 224, 327
Kruth 164
Kuhn, A. 51, 57
Kuhn, Thomas Samuel 294
Kühnert 36
Kukenheim 146, 156
Kussmaul 230, 235
La Harpe 55
La Mettrie 296, 297
Labrador 164
Lakoff 270, 277
Lambert 87, 100
Lambertini 211
Lambley 124, 126, 129, 132
Lancelot 73
Langendoen 277
Langer 355
Lardet xvi, xxiv, 349
Laronde 249
Laveaux 49, 50, 51, 52, 53, 54, 55, 56, 57
Lavoisier 174
Law v, xvi, xxiv, 7, 15, 27, 28, 37
Lazarus 255, 259
Lazius 349
le Ver 352
Lehnert 184, 190
Leibniz 111, 174, 175, 204, 207, 210, 212, 343, 351, 356
Leitzmann 306
Leont'ev 327
Leopold xvi, xxvi, 284, 288, 350
Lepsius 252, 259
Leupenius 195, 196, 198, 201
Levinson 346
Lewandowska-Tomaszczyk xvi, xxvii, 350
Lewry 29, 37
Lhomond 81, 82, 84
Lhuyd 88, 96, 100
Liberman 234, 235
Lichtenberg 169, 170, 171, 172, 174, 175, 176, 179, 180, 181
Lieberman 234, 235
Lightfoot 274, 275, 276, 277
Lily 183
Lindsay 12, 15
Linguist's Software xii
Linné 174
Lipps 309, 313
Lipsius 68, 92
Llull 351
Locke 74, 137, 204, 212, 330
Lodwick 183
Löfstedt 8, 9, 11, 15, 36
Lope Blanch 152, 156
López Madera 332
Lörenczi xvi
Louvain 85
Lovejoy 20, 26
Lovelock 291, 293, 306
Lowth 339, 359
Lucretius 170, 172
Luhtala v, xvi, xxiv, 39
Lull 176
Lully 351
Lummi 271
Lusignan 128, 133
Luther 334

Mac Aingil 86
Mac an Bhaird 86
Mac an Iomaire, Máirín xvii
Mac an Iomaire, Peadar xvii
Mac Aogáin 101
Mac Caghwell 86
Mac Cruitín 87
Mac Curtin 87, 91, 95, 96, 97, 98, 99, 101
Mac Eoin, Gearóid xvii, xxi, xxiii
Mac Eoin, Gimma xvii
Mac Íomhair xvii, xxi
Mac Muirí xvii, xxi, xxvi
Macintosh xii
Mackert vii, xvii, xxvi, 251, 255, 259
Mancinelli 334
Maratte 337
Marchello-Nizia 129, 133
Marenbon 29, 37
Marius Victorinus 30, 31, 32
Markowski 29, 37
Marmo 211
Marmontel 55
Martianus Capella 29
Martinet 1, 266, 357
Martínez Gavilán vi, xvii, xxv, 145
Marty 52, 331
Mashkur 267
Mathias 79, 84
Mathieu 348
Maupas 137, 143
McArthur 20, 26
McCawley 277
McClelland 330
McKenna 87
McMahon xvii, xxiv, 176, 351
Megiser 104
Meier 203, 204, 206, 207, 208, 209, 210, 212
Meigret 348
Meijering 65, 71
Meillet 237, 238, 245, 247, 248, 249, 250, 357, 364, 365
Melanchthon 334
Melis 237
Ménage 55
Mendenhall 346
Merlo 248
Merrilees xvii, xxv, 123, 125, 133, 352
Merula 68
Meshkot Dini vii, xvii, xxiv, 266, 267
Messen 86
Meurier 130, 132
Meyer, A. 295, 298, 305
Meyer, Kuno 3
Mhic Dhonncha xvii, xxi
Mhic Íomhair, Máire xvii
Michael 196, 201
Middendorf 113, 114, 122
Millett 85
Millon 84
Moʕin 267
Molière 54
Moltzer 280, 285, 286, 287, 288
Monboddo 341
Montaigne 74
Moody 101
Moonen 195, 196, 198, 199, 200, 201
Mooney 86, 101
Moore 204
More 334
Morelly 80
Morveau 80
Mugdan 328
Muller xvii, xxv, 33, 353
Müller, George Elias 309
Müller, Max 252, 257, 259, 282, 283, 284, 285, 286, 288
Müller, Nicole xviii, xxi
Mulligan 314, 316, 317
Münster 349
Murethach 8, 10, 11, 12, 13, 14
Murphy's Brewery x, xxiii
Nabais xviii, xxvi, 354
Nagle vii, xviii, xxiii, xxvii, 269, 274, 277
Nahvi 262
Najafi 267
Naumann 307
Nazemul-Atebba 264
Nebrija 121, 122, 146, 147, 148, 155, 156
Negev 346
Nelson 14
Nerlich xviii, xxvi, 354

Neumann 303, 306
Newton 174
Nicolai 106
Nicole 54
Niederehe ii, ix, x, xxi, 123, 124, 133, 156, 288
Niederehe, Hans-Josef xii
Niedermann, 250
Noordegraaf vii, xviii, xxvi, 202, 279, 281, 285, 288
Nowak vi, xviii, xxvi, 157, 163
Nuchelmans 317
Nuñez de Arenas 336
Ó Briain xviii, xxi, 86, 87, 88, 101
O'Brien 95
O'Brien, Sylvester 100, 101
Ó Casaide 91, 101
Ó Cléirigh xviii, xxv
Ó Clérigh 87, 101
O'Clery 87
Ó Concheanainn 87, 101
Ó Cuív v, x, xviii, xxiii, xxv, 1, 85, 87, 91, 101
O'Donovan 91
Oehrle 271
Ó hAodha, Donncha xviii, xxi, xxiii
Ó hAodha, Máire xviii
Ó hEocha x
Ó hEósa 87
O'Hussey 86
Olearius 158, 167
Ó MaoilChonaire 86
Ó Maolmhuaidh 88, 100
O'Molloy 88, 91, 92, 93, 94, 95, 96, 98, 99, 100, 101
Oosterhout 64, 71
Opitz 69
Oré 113, 122
Orwell 179, 291
Osthoff 243, 250
Ó Súilleabháin 85
Otfrid 69
P.T. 359
Padley 143, 145, 149, 152, 153, 156, 201
Paget 234
Pallas 353
Palma 104, 107, 111
Palmer 37
Paris 237, 238, 248
Paul 238, 243, 249, 250
Paulinus a Sancto Bartholomaeo 353
Pedersen 287, 288
Pellegrini 342
Penon 288
Percival xxi, 45, 48, 294, 298, 306
Périon 349
Peru 113, 114, 116, 122
Petitot 354
Petrarca 25, 145
Petrilli xviii, xxiv, 355
Petronius 66
Petrus Helias 27, 46, 48
Petrus, Suffridus 68
Phèdre 76, 78
Phocas 28
Pichon 337
Picht 25
Piedmont 50, 57
Pillsbury 233, 235
Piper 33, 36
Pirozynski 126, 128, 133
Plank 274, 277, 307
Plantin 133
Plato 172
Platon 309
Plitt 203, 204, 206, 208, 209, 210, 212
Pluche 80
Pollock 272, 277
Polomé 354
Pombo xviii, xxv, 356
Pontano 334
Popham 184
Poppe xviii, xxvii, 85
Porphyry 29
Port-Royal 73
Postel 103
Pott 284, 288, 300
Powell 252, 259
Pozuelo 146, 147, 156
Presence 344
Pringle x, xii
Priscian 7, 8, 9, 10, 11, 12, 13, 14, 27, 28, 29, 30, 34, 35, 36, 39, 40, 41, 43, 44, 45, 46, 47, 48, 61, 362

Promies 181
Proß 211
Přívratská xviii, xxiv, 356
Psichari 249
Pullum 271, 273, 276, 277
Putnam 179
Quemada 357
Quilis 156
Quintilien 146
Raabe 133
Racine 54
Radonvilliers 78, 79, 84
Rambaud 348
Ramus 21
Rask 345
Razi 261
Regnaud 243, 249
Reichelt 261, 267
Reid 313, 318
Reimarus 206, 207, 210, 212
Reinach 309, 311, 312, 313, 314, 315, 316, 317, 318
Resen 158, 167
Richelieu 54
Riché 7, 15
Rickard 123, 124, 129, 133
Ricken xxi, 143
Ricœur 354
Riemens 124, 133
Ripoll 34
Rischel 158, 159, 160, 166, 167
Ritter 305, 307
Rivard 78, 79, 80, 84
Rivarol 50
Robert, Gruffydd 87
Roberts 274, 277
Robins ii, iii, iv, xi, xii, xviii, xxi, xxiv, 37, 184, 190
Rocher ii
Rodman 234, 235
Röd 295, 306
Roeder 211, 212
Roget 22, 23, 26
Roggenhofer vi, xix, xxiii, 169, 170, 172
Romaine 275, 277
Roques 336, 357
Röseberg 295, 305
Rosén, Haiim B. xix, xxv, 357
Rosén, Hannah xix
Rosenbaum 276
Rosier ii, iii, iv, xi, xii, xix, xxi, xxiv, 15, 27, 37, 40, 48
Ross 270, 277
Rothwell 124, 129, 133
Rousseau 53
Rüdiger 353
Rudnicki 213, 217, 224
Rumelhart 330
Sadeghi 266, 267
Sag 273, 276
Saint-Gérand xix, xxiv, 357
Salmon ii
Sánchez Perez xviii
Sanctius 74, 146, 148, 149, 151, 156
Sapir 257, 259
Sarmiento xxi
Sauer xix, xxvi, 358
Sauter 302, 306
Sauvageot 1
Savigny 317
Sayce 257
Scaglione ii, 136, 143
Scaliger 185
Scaurus 30
Scheere 295
Scheerer 298, 305
Schelling 300
Schiller 301, 306
Schindler 105, 108
Schlanger 295, 306
Schlegel 298, 300, 301, 302, 345
Schleicher 238, 240, 248, 280, 283, 285, 286, 287, 288, 300, 303, 304, 321, 322, 323, 326, 328
Schlieben-Lange xxi
Schmidlin 50, 57
Schmidt 298, 301, 302, 306
Schmidt-Biggemann 294, 295, 307
Schmitter vii, ix, xii, xix, xxv, xxvi, 291, 292, 294, 295, 302, 303, 307, 329
Schneider 40, 48
Schreyer xix, xxvii, 359
Schuchardt 237, 238, 240, 241, 242, 244, 245, 249, 250

Schuhmann 313, 318
Schwab 50
Schwarze 293, 307
Scott 88, 101
Searle 309, 311, 316, 318
Sebeok 156
Sechehaye 141, 144
Sedulius Scottus 8, 9, 10, 11, 12, 15, 32, 33, 36
Seiffert x, xxi, 360
Sells 269, 277
Servius 31
Séwel 199, 202, 360
Shackleton xvi
Shankweiler 235
Shoʕar 267
Sibvayh 261
Siccama 66, 70, 71
Silke 86, 101
Simon 211, 306, 339
Sipma 71
Skarga 327
Skårup 158, 167
Skinner 330
Smart 330
Smith xix, xxvi, 360
Smith, Adam 341
Smith, Barry 318
Södergård 124, 131, 133
Spedding 173, 175, 176, 181
Spinoza 174
Spurzheim 232
St Augustine 29
Stach, Christian 159
Stach, Matthäus 159
Stankiewicz 328
Starcky 346
Statius 334
Steele 271, 272, 276, 277
Stein 17, 26
Steiner 305
Steinthal 255, 259, 300, 322, 323, 326, 331
Stengel 123, 131, 133
Stocking 259
Stokes 15
Strachan 3, 9, 15
Streitberg 249
Streuber 128, 133
Stricker 227, 228, 229, 230, 231, 232, 233, 234, 235
Struve 319, 320, 324, 325, 326, 327, 328
Studdert-Kennedy 235, 330
Subbiondo vi, xix, xxvi, 183, 190
Sundby 184, 190
Sweet 3, 4, 5, 249, 337
Swiggers vi, xix, xxiv, xxvii, 85, 86, 100, 132, 237, 248, 361
Tabarroni 203, 211, 212
Taleghani 264
Tanner 69
Tannery 174, 176, 181
Tausk 7
Taylor, Daniel J. xix, xxv, 362
Taylor, Talbot J. xix, xxvii, 363
te Winkel 279
Techmer 252, 259
ten Kate 200, 201
Terwey 199, 202
Tesauro 342
Tesnière 337
Teyssier 337, 338
Themistius 29
Thijm 284, 287
Thilo 294, 307
Thomas 248, 250
Thomason 341
Thurneysen 87, 101
Titone 123, 133
Tjallings 59
Todd 277
Tolson 48
Tooke xi, xii
Top 158, 159, 160
Tourneur 87, 101
Trabant 291, 292, 293, 302, 307
Trippault 348
Trnka 1
Trojahn xix, xxvi
Tsiapera xix, xxvii, 364
Tyrell 88
Uhlig 40, 48
Ullmann 19, 26
Uppendahl 169
Urmson 317

Usuard 29
Valdés 146, 147, 151, 152, 156
Valyi 353
Van de Velde 69, 71
van der Meer 71
van der Wal vi, xx, xxiii, 191, 192, 194, 202
van Driel 202
Van Hellemont 237
van Heule 194, 196, 197, 198, 201
Van Hoecke 132, 241, 248
van Kemenade 274, 277
van Marle xvii, xxvii, 351
Van Overbeke 95, 101
Vanhelmont 237
Vanière 78, 84
Varro 362, 363
Vaugelas 53, 55, 132
Vaughan 101
Vendryes 1, 250
Vergeries 334
Versteegh xx, xxv, 365
Vico 340, 342
Vidal 135
Villalón 147, 156
Villar 148, 149, 154, 155, 156
Visser 279, 289
Vivre 132
Voet 130, 133
Voltaire 53, 54, 55
von Rahden 279, 288
von Raumer 345
von Wartburg 22, 25, 357
Vonk vii, xx, xxvi, 309, 314, 316
Vries 64, 71
Vulcanius 68
Wagner 358
Wall 87, 102
Wallis 183, 184, 185, 186, 187, 188, 189, 190
Walton 105, 106, 107, 108, 111
Warburton 339
Ward, Hugh 86, 101
Ward, Seth 184
Warren 223, 224
Wąsik xx, xxvi, 366
Wasow 270, 271, 272, 276
Waswo 19, 26
Waterbolk 68, 70, 71
Watson 233
Waugh 235
Weiland 199, 202
Weischedel 306
Weiß vii, xx, xxiii, 56, 203, 205, 210, 211, 212, 298, 307
Welke 306
Wellberry 207, 212
Wells 251, 259
Werner 354, 355
Wernicke 227
Wessels 280, 283, 284, 285, 287, 289
Whatmough 2
White 88, 101
Widell xx, xxiv
Wiener 306
Wiggershaus 318
Wilkin xxvi
Wilkins 21, 24, 25, 183, 351
William of Conches 35
Williams vii, xx, xxvii, 319, 320
Wilson 271, 277
Winnett 346
Withals 26
Wittgenstein 23, 169, 170
Wolff 206, 207, 208, 209, 210
Wright, Joseph 245, 249
Wright, Thomas 17, 26
Wülcker 26
Wunderlich 293, 307
Wundt 232, 233, 235, 253, 254, 255, 259
Yllera 148, 149, 156
Young 204, 212
Zabrocki 213, 214, 215, 216, 217, 218, 219, 223, 224
Zachrisson 184, 190
Zollna xx, xxv
Zupitza 18

Index Rerum

absolute 41
Absolutio 348
Abstracts viii, 329
Académie Française 49, 50, 51, 52, 54, 55, 57
Adamic language doctrine 285
ἀδιαβίβαστον 41
ἀκολουθία 42
Aktstruktur
  des Versprechens 315
alphabet 116, 117
alternating apperceptions 257, 258
alternating sounds 251, 252, 257, 258
alternating sounds. 256
analogie 239, 241, 242, 243, 248
analogon rationis 209
analytic passive 191
Animal Language 203, 205, 210
animal-machine hypothesis 204
Anspruch 311, 314
antinomie 244, 246
Antinomies 249
antinormativiste 146
aphasia 227
apperception 251, 252, 255, 256, 258
apperception. 256
Ars Brugensis 32
Ars Laureshamensis 8, 10, 12, 13, 15, 32
art
  grammatical 150
  naturel 150
Asian origin of Frisians 67
auditory images 228
αὐτοπάθεια 42
αὐτοτελής 41
autorité 146
Aux 269, 270, 271, 272, 275
  autonomous 270, 275
auxiliaries
  modal 269
Biblia Sacra Polyglotta 105, 106, 107, 108
bilingual dictionary 49, 51
Bio-Bibliographical Handbook 335
Biologismus 303, 304
Carolingian linguistics 27
Carolingians 29
cas 337
catégorie 355
clang 252
colloque 124, 125, 129
common noun 34
comparatisme 339
comparative
  description 103
  table 108, 110
  work 104, 109
comparative work 105
comparative-demonstrational linguistics 110
comparative-historic
  approach 110
  linguistics 110
comparativism 103
comparison 104
concept 256, 257, 258
concord 42
Conditional 365
confusivum 218, 219, 220, 221, 222
consciousness 229
constance 240, 241, 242, 246, 247
Contact Languages 340
contrastive discourse analysis 138
coreferentiality 44
cryptographie 361
dastur 263
decline of Frisian 59
deductive approach to the dictionary 108
definition 32
definitions 30, 35

Demonstrative 263
descriptive linguist 121
development of languages 106
diacrisis 217, 221, 222, 223
dialectic 29, 30, 31, 33, 34, 35
dialogue 124, 125, 127, 129
διάβασις τοῦ προσώπου 41
διάθεσις 40
dictionary 17, 19, 52, 53, 352
differential threshold 252, 258
diffusivum 218, 219, 223
early comparativists 110
ellipses 75
empiricism 172, 173
enseignement des vernaculaires 123, 126, 128
ergative 161
ergativity 165
evolution 282, 284, 286
evolutionary theory 279, 280
facultas characteristica sensitiva 209
Fechner's law of thresholds 258
Fly-Bottle 363
Fremdpersonalität 315
functional 138
fundamental tone 253
gallicisme 81
gestural complex 230
gloss 8, 9, 11, 12, 13, 14, 17, 19, 20, 28, 29
Government-Binding theory 266, 272
gramática general 336
grammaire 123, 125, 127, 128, 129, 148, 333, 355
  descriptive 148, 155
  générale 136
  normative 148, 151, 155
grammar 29, 33, 34, 115, 120, 137, 344, 358, 360
  Generative 269
  of Labrador 159, 164
  of Persian 262
  particular 183, 184
  philosophical 183, 184, 185, 188
  Phrase-Structure 330
  school 184
  traditional 265
grammarian 35, 54
Grammatica Latino-hibernica 88
grammatical universal 137
Handlung 316
Harmonic 103, 104, 105, 106, 107, 108, 109, 110, 111, 356
  overtones 253
harmonization 109
harmony 110
hétérogénéité 245
Historical Linguistics 348
History Writing 329
ideational type 228
ideological dictionary 22
inconscience 245
INFL 270, 272, 273, 275
  INFL Phrase 272
information
  dictionary 53
  encyclopaedic 53
Intentionalität 315
intransitio personarum 46
intransitive 41
intransitivity 199
inversion 138
inversions 75
Invisible Hand 359
involuntary assimilation 256, 258
Irish
  grammar 85
  grammatical terminology 96
  phonetics 93
Jacobin 51
Jolley 204, 212
Karlsruhe MS Aug. cxxxii 10, 11
κατάλληλον 42
Kazań 224
  School 213
langage
  appris 244
  transmis 244
language
  change 59, 341
  History 341
language ability localisation 228
langue
  quotidienne 127, 129
  spécialisée 127

Latin model 90
latinisme 81
Lautgesetze 248
Lautsymbolik 281, 285
law of differential thresholds 258
lexicographer 51, 54
Linguistic Dynamics 354
Linguistics 321, 329, 334
    and philosophy 324
    autonomy of 320
    General 366
    Romani 353
    vs. Philology 319
linguistique
    développement de la 336
Literary Theory 329
lois
    phon(ét)iques 237
    phonétiques 246
    phoniques 238, 240, 241, 242, 243, 244, 245, 246, 247
    physiologiques 239, 240, 241, 242
manuel de conversation 124
Maschine 291
Meaning 354
Metalanguage 352
Metaphor 341
μετάβασις τοῦ προσώπου 41
méthodes 74
modal 270
modality 269
Moravian
    Brethren 159, 160
    orthography 164
    Society 159, 164
morphology
    distinctive 217, 219, 223
    natural 223
    of Persian 262
motor images 228
Moyen Age 123, 126
MS Leiden BPL 67 12
néogrammairiens 238, 240, 241, 243, 247
neologism 221, 223
new science 184, 189
Nomenklatur 177, 178
normativiste 146
norme
    cultivée 146
    grammaticale 145
    vulgaire 146
number 264
object 157, 165
occultation 357
ordre des mots 77
organiciste 238, 239, 248
Organismus 291
Organismusmodell 293
origin
    of human speech 205
    of Language 279, 280, 281, 282, 283, 285
orthography 163, 164, 344
Paradigm
    Conflict 340
Paradigmatic Dimension 351
partial tones 253, 254
parts-of-speech-framework 263
pédagogie 73
percept 256, 257, 258
Perceptual recognition routines 234
Philology
    classical 321
    comparative 321
    vs. Linguistics 321
philosophical language
    movement 183
philosophy
    of language 170, 174, 180, 275, 324
    of nature 324
phrenology 232
physiologique 243
Port Royal 187
position
    normativiste 154
Positivismus 303
Poznań 213
Prague School 217, 219
Prix Volney 350
process
    phonetic 215, 216, 217
    phonological 213, 214
    substitution 213, 215

  substitution 215, 216, 217
  surface
    deep 213, 214
productivity 220
psychophysics 229
Purist 338
rationalism 172, 173, 174, 203, 204
Reconnaissance 357
reflexive 44
reflexive construction 42
Renaissance 123, 126, 128, 130
  Conception of Language 332
retransitio 45
rhetoric 29, 137
rhetorician 35
Royal Society 184
rule borrowing 215
Sachverhalt 313
Schematism 354
science
  historical 321
  physical 321
second language acquisition 7
semantic
  Change 354
  load 222
Semantics
  cognitive 350
  componential 351
sens du langage 343
sensory
  images 231
  perceptions 230
Sensualism 203, 204, 210
sentence 138
Shem 107
signs 204, 205, 208, 210
similarity between Frisian and English 66
Sound Physiology 345
sound shift 103, 110
sound symbolism 222, 223
soziale Akte 311
Speculative Lexicography 17, 19, 20, 21, 22, 24
Spontaneität 315
Sprachgefühl ix
Sprachphilosophie 331
Sprachwissenschaft 321
Sprechakten 309
Sprechakttheorie 310
St. Anthony's College 86
St. Gall MS 904 9, 10, 11, 12, 13, 15
Stoic predicate types 40
Structuralism 364
Strukturalismus 293
Strukturmomente des Versprechens 313
Subconscious and Social 346
subject 157, 165
subvocal responses 233
suffix reinterpretation 220, 223
sympathetic vibration 254
syntax 365
  of Persian 262
  X-bar syntax 266, 271, 273
Systembegriff 291
Systemmodell 293, 304, 305
tendance
  antinormative 148
  normative 147
terminology 176, 177
TGL = théorie générale du langage 77
theoretical innovation 27
Theorie der sozialen Akte 309
theory of meaning 170
topical glossary 19, 20, 22
Tower of Babel 185
traductions interlineáires 74
traductions interlinéaires 74
Träger 314
transitio personarum 46
transitivity 39, 43, 157, 161, 199
  of pronoun. 39
  of verb 39
translation 137, 140
Uhrenmetapher 294, 295
uniformitarian principle 283
universal language 356
universaux 148
universaux de langage 81
usage 145, 146
  commun 146, 148, 150, 153, 155
  cultivé 148

Verbal 263
verbal voice 40
Verbindlichkeit 311, 313, 314
Vernehmungsbedürftigkeit 315
Versprechen 311, 312
vocabula usu trita 241, 244
vocabulaire 123, 125, 128
voice 230
Wolffian classification of ideas 207
word images 231
word order 136, 138
Writing Systems 346

In the STUDIES IN THE HISTORY OF THE LANGUAGE SCIENCES (SiHoLS) series (Series Editor: E.F. Konrad Koerner) the following volumes have been published thus far:

1. KOERNER, E.F. Konrad: *The Importance of Techmer's "Internationale Zeitschrift für Allgemeine Sprachwissenschaft" in the Development of General Linguistics.* Amsterdam, 1973.
2. TAYLOR, Daniel J.: *Declinatio: A Study of the Linguistic Theory of Marcus Terentius Varro.* Amsterdam, 1974. 2nd pr. 1989.
3. BENWARE, Wilbur A.: *The Study of Indo-European Vocalism; from the beginnings to Whitney and Scherer: A critical-historical account.* Amsterdam, 1974. t.o.p. 2nd pr. 1990.
4. BACHER, Wilhelm: *Die Anfänge der hebräischen Grammatik* (1895), together with *Die hebräische Sprachwissenschaft vom 10. bis zum 16. Jahrhundert* (1892). Amsterdam, 1974.
5. HUNT, R.W. (1908-1979): *The History of Grammar in the Middle Ages. Collected Papers.* Edited with an introduction, a select bibliography, and indices by G.L. Bursill-Hall. Amsterdam, 1980.
6. MILLER, Roy Andrew: *Studies in the Grammatical Tradition in Tibet.* Amsterdam, 1976.
7. PEDERSEN, Holger (1867-1953): *A Glance at the History of Linguistics, with particular regard to the historical study of phonology.* Amsterdam, 1983.
8. STENGEL, Edmund (1845-1935), (ed.): *Chronologisches Verzeichnis französischer Grammatiken vom Ende des 14. bis zum Ausgange des 18. Jahrhunderts, nebst Angabe der bisher ermittelten Fundorte derselben.* Amsterdam, 1976.
9. NIEDEREHE, Hans-Josef and Harald HAARMANN (with the assistance of Liliane Rouday), (eds): *In Memoriam Friedrich Diez: Akten des Kolloquiums zur Wissenschaftsgeschichte der Romanistik/Actes du Colloque sur l'Histoire des Etudes Romanes/Proceedings of the Colloquium for the History of Romance Studies, Trier, 2.-4. Okt. 1975).* Amsterdam, 1976.
10. KILBURY, James: *The Development of Morphophonemic Theory.* Amsterdam, 1976.
11. KOERNER, E.F. Konrad: *Western Histories of Linguistic Thought. An annotated chronological bibliography, 1822-1976.* Amsterdam, 1978.
12. PAULINUS a S. BARTHOLOMAEO (1749-1806): *Dissertation on the Sanskrit Language.* Transl., edited and introduced by Ludo Rocher. Amsterdam, 1977.
13. DRAKE, Glendon F.: *The Role of Prescriptivism in American Linguistics 1820-1970.* Amsterdam, 1977.
14. SIGERUS DE CORTRACO: *Summa modorum significandi; Sophismata.* New edition, on the basis of G. Wallerand's *editio prima,* with additions, critical notes, an index of terms, and an introd. by Jan Pinborg. Amsterdam, 1977.
15. PSEUDO-ALBERTUS MAGNUS: *Quaestiones Alberti de Modis significandi.* A critical edition, translation and commentary of the British Museum Inc. C.21.C.52 and the Cambridge Inc.5.J.3.7, by L.G. Kelly. Amsterdam, 1977.
16. PANCONCELLI-CALZIA, Giulio (1878-1966): *Geschichtszahlen der Phonetik* (1941), together with *Quellenatlas der Phonetik* (1940). New ed., with an introd. article and a bio-bibliographical account of Panconcelli-Calzia by Jens-Peter Köster. Amsterdam, n.y.p.
17. SALMON, Vivian: *The Study of Language in 17th-Century England.* Amsterdam, 1979. Second edition 1988.

18. HAYASHI, Tetsuro: *The Theory of English Lexicography 1530-1791*. Amsterdam, 1978.
19. KOERNER, E.F. Konrad: *Toward a Historiography of Linguistics. Selected Essays.* Foreword by R.H. Robins. Amsterdam, 1978.
20. KOERNER, E.F. Konrad (ed.): *Progress in Linguistic Historiography: Papers from the International Conference on the History of the Language Sciences, Ottawa, 28-31 August 1978.* Amsterdam, 1980.
21. DAVIS, Boyd H. and Raymond K. O'CAIN (eds): *First Person Singular. Papers from the Conference on an Oral Archive for the History of American Linguistics. (Charlotte, N.C., 9-10 March 1979).* Amsterdam, 1980.
22. McDERMOTT, A. Charlene Senape: *Godfrey of Fontaine's Abridgement of Boethius the Dane's 'Modi Significandi sive Quaestiones super Priscianum Maiorem.* A text edition with English transl. and introd. Amsterdam, 1980.
23. APOLLONIUS DYSCOLUS: *The Syntax of Apollonius Dyscolus.* Translated, and with commentary by Fred W. Householder. Amsterdam, 1981.
24. CARTER, M. (ed.): *Arab Linguistics, an introductory classical text with translation and notes.* Amsterdam, 1981.
25. HYMES, Dell H.: *Essays in the History of Linguistic Anthropology.* Amsterdam, 1983.
26. KOERNER, Konrad, Hans-J. NIEDEREHE and R.H. ROBINS (eds): *Studies in Medieval Linguistic Thought,* dedicated to Geoffrey L. Bursill-Hall on the occasion of his 60th birthday on 15 May 1980. Amsterdam, 1980.
27. BREVA-CLARAMONTE, Manuel: *Sanctius' Theory of Language: A contribution to the history of Renaissance linguistics.* Amsterdam, 1983.
28. VERSTEEGH, Kees, Konrad KOERNER and Hans-J. NIEDEREHE (eds): *The History of Linguistics in the Near East.* Amsterdam, 1983.
29. ARENS, Hans: *Aristotle's Theory of Language and its Tradition.* Amsterdam, 1984.
30. GORDON, W. Terrence: *A History of Semantics.* Amsterdam, 1982.
31. CHRISTY, Craig: *Uniformitarianism in Linguistics.* Amsterdam 1983.
32. MANCHESTER, M.L.: *The Philosophical Foundations of Humboldt's Linguistic Doctrines.* Amsterdam 1985.
33. RAMAT, Paolo, Hans-Josef NIEDEREHE and E.F. Konrad KOERNER (eds): *The History of Linguistics in Italy.* Amsterdam, 1986.
34. QUILIS, Antonio and Hans J. NIEDEREHE (eds): *The History of Linguistics in Spain.* Amsterdam, 1986.
35. SALMON, Vivian and Edwina BURNESS (comps): *A Reader in the Language of Shakespearean Drama.* Amsterdam, 1987.
36. KOERNER, Konrad (ed.): *Edward Sapir. Appraisals of his Life and Work.* Amsterdam, 1984.
37. Ó MATHÚNA, Seán P.: *William Bathe, S.J., 1564-1614: a pioneer in linguistics.* Amsterdam, 1986.
38. AARSLEFF, Hans, Louis G. KELLY and Hans-Josef NIEDEREHE (eds): *Papers in the History of Linguistics. Proceedings of ICHoLS III, Princeton 1984.* Amsterdam, 1987.
39. PETRUS HISPANUS: *Summulae Logicales.* Translated and with an introduction by Francis P. Dinneen, S.J. Amsterdam, 1990.
40. HARTMANN, R.R.K. (ed.): *The History of Lexicography. Papers from the Dictionary Research Centre Seminar at Exeter, March 1986.* Amsterdam, 1986.

41. COWAN, William, Michael K. FOSTER and Konrad KOERNER (eds): *New Perspectives in Language, Culture, and Personality. Proceedings of the Edward Sapir Centenary Conference (Ottawa, 1-3 October 1984)*. Amsterdam, 1986.
42. BUZZETTI, Dino and Maurizio FERRIANI (eds): *Speculative Grammar, Universal Grammar, and Philosophical Analysis of Language*. Amsterdam, 1987.
43. BURSILL-HALL, G. L., Sten EBBESEN and E.F. Konrad KOERNER (eds): *De Ortu Grammaticae. Studies in Medieval Grammar and Linguistic Theory in Memory of Jan Pinborg*. Amsterdam/Philadelphia, 1990.
44. AMSLER, Mark: *Etymology and Discourse in Late Antiquity and the Early Middle Ages*. Amsterdam/Philadelphia, 1989.
45. OWENS, Jonathan: *The Foundations of Grammar*. Amsterdam, 1987.
46. TAYLOR, Daniel (ed.): *The History of Linguistics in the Classical Period*. Amsterdam, 1987.
47. HALL, Robert A. Jr. (with the collaboration of Konrad Koerner) (ed.): *Leonard Bloomfield, Essays on his Life and Work*. Amsterdam, 1987.
48. FORMIGARI, Lia: *Language and Experience in 17th-century British Philosophy*. Amsterdam/Philadelphia, 1989.
49. DE MAURO, Tullio and Lia FORMIGARI (eds): *Leibniz, Humboldt, and the Origins of Comparativism. Proceedings of the international conference, Rome, 25-28 September 1986*. Amsterdam/Philadelphia, 1990.
50. KOERNER, Konrad: *Practicing Linguistic Historiography. Selected Essays*. Amsterdam/Philadelphia, 1989.
51. NIEDEREHE, Hans-Josef and Konrad KOERNER (eds): *History and Historiography of Linguistics*. Amsterdam/Philadelphia, 1990.
52. JUUL, Arne and Hans F. NIELSEN (eds): *Otto Jespersen: Facets of his Life and Work*. Amsterdam/Philadelphia, 1989.
53. OWENS, Jonathan: *Early Arabic Grammatical Theory. Heterogeneity and Standardization*. Amsterdam/Philadelphia, 1990.
54. ANTONSEN, Elmer H. (ed.) with James W. Marchand and Ladislav Zgusta: *The Grimm Brothers and the Germanic Past*. Amsterdam/Philadelphia, 1990.
55. HALL, Robert A., Jr.: *A Life for Language. A biographical memoir of Leonard Bloomfield*. Amsterdam/Philadelphia, 1990.
56. VERSTEEGH, Kees and Michael G. CARTER (eds): *Studies in the History of Arabic Grammar II*. Amsterdam/Philadelphia, 1990.
57. STARNES, de Witt T. and Gertrude E. NOYES: *The English Dictionary from Cawdrey to Johnson 1604-1755*. Reprint of the 1946 edition, updated and with an introduction by Gabriele Stein. Amsterdam/Philadelphia, 1991.
58. DINNEEN, Francis P. and E.F. Konrad KOERNER (eds): *North American Contributions to the History of Linguistics*. Amsterdam/Philadelphia, 1990.
59. NERLICH, Brigitte: *Semantic Theories in Europe, 1830-1930*. Amsterdam/Philadelphia, 1992.
60. KIBBEE, Douglas A.: *For to Speke Frenche Trewely. The French language in England, 1000-1600: its status, description and instruction*. Amsterdam/Philadelphia, 1991.
61. KOERNER, Konrad: *First Person Singular II*. Amsterdam/Philadelphia, 1991.
62. LEITNER, G. (ed.): *English Traditional Grammars: an International Perspective*. Amsterdam/Philadelphia, 1991.
63. SUNDBY, Bertil, Anne Kari BJØRGE and Kari E. HAUGLAND: *A Dictionary of English Normative Grammar 1700-1800*. Amsterdam/Philadelphia, 1991.

64. NOORDEGRAAF, Jan, Kees VERSTEEGH and KONRAD KOERNER (eds): *The History of Linguistics in the Low Countries*. Amsterdam/Philadelphia, 1992.
65. ITKONEN, Esa: *Universal History of Linguistics. India, China, Arabia, Europe*. Amsterdam/Philadelphia, 1991.
66. NAUMANN, Bernd, Frans Plank and Gottfried HOFBAUER (eds): *Language and Earth. Elective affinities between the emerging sciences of linguistics and geology*. Amsterdam/Philadelphia, 1992.
67. SUBBIONDO, Joseph L. (ed.): *John Wilkins and 17th-Century British Linguistics. A Reader*. Amsterdam/Philadelphia, 1992.
68. AHLQVIST, Anders (ed.): *Diversions of Galway. Papers on the history of linguistics from ICHoLS V*. Amsterdam/Philadelphia, 1992.